FORD FRICK

FORD FRICK

Baseball's Third Commissioner and His Four Decades of Shaping the Game

DAVE BOHMER

University of Nebraska Press | Lincoln

Acknowledgments for the use of previously published material appear on page 283, which constitutes an extension of the copyright page.

The University of Nebraska Press is part of a land-grant institution with campuses and programs on the past, present, and future homelands of the Pawnee, Ponca, Otoe-Missouria, Omaha, Dakota, Lakota, Kaw, Cheyenne, and Arapaho Peoples, as well as those of the relocated Ho-Chunk, Sac and Fox, and Iowa Peoples.

For customers in the EU with safety/GPSR concerns, contact:
gpsr@mare-nostrum.co.uk
Mare Nostrum Group BV
Mauritskade 21D
1091 GC Amsterdam
The Netherlands

Library of Congress Cataloging-in-Publication Data
Names: Bohmer, Dave, author.
Title: Ford Frick: baseball's third commissioner and his four decades of shaping the game / Dave Bohmer.
Description: Lincoln: University of Nebraska Press, 2026. | Includes bibliographical references and index.
Identifiers: LCCN 2025021894
ISBN 9781496243492 (hardback)
ISBN 9781496246578 (epub)
ISBN 9781496246585 (pdf)
Subjects: LCSH: Frick, Ford C. | Baseball commissioners—United States—Biography. | Baseball—United States—History—20th century.
Classification: LCC GV865.F68 B64 2026 |
DDC 796.357092 [B]—dc23/eng/20250615
LC record available at https://lccn.loc.gov/2025021894

Set in Lyon Text by A. Shahan.

It’s amazing what you can accomplish if you
do not care who gets the credit.

—HARRY S. TRUMAN, Truman Library Institute

CONTENTS

ILLUSTRATIONS

PREFACE

A Tool of the Owners?

I was a first-semester freshman at DePauw University in October 1965. The trustees always met that month around homecoming; then, an upperclassman informed me that a trustee was the baseball commissioner. I shrugged my shoulders, responding, "Who cares? If it were Rocky Colavito, I'd be impressed." Growing up in Cleveland, I made Colavito my childhood idol until he was traded in 1960. I was aware Ford Frick was commissioner—his name had a wonderful alliteration—but I was clueless on what was involved with being a trustee, let alone a commissioner. Nor did I care.

Flash forward three decades. In 1995 I returned to DePauw as director of the Center for Contemporary Media. During my years in telecommunications, I hadn't thought about Ford Frick. By 1995 I had served on numerous boards and understood about being a trustee. Though not a journalist, I admired the profession and took pride in the media executives and journalists DePauw had generated, some inducted into its Media Wall of Fame, featured at the center. I learned Frick was not only an alum but also a successful sportswriter for Hearst newspapers in New York, Babe Ruth's ghostwriter, and an announcer for New York's baseball teams and for college football. He hosted the first radio show in the United States devoted exclusively to sports, on WOR. That work resulted in naming the annual Hall of Fame broadcasting award for Frick. With his background, Frick was inducted into DePauw's Media Wall of Fame. Whatever he may have accomplished in baseball, he clearly succeeded as a sports journalist.

My appreciation grew after teaching a class on baseball history, which had prompted considerable reading and research for over a decade. From that, it appeared Major League Baseball experienced dramatic changes during Frick's commissionership. It went from ten cities in the northeast quadrant to clubs in all sections of the country, expanding from sixteen to twenty teams. It instituted a draft similar to pro football's. There were other major changes, including some during his years as National League president. Yet, Frick was usually viewed as ineffective, largely dominated by the owners, which doesn't correspond with the profound changes from 1934 to 1965. That piqued my curiosity to examine the discrepancy—hence this book.

Indeed, I believe Ford Frick was an effective executive, impacting baseball more than almost all other commissioners. Beyond franchise relocation, expansion, and the draft, Frick also oversaw stabilization of the Minors and preservation of baseball's antitrust exemption. As National League president, he assisted integration and kept four clubs from bankruptcy. He had a major role in baseball's continuation during World War II and was instrumental in the Baseball Hall of Fame and Museum. There were other accomplishments. Yet, the view of Frick remains a person who served the owners' bidding.

To understand that view, begin with Frick's predecessor, Albert Benjamin "Happy" Chandler, baseball's second commissioner. Frick had been a candidate, though Chandler's selection didn't appear to cause friction between them. In fact, Chandler promptly met with him, stating, "I merely invited Frick down to fill me in for personal guidance since he knows as much about baseball as anybody."[1] Their goodwill didn't last. Chandler and league presidents conflicted before the 1945 World Series when he suggested in the presence of the umpires that their compensation should be doubled. Both Frick and Will Harridge, his American League counterpart, blocked it, with Harridge adding, "The engaging and discharging of umpires was wholly a league affair and none of the commissioner's business."[2] By then some owners were dissatisfied with Chandler for other reasons, though matters later stabilized.

Although Chandler would continue to conflict with owners, there is little evidence of such with Frick, with Chandler coming to understand the independent jurisdiction of league presidents. However, he failed to comprehend his limitations with the magnates. As his contract neared expiration, he pushed for an early renewal, needing twelve votes from the sixteen owners. Instead, with a 9–7 favorable margin, he fell three votes short. Eight months later, Frick was named commissioner, with Chandler offering no reaction.

Obviously, he wasn't pleased with his first political defeat and logically might blame the successor, even if he wasn't vying for the position. The resentment surfaced during Frick's second year, as misunderstandings fostered player anger about their pension plan. As discussed in chapter 11,

Frick intended to meet with player reps in December 1953, without lawyers, so he could explain the situation fully. Before, reps contacted Chandler, who advised them not to attend without their attorney. When Frick still insisted on no lawyers, the players boycotted.[3] Chandler appeared to be undermining Frick's dealings with players.

Chandler was less reticent later. With New York losing both National League clubs and antitrust hearings in Congress escalating, Chandler took the opportunity to comment, this time while governor of Kentucky. Claiming the commissioner's office was abandoned, he added that owners "put in a stooge who would do their bidding first and foremost. Because of the selfishness and greed of the Major League club owners acting through a puppet commissioner, baseball has forfeited the right to be dealt with as a sport instead of as a business."[4] A year later, Chandler elaborated: "So far as leadership is concerned, baseball is bankrupt. Frick knows nothing of baseball and spends more time in Toots Shorr's than he does on baseball matters."[5] The person who once thought Frick highly knowledgeable now considered him ignorant.

Chandler carried that further when Frick was elected to the Hall of Fame: "Next thing you know they'll be voting in Charlie McCarthy. He's a dummy, too, you know. All he [Frick] ever did, for goodness sake, was 'saw logs.' Why, he slept longer in office than . . . Rip Van Winkle."[6] His comments were consistent, if inappropriate, though they may also have reflected jealousy over Frick's induction. At the same time, having been commissioner lent credibility, helping shape the perception that Frick only did the owners' bidding.

Chandler, however, was not the only baseball person with a negative view. Bill Veeck, after selling the White Sox, provided a more expressive assessment in 1962, in what became a widely read book—*Veeck as in Wreck*. While Chandler's comments in sports pages could be glossed over, Veeck's insights in book form had a resonance that built on Chandler's image of a do-nothing commissioner. The key chapter was "The Asterisk King," a play off Frick's infamous home run ruling. Veeck offered some select perceptions: "Given the choice between doing something right or something wrong Frick will usually begin by doing as little as possible. It is only when he is pushed to the wall for a decision that he will almost always, with sure instinct and unerring aim, make an unholy mess of things."[7] Referring to Maris's sixty-first home run at a half-full Yankee Stadium on the last day, Veeck called it "the greatest single promotional opportunity in the history of baseball and they blew it!"[8] He added, "Baseball doesn't want a Commissioner, it wants a figurehead, preferably a live one. In Frick, baseball got what it wanted."[9] Later, addressing Frick's leadership, he said, "It's perfectly apparent that he is unimaginative and vacillating. . . . You can revolt against a tyrant but it's hard to feel anything but a faint squeamishness about a man who has great power in any field and often uses it only in little ways to hang on to his job. . . . That is why I have always opposed Frick. Not because I dislike him but because I believe him to be inept. Because he has done almost nothing without prodding to address himself to the problems of baseball or the structure of the game."[10] Veeck's comments reflected frustrations from often being on the losing end in his efforts, though, unlike Chandler, his comments conveyed less jealousy and more credibility.

Both perceptions were impactful since they came from those who worked with Frick. It's also clear they held grudges. David Quentin Voigt, an early baseball historian and author of a three-volume set, the last of which was published in 1983, accepted their viewpoints. He didn't devote much to Frick's commissionership but was succinct: "a figurehead who would represent the game, while keeping his nose out of important decisions." Assessing Frick a follower rather than a czar, Voigt added, "Frick stood by as carpetbagging owners abandoned ancient franchises; as the first expansion weakened clubs; as Congressional committees probed for anti-trust violations; as players formed a protective association; as owners vied for bonus babies; as television became a reshaping force; and as the minor leagues sickened onto death. At a time when critical leadership was needed, Frick offered none."[11] While mentioning baseball's major challenges, Voight implied Frick was Nero, fiddling as baseball burned.

His criticisms were damaging, affecting other scholars. In his study of baseball during Chander's commissionership, William Marshall echoed Voigt, concluding, "Instead of facing the major issues of the day such as increased competition from other sports and leisure activities, labor relations, reserve clause challenges, realignment and expansion, the demise of the minor leagues, attendance issues, and the rise of television, he allowed the owners to run amok."[12] In a study of commissioners through Bud Selig in 2006, Larry Moffi called Frick's tenure "years of hibernation of the conscience of the office."[13] A more recent study by Russell D. Buhite concluded, "Frick, though a likeable man, . . . was not a leader or a man of intellectual depth. . . . [H]e was not prepared to resist the pressures of the owners."[14] Those comments summarize the current prevailing scholarly assessment of Frick.[15]

Even his biographer did not provide a favorable impression, although John P. Carvalho's book, published in 2016, was more positive. It discussed many issues Frick faced during his thirty-one years—bankruptcies, World War II, integration, relocation, expansion, antitrust, and the Minor Leagues. In conclusion, however, it considered Frick more passive observer than activist change agent. Carvalho asked, "So how should Frick be remembered?" He offered, "The powerless, compliant owners' servant is a tempting analogy. Perhaps it would be better to consider whether Frick stayed close to his journalism roots. He was not there to make things happen. He was there to gather information, analyze it, and present it in a way that informed his audience—the owners in this case."[16] As will be demonstrated, I disagree with the view of Frick as an ineffective commissioner manipulated by owners.

Not just historians cultivated this image. In 2001 Billy Crystal produced a Home Box Office (HBO) movie titled *61**, the story of the pursuit of Ruth's record. Frick made his infamous ruling in mid-July that the 162-game season meant any record taking longer than the traditional 154 games would be treated separately. Crystal portrayed Frick as obsessed with Maris's threat, frequently watching games with the hope he wouldn't succeed. Maris was cast as the forlorn hero, Frick the antagonist blocking success. As will be discussed, the situation was more complicated. While only a small part of Frick's career, that ruling and Crystal's portrayal helped shape the unfavorable image.

Not all assessments have been negative, with the most positive written by a fellow journalist, Jerome Holtzman. In a book examining commissioners through 1998, Holtzman concluded Frick and Selig were the best. Dealing with the perception Frick was a do-nothing commissioner, Holtzman quoted him directly: "I got panned very frequently for saying 'This was a league matter.' The owners try to throw a lot of their disputes in the commissioner's lap that were never meant for the commissioner to decide. You can't remain on a judicial level, protecting honesty and integrity and holding the confidence of the fans, if you're going to be required to roll in the dirt down at a lower level."[17] Holtzman stressed Frick didn't involve himself in lesser matters, adding, "Also, he seldom, if ever, fed his ego and refused to bang the drum on his own behalf." The owners made the rules; the commissioner's job was to enforce them.[18] A quarter century later, Holtzman's assessment remains the outlier.

One reason stems from Frick's referring to issues as "a league matter." Throughout Frick's tenure, that distinction was significant. The commissioner administered and had full authority over the World Series. When the All-Star Game was created, it was added. Beyond that, the commissioner was responsible for anything considered in the "best interests of baseball." The term was purposedly vague but also empowering. Hence, the first commissioner, Kenesaw Mountain Landis, banned eight Chicago White Sox for fixing the 1919 World Series, after they were exonerated by a jury. He also suspended the iconic Babe Ruth for violating barnstorming rules. Beyond that clause, though, the position was limited because each league had a president who administered the policies its owners established. When the leagues met jointly, most matters were resolved. If not, the commissioner broke the deadlock. To label an issue "a league matter" was delegating a decision to its proper place, not shirking responsibility, though the distinction was rendered moot when Selig eliminated the league presidents.

League presidents had many duties until then. They established the forthcoming season schedule; recruited, directed and scheduled the umpires; and approved every player placed on a club's roster before he could play. The presidents disciplined for misbehavior, such as excessive arguing or delaying a game. Only if the behavior involved gambling or moral behavior did the commissioner become involved. The presidents were also responsible for the financial well-being of their league and club solvency, especially relevant for the National League during the Great Depression. They recruited new owners occasionally.

As commissioner, Frick understood this demarcation better than predecessors or successors, who perceived the position as more powerful. Having been a league president certainly helped because others—until Bud Selig—were more involved in details a league president should have resolved. Landis, who considered himself a czar and behaved as such, was able to do it given the magnates' fear of gambling, along with the Depression and World War II. However, owners were becoming more dissatisfied before his death. Such overstepping by later commissioners often cost their job, though Frick, due to his experience, avoided such turmoil.

Although his 1973 memoir isn't well regarded, perhaps because he avoided discussing many controversies, in it he did describe his management style. He believed the commissioner was a judge, overseeing and enforcing the rules established by owners. Only when something became detrimental did he have investigatory power.[19] He added, "As a matter of record, 90 percent of the work of the commissioner's office involves violations by clubs and individuals of the rules that they, themselves, have set up. All transactions of any nature involving leagues, clubs or players, must be filed immediately with the commissioner. . . . These documents and records constitute an effective basis for the 'policing' job that is so great a part of the commissioner's duty."[20] Frick also stressed being able to cast the deciding vote when leagues disagreed, but of greater importance was persuasion. As he put it, "A telephone call or a man-to-man conversation frequently will head off a sticky situation before it develops into a reality."[21] That style alone explains why Frick left little documentation: "Today's commissioner must be more a diplomat and less a czar, more an executive and less a rugged individualist. He must be more an arbitrator than a supreme judge."[22] In those few comments, Frick laid out his management style during his time in baseball. However, the lack of documentation left behind from such management explains why his commissionership is misunderstood.

My own background in business and management, coupled with training as a historian, has shaped my perspective on Ford Frick—though business experience doesn't necessarily provide a different perspective. Robert F. Lewis examined the first nine baseball commissioners using the model of hard, soft, and smart power, from the work of Joseph S. Nye Jr., former dean of the Kennedy School of Government. Hard power refers to coercion, common in hierarchical organizations or in economic enticements. Soft power relies on persuasion or collaboration. Smart power reflects the utilization of both, depending on the circumstances. Lewis utilizes Nye's model and his own thirty-five-year corporate background to conclude Bud Selig was baseball's most effective commissioner. At the same time, he considered Frick one of the weakest, having "remarkedly little influence on the game" and demonstrating "the fallacy of relying too much on soft power."[23] I don't know Lewis's business background, but my own experiences lead me to conclude the opposite.

Over seventeen years in telecommunications, I worked in a variety of areas, from a regulated utility to competitive sales. Twice I worked in government relations, at both state and federal levels. I was also president of a company operating in seven states with a thousand employees. I served on numerous boards, including that of a hospital, a start-up company, and a trade association. I have also been on homeowners' associations, charity boards, and a local bank board. I spent twenty years as a university administrator, all of them providing perspectives useful in analyzing Frick's management skills. So did a semester at Harvard Business School in the mid-1980s, emphasizing case studies. Many chapters are case studies of challenges Frick faced while National League president and commissioner.

Any assessment of his success must be made within the structure of the organization he managed. Every corporation, association, university, or board of directors has its own culture and character. I experienced many. Each had its own political realities, in large part based on either dominant personalities or primary missions. University politics differed dramatically from corporate politics, as did the politics of a regulated utility from those of a competitive organization. Frick found himself in a rather unique organizational structure.

Baseball—or for that matter, any professional sports organization—has peculiarities. Baseball's peculiarities stem from the creation of the National League in 1876, when players were placed in a subservient position to owners and the league existed to administer the rules. Each team was privately owned and managed but required coordination because it also competed. That structure, created by William Hulbert, remains essentially the same today, with the only change the creation of commissioner after the fixed 1919 World Series. Before that, the commissioner was a figurehead. Even Landis's powers were limited, other than for the best-interests clause. The commissioner had other restrictions. Most important, he was hired by the owners and paid by the owners, and—if the magnates weren't satisfied—they could dismiss him or not renew his contract. Of the first nine commissioners, five were terminated, two—Landis and Bart Giamatti—died in office, and the others, Frick and Selig, chose to retire. Needless to say, the position has not been secure. The magnates have never been collectively easy to please.

Part of that is due to their varied backgrounds and perspectives. In the early days, some owners came from baseball, including Charles Comiskey, Clark Griffith, and Connie Mack. Even then, many magnates used riches earned elsewhere to acquire clubs, and with varied backgrounds, they often disagreed. The two leagues have also had differences, requiring resolution from the commissioner. If he became too involved, though, he received the wrath of league presidents, as happened to Chandler, or if he tried to resolve matters that should have been handled at lower levels, he encountered backlash, sometimes ending his commissionership. When dealing with various personalities, commissioners had to tread cautiously because the position was highly sensitive politically.

The closest organizational parallel is a trade-association director. Each member of the association represents an organization whose employees sometimes compete against each other while also collectively sharing many objectives. The members hire the director, pay the salary, and dismiss him or her if displeased. In many ways, baseball's commissioner fits that model, the most notable exception being the league presidents, who already performed many of the duties. The commissioner thus had the added challenge of not interfering with them. That problem, one many trade-association directors don't have, made the position even more politically sensitive, and many commissioners unintentionally stepped on land mines.

Why do I consider Frick and Selig the most successful? The basic answer is they better understood the politics. Frick spent seventeen years as president of the National League before becoming commissioner, working with half the owners and even recruiting some. He was also acquainted with American League owners through joint meetings and other events. In effect, he had already built personal relationships. Similarly, Bud Selig owned the Milwaukee Brewers for decades before being named acting commissioner in 1993. He was part of the group. Both learned how to deal with various personalities to effect change and at the same time understood the need for patience to achieve it. No other commissioner, other than Rob Manfred currently, had similar exposure when named to the position; thus, learning curves hampered their effectiveness. In contrast, both Frick and Selig hit the ground running, accomplishing more sooner.

Most chapters focus on Frick's achievements in baseball, first as National League president and then as commissioner. Major contributions are addressed in separate chapters; lesser, but still important, accomplishments are discussed later.

This is a revisionist history. If one examines baseball from 1934 to 1965, one acknowledges the game changed considerably, usually for the better. That occurred either in spite of or in part due to his efforts. I contend the latter is unquestionably the case. He did not address all the challenges faced in the 1950s and early 1960s. Attendance problems persisted. Television, while providing baseball a growing revenue stream, was more conducive to football, helping its popularity at baseball's expense. It's questionable what Ford Frick could have done regarding those challenges. He did, however, address others, shaping and changing baseball in doing so.

Although this book deals primarily with Frick's baseball impact, it touches on his background earlier, along with his selection as commissioner. There was certainly a personal side to the man, provided by four close to him: Buzzie Bavasi, for whom Frick was a surrogate father; Jeri Frick, his daughter-in-law; Kelly Frick Richards, his granddaughter; and Ford Frick, his grandson. All provided perspectives worth mentioning. For Bavasi, Frick was responsible for having him attend DePauw with his close friend Fred Frick, Ford's son. He also arranged his first job with the Brooklyn Dodgers, leading to a long executive career with three clubs. For daughter-in-law Jeri, he offered support when her new husband was stationed overseas during World War II. They rode the train together to work and met once a week for lunch at Toots Shor's Restaurant. For the two grandchildren, he was a warm, caring man who loved telling stories.[24]

The composite assessment is of a successful man not encumbered by ego. He was proud of his achievements but didn't let them interfere with his goals or relationships. He wasn't bothered by criticism, usually not reacting to it unless requiring clarification. If his goal was achieved, he rarely cared who was credited. He usually didn't hold grudges, realizing there was always a next time, thus rarely responding publicly to criticisms. He possessed a strong intellectual curiosity, demonstrated throughout his life. He was not a saint and sometimes made mistakes, but he always attempted to be fair—not easy given his administrative responsibilities. Much of this will become clear in the chapters.

FORD FRICK

1

Before Reaching the Majors

Frick had an interesting journey before becoming a baseball executive. He was born and resided in two small Indiana railroad towns. After graduating from high school at fifteen, he spent a year in Fort Wayne, working as a copyboy for the newspaper. At sixteen he matriculated at DePauw University in Greencastle, Indiana. Those four years offered Frick numerous extracurricular opportunities that assisted in his development—one, ironically, was failing to make the baseball varsity. After graduation, he headed to Walsenburg, Colorado, fulfilling his interest in the West. He spent seven years in the state, mostly at a local newspaper in Colorado Springs. A story on the 1921 Pueblo flood led to a job offer with a New York newspaper, where he covered the New York Yankees. By the early 1930s he hosted shows on WGN radio and broadcast both baseball and college football games. He was already prominent when hired by the National League.

A NOBLE UPBRINGING

Ford Frick's family had been in Noble County, Indiana, for over forty years when he was born in December 1894. His grandfather Christian, born in 1819, and great uncle John, born in 1820, immigrated from Erlenbach, Switzerland, a small community south of Zurich. Evidence suggests their family were members of the conservative faction of the Swiss Reformed Church and were concerned after the Zurich liberal faction regained control in the early 1840s. The brothers left for America soon after, stopping in Ohio before settling in Noble County, Indiana. Christian came first, residing with another Swiss family in 1850 and soon acquiring property. His brother bought land in 1853, adjacent to Christian's in Elkhart Township. By then Christian was married, and his first son, Jacob, was born. Both brothers had large families—descendants, mostly from John's side, still reside there. The brothers had sizable, profitable farms by 1870, benefitting from completion of a railroad in the late 1850s.[1]

Jacob Frick's career and Ford's childhood centered around that railroad. When Christian died in 1880, Jacob, then twenty-seven, was married and residing next door. Jacob met his wife, Emma Jane, when her father, Jacob Prickett, ministered the family's Baptist church in Cosperville, three miles north of Wawaka. By 1879 they had their first child, Sophronia. Little is known about Jacob Frick's childhood, though it certainly included farm chores and school. Evidence suggests education was important, as Jacob was considered "a very ardent learner and reader." With help from neighbors, he built a log-cabin schoolhouse, becoming one of the first teachers in Noble County.[2] Indeed, the Elkhart Township plat map of 1893 shows Union School on Frick property.[3] Farming remained Jacob's primary livelihood until he made a career change in 1889. He sold his interest in the farm and moved to Wawaka, where Ford was later born, receiving $450 for the sale of three parcels of land.[4] The 1890 census is destroyed, but the family was likely in Wawaka by then. In 1900 Jacob was a railroad laborer, renting a house in Wawaka. Why Jacob sold his interest in the farm is unknown; perhaps he was lured by a more stable income. It proved fortunate. Whether due to bad management or excessive debt during the 1893 depression, his brothers lost the farm in a sheriff's sale in 1895.[5] At that point, Jacob may have been relieved.

Still, residing in a railroad town and working along the line wasn't easy. Such towns were located roughly five miles apart so engines could stop as needed to replenish water or wood. Although engines later burned coal, water needs remained unpredictable, and fuel still needed refilling. The track had to be maintained regularly and cleared during winter storms. There was always work with a steady, albeit not large, paycheck. Unfortunately, railroad towns lacked the charm of many communities. The constant traffic of steam engines belching smoke coated streets, lawns, and houses with soot, and they were quite noisy. A Wawaka resident described it vividly: "Finally around the bend came the train, a pall of inky smoke coming from its stack, rolling and rumbling along, its wheels clicking, the bell clanging away as it swept past us."[6] Once steam engines were replaced, Wawaka lost it function, existing today as a shell of what it was when Ford was born.

Yet, in spite of the soot and noise, the town was vibrant. In 1900 there were over 250 residents, making it the largest community and hub of Elkhart Township, which had a population of 1,400. Ten railroad workers were in Wawaka, along with a restaurant, barbershop, hardware store, grocery, bakery, general-merchandise store, and sawmill. Scattered throughout the township were nine teachers, twenty-one artisans, two doctors, two ministers, and a veterinarian. When the family moved to Brimfield, with Jacob promoted to section foreman, they found a similar community, though Orange, its township, was more diverse. Brimfield was smaller than Wolcottville and Rome City, the latter where a sanatorium and summer chautauqua (a group that held adult-education courses and entertainment) generated activity. Brimfield had about sixty fewer residents than Wawaka, though was similar otherwise. As many railroad workers were there, though Brimfield was more specialized, with two signal workers, two telegraph operators, and an electrician.[7] During young Ford's years, the town had a weekly newspaper, which proved formulative, and Orange Township was more vibrant during his school years.

Brimfield is the town Frick refers to in his memoir, *Games, Asterisks, and People*, with the entire prologue devoted to the village. He mentions playing baseball and highlights his idol, Ed Morley, a pitcher for semipro clubs in Fort Wayne and South Bend who also published Brimfield's newspaper. Frick credits Morley with sparking his journalism interest: "[He was] the editor, publisher, and printer of our local four-page newspaper, which he turned out single-handed on an antique hand-operated Franklin press. It was in his shop that I first got the smell of printer's ink in my nostril, and the lure of news reporting in my heart."[8] Edgar J. Morley lived in Brimfield in 1900, residing with his stepparents and listed as a printer.[9] Other historical records indicate a newspaper then, the *Brimfield Call*.[10] It is unknown how long it was published, but a town of Brimfield's size did not assure success. By 1910 Morley resided in Elkhart, Indiana, no longer a printer, though he had clearly influenced a future journalist.

Some other childhood recollections by Frick seem embellished. In his memoir and many speeches, Frick claimed he was a farm boy, though he always resided in railroad towns. He also claimed to attend a Cubs exhibition game in Kendallville, Indiana, in 1907. Allegedly, Frick waited outside the ballpark before the game, and Cubs catcher Johnny Kling snuck him in by letting Ford carry his shoes, allowing the twelve-year-old to sit by their bench. Frick claimed that cemented his love of baseball.[11] Yet there is no evidence the game occurred, though such exhibitions were then common.[12]

Baseball was played everywhere. Kendallville was large enough to have a semipro club, where Ed Morley exhibited his skills to boys like

Ford. And though some of Frick's recollections were embellished, his memories of playing baseball seem likely: "It was a land of open spaces. All we needed was . . . three grain bags, cut to size, and pegged down for bases; and a shingle set in the ground to serve as home plate. We were in the baseball business. More important, it was a land of farm villages and hamlets. . . . These villages, intensely proud and violently competitive, were the battlegrounds of our baseball wars."[13] Playing organized ball, however, was less likely. His high school class in Rome City graduated only four boys, with most others having stopped schooling after eighth grade. Informal pick-up games were the primary option.

Although the move to Brimfield would be formulative for Frick, it had little impact on his family's lifestyle. Being a section foreman was a step up in job status and wages, but it was not substantial. The lot for the house Jacob purchased was small, and even though the house was large enough for a boarder, in addition to Ford and his younger sister, Emma, living quarters were tight. The house had no indoor plumbing; instead, an outdoor pump was for water, and a privy accommodated other needs. Their house was also close to the tracks. Said Ford's granddaughter, "Jacob had a spot he liked to sit in the dining room where he could watch the trains come through on the tracks, just across the road from the house."[14] Besides these four family members who lived together, both older, married daughters lived close by, one in Brimfield and one on a farm.[15] Ford's grandmother, along with aunts and uncles, resided in Wawaka or farms in Elkhart Township.

Overall, young Ford had a normal childhood. He went to elementary school through eighth grade, three blocks from his home. Beyond earning money working with Ed Morley, Frick likely had other jobs, especially during the summer. He may have helped his sister and brother-in-law on their farm, hence his later references, or worked with his father on the railroad. Only fifteen when he graduated from high school, he likely skipped grades, suggesting a serious student. Other than his exposure to journalism and apparent eagerness to learn, Frick's childhood appeared typical for a small town, midwestern boy in the early twentieth century.

Frick's high school in Rome City was almost six miles away, with no railroad connection. It was a long walk for a boy of twelve or thirteen. Though Rome City was double Brimfield's population, it was far more vibrant due to its sanatorium and the chautauqua. However, changes in railroad rate schedules in 1908 ended the chautauqua, slowing Rome City's pace by the time Frick started school. His graduating class had eleven students, and the high school at most sixty students with twenty boys. There is no evidence of formal sports, and Frick may have been too short. "It is said that he graduated from high school still wearing knee pants, he was so small."[16] His graduation ceremonies went on for a week; activities included plays and music, with one night at the Methodist church in Brimfield.[17] Looking back, Frick recalled, "When I graduated from high school, I decided I was going to be a newspaperman. I was a young kid, 15 or 16, and somebody told me you had to know how to type."[18] That determined his next step.

That summer, in 1910, he moved to Fort Wayne, enrolling at the International School of Business. He "took courses in typing and stenography.... There were no journalism schools in those days and I figured that sort of stuff could be the beginning thing."[19] The courses paid major dividends later, as Frick was typing 150 words a minute when in New York, though benefits came sooner because he was hired by the *Fort Wayne Journal-Gazette* as an office boy and police reporter for $3.50 a week.[20] Because bylines were rare, the extent of his reporting is unknown, though the experience opened new horizons. With no relatives in the city, he had to find and pay for his own room and board, and with a population of over sixty thousand, the city dwarfed Brimfield. The *Journal-Gazette* offered considerable journalism experience. The year in Fort Wayne developed skills and experience not available in Noble County.

His time at the newspaper perhaps helped to determine his next step. While college journalism programs were scarce, many universities published campus papers and had departments of English Composition. Frick's time at the *Journal-Gazette* might have directed him to a particular school to pursue his news-writing interests. The reporters with whom he worked were likely aware of colleges in Indiana with daily newspapers and knew that Sigma Delta Chi (SDX), the precursor of the Society for Professional Journalists, had been founded two years earlier at DePauw University. That, along with DePauw being the smallest Indiana school to publish a daily paper, enticed Frick to matriculate in the fall of 1911. The next four years would prove formative.

"GREENER CASTLES"

With a population of three thousand, the town of Greencastle didn't match Fort Wayne's urbanity. Still, the town was over ten times the size of Brimfield and a considerable hub. Three railroads passed through the county seat, enabling residents to reach Chicago, St. Louis, and Louisville in hours. For closer trips, the interurban railroad connected Greencastle with both Indianapolis and Terre Haute in an hour. Beyond the rail lines was industry—with much industrial activity dependent on local limestone quarries—along with the stores, restaurants, and hotels expected in a county seat.

DePauw University was a major asset. Starting as Indiana Asbury University in 1837, the school grew considerably, admitting women after the Civil War and receiving a major endowment from business philanthropist Washington C. DePauw in the 1880s. That gift stabilized the school financially and ensured the Methodist church continued its oversight. The gift created a school of music and was renamed for its benefactor. Upon Frick's arrival, ten fraternities and eight sororities were on campus. Most students were affiliated, with many men joining before arriving on campus.[21]

Based on the campus newspaper, the *DePauw Daily*, the school of liberal arts had around 660 students and the school of music 140 during Frick's years, with slightly more men than women. Over 85 percent were from Indiana. The most popular career pursued was teaching, with around 40 percent planning to enter an education profession. Women in particular chose this career, given the limited opportunities available to them. The next most popular pursuit was the ministry, followed by business, law, medicine, and journalism.[22] That education and divinity were the most popular is unsurprising—in 1910 other careers rarely required a college degree, though law, medicine, and journalism were becoming more difficult to pursue without one. That may have factored in Frick's decision.

Attending college away from home was expensive for Frick's family. Based on the school's 1914–15 catalog for Ford's last school year, the cost of tuition each semester was $30, with a $2 athletic fee and a $5 charge for a diploma. Room and board costs were estimated at $4.25 a week; the former cost $1.25. According to the catalog, the overall costs "need not ordinarily exceed $300 for the year."[23] It also indicated that "the faculty earnestly recommends that friends or parents of students insist upon a regular and systematic accountability for the funds placed at their disposal, believing that economical habits should be acquired during college life by those of large as well as those of limited means. It is the earnest effort of the university administration to keep the life of the institution simple and inexpensive."[24] What that meant for young Frick, whose father earned around $700 a year, was the need for employment during the school year to cover some costs.[25] That work is unknown, but stoking furnaces and waiting on tables in living units were the most common.

Whether working or not, students were required to take between 20 and 22 hours of class a week each semester. A total of 168 hours were required for graduation, and all students had to complete work in four groups: 16 hours in a single language other than English, 8 hours in English and public speaking, a minimum of 10 hours in a single math or science subject, and at least 10 hours of course work in the social sciences. They also completed 120 hours of elective work. Freshmen were further required to take 2 hours of gym a week both semesters.[26] Any jobs a student had were obviously scheduled around classes.

While classes were demanding, extracurricular activities offered further opportunities. Men interested in sports had football in the fall, basketball in the winter, and baseball, track, and tennis in the spring. All five competed against other schools and were limited to men. Students not enrolled in music could participate in the band or glee club, both of which provided performance opportunities. There were also oratorical competitions. The campus newspaper was published daily five days a week, except during final exams, and members of the junior class produced a yearbook—the *Mirage*. There was also student government and other committee work, and Greek units offered positions of responsibility. The *DePauw Daily* estimated two-thirds of DePauw students affiliated with a Greek organization.[27]

Frick attended DePauw at an interesting time due to progressive reform movements, in particular women's suffrage and prohibition. Both had major student support. The suffrage movement had a growing number of coeds, and even some men were involved. Outside speakers were brought in, featuring alumnae like Mary Beard, and faculty members predicted women would soon gain the right to vote. Given DePauw's ties to the Methodist Church, the emphasis on prohibition wasn't surprising. During the second semester of Frick's junior year, faculty spoke on the dangers of alcohol consumption, due to Greencastle officials establishing a referendum to rescind its ban on saloons. More than any other issue, this became the focus of the *DePauw Daily*, which ran four front-page editorials favoring prohibition's continuation and encouraging students of age to return during winter break to vote against the proposal.[28] The referendum was defeated by over two hundred votes, and DePauw president George Grose thanked students who voted to keep Greencastle dry.[29]

Each semester had a special day without classes, but one football game against all-male Wabash College—located twenty-seven miles north in Crawfordsville—was gaining prominence over other events. Coverage by the *DePauw Daily* made clear this contest surpassed other campus sporting events. During Frick's first year, the teams tied at Wabash. The following year, before a large DePauw home crowd, enthusiasm was stifled quickly with a crushing 62–0 Wabash victory. For at least two days after, practices were canceled due to the coach suffering "a severe attack of indigestion,"[30] and a month later, concerned DePauw alumni met to take more control of athletics.[31] That involvement strengthened sports, also providing Frick an opportunity.

While the university offered many activities, it also imposed restrictions. As a Methodist college, DePauw expected students to obey church guidelines, even if not affiliated. Major violations resulting in expulsion included drinking and gambling, the latter tied to card-playing or billiards.[32] While not in the same category, dancing was also forbidden on campus, and students were aware violators faced penalties. Male students did not always obey rules, but transgression was undertaken cautiously. Coeds had additional restrictions. Hours of visitation with men were limited, and "college women must not visit men's fraternity chapter halls at any time other than on the occasion when special chaperones are provided."[33] Whereas men were largely free to come and go as they pleased, coeds were tightly confined to living units or campus activities. Although there were some protests, nothing changed during Frick's tenure.

Though the administration didn't seem to approve, as the president considered it a greater problem than drinking, one vice tolerated was smoking.[34] Perhaps that was due to estimates that half of the men smoked. Numerous events on campus were called "smokers," some even attended by the president. Evidence indicates Frick was among those who smoked, as he did through most of his life.

In spite of the restrictions, DePauw did not lack social activities. Along with smokers, fraternities hosted other activities for men, including meetings for Sigma Delta Chi, the journalism honorary, and Kappa Tau Kappa, the interfraternity honorary. Whereas fraternity houses were generally off limits for coeds, Greek units hosted a variety of outdoor, off-campus events. Phi Kappa Psi, Frick's fraternity, hosted a hayride before Halloween his senior year.[35] Other annual arranged trips, generally during warmer weather, to a restaurant along the Old National Trail in Mount Meridian or to Eel River Falls included coeds.[36] These longer trips necessitated horses and buggies, but some locations were within walking distance. The most popular was McClain's Springs, just south of the university across the Vandalia (later Pennsylvania) Railroad tracks, a common site for picnics.[37] Places to hang out were nearby, the most popular being "the little drug store," which moved to new quarters during Frick's junior year. The *DePauw Daily* expressed concern, stating that it would be a long time before "the new place shed one ray of the congenial warmth with which the old place glowed, a warmth which made it the cheeriest spot on campus."[38] Frick mentioned another popular hangout, Charley Bells', where "the ungodly" went "for a quick coke and a hot ham sandwich during Chapel period while the saintly were enjoying prayers at Chapel."[39] Thus, in spite of restrictions, DePauw students still could engage in many joint activities.

BIG MAN ON CAMPUS

Frick may have chosen DePauw due to the opportunities provided, especially its newspaper, but he was slow to take advantage of them. Although he may have reached normal height when matriculating, he was younger than most freshmen and may not have had time. Given his father's annual income, he needed to help cover expenses. That started to change during the second semester of freshman year.

Pursuing his primary objective, Frick tried out for sophomore editor of the *DePauw Daily* in March. The campus paper held two tryouts a year, in November and March. Frick skipped the first but succeeded in the spring. What was required for the tryout is unknown, but he won against four competitors.[40] The *DePauw Daily* was not Frick's only endeavor, for he also joined a twenty-member band in which he apparently played trumpet,[41] seemingly a skill developed before college. He did not try out for baseball, nor did he pledge a fraternity, unlike most freshmen. For that he waited until second semester sophomore year, both age and money the likely reasons for hesitancy.

Frick did increase his extracurricular activities during his sophomore year. At the start, he joined Darsee Club, a "rooming club" for men, dropping out when pledging Phi Kappa Psi in second semester.[42] It is unknown why Frick joined Darsee, though given the state of many campus rooms, it may have been an upgrade of living conditions. The *DePauw Daily* described the typical campus room as "a simple square box, with faded paper on the wall, yellow time-stained curtains on the window, patched up matting and linoleum on the floor."[43] He joined the band again sophomore year, the last time he did so. He was also a member of the Philo Society, "one of the oldest and most potent of the organizations in the university . . . established at DePauw in 1848. The aim of the organization is the development of the literary, musical, debate, and oratorical talents of its members."[44] Its importance on campus was waning when Frick joined, but he may have found it helpful when he engaged in campus politics.

Frick entered that realm in the fall of sophomore year, running for student council as one of two class representatives. DePauw encouraged a democratic environment, if judged by the number of positions chosen by popular vote. They included class president, vice president, secretary, treasurer, scrap captain, yell leader, football captain, football manager, basketball captain, basketball manager, historian, prophetess, poetess, and sergeant-at-arms. Frick belonged to the Independent Party ticket, which swept the entire election in 1912 by an average 47–35 margin.[45] Based on reporting from the *Daily*, party coalitions and names changed yearly, with the coalitions stemming from Greek units and campus clubs. The alliances were apparently fluid. Frick's membership in Darsee and Philo, along with his involvement with the *Daily*, possibly were factors encouraging him to run. There is no record of issues the student council faced, but representing his class increased Frick's campus presence.

Beyond the council, Frick also tried out for baseball sophomore year, one of thirty doing so.[46] Tryouts were shortened due to a wet spring, and the season started four days later. Frick didn't make varsity, though he was noted twice, once for surviving the first cut and the other for spiking Wilson of the varsity "when he slid into him in the fifth frame" of a scrimmage game.[47] A later issue of the *DePauw Daily* mentions the coach was unable to schedule games for the scrubs, which likely affected Frick, as scrimmages were the only baseball action he saw. That proved a prelude for the rest of his baseball experience at DePauw. Even without making the varsity, though, Frick's sophomore year was far more active than his freshman year.

It was likely not just more confidence that led to his activities but also a change in Jacob's occupation. Sometime in 1913, perhaps as early as late March, his father was named postmaster for Brimfield, a political appointment. In November 1912 Democrat Woodrow Wilson was elected president. Although there is no record of Jacob's political involvement, the appointment, as well as family history, suggests he was a Democrat.[48] Most relevant to Ford, his father's salary went from roughly $700 to $1,200 yearly, a substantial increase.[49] That meant Jacob was more able to assist his son with expenses, providing him more free time.

The most important aftermath of improved family finances was Ford pledging Phi Kappa Psi fraternity, starting a relationship for the remainder of his life. Little is known of Ford's time as a pledge, but the burdens were likely onerous. Though hazing of pledges continues today, it was far more burdensome a century ago. Frick alluded to it in his centennial address, recalling the "cold baths; the demerit board; freshman week and Hell week—all happily defunct now."[50] Because he joined second semester with one other pledge, he may have received more unwanted attention than usual. By senior year, though, he was a chapter leader, serving in the two most important positions—recruitment chair in first semester and president in second.

The minutes from chapters meetings in 1914–15 provide a snapshot of DePauw fraternity life over one hundred years ago. At a fall meeting, while recruitment chair, Frick commented that many in the chapter were "a contented bunch of loafers." Action was taken against "men coming in the house and getting drunk." Later that semester, concern was expressed about low freshmen grades. In the spring, a member griped about "superfluous pool playing," and later one urged that "betting in the house must be stopped."[51] It's clear a number of DePauw's rules were not followed by some members, providing challenges to the officers.

What's also clear from the minutes is that fellow members respected Frick. His comments were impactful, as motions were often changed when he spoke against them. When elected president, the other officers proceeded to "treat the chapter to ten cent drink" in Frick's honor after the meeting.[52] Soft drinks sold for five cents, so one can infer the nature of a more costly celebratory beverage. Respect was further shown by naming him their representative to Kappa Tau Kappa, the honorary organization for DePauw fraternities, and sending him to Chicago to represent them at Phi Psi's district convention in May 1915.[53] Fifty years later, in 1965, Frick was again honored by his chapter, selected as the featured speaker for the centennial celebration of DePauw Phi Psi. His speech was filled with warmth and affection, perhaps best expressed by his comments that "it demands of each of us temperance within reason, good humor and good sportsman ship. In return it offers laughter for the happy, understanding for the worried, sympathy for the sufferer and a hand of friendship for the stranger."[54] His ongoing involvement after graduation, especially when son Fred and Buzzie Bavasi affiliated with the fraternity in 1934, further demonstrated Phi Psi's importance to Frick.

While his fraternity membership had, perhaps, the greatest impact on him, the *DePauw Daily* was a close second, especially in preparing him for early careers. It was the only activity in which he was involved all four years. Along with being the sophomore editor, he was one of three junior editors, part of a staff of seven who rotated responsibility for overseeing the output. If Frick attempted to be editor-in-chief his senior year, he wasn't successful, though he served as third editor behind the chief and the assistant and still participated in editorial decisions and contributed stories. For some reason, perhaps due to other responsibilities, he stepped down in late October senior year, returning in early March, remaining with the *Daily* until seniors relinquished their duties.[55]

Because the *Daily* rarely contained bylines, Frick's contributions can't be gauged. Only two stories were credited, offering an early hint of the sportswriter he would become. Both dealt with sports. The first, written during sophomore year, discussed an upcoming football game against Earlham College: "With final scrimmage done and all the men in fine condition, sixteen members of Coach Cunningham's squad will make the trip to Richmond tomorrow determined to show the Quaker 'home-comers' a new wrinkle in scientific football. . . . Dope on the two teams seems to favor DePauw but a comparison of the two promised one of the hardest battles of the year for Coach Cunningham's scoring machine."[56] The other was written in the fall of senior year in a series about DePauw's administrators. Frick's story featured Heber Ellis, an alumnus serving as athletic director. Discussing Ellis's student days in the 1890s, Frick wrote, "He was not particularly prepossessing, this particular specimen. . . . True enough he had a voice like a real-for-sure New England foghorn; was built much on the lines of the famous Stone Wall and had a punting foot good for sixty yards on a wet field—but then he was only a freshman and could only expect to be shadowed by the glowing radiance of his upperclassmen." Today, with Ellis overseeing DePauw sports, "he is the first man to wish the boys luck; after a hard dusty practice he is the first man in the gym ready with a towel and a bottle of rub down. When there is hard work to be done, he is the first man called on. In his pocket he carries the key to DePauw athletics; in his heart he carries and cherishes the best wishes of the student body."[57] Frick's embellished writings reflect the period's style and demonstrate the foundation for his work during the next two decades.

Along with the challenges and benefits Frick and others experienced working at the *DePauw Daily* was the freedom to print independently. While the *Daily* rarely took the administration to task during Frick's years, it was allowed to disagree, the best example being editorials against social restrictions on females. Although DePauw did not alter policies, it did not hamper the *Daily* from disagreeing. Professor Tilden, the faculty advisor to the paper, affirmed this independence: "The paper should be a student organ in the columns of which the students would have perfect liberty of expressing their opinions and spirit. There has been no thought as far as I know of the faculty controlling *The Daily*."[58] In the same article, Tilden expressed concern for coverage of the *DePauw Daily*'s expenses, paid by student subscriptions, as fewer than half subscribed at a cost of $2.50. That problem was solved before Frick graduated, with students voting to support the paper through a tuition increase.[59] Its independence wasn't affected.

The *Daily* was not DePauw's only student publication. Like most universities, students published a yearbook—the *Mirage*. By tradition the junior class was responsible, though every year it required approval by a faculty committee, thus not a certainty. During Frick's junior year, the faculty demanded proof of support, agreeing to allow work only after students raised $1,000.[60] Unlike the *Daily*, which chose its staff through tryouts, *Mirage* positions were elected by the junior class, with the two parties slating candidates. Frick was nominated to be editor by the Liberal Party, and his ticket swept all but one position.[61] How candidates were nominated is unclear, but the only input a potential editor had in the selection was by convincing students to run—and their election wasn't guaranteed. That presented challenges for the editor, as Frick's yearbook comments implied.

Frick did have an advantage in promoting the *Mirage* because he was also an editor at the *DePauw Daily*. Numerous times the paper generated publicity. In January Frick announced in the *Daily* that the *Mirage* would devote seventy-five pages to sports, and late in February he highlighted two new sections, on coeds and dramatics.[62] As the book was almost ready, Frick asserted, "Well boys, they'll all be jumping on my neck by this time tomorrow," emphasizing it was the best *Mirage* "put out this year." The *Daily* begged to differ with that humble assessment, claiming it was "the unanimous verdict of those who have already seen the book that the last two words should be stricken."[63] Compared with yearbooks the year before and after, Frick's production definitely contains more humor, perhaps reflecting the editor's wit. Even in his personal bio in the *Mirage*, Frick stated, "This is the perpetrator of this collection of beauty, wit and literary perfection. I'd like to have a *Mirage* board that works."[64] Later in the book, Frick offered a father's advice to his son: "Go to college, my boy, but for the love o'mike, don't try for a *Mirage* job."[65] It appears his editor duties were challenging, but he maintained his sense of humor throughout. The *Mirage* appeared to be well received, reflecting his personality and wit, along with his editorial efforts.

Frick's baseball efforts junior and senior year were less successful. Although he later claimed to play baseball at DePauw, he never made the varsity. DePauw hired a new coach Frick's junior year—John Grim. Unlike his predecessor, Grim played in the Majors, mostly as a catcher and first baseman for National League clubs in Louisville and Brooklyn. The new coach didn't help Frick. His junior year he survived the first cut and was one of twenty-five players who practiced, fourteen seeing varsity action and listed in team statistics—but not Frick.[66] The following year, the *DePauw Daily* was optimistic about his chances, claiming he "will try to put the skids on one of the outfield spots."[67] He was listed with the larger squad as one of six outfielders, and he saw action at first base in a game between the varsity and "Yannigans," playing with the scrubs.[68] His team lost, 9–3. By the end of April he wasn't even in scrimmages, suggesting he was no longer involved. Frick tried out but never got beyond practices or a few scrimmage games.

He did travel with the team during his senior year. In the fall, Frick was voted the baseball captain—a team coordinator—by his classmates. Although the extent of his responsibilities wasn't defined in the *Daily*, he traveled with the team to Oxford, Ohio, and Lexington, Kentucky, for games with Miami and Kentucky.[69] He also announced in November 1914 that he would manage a freshman basketball squad. Due to poor facilities, DePauw had not played basketball since Frick's sophomore year. Declaring the Greencastle armory an adequate place, he claimed that "it will be possible to make enough money on home games . . . to enable them to have several good trips to various parts of the state where they will probably play other freshmen teams."[70] Unfortunately, his plans were for naught, except for a few practices, as two weeks after his announcement, a committee chaired by Heber Ellis declared the armory unsafe.[71]

His commitment to sports went even further, as he was elected chairman of the Vigilance Committee at the start of second semester senior year.[72] According to the *Mirage*, its purpose was "getting new men, especially athletes, to enter DePauw. . . . The representative of each fraternal organization in school cooperates with the graduate manager of athletics to secure the names of new students and by personal work under his direction to bring desirable men and women to DePauw."[73] The program was a byproduct of DePauw's humbling loss to Wabash in 1912, and Frick worked closely with Heber Ellis to strengthen its athletics.

In early February 1915 Frick was appointed by the senior class president to chair the Coming Out Committee responsible for planning graduation. Frick worked closely with the university president and two other seniors to recruit a speaker. By the end of the month the *Daily* announced Bishop William A. Quayle would give the address, calling him "one of the most able lecturers on the American platform." The paper went on to say, "Ford C. Frick, together with President Grose, was instrumental in bringing Bishop Quayle here."[74] Frick's committee asked the administration to consider holding graduation outdoors, though it's unclear whether such occurred.[75] In his last duty, Frick announced class-day exercises, held three days before the June 9 commencement, which included a faculty address, senior response, class oration, and other activities.[76] His senior committee and sports experiences, coupled with his work on the *Daily* and *Mirage*, offered Frick considerable interaction with the administration and faculty, which would prove invaluable later.

Frick was also inducted into two honorary organizations. The most active was Sigma Delta Chi (SDX), the journalism honorary group founded at DePauw. The main duty of the local chapter was bringing journalists to speak and interact with students, along with other activities. During his junior year, SDX conducted a play, called *One for the Faculty*, written as a spoof of the *Daily*. Frick was cast as office boy Hearst, who worked with another character, Arthur Brisbane, the editor of the *New York American*, a Hearst newspaper. Both were real. Coincidentally, eight years later it would be Brisbane who dramatically affected Frick's career. The performance did not launch an acting career, though the *DePauw Daily* stated, "The work of . . . Ford Frick as Hearst, the office boy, is . . . worthy of special comment."[77] The other organization was Kappa Tau Kappa, a local honorary interfraternity mentioned earlier.

Little documentation of Frick's college personal life exists, though inferences can be drawn anecdotally. There is no record of his dating, but he was involved with organizations with coeds, like the newspaper and yearbook. He also participated in coed social events, such as the trip to Eel River Falls.[78] No evidence suggests that he dated seriously, a possible indication that DePauw's coeds lacked appeal.[79] Anecdotal evidence relates to other aspects of his social life. When Frick gave the keynote speech for Phi Psi at his fiftieth reunion in 1965, he referenced four major taboos during his time as a student: dancing, billiards, card games, and alcohol. During his speech, he alluded to "clandestine dances at Calumet Hall," "Little Feller out-slicking the slickers at Pete Stoner's Pool Hall," "hot hand games in the smoker," and "surreptitious trips to Brazil."[80] The reference to dances, billiards, and card games are obvious, surreptitious trips less so. Brazil, Indiana, the next town west on the interurban line, didn't prohibit alcohol and was sufficiently close for students who wished to imbibe but far enough to avoid being caught. In essence, fifty years after graduation, while still commissioner, Frick implied he violated almost every social restriction while in college.

In spite of extracurricular and apparent clandestine activities, Frick gave studies high priority. He was a B student. His best grades of A were in two English Composition classes, reflecting his main interest. If there were a mentor among professors, it was likely Nathaniel Barnes, who taught English Composition.[81] Barnes may have also been advisor to the *DePauw Daily* or *Mirage*, as the yearbook Frick edited was dedicated to him. Ford's worst subject was German; he received an F his sophomore year, his only failing grade. When he retook the course, he received either a B or P, the latter signifying all requirements were met. Though a decent student, Frick didn't graduate with honors, nor was he inducted into Phi Beta Kappa. While not an honor student, and in an era preceding grade modifiers of plus and minus, Frick was solid academically.[82]

Graduation ceremonies were held on June 9, and the local newspaper noted, "The weather could not have been any better had it been made to order, except ten degrees more of Old Sol's would have been welcomed." It stated that Bishop Quayle's oration was "one of the best ever delivered at DePauw and of a practical nature."[83] The graduating class consisted of

130 students. Regarding graduation, Frick described the ceremony as "the unforgettable final farewell as you walk from the Chapter house, out the drive, across the campus and into the world of the alumni, still clinging fast to the hopes and the dreams."[84] Whatever his ambitions were, they didn't include commissioner of baseball, which didn't exist in 1915.

Although his DePauw years aren't mentioned in Frick's memoir, they were clearly formative. In later decades he devoted considerable time to his alma mater, first on the alumni board and then on the trustees for over a quarter century. He sent his only child, Fred, to DePauw, even though he preferred being closer to home.[85] He also convinced Buzzie Bavasi's mother that DePauw would be a good experience, causing a last-minute switch from Notre Dame.[86] On numerous occasions, Frick, by then a baseball executive, would visit.

More significant, his course work and extracurricular activities paid major dividends for his career. His work at the *DePauw Daily* was beneficial for his journalism both in Colorado and New York. While the *Mirage* involved less writing, the experience directing a less-than-committed staff provided a lesson in management. So was his work as baseball manager, likely more beneficial than had he played. His committee work, along with fraternity leadership, taught him to work with people of different mindsets to achieve consensus. Further, his experiences helped develop a congenial personality even when dealing with people of strong differences of opinion. Frick may have been undecided on a career when he walked across the graduation stage, but those DePauw years helped pave the direction.

"GO WEST, YOUNG MAN"

Frick moved to Colorado after graduation. As a boy, he was fascinated with Native Americans, reading extensively about them. Colorado offered the opportunity to be closer and also satisfied his wanderlust, which stemmed from growing up by the railroad. Before, he rarely traveled outside Indiana, but he had a job when he arrived. When Frick was in third grade, the principal of his school, S. M. Andrews, boarded with his family. Andrews was now superintendent of Walsenburg schools and offered the new graduate a teaching job at the high school, though it is unclear who initiated the contact. Ford was hired to teach in the commercial department and offered the first journalism class.[87] His other classes are unknown. He may have played semipro baseball the summer before and following the school year, claiming years later, "I lost my amateur standing in Walsenburg, where I played first base on the Colorado Fuel and Iron Company team. I had played in college, but now I was a professional. Was I good? Listen, they asked me to come back the following summer."[88] During his time in Walsenburg, it appears Andrews returned Jacob's hospitality, renting Ford a room in his home.[89] Frick also met and later married Eleanor Cowling, whose father owned a general store. They married in September 1916 at her parents' home, but by then Frick resided in Colorado Springs.[90]

Ford and Eleanor remained together until he passed away in 1978, raising one son. She seemed happy to escape Walsenburg, preferring larger cities. Their marriage was solid. She tolerated his long trips as a sportswriter, radio broadcaster, and baseball executive. At times, she joined him during spring training and his trips to Japan. She rarely returned to her Colorado home and only once visited Frick's family in Brimfield, shortly after their marriage. She enjoyed her social life in Bronxville along with its proximity to New York City. To her grandchildren, she seemed more aloof than affectionate, both of them feeling closer to Ford.[91] Perhaps because baseball then was essentially a man's world, she usually stayed distant, quietly supporting his activities.

Unsurprisingly, Frick and his bride relocated, given Walsenburg in 1915. Colorado Springs was attractive, then the state's second-largest city, though Walsenburg was the primary impetus for their move. The town, not much larger than Greencastle, had thirteen mining operations nearby, increasing its population. While Greencastle was a dry town, Walsenburg had as many as forty-five saloons.[92] According to author Dorothy Rose Ree, it was a "tough place to live." Although the town was prosperous due to the mines, prostitutes were common on the streets, and most saloons had back rooms with rear entrances to accommodate that, along with gambling parlors.[93] Patrons were usually mine workers, recent immigrants from Italy, Greece, the Balkans, or Asia.[94] The area had numerous strikes, the most famous—the Ludlow massacre—occurring outside Walsenburg the year before Frick arrived, reflecting the rough, raucous community.

Frick appeared to have a similar teaching job at Colorado Springs High School in 1916–17, at least according to contemporary sources. The wedding announcement on September 19, 1916, mentions it being his job. The other source was Frick's draft registration card dated June

5, 1917, classifying him a "teacher at high school."[95] Both suggest he held the job the entire year, though he wasn't listed in the school yearbook, and nothing in its archives verifies his presence. The yearbook may have overlooked him, but the wedding announcement and draft card were likely accurate and a logical transition from his Walsenburg job.

Sometime during 1917, perhaps when school ended for the summer, Frick began work as a sports reporter for the *Colorado Springs Gazette*, with articles decades later suggesting he was sports editor. Since there were no bylines, his work there cannot be assessed. Further, it may not have been full-time because he also became a part-time professor at Colorado College in 1918. However, when the *Gazette* ran the birth announcement of son Fred in 1917, it stated Ford was employed by the paper.[96] Thus, it appears that from summer of 1917 through fall of 1918, when Frick was called to military duty, employment at the *Gazette* was at least part-time.

Regarding his teaching job, Frick was mentioned in the Colorado College's *Tiger*, the student newspaper, in October 1918, in an article about new professors. The story describes Frick as "formerly instructor of journalism at DePauw University and instructor of English at the local high school."[97] Frick never taught at his alma mater, having left after graduation. The college's yearbook for 1918–19, the *Pikes Peak Nugget*, listed him as an instructor of journalism, its subhead stating he graduated Phi Beta Kappa and received a master's degree in 1916 from DePauw.[98] In fact, Frick left a year earlier, attaining neither honors nor a master's. It appears Frick embellished his past, a habit that continued even when becoming a baseball executive. The campus catalog described his course: "Journalism—news gathering, news writing, and news editing; practical field work; analysis of news of the day. Each half year, 3 hours."[99] The catalog also indicated it was the only course taught by Frick and was only for first semester. The most notable event during his brief tenure was the outbreak of the Spanish flu on the campus, shutting down classes in October.[100] In any case, his relationship with Colorado College soon ended, perhaps before the semester did.

Even though Frick was definitely of draft age during World War I—twenty-two when war was declared in 1917—he was not called to duty until late in 1918, which may have abruptly ended his Colorado College tenure. His duties sent him to Denver as a training supervisor for four states—Colorado, Wyoming, Utah, and New Mexico—in the Rehabilitation Division of the War Department.[101] How long he served is unclear, but the 1920 U.S. Census, taken in January, placed him in the job, classifying him a "supervisor in an educational business." Along with spouse and his son, Fred, Eleanor's younger brother, also named Frederick, resided with them.[102] At the time, he owned a house with a mortgage near downtown. His neighbors were working as car mechanics, teamsters, truck drivers, and meat cutters. His military assignment may have been ending, as he was also employed with the *Rocky Mountain News*.[103] In any case, that job was short-lived, as Frick returned to Colorado Springs in late 1920.

His return involved two jobs, one with the other newspaper, the *Evening Telegraph*, as manager and writer of the editorial column, and the other creating an advertising agency.[104] It is unclear whether the agency was solely his. In late 1920 the *Colorado Springs Evening Telegraph* announced it would "publish a series of Indian legends of the Pikes Peak region written by Mr. Frick during the coming weeks"; he was finally able to pursue his interest in Native Americans.[105] Most of his focus at the *Telegraph* was on editorials, but he also did some reporting. In fact, one story Frick covered opened the door for his New York career.

In 1921, Pueblo, Colorado's largest city, was a steel-manufacturing hub and the center for saddle making, given its location along a major cattle drive. A disaster struck that year. A series of severe rainstorms, both in the mountains and over the city, fed the various tributaries of the Arkansas River. Reaching Pueblo, rain caused severe flooding and extensive damage to buildings, railroad cars, and bridges, with hundreds of lives lost. Any reporter present was stranded, unable to send out a story due to a power outage. Frick took a different approach. He hired a pilot in Colorado Springs to fly over Pueblo, where Frick took detailed notes and perhaps photos. Then, either Frick instructed the pilot not to land or he was unable to, so instead the pilot returned to Colorado Springs. Frick was thus a day ahead of other reporters and scooped the story. His description was vivid: "Everywhere water—brown, muddy waters—sucking, grasping, pulling at homes and store buildings alike—here and there a raft with its freight of human lives—everywhere desolation and death."[106] His story appeared across the country.

Frick initially received no reaction to his work, but he did benefit from a retirement home for newspaper printers in Colorado Springs. Resident Hyde Rogers had worked for the *New York American*, the Hearst morning newspaper in New York, and knew editor Arthur Brisbane. He brought the story to Brisbane's attention, recommending he consider Frick for a position. Sometime after, Brisbane telegraphed Frick, inviting him to New York for an interview, though Frick initially "thought the wire was a practical joke and almost missed the opportunity to go."[107] He did go after verifying the telegraph, accepting a job in 1922. Altogether, Frick spent seven years in Colorado, moving four different times. He gained more reporting and managerial experience, both of which proved useful in New York.

"IF I CAN MAKE IT HERE . . ."

At the time, both Brisbane and Hearst newspapers were preeminent in the city. Brisbane was known to be a tough and demanding editor, producing a well-regarded paper. As much as Frick enjoyed Colorado, it was difficult to decline working for a prestigious editor. It wasn't coincidental that Brisbane's name had been used in the DePauw spoof. Frick summed up his boss: "Brisbane was a rough, tough guy, a smart guy. He was very opinionated, very cold. . . . Brisbane was the biggest name in New York in those days, both as a writer and editor. . . . He was a brilliant man, quite a brilliant mind. You saw him only when he wanted to see you . . . and he was always a thought ahead of you."[108] Frick added that he wasn't Brisbane's protégé, though a spontaneous decision by his boss produced a bonanza for Frick's baseball career.

The decision was to move Frick from the *American* to the *Evening Journal*, the other New York Hearst paper. Frick explained:

> I was covering the Giants. The game was rained out and I was in the office writing a rainy-day story, and the office boy came in and said, "Mr. Brisbane wants to see you." I went to Mr. Brisbane's office and he told me he was taking over the *Journal* and was switching me over. He already had an assignment for me. . . . I started to walk away, and he said, "Where are you going?" "I'm going back to the *American* to finish my story." And he said, "To hell with the *American*. You're working for the *Journal*." I never did go back. As far as I'm concerned that rainy day story, on the Giants, is still in the typewriter.[109]

Frick switched to covering the Yankees at a time when the team surpassed John McGraw's Giants as the premier club. It was the heyday of Babe Ruth and later Lou Gehrig, and the job created opportunities Frick wouldn't have had covering the Giants.

Frick became personally acquainted with Ruth, a relationship that lasted until Ruth's death in 1948. Frick conveyed that significance in his memoir: "The Babe had 'charisma.' . . . He captured the imagination of the public as no man before or since. . . . Through it all, to the sports public, Babe Ruth was No. 1."[110] Frick became Ruth's primary ghostwriter, also writing for Gehrig and manager Miller Huggins. Frick later claimed, "I was Babe's ghost-writer from 1924 until I stopped working. I think we wrote a schedule of three stories a week. I know we did more than one. . . . I lived with the old guy, really."[111] Even after baseball hired Frick, he maintained a relationship lasting the remainder of Ruth's life, either on the golf course or by playing bridge with spouses.[112]

Frick considered his sports reporter job the best of his career, asserting such in his memoir and claiming the 1920s in New York was the best time for sportswriting. "I know I'm a prejudiced witness, but sentimentally I have always felt the heyday of baseball writing occurred in the decade following the end of the First World War. . . . It was a fun period—fun for the writers, fun for the players, and fun for the fans."[113] He mentioned meeting some of the great writers, including Damon Runyon, whom he considered a mentor, along with Grantland Rice, Heywood Broun, Ring Lardner, and Freddy Lieb.[114] Modesty prevented Frick from putting himself in that group, but he clearly became a premier sports reporter during that era.

He was also proud of his involvement with the Baseball Writers' Association of America in its largest branch—New York City. The association was founded in 1908 to protect baseball writers' interests, especially access to dugouts and press boxes. It also offered companionship for writers from other newspapers. The New York club was special because it hosted baseball's top brass—owners, managers, coaches, and players—at an annual dinner during the scheduling meeting of the two leagues, usually in early February. The reporters conducted a roast, done in the form of a minstrel show, blackface being the norm for participating writers. Frick took a lead role as the interlocutor. The participants performed gags, hitting "some of those present pretty hard."[115] Frick served as president of the New York chapter until joining the National League's offices.[116]

His shift into baseball was also facilitated by his work in radio, a natural transition, as WOR was also owned by Hearst. That brought Frick national recognition. He started in 1930, hosting a fifteen-minute show on sports five days a week. Frick explained that the opportunity was serendipitous:

"I had never been on the air. I was sitting in the office one morning when the managing editor came to me and wanted to know if I would be willing to do a 15-minute spot on the air that day, substituting for the regular news editor, who was ill. I went on the air for two days, as I recall, then went on the road with the Yankees to Washington. When I came back, I found that I had been transferred to a radio performer, and from that time on have been closely identified with radio."[117] He was a regular on that show until becoming National League president, explaining that "his new office would force him to retire from this field with the expiration of his present contract next month."[118] By then he had been a regular for over four years.

That wasn't his only radio accomplishment. In an interview with Dan Daniel in *The Sporting News* when he began working for baseball, Frick elaborated, "During the past two years there have been various commercial jobs, also, at present, I have three commercial contracts—one with the Dodge Motor Company, one with the Mennen Company and one with the Liggett & Myers Tobacco Company, on the Chesterfield Program. I go off the air on these contracts late in December."[119] Frick also broadcast games, especially for the New York baseball clubs and nearby college football teams. In 1930 he teamed with Graham McNamee to broadcast the World Series nationally.[120] That same year, he covered the Army-Navy football game, the nation's biggest football game at the time.[121] Frick was a broadcast celebrity.

Whereas his work with the New York Baseball Writers' Association of America provided Frick baseball notoriety, it was his radio shows, carried nationally, that made him a household name. Furthermore, even after leaving journalism for the National League Service Bureau, its public information division, he continued his radio contracts until becoming president. When Ford Frick was named to that job, he was well known to sports fans and others. In many ways, he was well prepared for his move.

2

A Depressing, Challenging Start

Frick's departure from journalism received little reaction from peers because, as head of the National League Service Bureau, he still interacted with them. He continued his radio shows. Nine months later, when named league president, sportswriters, aware of the challenges the league faced from the Great Depression, showed far more interest. At his first league meeting, Frick faced two controversies. Although the Cincinnati Reds were more secure financially than they had recently been, they were proposing night games to improve attendance. At the same time, the Boston Braves hoped to improve their financial difficulties by allowing dog races. Two other clubs struggled during Frick's first years, a situation not resolved until after World War II began. The young president emerged from these struggles a stronger executive.

AT THEIR SERVICE (BUREAU)

John Heydler, National League president, was tired. He had headed the league for fourteen years, deciding in 1932, as attendance dwindled, to keep his Service Bureau position vacant. Instead, he and Secretary Harvey Traband absorbed the duties to save money as the economy declined. By early 1934 Heydler reassessed the situation. He felt public relations duties either were too strenuous or had been seriously neglected. Either way, at the league's meeting in February, the Service Bureau was the top agenda item, and the president had a candidate to present to owners: "My thought was that we either go on as we are or get a man who was going to be the outstanding man in the newspaper profession. With that in mind, I approached Ford Frick about whether or not he would consider a proposition of this kind, and after he thought it over for a week or so, he said he . . . would go on here for one year at $10,000 for the year."[1]

The surprise of the eight club owners suggests Heydler had not provided advance notice, though their reaction was definitely positive. Samuel

Breadon, St. Louis Cardinals owner, exclaimed, "Ford Frick is the best man in the country, without a question." Charles Stoneham, New York Giants magnate, added, "Speaking only for New York, Ford Frick is acknowledged by the newspaper men themselves to be—he is Ford Frick, that is all there is to it."

The discussion turned to whether he would agree to a long-term contract, to which Heydler responded, paraphrasing Frick, "If I cannot make good in one year, I won't make good at all." Next, owners examined Frick's other duties, noting that he would resign as a sports reporter for the *Evening Journal* but continue his radio broadcasts, which they considered an advantage. Heydler, with such positive response, announced Frick was present to join them for questioning before he was to start the job in March. Heydler introduced him: "Gentlemen, it gives me great pleasure to present to you a man that we not only know in this League, but that everyone in this whole country knows, in the world of sports." He nodded toward Frick. "I think it is the kind of work that is going to appeal to you, and you are the right man in the country to tackle it." Responding modestly, Frick stressed he could not do his job without the cooperation of the owners and their clubs. He added, "I think I know the newspaper slant and what the boys are interested in. I think if you will help me . . . year by year we can build this thing up."[2] With that, Frick's thirty-one-year baseball adventure was to begin.

Whereas the National League magnates were enthusiastic, sportswriters' reactions were subdued. *The Sporting News* announced the hiring, but at the bottom of a page 5 article covering the annual banquet of the New York Baseball Writers' Association of America. It offered a positive spin: "The appointment of Ford Frick as publicity man for the National League was received with general favor here. Ford, an able and experienced baseball writer, is well qualified for the post by person of his background, his energy and his personality. . . . Ford has a number of excellent ideas he will put into effect."[3] The *New York Times* was less excited, placing it near the bottom of a story on the league meetings, without elaboration.[4] The sports world seemed nonplussed.

There is little evidence to assess Frick's achievements during his nine-month tenure, though it suggests his efforts were productive. *The Sporting News* mentioned Frick sending bulletins to local sportswriters when a club visited another city, letting them know where the team was staying.[5] The most notable endorsement came from Heydler in his last comments before retiring. He noted that through another difficult season, attendance had increased more than thirty-seven thousand. He added that "new life and vigor was instilled into our publicity department under the able management of Ford Frick. I do not recall a year when baseball so continuously predominated the sports columns, the radio and the screen, which constitute the three life arteries of publicity."[6] Apparently, his work merited promotion.

PRESIDENTIAL MATERIAL

John Heydler's retirement announcement surprised the league's board of directors at its regular November meeting. The public announcement said, "With deep regrets . . . owing to his desire for complete separation from the duties of the office, and in order to restore his health, [Heydler] had decided to retire as president, secretary, and treasurer of the National League, the same to take effect at the close of the present fiscal year, namely December 11, 1934."[7] The directors scheduled a meeting of club owners in New York six days later, without discussing a replacement. Nor was anyone discussed prior to or at the November 8 meeting. Instead, after designating Heydler "chairman of the board" for life, with a salary of $5,000, "on motion by Judge Fuchs, seconded by practically everyone in the room, Mr. Ford C. Frick was unanimously elected President of the National League for the period covering the fiscal year of the National League, to be effective from the annual meeting held in December 1934 to the annual meeting to be held in December 1935, at the salary of $18,000 per year." Harvey Traband, Heydler's secretary, was chosen secretary and treasurer for the same term.[8] Whether other options were considered is unknown, but apparently Frick was always the first choice with no alternatives discussed.

That didn't stop sportswriters from speculating. In his weekly *Sporting News* column, Dan Daniel suggested owners attempted to hire Emil Fuchs, a Boston Braves' owner.[9] The *Chicago Tribune*, on the day of the announcement, suggested that four besides Frick were considered, including Fuchs and Branch Rickey.[10] The *New York Times* offered a similar assessment, though designating Frick the favorite.[11] Such speculations were the only evidence of other candidates, lacking any such mention in the league minutes.

In fact, in its public statement the National League stressed that Frick was the only candidate. According to the *New York Times* report the day after, "Moving swiftly and apparently in perfect harmony, the eight club owners of the National League consumed a little more than an hour yesterday to name a successor." The article provided an official statement that "no other candidates were considered for either office, it being the feeling of the owners that the National League affairs could best be conducted by men who had been in the organization."[12] Heydler related that Frick was the choice all along. Other evidence suggests that as well. J. Taylor Spink, *The Sporting News* editor, noted, "Encroaching age and illness brought warnings that the veteran executive must slow up. . . . Heydler must have foreseen the inevitable a year ago when he induced Frick to give up newspaper work with the *New York Journal* to take charge of the Service Bureau and become acquainted with the interworkings of the league."[13] Indirect evidence also indicates that was Heydler's intention. He offered no other option when Frick was selected for the Service Bureau, giving him nine months to become familiar to magnates. When Heydler announced his decision, Frick's selection seemed obvious.

The hiring of Frick generated considerable positive response, far greater than his Service Bureau selection. In a *Sporting News* column, Dan Daniel couldn't contain his pleasure: "In electing Frick, the National League has assured itself of a capable leader, a good diplomat and a strong representative in its relations with the great army of American fandom. Frick has been a baseball writer. He has been a radio sports commentator. He knows his stuff from AA to ZZ. He knows the psychology of those who cover baseball for the newspapers. He knows the psychology of the fan and after a year's connection with the league, is familiar with the problems and reactions of the club owners."[14] Daniel spoke for other sportswriters, who felt they had one of their own in baseball leadership, echoing similar reactions. In the same issue, Daniel proved prophetic: "It is expected, however, that he will wear long and well as the circuit's chief executive."[15] Frick would serve for seventeen years, longer than his predecessors.

Frick was aware his former compatriots would make him pay for his success. In recognition, the New York Baseball Writers' Association of America hosted a dinner during the Winter Meetings in December. The guests included magnates from both leagues, along with managers and sportswriters. Commissioner Kenesaw Mountain Landis was among the 140 attendees. Poking fun at Frick, Landis offered to teach him the rudiments of addressing "newspaper men" in a manner befitting of his high position. Coming off his first year as the Brooklyn manager, Casey Stengel offered, "There's nothing like letting our new executive know without delay who his bad umpires are. Or perhaps it would be better to name the good ones. That wouldn't take so long." Frick was on the receiving end "of a heavy barrage of barbs from his former colleagues," accusing him of "jumping to the enemy" and asking if he was still permitted to be the interlocutor at their annual minstrel show. Adopting an official tone, Frick responded, "I can't answer that just now, the matter has not yet been discussed."[16] At the main banquet in February Frick wasn't the guest of honor, but his presence on the dais precipitated numerous barbs from former colleagues—"an unmerciful shellacking," addressing the new president "in a boisterous and tempestuous vein."[17] Frick must have been relieved when the events were over.

A byproduct of Frick's promotion was found in his short biography in *The Sporting News*. Dan Daniel authored the story, but Frick was quoted directly, embellishing two enduring myths, the first that he was raised on an Indiana farm. Frick may have spent time as a child with farming relatives, but he resided in railroad villages. The other myth was playing baseball for DePauw. Attempting three times, he never made the varsity. He may have played semipro ball in Walsenburg, Colorado, like many did in the early twentieth century, but never on varsity in college.[18] Those two myths would persist, though, throughout his baseball career.

Myths aside, he was a logical choice for league president. He was already prominent in New York City and nationally, especially on radio, reaching a large audience outside baseball. He had done substantial sports broadcasting, including the 1930 World Series.[19] Between his coverage of baseball, ghostwriting, radio work, and leadership in the New York Baseball Writers' Association, he was a known quantity, from owners to fans. In particular, he was highly regarded by sportswriters. Still, he accepted the position at a challenging time, hitting the ground running out of necessity in late 1934. Although the Cincinnati Reds had support from most owners for night games, the issue was still unresolved. The other issue was the Boston Braves' proposal to permit dog racing at the ballpark, with its gambling associations. Such a connection would not sit well with Commissioner Landis or others, given the lingering shadow of the Black Sox scandal from fifteen years before. Frick faced those challenges head-on.

NIGHTTIME IS THE RIGHT TIME

Night baseball was the main topic when Frick took charge of the December meeting, with the only preceding item the Browns' attempt to block radio broadcasts by both St. Louis teams, believing it reduced attendance. The Cardinals strongly opposed the measure, as their broadcasts reached much of the South. Although the three New York clubs had recently entered a five-year agreement prohibiting local broadcasts, the Dodgers and Giants opposed doing such to their league's sister club in St. Louis. Drawing from his experience, Frick noted that by using Western Union, a ball game could be broadcast without someone being present. Because Western Union was a public carrier, it would be difficult to block.[20] The concern that broadcasts reduced attendance foreshadowed similar worries later about television. Both persisted through much of Frick's tenure. Once Cardinals broadcasts were protected, focus turned to night baseball.

Larry MacPhail, Reds general manager, spoke first. He downplayed the issue, stressing that the Reds only requested seven night games, adding that any visiting team could opt out. He emphasized that weekday games were sparsely attended, especially in Cincinnati's smaller market. MacPhail cited experiences of Minor League clubs that played at night over the past five years, noting that numerous clubs had been saved financially. The cost of installing lights would be paid off after two games by increased attendance, he said. A long discussion followed. Only Giants owner Horace Stoneham didn't support it but agreed not to block it. The remaining discussion focused on wording, in particular limiting the games to seven.[21] Otherwise, there was no opposition.

Not all magnates lacked experience with night baseball. MacPhail had installed lights while general manager of the Columbus, Ohio, Minor League club two years before. He witnessed firsthand the substantially larger crowds, with his club breaking attendance records and being the league's only club operating in the black.[22] Other Minor League clubs also had huge gains. Indirectly, Cardinals owner Sam Breadon and General Manager Branch Rickey also had experience, as St. Louis owned the Columbus team and two other clubs that had installed lights. In fact, during the discussion, Breadon indicated his desire to install lights at Sportsman Park, except that the Browns' and stadium owner, Phil Ball, blocked him. Without question, Breadon supported MacPhail's efforts, agreeing to play any of the seven games other clubs declined.[23]

Frick was passive during discussions, interjecting himself only when owners were uncertain of resolution wording on how to prevent more than seven games and whether the accord should be in the league's constitution. Frick suggested, with agreement, that final wording be prepared for resolution at the next meeting in February. The official establishment of night baseball, even just for one season, would wait another two months, officially adopted then with a strict limit of seven games.[24] Despite staying mostly out of the discussion, Frick was definitely supportive. As remained typical throughout his career, he was low-key, not attempting to affect the outcome. Following the December meeting, Frick was interviewed for the first 1935 issue of *The Sporting News* by J. G. Taylor Spink, its publisher. He initially opposed night baseball, he said, but now believed it was inevitable. Reflecting comments during the meeting, he stressed how night games helped Minor League clubs weather the depression. He also mentioned the fan who worked during the week and golfed on weekends but would attend a night game.[25] He generally echoed the meeting's discussions.

Though Frick was supportive, Commissioner Landis decidedly was not. MacPhail had approached Landis, hoping for his support. The "czar of baseball" responded succinctly: "Young man, you can write this down. Not in my lifetime or yours will you ever see a baseball game played at night in the majors."[26] In fact, there would be many night games before Landis died in 1944. MacPhail concluded that the issue of night games was a league matter, not under the commissioner's jurisdiction. Landis, scheduled to throw out the first pitch, did not attend the first game on May 25, 1935, allegedly due to illness.[27]

Instead, Frick tossed the game ball, after President Franklin Roosevelt flipped a switch in Washington to turn on the Crosley Field lights. Newspapers outside of Cincinnati gave little coverage, but it was the central feature of the subsequent *Sporting News*. Noting that over twenty thousand fans attended on a cool and misty night, one reporter concluded, "It appears the Cincinnati club has tapped into a fine source of revenue by going in for electric light baseball."[28] Another writer felt the ball was easier to follow than in the sunshine. Interviewed after the game, Frick proudly exclaimed, "It's up to the fans now. I can't see anything else wrong with it."[29] Even in less-than-ideal weather, the Reds had drawn almost ten times as many than the team would have if the game been played that afternoon. The Reds went on to play all seven of their allotted night games in 1935, drawing fans in such quantity that they more than doubled their attendance from the previous season.

Cincinnati continued to play seven night games during the next two seasons, with similar results, yet no club followed suit. Only in 1938, after three years of success, did another club play games under the lights—the Dodgers, with their new general manager, Larry MacPhail. Powell Crosley, the Reds' owner, and MacPhail had parted following the 1936 season.[30] (MacPhail's hiring by the Dodgers will be discussed later.) It would take another season before any American League team played at night. After that, night baseball became more common, thanks to World War II. By the end of Frick's tenure as league president, only the Cubs were playing all their games in daylight. Further, the Reds were solvent after 1935 for the first time in many years, helped both by night games and a rebuilding effort.

A BRAVE UNDERTAKING

The night-baseball controversy was child's play compared to Frick's struggles with the Braves. Coming off a major decline in attendance and resulting financial difficulties, owner Emil Fuchs proposed his solution of leasing the ballpark for dog races. Commissioner Landis, who owed his position to the Black Sox scandal, had certainly not changed his opposition to gambling. While betting still occurred—Boston was notorious for it—baseball needed to keep itself detached for the sake of image. Fuchs's plan was known at the 1934 annual meeting, but it wasn't on the agenda to be discussed. That didn't prevent Frick from acknowledging the problem.

The Braves were ripe for a financial crisis. Fuchs did not own the ballpark that was built by James Gaffney in 1915, following the championship season of his "Miracle Braves." Though he sold the team soon after, Gaffney maintained ballpark ownership. Fuchs paid $40,000 a year in rent to Gaffney's heirs (James Gaffney died in 1932) and was in arrears by 1934. Fuchs, who immigrated from Germany as a child, had purchased the Braves on a whim. Although he was a successful New York lawyer and a one-term judge, he still needed other investors to complete the 1923 purchase. It went smoothly for the first few years, especially when Boston permitted Sunday games in 1928, for which Fuchs had invested $200,000 in political donations. The increase in attendance, however, was offset by the Depression. The team remained profitable, but improvement expenses by 1932 caused Fuchs to lose control to partner Charles Adams. Dog racing was Fuchs's ticket back to solvency.[31]

Though Fuchs's financial difficulties were not brought up formally in December, they were mentioned. At the Board of Directors Meeting in November, Fuchs, a director, expressed hope there would be no publicity about his club's problems. He made no reference to dog racing but did mention his intent to resolve the financial concerns, including meeting with Landis.[32] At the December meeting, Frick suggested Fuchs make a statement to sportswriters about the Braves' financial issues. Fuchs responded, "I believe I can work out my problem in a manner that would protect the league." Although dog racing had not been mentioned, it was understood to be his intention, since Fuchs had conveyed such to Boston media a week before the Winter Meetings. He planned to convert the baseball field to a track and play his games at the Red Sox's Fenway Park, expressing confidence "that the other directors will sanction every action of mine when I present them with the facts." Frick acknowledged Fuchs had a financial problem and was aware of his dog-racing plans but offered a stark opposing view: "I cannot speak for the board of directors, of course, but such an alliance is absolutely preposterous and entirely at variance with the principles for which baseball has battled so strenuously. . . . Organized baseball has outlawed players for gambling. It has waged a ceaseless campaign to wipe out even the slightest signs of gambling at ball parks. Not only is it inconsistent, but it is ridiculous to conceive that baseball could now permit a sport founded on gambling to move into the same premises as it." A similar view was expressed in the *Chicago Tribune*.[33] Fuchs's plans and Frick's reaction had gone national before the latter was officially named president.

A special meeting of league magnates was held in mid-January to address the issue, but by then the matter had grown more complicated. The Braves had fallen in arrears by $11,000 on ballpark rent, and Gaffney's estate had granted a lease to the Boston Kennel Club, which coordinated the dog races. The kennel club then filed for a license to operate and install a betting apparatus. That meant the Braves could not play at their ballpark, but Fenway was not an option because owner Tom Yawkey prohibited the Braves from playing there. As the magnates met, it appeared the Braves had no home, though there were offers from Montreal and Baltimore to purchase and move the franchise. To add confusion, Charles Adams, the major Braves investor, had no interest in overseeing the club.[34] Going into the meeting, Frick faced a dilemma.

There is minuscule documentation of the discussion because most of the meeting's thirteen hours were conducted in executive session. Frick set the tone: "The matter of who is responsible for the dog racing application . . . does not concern us." What does "is trying to solve the difficulties of the Boston Club."[35] When the owners finally finished before midnight, they recommended the league take possession of the ballpark's lease for its eleven-year duration, guaranteeing payments to Gaffney's heirs.[36] The Braves still had their park. At the press conference, Frick allowed no questions. He announced that the league reaffirmed its ban on dog racing—unanimously—and the Braves would remain in their ballpark. He added, "The entire situation, we feel confident, will be clarified and definitely settled at the schedule meeting on February 5. We believe that the Boston baseball public will be entirely satisfied with the solution of the problem." No specifics were provided.[37] True to Frick's promise, the February meeting provided clarity, seemingly resolving the Braves' dilemma. The league would guarantee rental payments to the heirs for the years left on the contract. The Braves would pay the lease, but the league guaranteed it. Further, Fuchs would still manage the ball club, with Adams remaining vice president and New England communities committing to help bolster attendance.[38] For the time being, the crisis appeared resolved.

Such was noted by J. G. Taylor Spink in *The Sporting News* preceding the February meeting, praising the leadership Frick brought. Noting that Frick had been put on the spot even before taking office, Spink concluded, "He came through the affair with colors flying, handling it with the aplomb and poise of a veteran long skilled in meeting difficult situations. The baseball world will hear a lot of Ford Frick in the years to come. He has proven his mettle." Spink also mentioned the new president had established three main points. First, no gambling would be connected with baseball. Second, original National League member Boston would retain its franchise. Finally, contrary to some writers, the league was in no danger of disintegration.[39] In spite of that optimism, though, the Braves' struggles persisted.

There was hope the Braves could boost attendance in 1935. The Yankees had declined signing Babe Ruth, leaving him free to play elsewhere. For $25,000, a sizable contract for the aging player, Ruth joined the Braves, part of the attraction being his return to the city where his career began. It is unknown how the deal was presented to Ruth, or Frick's involvement.

Given his relationship with the Babe, it seems likely Frick assisted, coinciding with the goal to improve attendance. Speaking on the West Coast, Frick proclaimed, "The Babe would be an asset to any club if he merely sat on the bench. As a player he will be a tremendous draw at the gate. Baseball needs color and Ruth will provide it in Boston." Days later, he ventured further, predicting Ruth would draw over five hundred thousand fans to games.[40] Frick wasn't prophetic. At the end of May, Ruth left the Braves, disagreeing with the club on taking a leave of absence to attend an event in New York. Not that it would have mattered—his home runs were fewer, his batting average below .200. There was a surge in attendance early, but it had tapered off, and by July, a month after Ruth's departure, it was clear the Braves would not achieve their previous season's attendance. Matters came to a head at the July meeting.[41]

Once again, the financial situation was a concern. Frick was disturbed because the club's troubles had already cost the league $26,000 in promised payments, which would deplete the treasury in three months, requiring an assessment from the other clubs. Fuchs countered that adding Ruth hurt the Braves, increasing indebtedness to almost $300,000. He also blamed the bad publicity stemming from being prevented to sell the club. Frick replied that the inability to sell was due to Fuchs and Adams setting too high a price and threatened to put the club in bankruptcy if a deal was not reached by August 1, unless the Braves paid what it owed the league. Because Charles Adams remained the major owner, Frick declined to discuss matters further with Fuchs.[42] The remaining discussion was off record, but Frick was resolved to address the Braves' problems, and only Adams could help accomplish that.

The two met soon after, with Adams taking control on August 1. Both he and Frick were aware his involvement was a short-term solution. First, Adams had little interest in managing the Braves, being involved with professional hockey, especially the Boston Bruins. More troubling, he was also invested in Boston's Suffolk Downs Racetrack, tying him to a sport connected to gambling.[43] Adams was financially able to stop the hemorrhaging that worried Frick, but neither his personal interests nor baseball's image were compatible with his presence. How concerned Adams was about the Braves is unknown, but he clearly had no interest in controlling the club long-term.[44] Frick needed to find a buyer or some way to diminish Adams's duties. In early November Frick met with Braves shareholders to discuss their financial future, accompanied by Bob Quinn, general manager of the Dodgers. When approached by reporters, Quinn denied rumors he'd become involved with the Braves. Rather, "Frick asked Quinn to accompany him as an advisor, recognizing Quinn's long baseball experience and particularly of his knowledge of the situation in Boston, where he was head of the Red Sox for nine years."[45] In fact, Quinn had only left Boston to join Brooklyn two years earlier, making his story credible. In reality, Quinn's involvement with the Braves was already being discussed.

Frick moved in that direction by calling a special owners meeting on November 26, 1935, to have the league take control of the Boston franchise. Adams was present, supporting the action, though he abstained when approving the transfer. Frick explained the action was taken "because of the failure of the Boston National League Baseball Company to fulfill its contractual obligations over an extended period of time." He added that this was "a friendly gesture to pave the way for a reorganization and to protect the minority stockholders from loss."[46] The owners, other than Adams's abstention, approved it unanimously. The National League controlled the franchise, though not for long.

At the Winter Meetings on December 11, it was announced the Braves' franchise was awarded to James Aloysius Robert "Bob" Quinn and his corporation, and although Adams would maintain an interest, Quinn would manage. Further, there were other shareholders. The action was approved unanimously, and the Dodgers thus released Quinn.[47] The league would no longer have any control, except for whatever debt it was still owed. In reality, little had changed. Regardless of what Quinn invested, Adams remained the major shareholder but without any direct management involvement. That satisfied Frick and apparently pleased owners, as they renewed Frick's contract with a salary increase. Sam Breadon, the Cardinals' owner, summarized their consensus: "I think we were most fortunate in electing our president."[48]

Quinn didn't make dramatic changes during the nine years he managed the franchise. The team improved from its disastrous 1935 season with fifth- and sixth-place finishes over the next three years. Attendance also improved. There was no new investment, however, because Quinn didn't have the wherewithal to finance major changes and Adams had little interest.[49] That picture changed in 1941 when Adams was bought out. The nine-member purchasing syndicate was led by Lou Perini, who obtained full control three years later. The syndicate purchased Adams's interest for $350,000, an amount obviously satisfying him. Quinn was retained as the main partner and general manager, but the new group added working capital. Quinn indicated no outside involvement was in the deal, suggesting Frick didn't play a role.[50] Though no evidence shows otherwise, that seems unlikely. From the time he was named president, the saga of the Braves was a major problem. Frick clearly had an interest in relieving Adams, given the latter's involvement in horse racing and his lack of desire to invest. In any case, Quinn remained in charge through 1944.

Perini, with two partners, bought out the syndicate in early 1944, acquiring whatever financial interest Quinn held. Even though Quinn remained president and on the board, the Perini group now had full financial control. Frick indicated his awareness of the pending deal, suggesting his involvement. When asked if the new owners had the means to produce a winner, he responded, "I fervently hope that's correct. From what I have been given to understand, I believe the new ownership will help the Boston situation a lot." He added that the Braves' difficulties had been his first real challenge.[51] Quinn retired after the 1944 season, but four years later, the Braves won the pennant, proving Frick correct.

The Braves difficulties not only were Frick's first major challenge but also remained an albatross for years. Bringing in Quinn was a brilliant move, as it relieved Adams of day-to-day worries and sidelined Adams's racetrack interests. That said, the National League had to balance its relations with Adams because he remained the major stockholder while baseball attempted to diminish its association with him. Whatever Frick's involvement—and he likely had a role in Perini's recruitment—the president was relieved when the syndicate bought out Adams. And Quinn, having held together a poorly supported franchise for nine years, now was free from those pressures. It took a decade, but Frick's efforts stabilized what was otherwise an insolvent franchise. Ironically, the Braves would present more challenges at the end of his tenure as commissioner.

DODGING A BULLET

Unlike the financial problems of the Reds, Braves, and Phillies, all of which were covered extensively in the press, the challenges of the Dodgers were rarely mentioned. In many ways, though, theirs was the most serious during Frick's tenure, tolerated only by the patience of the Brooklyn Trust Company that held the mortgage. The organization was apprehensive following the 1937 season, however. The Dodgers had finished in the second division every year since 1932. Although their attendance was better than either the Braves or Phillies, four hundred thousand fans per season proved insufficient; the franchise was unprofitable since 1930.[52]

Part of the problem was created by divided ownership. When owner Charles Ebbets constructed his ballpark in 1912, he needed partners to help finance it. He recruited the brothers Ed and Steve McKeever, who received 50 percent interest. Both Ebbets and Ed McKeever died in 1925. Steve remained involved until his death in 1938, but the club remained divided evenly between the heirs. Due to that split, management was weak, decisions were deferred, and the ballpark was deteriorating. Because Steve McKeever was in declining health, his son-in-law, Jim Mulvey, attended most meetings since Frick became president. Mulvey approached him after the 1937 season about hiring a new general manager.[53]

Previously, the Dodgers seemed about to be sold in early 1936. The club's vice president and de facto general manager at the time, Joseph Gilleaudeau, announced Steve McKeever was willing to sell for $2 million.[54] Later that year a buyer emerged—Tillinghast L. Huston, formerly part owner of the Yankees. Huston had met with Frick about purchasing the club and making Babe Ruth the manager, but he also indicated the asking price was too high. Around the same time, Larry MacPhail was also rumored to be the future general manager, immediately after leaving the Reds. The article mentioned that "Ford Frick, president of the National League and ardent booster of night baseball, and MacPhail have convinced those concerned that the circus stuff which saved the Cincinnati club is their only possible salvation, and that MacPhail . . . is their man." It indicated Frick made that suggestion to the Dodgers.[55] Either the article was prophetic, or there were already speculations about MacPhail.

Fourteen months later, those rumors were validated; MacPhail was named vice president and general manager. However, the stories differ on how it developed. Some sources suggest Branch Rickey was approached to run the club but declined and recommended MacPhail. Although Frick was involved, having suggested Rickey and later approving MacPhail, Rickey would have received the credit. Rickey even asserted such, and other sources have supported it.[56] MacPhail denied Rickey had any involvement, perhaps reinventing history after their 1947 fallout, but strong evidence indicates Frick was the driving force, even if he had suggested Rickey initially. It was Jim Mulvey who conducted the search and had worked closely with Frick for years. Further, Frick and MacPhail had worked closely on night baseball. Given that MacPhail was available and Frick had hired away the Dodgers' general manager to manage the financially strapped Braves, the league president's role seems more likely.[57] In any case, hiring MacPhail reversed the Dodger fortunes overnight.

He wasted no time changing how the club was managed. He immediately took advantage of the rule he helped establish, announcing the club would play seven night games during the 1938 season. After drawing over sixty thousand fans for the first two games, even American League president Will Harridge concluded that baseball under the lights was both inevitable and lasting.[58] In the hope of attracting more fans, MacPhail hired Babe Ruth as a coach, though stressing he would not become manager. Frick was "greatly pleased" by the decision, suggesting he may have been involved with Ruth as well.[59] In December MacPhail announced the Dodgers would broadcast all their games in 1939, surprising the other New York clubs because two years remained on the agreement to black out radio in the city. Again, Frick seemed aware: "I have no comment to offer. The matter is strictly a club affair." MacPhail also painted and cleaned the ballpark and started trading and signing players.[60] MacPhail believed a ball club had to spend money to make money.

That conviction was soon rewarded. Although the Dodgers finished in seventh place in 1938, lower than the season before, they drew almost two hundred thousand more fans due to night games. A year later, they finished third, their first time out of the second division in seven years, and they drew an additional two hundred thousand. By 1941 the Dodgers won their first pennant in twenty-one years, drawing over a million fans. In his first year, MacPhail cut the losses to under $4,000 and a year later operated well in the black. To the pleasure of the Brooklyn Trust, the mortgage was reduced substantially.[61] The Dodgers had rapidly gone from a troubled franchise to one of the most successful.

Whatever role he had in hiring MacPhail—and evidence suggests it was major—Frick was pleased. During his first five years as president, he had stabilized or improved the finances of three franchises. Whereas the Braves were still struggling, albeit stable, the Reds and Dodgers had achieved major improvements financially. While the country was still in the Great Depression, Frick had reason to feel confident that better days were ahead. Unfortunately, one club had barely survived the Depression, and for the next five years, the Philadelphia Phillies would be a huge burden.

The Phillies were the last club financial challenge Frick faced and also the most vexing. First, its difficulties percolated longer before reaching a crisis and thus became more problematic. Second, the limited funds available for rainy-day challenges were taxed beyond their capabilities, given problems like the Braves' situation. Third, the Phillies' ownership was inflexible in acknowledging the severity of the problem, even after the league became involved. Finally, when a solution materialized with new ownership, that also became a problem. The Phillies were Frick's longest and most complicated challenge.

Like the Braves, Philadelphia's difficulties went back decades, when William Baker gained control in 1913. Baker, a wealthy New Yorker and former police commissioner, took charge after his predecessor died. It began well. The Phillies won their first pennant in 1915, and the ballpark was unofficially renamed the Baker Bowl. From there, things went downhill. Baker was not a baseball man in knowledge or experience, though that didn't prevent him from making decisions. He didn't invest his own money and notoriously made bad trades.[62] Until his death, the results were predictable. After two second place finishes following the pennant, the club dropped to the second division, often last, until Baker died in 1930. After limited improvement for two years when Baker's partner ran the club, the situation grew worse.

Gerald Nugent and his spouse, Mae, gained significant control at Baker's death and total control when Baker's wife died four years later. With no Baker offspring, the Nugents inherited the franchise. Mae was Baker's secretary, and after she married Nugent, he was hired as business manager in 1925.[63] From 1933 on, Gerald Nugent ran the club. Unlike Baker, he understood baseball, but like Baker, he wouldn't invest his own money. In his first five years, the team finished seventh four times and last once. Over the next five years, the club was a perennial bottom feeder, losing over 100 games each season. Even after Philadelphia legalized Sunday baseball in 1934, poor play and a lousy ballpark discouraged fans. To save upkeep costs, Nugent rented sheep to maintain the field.[64] The facility deteriorated so badly Nugent was forced to rent the A's ballpark in 1938, though the new environs didn't help the gate. It still took three more years before the depth of the problems came to a head.

Since the league had loaned money to both the Reds and Braves to maintain solvency, Frick and the magnates considered establishing a rainy-day fund for struggling clubs. The subject was brought up in July 1935 as the league confronted the Braves' challenges. Frick brought it center stage at the November special meeting: "The only moneys the League offers as an organization is enough money to conduct their current expenses from one end of the year into another. They don't have surplus funds." He also stressed there were no funds from Landis's office. In 1936, at the February meeting, a motion was entertained to help struggling second division clubs by increasing their revenue split for away games, though the thriving clubs—the Cubs, Pirates, and Giants—voted it down. The matter wasn't considered again for four years, surfacing in 1940 when Sam Breadon noted the American League had a contingency fund of around a million. By comparison the National League's reserve was $155,000.[65] Still, no action was taken, though it came up again in December, when magnates finally recognized the seriousness of the Phillies' plight. Following Nugent's presentation of his problems, Frick proclaimed, "In times like these, . . . when we have clubs that are having difficulties, when we do not know what is going to happen, there should be a reserve fund in our league that is easily liquidated, readily accessible, containing money that can be used 'right now' to meet an emergency, if and when it arises."[66] For years, the league was aware of the fund's inadequacy, but the Phillies' crisis brought it front and center.

At the 1941 July meeting, Nugent outlined his club's finances, stressing his personal sacrifices. Frick followed, acknowledging the problem and lack of funds: "I am not an alarmist, I am not trying to frighten anybody but, unless some relief can be devised—unless some plan can be suggested for the operation of the Philadelphia ball club, you men face the serious problem of having [the team] not be able to operate beyond the 15th of August or 1st of September." Discussion focused on how to assist the club, authorizing Frick to seek investors. In that, there was some success, for in September a syndicate headed by John B. "Jack" Kelly offered Nugent $500,000, thereby absolving their debts. Nugent rejected it, and a frustrated Frick claimed he was powerless to act.[67] The club somehow skated through 1941 with its problems unresolved.

For whatever reason, the perilous state of the Phillies was not a topic during the annual meeting, other than to allow the club to amortize its obligations to the league over five years. Instead, a special meeting was called for January.[68] The situation was clearly urgent, with the $55,000 club bank note due at month's end. The magnates rejected the Phillies' proposal to sell players to pay down debt, and with limited capital opportunities, Nugent requested the that the league pay the debt and loan another $30,000, secured by his stock, paid by year's end. World War II, however, made the situation more precarious, as baseball could be stopped at any time. The magnates agreed to stopgap measures, putting off final action for a month.[69]

The war was the focus of the February meeting, especially President Roosevelt's request for more night games. There was already a shortage of ballplayers, as many volunteered or were drafted. When the owners focused on the Phillies, they authorized a loan of $85,000 beyond the $60,000 already provided, secured by Nugent's stock. The lease for the Athletics' Shibe Park was also amortized. Frick stressed it was imperative to find a buyer quickly, by December 1, 1942. Further, he deliberately kept the Phillies' situation from reporters; he was concerned about adverse publicity given the war, noting publicly that its plight had not been the meeting's purpose.[70] He was thus successful in avoiding rumors during the season.

That would change with the season's end, however, because the situation grew worse, causing Frick to schedule the Board of Directors Meeting at the start of November. Nugent was not a director but was invited because his club was the primary subject. The league's investment in the Phillies, now approximating $150,000, had brought matters to a head. Although the Braves still had obligations totaling $70,000, Frick stressed, "I am not so concerned about Boston at the moment. I am concerned about Philadelphia." He further emphasized the situation could produce "an utter financial collapse of your League." While appearing sensitive to Nugent and trying not to prejudice the case, Frick noted that Nugent overvalued his franchise, none of his plans were viable, and selling players jeopardized the league's loan. Frick's goals were to keep the league intact and protect it financially, but the Phillies' debt brought their plight to crisis levels.[71]

If there were an optimistic note, it was that both Nugent and Frick had been approached by a prospective buyer—Bill Veeck. Veeck owned a successful Minor League team in Milwaukee and told Nugent he had capital backing. Frick added that Veeck had contacted him separately, with an interest in spending between $200,000 and $400,000, noting the lower amount was unacceptable to Nugent. In both cases, the contacts occurred weeks before, and neither had heard back. As the meeting ended,

Frick advised Nugent to be more flexible, emphasizing again not to sell players.[72] There was still little news coverage, though one paper surmised the league would run the club if no buyer came forth.[73] The discussion continued at the regular Directors Meeting the last day of November. At that session, Frick indicated there was a potential buyer, though he was not at liberty to disclose who, stating the prospective owner would be "a credit to baseball." Frick also outlined the club's indebtedness to the league—now $168,000—and concluded that "the Club has no means of fulfilling its contractual obligations to the League and other creditors" and that "the aforesaid failures and refusals of the Club to fulfill its contractual obligations to the League presents a case for termination of the membership of the Club in the League." The board attached a resolution to have the Phillies' owners present their case within ten days.[74] Directors still avoided drastic action, hoping for a buyer.

The discussions continued at the Winter Meetings. It was suggested the league take over the franchise, moving toward a forfeiture, liquidation, or relocation. Frick explained the disadvantages of each and why any such move was too costly. The discussion became more focused with Frick's disclosure that the potential buyer had backed off. The owners were back to square one, and any action proposed could seriously affect finding a buyer. Even worse, Nugent was threatening counteraction if the league executed its threats. Frick still was able to keep this from reporters, the only information printed being the franchise's major debt to the league and the league's need to find a buyer or take over the franchise.[75] As the 1943 season loomed, the crisis grew worse. It was certainly not a good time to find a buyer. The large debt and the expectation that an owner would assume it provided a roadblock. So, too, was Nugent's expectation of compensation for his stock, valuing it higher than any prospective buyer would. Compounding the problem for Frick, now the broker for any deal, was the war, as baseball could still be shut down by Washington at any time. Even if allowed to continue, the loss of most players had impacted the gate, with 1942 attendance down at most parks. That was Frick's dilemma starting the new year.

When the magnates met in February, though, a potential buyer surfaced—a syndicate headed by William Cox, a lumberman from New York City. The offer was serious, though it generated considerable haggling. Nugent expected more for his stock than Cox was willing to offer, and the league had to forego debt payments until the franchise became profitable. Horace Stoneham expressed personal concern about Cox but did regard his partners highly and agreed to the deal. The other moguls were more concerned with resolving a problem that had dominated their meetings for years. Frick summarized, "The League is in a position where it gets nothing now, with the potential of getting something in the future if the thing makes a profit."[76] He added that it avoided both the league putting in more money and litigation. Without a deal, the league might have to take over. Those considerations made Cox's offer seem more attractive.

The final deal was a transfer of stock from the league to the Cox syndicate, with the league having obtained the vast majority of shares, including Nugent's. Doing so meant the league would manage the franchise if the deal fell through, but it also facilitated the franchise transfer. Two weeks later, Frick appeared with Cox to announce the deal, introducing the lead owner and realistically assessing the matter: "I believe we have solved the Philadelphia problem. He [Cox] is not a miracle man. I don't want anyone to think the Phils will get into the World Series this year. We all know it will take years to build this club up." In his weekly column, Spink credited the president: "The superlative salesmanship of Ford Frick . . . cannot be ignored. . . . Frick found his buyers, impregnated them with his enthusiasm, and now Philadelphia of the National League is straightened away to a more pleasant life."[77] Unfortunately for Frick, that "more pleasant life" remained distant.

Although Cox stayed in New York, he had no intention of being an absentee owner. He moved quickly to rebuild the club, hiring an experienced manager, Bucky Harris, and tapping into the limited player talent. He also promoted his club. The team lost fewer than 100 games for the first time in six years, and attendance more than doubled, a major accomplishment for a seventh-place team. Those results had a price, for Cox developed a reputation for being talented at "capturing headlines and creating turmoil."[78] Upset at Frick's rulings against his club in two games it lost, he proclaimed, "We have no confidence that the rule book is the backbone of baseball law. It is merely a vehicle to be interpreted at the whim of the president of the National League. We have no faith whatever in any decision coming from the League office." Unsuccessful on appeals, he complained at the Summer Meetings about umpires—a topic dear to Frick—behaving as a pushy know-it-all for someone new. Following the meeting, he tempered his comments: "I have the highest regard for Mr. Frick's integrity and would be the last person to question it."[79] However, his strained relationship with Frick would become the least of Cox's problems.

At midseason, Cox, unhappy with his manager, replaced him. That proved a huge mistake. Harris made it known his former boss was betting on the Phillies, committing baseball's cardinal sin. Frick and Landis undertook an investigation, and the outcome was not good for Cox. He denied the allegations initially but then admitted betting $25 to $100 that the Phillies would win, stopping in late May after realizing he violated the rules. Landis banned him for life.[80] A week later, thanks to Frick, Robert Carpenter, part of Cox's syndicate, purchased the Phillies outright and named his son, Robert Jr., club president.[81] Part of the DuPont family, Carpenter had both the wealth and willingness to invest. The club's financial straits stabilized, with the Phillies no longer presenting Frick with problems for the remainder of his baseball tenure.

A SOLVENT, SUCCESSFUL LEAGUE

Early in the discussions concerning the Phillies' plight, Frick emphasized to owners, "Certainly, the League cannot do a thing without the authorization of the League. The League president can only call your attention to the seriousness of the situation." He then asked for authorization to find investors.[82] That statement demonstrated his management style, conducted with consistency during his clubs' financial crises. He did not get out in front of the owners, excepting the financially troubled club whose interests were not in concert with the league's. He managed by consensus, obtaining agreement before he acted, conducting many meetings and phone conversations with individual owners, all undocumented. In his actions on night baseball and the financial challenges in Boston and Philadelphia, he clearly had the magnates' support. He likely had their support when assisting the Dodgers in hiring MacPhail. The solutions took time, especially with the Braves and Phillies, but they also avoided controversies.

His actions in dealing with the financial challenges left the National League in much better shape. After Powell Crosley bought the Reds and lights were installed, the team made it to the World Series twice in the late 1930s, winning once. After MacPhail joined the Dodgers, they won the pennant three years later. The challenges of the Phillies and Braves took longer to address. The Phillies didn't reach the World Series until

1950, and the Braves won their last pennant in Boston in 1948. Frick was league president when both occurred, new ownership in both cases successful in turning around the weak franchises. As Frick stepped down as president in late 1951, he could look back with pride at his accomplishments in rescuing troubled franchises and their subsequent successes.

3

Staying Alive

The Depression presented baseball and Frick with many challenges, some remaining as war loomed. Though few magnates had been around to experience the impact of World War I, those who did recalled its disruption to baseball. Once again, the threat of losing players was real, along with the possibility of the game being halted. The loss of players became a reality, but the Major League clubs persisted throughout the war by adapting to major challenges. Frick played a crucial role, instrumental in keeping baseball alive. At war's end, Frick had learned lessons that proved helpful throughout the remainder of his baseball career.

WALKING A TIGHTROPE

As early as October 1940, baseball magnates sensed war was eminent. Both the Majors and Minors would face talent depletion. Unless under eighteen or over thirty-five, ballplayers were candidates for military conscription, most in good physical shape to qualify. Historical precedent was not encouraging. The 1918 season shut down a month early, mainly due to the loss of players. The federal government offered no exemptions for professional ballplayers then, and that seemed likely again, posing the possibility of shutdown. The sport could be perceived as patriotic, accepting substantial losses of players, or attempt to procure exemptions and appear unsupportive. Frick grasped the dilemma, encouraging owners to take a supportive yet cautious approach to draft possibilities.

In the euphoric aftermath of his league's first World Series victory in 1940 since becoming president, Frick was asked to comment on the European war's impact. He walked a tightrope, as he did for the next five years: "We are fully awake to the national and international situation as it pertains to baseball. However, we are going along as before. Some of our men will be conscripted, and if a greater emergency arises, we will meet any demands made upon us. Even in war-torn Europe, sports have continued and I feel that our government will want us to continue baseball."[1] In that statement, intended for both government officials and the public, Frick offered support for the war effort while signaling baseball's intention to continue.

Pearl Harbor was bombed during the 1941 Winter Meetings. Responding, Frick was candid with owners, and their discussion focused on how baseball could support war efforts. It had already organized the Bat and Ball Fund, providing baseball equipment to hundreds of military camps in the United States and abroad. Owners decided to raise money for the army and navy relief programs and the Red Cross, with each club donating the proceeds from one game. They also agreed to sell war bonds at all games and donate a portion of All-Star Game and World Series revenues. Any service man in uniform would be admitted free. In subsequent discussion with owners, Frick stressed, "Without being too somber or too serious, I think all of you must recognize that the immediate future of baseball is in no small way dependent on the way we fall in line with the war effort."[2] In essence, the efforts provided a means for baseball's survival.

Frick also reminded owners why it was critical for baseball to continue, regardless of loss of talent, focusing on fixed costs every club would face: "If we have to close, . . . then we have idle parks and we still have rentals to pay; we still have commitments; we still have all those things that will break us a damn sight more than giving away our profits now will break us."[3] Basically, he reinforced that baseball should support war efforts, even if profits diminished due to lower attendance.

While one end of the tightrope was the owners, the other was war officials. Frick made numerous trips to Washington, in spite of Landis prohibiting such meetings without the commissioner present. There, he conveyed the importance to the country of baseball continuing. He emphasized that not only would the season be lost but also there would be no sports pages, radio broadcasts, or soldiers cheering their teams.[4] Together, these arguments helped maintain commitments from owners and war officials. In the end, though, even more would be required to maintain continuity.

Well before Pearl Harbor, Frick had sensed the challenges if the United States entered the war. It was traditional for the league presidents to assess the upcoming year as the season opened. Frick would always predict a hotly contested race involving many of his clubs, a balanced assessment, as much for owners as fans. In 1941 he added a caveat: "How this will be modified by the events of the weeks and months to come no man can foresee. Baseball has its place in a nation preparing for national defense just as in a land at peace and engaged in the industries of normal civilized times. That place will be defined as events shape themselves. The National league will be prepared at all times to do its part."[5] Those challenges would evolve with the war.

Shortly after war was declared, Frick offered a statement that remained consistent throughout the engagement. As he traveled to Washington for the annual ritual of providing season passes to the president, he assured the public that baseball would fully support the war effort and continue play. "Baseball men are not worried about baseball. Their paramount concern is the winning of the war and preserving our way of life and our country. Because as long as there is America, there will be baseball."[6] His comments portrayed a confidence not shown at league meetings but did suggest flexibility to adapt to war demands. From all indications, Frick led baseball's way in walking the tightrope, helping to ensure continuity. That effort would also shape baseball after the war, developing an awareness, previously nonexistent, of Washington and the public-policy process.

NIGHT FEVER

Kenesaw Mountain Landis, baseball's first commissioner, was often called a czar, suggesting absolute power. In reality, it was limited. The commissioner oversaw the World Series and the All-Star Game. When the two leagues disagreed, he cast the deciding vote. He also rendered rulings "in the best interest of baseball," as Landis did by banning eight players for life for fixing the 1919 World Series. When Larry MacPhail proposed installing lights in Cincinnati, Landis assured him it wouldn't happen, yet when Landis died, most clubs played night games. In reality, most power rested with the league presidents.

His position on night baseball indicated Landis disliked change, which included the New Deal.[7] It was largely that disdain that caused Landis to prohibit executives from meeting with Washington officials except when league presidents presented the president with season passes. Frick ignored Landis's prohibition numerous times, to baseball's benefit. After Pearl Harbor, however, Landis did become more supportive of FDR, asking him to decide baseball's fate. In a letter dated January 14, 1942, he placed the season in the president's hands: "If you believe we ought to close down for the duration of the war, we are ready to do so immediately. If you feel we ought to continue, we would be delighted to do so. We await your order."[8] In his famous response, the green-light letter, FDR gave the go-ahead: "I honestly feel that it would be best for the country to keep baseball going. There will be fewer people unemployed and everybody will work longer hours and harder than even before. And that means that they ought to have a chance for recreation and for taking their minds off their work even more than before." He left the decision with baseball, adding, "I hope that night baseball can be extended because it gives an excellent opportunity to the day shift to see a game occasionally."[9] That comment became the focus of debate at ensuing league meetings.

Although FDR's letter shifted dynamics, the number of night games played had been debated long before the war. Most matters were resolved at the separate league meetings, but the night-game controversy carried over to the joint meeting in 1940, with arguments on whether night games were a league or joint matter. Will Harridge, American League president, argued each league should decide for itself, noting the National League had allowed night games in Cincinnati and Brooklyn without consulting his league. As such, they were free to allow the Browns, which just installed lights, to play fourteen night games, even while the National League was limited to seven. Frick countered that in two-club cities, one playing additional night games could ruin day games of the other, adding, "Pretty soon you could be playing all your games at night."[10] After listening, Landis intervened, siding, not surprisingly, with the National League and reminding owners that no one wanted night baseball being more than a novelty.[11] Baseball remained limited to seven until the next Winter Meetings.

By then there were two major changes: Pearl Harbor and the installation of lights in Washington, the eleventh club to do so. The remaining five—the Braves, Red Sox, Yankees, Tigers, and Cubs—played without lights until war's end, with the Cubs taking four more decades for night baseball. Night games were crucial to Washington's club due to the war. Few government employees were free during the day, causing Clark Griffith, the Senators' owner, to propose allowing all clubs fourteen night games, joined by the struggling Browns. Frick strongly opposed, arguing it would set precedent, countering that the seven-game limit be strictly enforced. Predictably, Landis reinforced him, stressing that too many night games pulled fans away from day games, thus ruining baseball.[12] The National League voted unanimously against additional night games and the American League unanimously in favor, with Landis again supporting the former.[13] The status quo of seven games remained until FDR's letter reopened the issue.

When the National League met in February 1942, FDR's letter was the focus; Frick stressed, "That request [for more night games] we cannot table." He recommended the league schedule fourteen games wherever there were lights.[14] Concern was expressed that the American League would go beyond the fourteen, perhaps even an unlimited number. Frick countered that any increase would be predicated on joint action. His league thus allowed additional games, while understanding their counterpart would do likewise.[15] Near meeting's end, Clark Griffith appeared, explaining that he needed to double the fourteen games, or his club couldn't survive.[16] The matter stayed unresolved until the joint meeting that summer.

By then low attendance created even greater concern for Griffith, causing him to propose playing all remaining home games at night, except on Sundays and holidays. Predictably, his league supported him unanimously while the National League opposed by the same, causing Griffith to ask why its owners voted no when some had indicated their support. Larry MacPhail responded, "I told you I would make a speech in favor of you because, as I have stated a hundred times, I thought the best thing to do was to let you commit suicide, if you wanted to. . . . But I changed my mind."[17] Considerable discussion followed. Breadon argued that all clubs should have the same opportunity, and Leo Bondy, lead counsel for the Giants, claimed Washington was actually doing well. The Browns owner argued that night games were far more accessible, but Warren Giles of Cincinnati countered that they would kill day attendance.[18] Once again, Landis supported the National League. He noted MacPhail's comments and added, "If he sees some fellow about to jump in the river, . . . keep him from doing it if he can." Griffith replied, "You want to push me in, then, rather than pulling me out."[19] Most clubs remained limited to fourteen night games, and none was allowed more than twenty-one, but night games were increasing.

As the war continued, pressure for additional night games persisted. By 1944, with attendance down significantly, both St. Louis clubs and the White Sox requested playing their remaining games at night other than Sundays and holidays. Breadon had switched, and the National League now was divided 3–2 in opposition, with three abstaining. The rival league remained unanimous in favor. Landis broke the "tie," permitting the St. Louis teams and Chicago, but only in 1944. Although the Giants, long opposing night games, now had lights, Giants executive Leo Bondy remained dubious about adding more games: "If you extend night baseball, you will have all night baseball after the war is over, and you are going to ruin and kill baseball."[20] In spite of such objections, the increase in night games was now inevitable.

There was an irony to the objections, especially from MacPhail and Bondy. Due to potential submarine attacks in coastal cities at night, the military prohibited night games in New York City, affecting the Dodgers and Giants. That concerned Frick because the 1942 All-Star Game was scheduled for the Giants' Polo Grounds; he noted that players coming from St. Louis couldn't get to New York for a day game and stressed its importance, as proceeds would go to the army and navy relief funds. Ultimately, by imposing universal daylight time, the dilemma was avoided and the game played in daylight with all players present. The dim-out policy applied to New York until the 1944 season, when the mayor lifted it.[21] That prohibition was the only remaining glitch in the growing night-game trend. Frick and Landis now found themselves in the minority because more owners were convinced night games increased revenue. By war's end and Landis's death, any limits on night games ended, and all but one club installed lights after the war. Night games were now normal, facilitated greatly by World War II and financial realities.

TIT FOR TAT

In the same July 1942 meeting in which the National League allowed only fourteen night games, Frick put forth an innovative proposal to extend the season by adding nine games to the World Series—a fifteen-game series, the winner needing eight wins. The first six games would be split, with three home games for each club. The last nine would be played in Minor League cities around the country.[22] No cities were mentioned, nor was how they might be selected. It was, however, a creative approach for baseball during challenging times.

Frick outlined the concept to National League owners, conveying advantages in broad terms. First, it would extend the season by two weeks, generating public interest longer and providing momentum for 1943. Second, it would bring the Series to cities never exposed, making Major League baseball available to many who had never witnessed it. Finally, it would raise money for the war effort, the first six games to be split, 50 percent to the leagues, players, and ball clubs, the other 50 percent to the war effort. Revenues from the remaining nine games would go fully to war relief.[23] In the ensuing discussion, owners seemed supportive. Frick had already discussed it with Landis and Harridge earlier, but only the *Chicago Tribune* reported the proposal, perhaps receiving the scoop from Landis or Harridge because their offices were there. The article mentioned extending the Series into Minor League cities, calling it a "cross country" idea. It also suggested there were too many obstacles—wartime transportation, weather, and small ballparks among them—and thus wouldn't be a good fundraiser.[24]

Whereas the *Tribune* presented a negative slant, that wasn't the impression Frick received from magnates in July. Horace Stoneham was intrigued, asking Frick what Landis had in mind. Frick responded, "Horace, if you can tell definitely what the commissioner had in mind, you are better than I am! But I think something like this is the plan he had in mind." Then turning pessimistic, he summarized Harridge's view: "Well, this has never been done before, and we shouldn't think of it." Frick also indicated at least two American League owners, including Clark Griffith, opposed it, thus adoption at the joint meeting that afternoon was uncertain. However, Frick's magnates voted unanimously in favor, then unanimously as well to prohibit Griffith from adding night games.[25] Those two votes laid the groundwork for the outcome.

Larry MacPhail was assigned to present it at the joint meeting, though Frick did most of the talking. Referring to the Minor League cities and their fans, he said, "If we have gone to them we will have established, it seems to me, the morale value of baseball in a stronger, more concise, more visible form. . . . Let's bow out of this thing, by George, with the flag waving and the curtain coming down on a good general chorus and ensemble." Branch Rickey eloquently offered support, filling ten pages of the minutes with stories and noting numerous cities where you could get Major League prices for World Series tickets. Even John Heydler supported the idea, stressing importance for "the boys" overseas, especially from cities hosting the games, and that radio broadcasts would be heard by many troops.[26] Those comments would be for naught.

The most vocal opposition came from Joseph Hostetler, chief attorney for the American League. Though not as long-winded as Rickey, his comments still took up five pages. Both Tom Yawkey and Eddie Collins from the Red Sox commented, questioning whether Minor League games would raise much money and doubting ball players would be supportive, especially if not paid for extra games, which Landis indicated wasn't possible. Tension was clearly present between the leagues, the greatest between Sam Breadon and Branch Rickey on one side and Clark Griffith on the other. The American League was clearly as opposed as the Senior Circuit had been supportive. With the two leagues polarized, Landis was left to decide, and he supported the status quo, as he did with night games. The proposal was voted down, and the Series was kept to the best of seven.[27] The arguments American League magnates offered against the proposal weren't convincing. Were Griffith and his league colleagues getting even with the National League owners for stymieing greater expansion of night baseball? If so, they had achieved revenge, blocking one of baseball's more innovative war responses. It was one Frick war effort that didn't succeed.

CAPITAL SESSIONS

Although there was no formal policy, Landis intended to be the only person dealing with Washington officials. He had his reasons. Besides being baseball's top person, he had worked in Washington during Grover Cleveland's administration and later served as a federal judge.[28] A good example of that tight control actually came after his death, following Frick and Griffith's visit with Washington officials in January when the 1945 season appeared in jeopardy. When Frick returned, his partners in the triumvirate governing baseball—Will Harridge and Leslie O'Connor, Landis's secretary—condemned the visit, stating Frick had no authority to do so.[29] Arthur Daley of the *New York Times* came to his defense. He noted that Frick was "criticized by some for shattering Landis' precedent by visiting Washington." Daley added, "What's the difference if Judge Landis ordered all baseball executives to stay away from Washington? The Judge is dead now. Is he to rule the sport from his grave?"[30] Harridge and O'Connor were convinced Landis had a prohibition on Washington lobbying that still needed to be followed.

Historically, there may have been rationale. The federal government had little to do with baseball. There were only two occasions before World War II where the sport was impacted by Washington—World War I and the Supreme Court decision *Federal Baseball Club v. National League* in 1922. World War I certainly disrupted the 1918 season, with numerous players lost to the war effort, sufficient enough to halt the season abruptly a month early and delay the 1919 season start for a week. There was little effort to lobby because the war started and ended quickly and matters returned to normal. As for the *Federal Baseball* ruling, the sport's main interest was avoiding treble damages for violating antitrust laws. It relied on attorneys to handle the case. No one in the executive ranks anticipated the ruling would provide a powerful antitrust exemption that largely provided baseball freedom from government interference, enabling Landis' tight control. Frick changed that precedence during the war.

Frick recognized the new reality, even when Landis and Harridge did not. As early as January 1941, well before Pearl Harbor, Frick visited war officials to determine what role baseball could play as Washington prepared for war. He met with General George Marshall—chief of staff for the army—about the draft and baseball's assistance with recreational programs. Marshall did not anticipate a need for contributions but did encourage exhibition games during spring training when teams were close to military camps. Marshall agreed that if a player was drafted midseason, he would be deferred until season's end. Although these requests and concessions were positive, Frick told his magnates, "It is a very ticklish proposition to go before the draft board, or to publicly make any move that would indicate that we are trying to duck some sort of responsibility." Concerned that Landis might intervene, National League owners offered to submit a letter to him, but Frick suggested staying mum: "It is the only way I know of to approach the thing properly. I don't think that Frick going to Landis, discussing the thing, is going to carry a damn bit of weight."[31] Apparently, no letter was sent.

A year later, at the 1942 February meeting, discussion focused on additional night games and the Bat and Ball Fund. The minutes, along with comments in *The Sporting News*, suggest Frick made another Washington visit, discussing FDR's letter and additional ways to support the war effort.[32] Already gaining magnate approval for additional baseball gear, Frick announced that the army requested him to give a series of lectures on athletics and physical training at camps. He agreed, giving up two weeks of his vacation and requesting permission from owners to cut short his spring training visits. He said the talks would focus on the value of organized sports in camps and compare German and American methods of physical training.[33] In his weekly column, J. G. Taylor Spink noted Frick had conducted numerous meetings with the War Department, leading Spink to decide that "here was a real talker with a real message, who should go among army men and spread the gospel of their mission and their destinies. . . . Washington . . . asked him to deliver a series of geo-political talks and he has been making them with tremendous success."[34] Again, there was no indication that Landis reacted to his visits.

By July 1943 Frick had again been to Washington, with the focus less on aiding the war effort than on how baseball could stay viable. His report to the magnates outlined reasons for concern and optimism:

> I have made it vague and broad for the simple reason that I feel there are certain confidences that I cannot disclose even to this group. . . . But I do want you to know that we have friendly feelings in Washington. We have men over there in the Army and in the Navy, and very close to the White House—men of considerable importance and considerable power—who feel strongly that a sports program should be adopted, and who are perfectly willing to go to bat for the program, but who feel that it should come from Baseball and from the sports people themselves, and should not be left for them to outline.[35]

Essentially, the game should go on, but it was up to owners to deal with manpower and travel limitations. This remained the primary emphasis until early 1945.

Frick's meetings in 1944 remained focused on keeping baseball alive and supporting the war effort. When his owners convened in February 1944, he mentioned having recently met with General Lewis Hershey, head of Selective Service, and his first assistant, Colonel Barry Howard. Frick conveyed to them a potential shortage of sixty players for 1944, and Howard was prepared to recommend releasing players in war industries during the season. Though it was a promising note, clubs had to work out details. Frick also mentioned meetings with legislators to whom he emphasized the benefits of allowing baseball to continue. Furthermore, he noted the war was not likely to end soon.[36] There was no mention of Washington visits at the Summer Meetings, nor was any opposition raised about Frick having gone to the capital.

Of all his visits, the most crucial occurred in January 1945, when the war offices seriously considered canceling baseball. Those sessions would ultimately salvage the season but also brought the negative reaction from Frick's cohorts. Two points stand out from all Frick's Washington sessions.

First, the league president had developed relations with members of the War Council, producing an ongoing exchange of information and a level of trust that helped when matters reached crisis level. Second, there was no public reaction from Landis, even though *The Sporting News* mentioned the meetings and National League owners were aware. No doubt, the meetings were instrumental in keeping baseball alive during World War II.

HELP

Frick's Washington meetings were not the only efforts that aided baseball's continuity. Even before the war, a number of ideas were developed, mostly in National League meetings, the first being the Bat and Ball Fund. A year before Pearl Harbor, as troops were mobilized and stationed in training camps, the league created a spring exhibition All-Star Game against a camp and a Major League team in proximity, using funds to purchase the equipment.[37] The game, while not a great success, initiated the fund, and Pearl Harbor catalyzed expansion. *The Sporting News* announced the program in January 1942, adding that it would replicate one implemented during the last war. Bats, balls, gloves, catcher's gear, and issues of *The Sporting News* were sent to military training bases in the United States and around the world. Clark Griffith, owner of the Senators, oversaw the program, having done so in 1917; Frick worked with Griffith, with Frick's New York office the headquarters.[38] In reality, Griffith was a titular head because all coordination was done from New York. The fund's creation was initiated by the National League to coordinate an overall effort by the eight clubs not only to provide the equipment but also to construct ball diamonds, accomplished by lending clubs' groundskeepers. Further, Major League clubs played exhibition games against camps close by to raise money, though most expenses were funded by All-Star Game proceeds. The American League responded favorably, setting the program in motion, though some reticence remained.[39]

At the National League meeting in February, concerns were raised about costs. The most vocal were Powel Crosley and Warren Giles, owner and general manager of Cincinnati. Giles raised the affordability issue, given the uncertain near-term future of baseball. After some back and forth, Frick conveyed strong support. He stressed how well the military brass appreciated the fund, as demonstrated by letters from Brigadier General Frederick Osborn of the Information and Education Division of Special

Service and General George Marshal of the U.S. Army. Frick added, "I think it is a hell of a program. It is a good baseball program, gentlemen. I think we are doing a real job if we continue to do that sort of a job, but it is going to take money, and it is going to take time, and it is going to take effort." Branch Rickey echoed, "Why in the hell are we running around trying to find something to do when we have a thing like that in front of us?" Larry MacPhail added that an investment of $200,000 to $250,000 would do "a hell of a job," adding that it could be totally funded by All-Star Games.[40] In spite of the burden the Phillies were placing on the National League, the Bat and Ball Fund was approved—by both leagues. Before the season, Frick announced that 1,850 kits had been sent to camps since Pearl Harbor, noting that funds were coming from two All-Star Games, one between leagues, the other between current players against those in the military.[41]

By the end of the year Frick announced the Bat and Ball Fund was already financed for 1943, with baseball having raised $200,000. Orders were placed for thirty-six thousand balls, nine thousand bats, and four hundred sets of catcher's gear, and Frick noted that similar equipment had already gone out to over four thousand units at nine hundred camps in forty-three states. Others were sent overseas to England, Iceland, Africa, Australia, Alaska, Hawaii, the Canal Zone, and the Caribbean. He noted that the gear had a positive effect on morale, building both spirit and cooperation among the troops.[42] The program was an obvious success, generating positive publicity both in Washington and with the public that continued until the end of the war.

Like the Bat and Ball Fund, the idea to have each club donate a game to support the war relief funds was initiated in the National League, suggested by Larry MacPhail. He was a huge booster of the efforts, soon even resigning to return to military duty. Shortly after the February meetings, he announced that proceeds from one of his home games would be donated to a serviceman's welfare agency. MacPhail said, "Baseball cannot content itself merely with giving paraphernalia to the soldiers and sailors of our country. Something more substantial must be done and this may be a beginning. I hope other clubs will follow suit." They did. Before the 1942 season, Landis, Frick, and Harridge, along with Minor League officials, met with Colonel John Taylor, head of the Army Emergency Relief Fund, and Lieutenant William Huggins Jr., director of the Navy Relief Society. The outcome was an agreement for each club to donate proceeds of one game.[43] Eventually, it would include the army and navy relief funds and the Red Cross.

Not surprisingly, there was again reticence from some owners because attendance was declining. Teams reduced the impact by earmarking their game for a weekday afternoon when the crowd was much smaller. The first games thus produced minimal funds, causing both league presidents to change policies. The remaining games were held on weekends or under the lights, guaranteeing larger crowds and greater proceeds. That produced better results, with the campaign raising over $500,000. A sum of $60,000 was also collected through the extra All-Star Game, played in Cleveland's huge Municipal Stadium between the American League and a team of players in the military. The league club was victorious, and sixty thousand fans were entertained by a huge display of military pageantry.[44] Those games were continued for the war's duration.

Although the funds raised the next two years were not as impressive, the war relief games still served two purposes: raising hundreds of thousands of dollars for the relief effort and providing baseball with positive publicity. In September 1943 Frick presided at an event designed to create public awareness, presenting checks to well-known sportswriters Grantland Rice and John Kieran, cochairs of the Red Cross's Sports Advisory Committee, and Prescott Bush, campaign chair of the National War Fund. The groups received checks for $163,279.42.[45] The following spring, addressing the New York Advertising Club, Frick again promoted baseball's efforts. He highlighted the number of ballplayers in military service, the fact that a million dollars was raised for war relief funds, the sale of over a billion dollars in war bonds at baseball games, and the donation of over a half million pints of blood. He said, "The real example of genuine democracy is on the playing fields of America. It is the one place American youth meets on common ground and the real lesson of democracy can best be preached."[46] Frick was diligent in ensuring the public's awareness.

While the Bat and Ball Fund and war relief efforts received more publicity, the most successful program was selling war bonds at all games. The program generated little costs other than labor to conduct the effort. Before the program started in 1942, Branch Rickey established precedent by motioning that all in baseball, other than players, donate ten percent of their salary to purchase defense bonds. Both leagues adopted bond sales, which continued until the war's end. Later in that 1942 scheduling meeting, Frick summarized that baseball undertook three things that a newspaperman could sink his teeth into: the bond program, letting men in uniform into games for free, and the Bat and Ball Fund.[47] Even though Frick did not initiate it, he became an enthusiastic supporter of the bond sales.

Most sales were at ballparks, but baseball organized other supplemental programs. The largest was a luncheon in New York City sponsored by the New York and Brooklyn chapters of sportswriters in June 1943. In attendance were 1,500 businessmen, bankers, and industrialists, among the wealthiest in the metropolitan area. Also in attendance were Frick and officials and players from the Yankees, Giants, and Dodgers. Opportunities to mingle with players were auctioned off, raising $123,850,000, some bidders agreeing to purchase additional bonds based on the performance of the player they purchased. Although Frick did not create the event, he had a major role in its organization.[48] It was another means to aid the war.

The money raised by the three programs never resulted in a comprehensive report of what was achieved overall. A cumulative summary was offered years later by Frick at a congressional hearing before Emanuel Celler's Antitrust Subcommittee in July 1951. Emphasizing baseball's benefits, he reported the sport had contributed $2,128,698.58 for the Bat and Ball Fund and war relief programs, along with raising $1,027,923,225 in war bonds. Given that it was offered under oath, it's likely the numbers were accurate.[49] It remains debatable, however, as to how meaningful baseball's war efforts were; a recent article suggested they "were limited in scope and had minimal impact on the war effort as a whole. Major League Baseball was capable of doing much more both financially and socially, though in the league's defense, it could have done much less and not many would have noticed."[50]

It is difficult to assess the overall impact of the efforts, though Frick believed they were substantive. As will be discussed, they may have been helpful when baseball was preparing for the 1945 season. Another way to assess the efforts is to translate the contributions into today's dollars, equating to $41.9 million in 2025 dollars for equipment and relief funds and the war bond purchases equating to over $20 billion. Whether baseball could have done more is arguable. Although initial resistance came from some clubs, executives later referred to their efforts with pride. Further, they would produce other unintended benefits.

As the 1942 season ended, baseball's executives faced additional challenges. The largest was finding players. The second was declining revenues—attendance in 1942 decreased by over a million. A third was supporting both the Bat and Ball Fund and the war-relief program, both cutting further into the declining revenue stream. On top of those problems, the War Office added another in October, requiring a reduction in travel for 1943.

Frick and Harridge met to discuss the problem during the 1942 World Series. Both leagues were historically divided between four eastern and western teams. For the National League, the eastern clubs were the Braves, Dodgers, Giants, and Phillies, and the western teams were the Pirates, Reds, Cubs, and Cardinals. The American League eastern teams were the Red Sox, Yankees, Athletics, and Senators; the western ones were the Indians, Tigers, White Sox, and Browns. Traditionally, they would travel four times a season to the other's section. To reduce travel, the presidents agreed to only three swings to the other, with each series now consisting of four rather than three games.[51] Frick stressed that baseball could keep the 154-game schedule, as one less trip was enough to achieve the mileage reduction.[52] The issue did have ripple effects, however.

One emerged quickly when an anonymous baseball official proposed realigning the leagues into eastern and western clubs; the reaction from owners explains why the person remained unknown. Landis refused to discuss the matter. Harridge claimed there was nothing to the idea. Frick asserted it wouldn't be necessary unless an unforeseen emergency occurred. Sam Breadon expressed owner sentiment: "If baseball is that hard up, it had better stop altogether."[53] The idea was rejected without discussion. The challenge did not disappear with the initial travel cutback, however. In letters to Landis, Harridge, and Frick in late November, Joseph B. Eastman, director of the Office of Defense Transportation, asked the leagues to find spring training sites as close as possible to the club's cities, the purpose being to free the railroads for military logistics. He also indicated that reductions of the 154-game season might be necessary.[54] Those requests became a major topic at the Winter Meetings.

Unfortunately, Eastman's letters arrived too late to be on the agenda, given baseball's thirty-day notification requirement. The reduction of east-west trips was discussed and adopted, claiming travel would decline by twenty-three thousand railroad miles, but the spring training issue remained unresolved.[55] This time, Landis went to Washington before the end of the year to discuss the matter with Eastman.[56] Upon returning, he called a special joint meeting in January, presenting their agreement. All spring training camps would be conducted north of the Potomac and Ohio Rivers, with the Missouri clubs finding in-state sites. Reducing regular season games to cut back train travel further was also discussed. Frick was adamant about preserving the 154-game schedule in place almost every season since 1901: "If baseball is worth preserving, if baseball is worth playing, if we have a place in this thing, then we need not apologize for our activities. . . . We don't have to apologize for this game of ours, why not play it on our regular schedule?" The magnates agreed but pushed the start of the season back a week given the likelihood of inclement weather at spring training sites.[57] Eastman was satisfied.[58] Although baseball faced many challenges, its basic structure—the same clubs in their respective leagues and the 154-game schedule—remained intact.

Even with travel reductions, further travel cuts remained an issue until the war ended, producing additional concessions, one a natural result of earlier reductions. With the pennant races decided, Cardinals and Yankees management met Harridge, Frick, and Landis, agreeing to reduce travel by playing three games in New York and the remainder in St. Louis.[59] The other reduction proved more difficult. Eastman had been replaced by Colonel J. Monroe Johnson, who pushed in February 1945 for an additional 25 percent travel reduction, suggesting an east-west realignment of leagues.[60] Frick and Harridge met with Johnson later that month, agreeing to cancel the 1945 All-Star Game and to reconsider the World Series if the war continued. There would be no realignment, and the 154-game schedule remained. Frick stated, "It's just what we wanted; now we know where we stand and can get down to the business of going ahead."[61] The next day, Frick remained supportive: "Mr. Johnson was fair all the way through. We're delighted with the results of a most friendly conference . . . and still able to plan definitely a proper Major League schedule."[62] When the war ended that summer, concessions were no longer necessary.

The travel restrictions presented challenges to baseball, though. Spring training in colder climates forced many clubs indoors. Railroad travel was more difficult to arrange. Through all of it, baseball maintained its regular season and the World Series without changing either league structure or the number of games. Like other war decisions, Frick had a major role in working out the issues and maintaining stability.

When the 1944 season ended, Frick felt comfortable. Baseball had complied with war restrictions, kept the game alive, and played a traditional season. In spite of losing players, the clubs accumulated enough talent to continue without requesting special treatment. In spite of controversies, the Majors played more night games, well beyond the initial fourteen. They had done much for the war effort, selling bonds, dedicating game proceeds, and donating equipment. Baseball had also proven flexible by relocating spring training and cutting travel. With the Germans in retreat, 1945 prospects looked bright. Frick had utilized all the ammunition in his arsenal to keep baseball alive for three seasons, but he would now need even more. In aggregate, his additional efforts likely saved the season.[63]

The challenge stemmed from the shifting status of the war. On the Pacific front, the retreat of the Japanese was slow and arduous, with battles undertaken to gain an island at a time. In Europe, where Germany's surrender appeared imminent, the Battle of the Bulge launched in December rendered that doubtful. Washington responded accordingly. In early January President Roosevelt asked Congress to make all men who were classified 4-F—exempted from the war—available, a request similar to the work-or-fight order from Secretary of War Newton Baker in 1918 that brought baseball to an early halt. Because 281 of baseball's 400 players were 4-F, no baseball in 1945 was a strong possibility.[64] When the War Office halted all East Coast horse racing in January, that threat increased.[65] Baseball had good reason for concern.

Frick voiced confidence following the racetrack ruling that all would work out: "So long as sufficient players are left and the government indicates it wants us to keep going, baseball will continue to operate. Baseball has asked no favors in the past and does not intend to do so now."[66] He was less optimistic after FDR's 4-F reclassification. Although Roosevelt had clarified his request at a press conference—implying that baseball should continue, if possible, without hurting the war effort—it did not provide Frick comfort. He traveled to Washington to gain a better sense of the ruling's effect.[67] Those mid-January meetings lasted almost two weeks.

During his visit, Frick met with the three officials most responsible for coordinating the war effort: James Byrnes, head of the Office of War Mobilization; Paul McNutt, chairman of the War Manpower Commission; and General Lewis Hershey, head of the Selective Service. Beyond the reclassification of 4-Fs, Frick was concerned about the decision to recheck the physical condition of 4-F athletes to reassess their fitness, seemingly a double jeopardy. Neither Frick nor Clark Griffith, also at the sessions, offered comments publicly, but Frick indicated he would present details to owners on February 3. Anticipating criticism, he said, "I did not go to Washington to plead the cause of baseball, but to obtain factual information which I could give to my club owners. . . . They will have to decide then whether under these conditions they will be able to open the 1945 season." He added nothing, though hinted there wouldn't be a ban, which suggested utilizing players above and below draft age.[68] Still, baseball's status for 1945 remained in doubt.

Frick had anticipated a backlash for his January meetings, and the other members of the triumvirate provided it. Harridge told the press he knew nothing about the meetings, stressing neither Frick nor Griffith acted in any official capacity. O'Connor claimed he hadn't heard from Frick, reiterating Harridge's position.[69] Coming to Frick's defense, Arthur Daley chastised Landis for refusing "to confer with Washington officialdom during his reign and hence baseball went on its fumbling way for the first three years of the war without ever knowing precisely what the score was." He called Frick and Griffith's efforts "a refreshing and sensible change for the better."[70] Daley sensed that Frick was bringing a new strategy to government relations.

That would come to a head at the National League scheduling meeting in New York on February 3, which proved to be extremely important. With the upcoming season in doubt, Frick altered his presiding style, still reporting but also lecturing magnates. The session began by discussing with whom Frick and Griffith met and what those officials thought about the upcoming season. The list of dignitaries was impressive. It included the three men mentioned earlier, along with Vice President Harry Truman, Under Secretary of War Robert P. Patterson, Stabilization Chairman Fred Vinson, and Senate Majority Leader Alben Barkley. Frick concluded that baseball's main concern was the byproduct of Germany's initial success in the Battle of the Bulge. Because the European conflict had turned favorably toward the Allies, that concern was diminishing. It was also felt the challenges facing baseball would be less acute when the season started. Frick pointed out that baseball was regulated by directives from the War Offices, not from legislation. He closed by emphasizing that Hershey was asked directly if baseball should continue in 1945. Pausing, Hershey acknowledged there was no tendency to order a stoppage, though he added the sport could expect no favors from him or the War Manpower Commission; the other officials expressed greater optimism.[71] Frick's report was clearly positive overall.

Frick then summarized pertinent points: (1) There would be no order to shut down baseball. (2) All players now in baseball from ages eighteen to forty-five would be subject to the manpower draft. (3) Players under eighteen and over thirty-eight would likely be available. (4) Men discharged for physical disability would likely be permitted to play. (5) Men with a 4-F who are over age thirty would not be called until all between eighteen to thirty were drafted. (6) Men reclassified from 4-F would be available until called. (7) Men in industries who are ballplayers would be available at the discretion of employers.[72] Frick thus outlined a road map for owners as they assembled their rosters.

Frick also presented magnates with long- and short-term options. Long-term, baseball needed to keep its issues before the decision-makers like other industries did. Almost all of the federal officials with whom Frick met said baseball's failure to present its case was a real shortcoming. The league president then phrased it more succinctly: baseball must become proactive in conveying its needs to Washington officials while communicating its benefits as well. As one official asked, "How can you expect us to know your problem when all these newspaper statements seem to indicate that you don't know it yourselves?" Frick stipulated that baseball had to take leadership in articulating positions and helping to shape policy. Later, Robert Carpenter, owner of the Phillies, asked Frick why baseball didn't have Washington representation beyond the fact-finding just undertaken. Frick replied, "Mr. Carpenter, you could lead me into a long speech on that. . . . We have not, through neglect." Later, the magnates returned to the Washington issue, specifically that of O'Connor considering Frick presumptuous for going to Washington. Frick responded, "I would not take that any more seriously than it should be taken." He added it was explained to O'Connor that he was not representing the National League or baseball.[73]

The discussion then turned to the short-term option—the upcoming season. That option was to play baseball, and Frick recommended that baseball plan to continue without equivocation. He added, "Certainly we face handicaps—but handicaps constitute the real test of our fighting spirit and ingenuity." He then stressed that baseball should make clear it supported every government move and would help the war effort in any way, noting, "The use in baseball of any single man who could better serve the war effort in other fields is just as distasteful to baseball as it would [be] to government or to the public."[74] In essence, Frick asked for and received unanimous support to not only proceed with the season but also remain in communication with Washington. The American League followed suit, agreeing to send Frick and Harridge to Washington to keep abreast as the season approached. The following day, the *New York Times* announced baseball would be played, with its leaders staying in contact with war officials.[75] Although baseball wasn't out of the woods, there was a commitment to play.

When the league presidents returned to Washington in late February, they received good and bad news. In their first meeting, with James Byrnes, they were looking for guarantees to be able to staff all sixteen clubs. Frick framed it precisely: "Either leave us with enough men to play baseball or tell us to stop. You can't expect us to play without players."[76] Although they did not receive a definitive yes or no answer, Frick was optimistic: "We're making every plan to carry on in 1945. . . . Nothing developed today to change my opinion that baseball can operate."[77] The following day's meeting, while discouraging, did not temper his optimism, as J. Monroe Johnson, head of the Office of Defense Transportation, requested another travel reduction. They agreed to eliminate the All-Star Game and exhibition games requiring travel and placed the World Series in limbo pending the war situation. Frick was positive: "It's just what we wanted; now we know where we stand and can get down to the business of going ahead."[78] In spite of additional road bumps, nothing dampened expectations for the season.

It took another month for the official green light; even then it was not definitive. On March 21, Paul McNutt ruled that all players in war-related industries would be available to play: "There is considerable evidence that it [baseball] adds to the morale on the home front in war time and that, therefore, there is a real justification for this action."[79] Frick was elated. In a carefully worded statement, he summarized: "Mr. McNutt's statement clarifies our situation. . . . Under the Washington ruling these men are now privileged to return to baseball. The use of these players should enable us to go through the coming season in good shape."[80] He now didn't see any obstruction for 1945.

Although written prior to that outcome, Spink's editorial in the first March issue applauded Frick's efforts:

> Baseball owes a large debt—to Frick. . . . It was through Frick's efforts that the Washington go-ahead finally was achieved. . . . It was Frick who, a long time ago, decided that to adhere to the policy established by the late Judge Kenesaw M. Landis, and remain away from Washington, could have fatal results. It was Frick who recognized the absolute necessity of bringing to the attention of bureau chiefs, by personal contact, the facts in the baseball picture. Frick went to Washington perhaps a dozen times before his presence there finally became a matter of public information, and Leslie M. O'Connor announced that Frick had gone to the Capital, not as the representative of baseball, but merely as president of the National League. It now develops that, right from the start, Frick was the representative of all baseball, and was so recognized by government officials. And a good thing for the game that he was! It is now a certainty that if baseball had adhered to the Landis injunction to stay away from Washington, the major league would face the padlocking of their parks for the 1945 season.[81]

As the season approached, Frick wrote his annual column on how he saw the National League taking shape. He was pleased to say it was business as usual, while noting that "our best ball teams have gone to war." He then emphasized that baseball would continue to do what it had already done during the war: play games for charity and adhere to travel restrictions. There would be no All-Star Game, and all men in uniform could attend any game for free.[82] Essentially, even with restrictions, supporting the war would continue. More important, so would baseball.

The season followed that course through Germany's surrender in May and Japan's in August, when all travel restrictions were lifted. While thrilled, Frick remained cautious: "It looks like this action paves the way for the World Series. It looks like we will go south for training next spring; it looks like we're back to pre-war days. From now on to the end of the season we're not going to run wild, of course. I think we will travel about as we have."[83] Even with everything back to normal, Frick wouldn't gloat.

That was consistent with his approach during the war and his reluctance to take credit. Yet, it is likely Frick's efforts were a major reason the game persevered. While no minutes exist from the meetings with war officials, it is clear they made him aware of plans and enabled him to emphasize baseball's contributions. He could have mentioned the Bat and Ball Fund, the games dedicated to raising money for relief efforts, and the value of war bonds sold at games. Additionally, he could have emphasized the role baseball played in maintaining troop morale. By keeping that information in front of officials, especially if they questioned baseball's importance, it impacted their decisions. Regardless of whether baseball had done all it could to support the war effort, those meetings helped in Washington, without Frick requesting any special treatment.[84] Frick, more than anyone else in baseball, had successfully walked the tightrope. World War II presented baseball with many challenges, but Ford Frick deserves considerable credit for ensuring the game stayed alive.

4

Change Is Going to Come

Breaking baseball's color barrier in 1947 was pivotal for the sport and for America. Ford Frick played an important role in the historic event, as he approved every player added to National League club rosters. His background offered no hints he would play such a role. He resided in white communities with little interaction with African Americans before becoming league president. Even then, his interactions were miniscule, limited to a few interviews with Black sportswriters, during which he was, at best, noncommittal on integration. Decisions reached the year before Robinson's signing likely facilitated the process. Subsequently, he supported Robinson at critical times. Frick clearly played a role both in changing who was allowed in the Majors and providing support necessary for success.

A SPORT IN CRISIS

Before the season, 1946 looked to be a banner year. With the war ended, there was much reason for optimism. Spring training returned to warmer climates, travel was no longer restricted, and star players were back. Major League attendance increased 23 percent in 1945, higher than any season in that decade. In the early weeks of 1946, attendance at every park increased significantly. By the All-Star break, magnates should have been savoring their success. Instead, they were panicked during the Summer Meetings, so concerned they conducted them in secrecy.[1]

Three issues created the apparent crisis. First, the Mexican League, headed by wealthy Jorge Pasquel, was enticing players with huge salaries. Although its recruitment success was limited, players like Sal Maglie and Mickey Owen had departed, ignoring the reserve clause. Pasqual called baseball an unfair monopoly and welcomed a legal test of the reserve clause that enabled a club to perpetuate a player's contract.[2] Magnates believed the game couldn't survive without it. Second, there was a threatened player strike by Pittsburgh in early June. Robert Murphy, a labor organizer, chose the Pirates as his initial effort to create a players' guild. Though he failed to garner sufficient player support initially, a second vote was planned.[3] Finally, owners were concerned over a Black man playing professionally in the highest Minors, raising worries about integration. Although no minutes of the meeting are extant any longer, it is known that a committee was established to address the problems.

There is evidence minutes existed. A report produced by the committee in late August quoted a resolution adopted unanimously by the National League at the July meetings: "RESOLVED; that the President of the National League appoint a Steering Committee of two Club representatives, the League President to be a member and Chairman of said Committee. The Committee is directed to employ counsel and to consider and test all matters of Major League interest and report its conclusions and recommendations. . . . The said Committee is also authorized to represent the National League in conference with a similar Steering Committee of the American League." It acknowledges a similar resolution adopted by the American League on the same date.[4] The report by the committee became known as the MacPhail Report, named for its chair, Larry MacPhail, part owner of the Yankees.

The report was presented and discussed at a special joint meeting on August 27, 1946, without minutes taken. They were transcribed at the meeting the following day, reflecting actions taken to address two of the concerns raised in July. Revisions were made to tighten the reserve clause. While not preventing players from jumping to Mexico, it strengthened the clause's legal standing. Significant financial reforms were adopted for the players, including a minimum wage, spring training money, moving expenses, and initiation of a pension plan.[5] These changes were intended to improve player relations. The third item, integration, was never mentioned at the August 28 meeting, though it remained a concern.

The original report didn't propose a position on integration, but the concerns expressed made its intention clear. First, it suggested no Black players were ready for the Majors, quoting as its authority Sam Lacey, an African American sportswriter. Second, it claimed integration would be the demise of the Negro Leagues. Finally, it feared a loss of revenue for Major League clubs who rented their ballparks to Negro League teams.[6] The report also feared integration would bring large numbers of Black fans, causing even greater reductions of whites. It added, "The individual action of any one Club may exert tremendous pressures upon the whole structure of professional baseball and could conceivably result in lessening the value of several Major League franchises."[7] In effect, the MacPhail Report was succinct on integration: go slowly! It was aimed at Branch Rickey's Dodgers, as Robinson was already at the highest Minor League level there. The report appeared to reflect its six members, including Frick. The others, MacPhail, Tom Yawkey of the Red Sox, Sam Breadon of the Cardinals, Phil Wrigley of the Cubs, and Will Harridge, were all signers. Frick's position was less clear, as will be discussed, but his signature was on the August meeting report.

Without minutes, the discussion on August 27 remains a mystery. Only indirect reference was made by Branch Rickey in a speech at historically Black Wilberforce College in Ohio, in February 1948. Rickey referenced an unnamed report that attempted to block or slow integration. He claimed the report was supported by owners, fifteen voting in favor, only the Dodgers dissenting. Copies were then allegedly collected and destroyed.[8] Rickey's speech suggested overwhelming opposition to integration at the meeting. The next day, the entire report was officially adopted—except the integration segment, which was also never discussed.[9] The alleged 15–1 vote never resulted in any formal action opposing integration.

The reason for that lack of action is unknown, though it's possible Frick helped to remove that section. By 1945 pressure was in New York City to provide opportunities for African Americans, including in baseball. The outgoing mayor, Fiorello La Guardia, an advocate of racial equality, established the Committee for Unity, inviting owners of the New York ball clubs to participate. Horace Stoneham declined, calling the committee a bunch of "professional do-gooders." Although MacPhail agreed to participate, he reflected Stoneham's view, branding the committee "social and political drum-beaters." Only Rickey was serious, developing a relationship with the executive director, New York University sociology professor Daniel W. Dodson, with whom he shared his integration plans. When La Guardia pushed further, Rickey arranged for a press conference in October announcing that Jackie Robinson had signed a Minor League contract. Though Rickey was not there—his son, Branch Rickey Jr., director of the farm system, was—he made sure the announcement was in Montreal, where Robinson would play, to appear independent from La Guardia's pressure.[10] Frick, as National League president and a resident near New York City, was well aware of the La Guardia committee.

He was also the only person other than the Dodgers who could block Robinson. In both leagues, all players had to be approved by the president. As he formulated his plans on Robinson, Rickey was aware of the requirement, having spent decades with the Cardinals' front office. Although it is uncertain when Rickey finalized his intent to integrate, it was likely after Commissioner Landis died and the war ended. A major motivator was passage of the Ives-Quinn Act by the New York Assembly in July 1945. The law established a state commission guarding against discrimination that could impose a $500 fine or one-year jail sentence on employers refusing to hire due to race.[11] That law further strengthened New York's Committee for Unity. Working in the city, Frick was aware of the law as well.

In addition, Frick and Rickey had worked together for over a decade after Frick joined the league, jointly attending numerous league meetings. They may both have been involved in the Dodgers' hiring of Larry MacPhail and likely had conversations when Landis threatened to break up the Cardinals' farm system. By the time Rickey joined the Dodgers in 1942, they had a long relationship. Given their proximity and the controversy associated with integrating baseball, Rickey and Frick likely had numerous discussions concerning Robinson. Further, the two men shared similar backgrounds. They grew up in small, midwestern communities, byproducts of deeply religious families, and were graduates of Methodist liberal arts colleges. They also spent time in western states before heading back to pursue opportunities connected to baseball. Given Frick's role in approving players, coupled with their long-term connection, Frick was likely aware of Rickey's intentions well before the meetings concerning the MacPhail Report.

Frick was also aware of baseball's involvement with La Guardia's Committee for Unity, as were Stoneham and MacPhail, whether they agreed or not with the pressures to integrate. Given the 15–1 vote against integration that allegedly occurred on August 27, something happened to exclude it from the report enacted the next day. Frick may have been that something. With the owners opposing integration, no one other than Rickey was inclined to remove it. Harridge may have had some awareness of New York's pressures, but not like Frick, who was exposed daily. He was the person best positioned to persuade magnates to postpone action on the integration segment. Baseball owners, while addressing the reserve clause and player unrest at the August meeting, left the integration issue to the Dodgers and Ford Frick by declining action on it.

Little in Frick's background prepared him for a role in baseball's integration. Growing up in small Indiana towns, Frick rarely crossed paths with African Americans, there being no Blacks in either Wawaka or Brimsfield. His year in Fort Wayne provided a more cosmopolitan environment, but Frick's experience was segregated, both at school and the newspaper. The same was true at DePauw. Few Black residents were in Greencastle, and the college had only one African American student, who attended the School of Music part time, separate from Frick's College of Liberal Arts.[12] In his various Colorado jobs, he interacted only with whites. Even in New York, he was employed as a sportswriter for newspapers geared to white clientele, working with white reporters, covering sports played by white athletes. He resided in Bronxville, an almost exclusively white suburb. No experience broadened Frick's horizons.

In fact, one of his New York experiences may have had the opposite effect. Soon after he started, Frick became active in the New York Baseball Writers' Association of America, an all-white group writing for the city's newspapers. Because baseball held its February meeting in New York, his branch traditionally hosted the formal dinner. With top executives present, it evolved into a roast of the game's executives and players, performed by the writers. From the 1920s through the 1940s, the roast was presented as a minstrel show, writers putting on blackface to portray the stereotypical image of minstrel singers. Soon after he arrived in New York, Frick became its interlocutor, putting on numerous parodies "that had many of the baseball celebrities squirming."[13] Frick effectively perpetuated racial stereotypes.

The 1933 performance was Frick's last because he was now employed by baseball and no longer part of the sportswriters' fraternity. He attended the dinners but was now one of those roasted. That didn't affect Frick's perception of minorities because the sport remained a white man's game. The only interaction between Black and white players occurred in off-season barnstorming games. There is no evidence Frick attended such games, even when featuring greats like Satchel Paige against Bob Feller.[14] Until integration, these games drew good crowds and provided supplemental incomes for participants though were never sanctioned by organized baseball. There was little reason for a league president to attend.

The Depression did produce pressure to offer Black players opportunities, though most of it came from Black and Communist newspapers.

One initiative was undertaken by Wendell Smith, assistant sports editor of the *Pittsburgh Courier*—a Black newspaper—who interviewed Frick in February 1939. They met in the lobby of a Pittsburgh hotel where Smith, later Jackie Robinson's traveling companion during his rookie season, hoped to ascertain the National League president's opinion on integration. It is unclear why Smith chose Frick, though as a newcomer relative to Landis and Harridge, he may have seemed more open to change. Because Pittsburgh was a National League city, he was also more accessible. Frick's comments, though, did not offer hope.

Frick contended that the greatest obstacles to integration were the players and the fans, claiming both would create problems. He also stressed that spring training in the South would present challenges due to Jim Crow. Even Major League cities had many hotels and restaurants that wouldn't accept Black guests, and Frick suggested such separation could impact a team's cohesiveness. He emphasized that owners were not the barrier since baseball had no formal policy prohibiting Blacks.[15] Smith published the interview but also tested Frick's assertions. During 1939 he interviewed league players and managers, their comments often not corresponding with Frick's claims they were reticent to integrate.

Some managers affirmed Frick, but others favored integration. Leo Durocher was one: "I certainly would use a Negro ballplayer if the bosses said it was all right." Pie Traynor, Pirates manager, asserted, "Personally, I don't see why the ban against Negro players exists at all. It is a known fact that there are plenty Negroes capable of playing in the big leagues."[16] On the other hand, Bill Terry of the Giants opposed integration, mostly because the team could not stay in hotels or eat meals together. Casey Stengel, skipper of the Braves, perhaps reflecting owners, contended that integration would hurt both the Negro and Major Leagues, adding that Black crowds would keep white fans from ballparks.[17] Even though Smith didn't find consensus, enough players and managers were open to integration to suggest they weren't the primary barrier. Rather, Smith concluded it was owners and executives who were the problem. Although Smith's findings never appeared in mainstream press, they suggested to later historians that Frick was one of those barriers.

Interestingly, a Frick interview three years earlier with the *Daily Worker*, a Communist publication, was both more disingenuous and forthright. It was more dishonest because Frick claimed he did "not recall one instance where baseball had allowed either race, creed or color to enter into the question of the selection of its players." He was more honest when adding that the issue involved all clubs and was "not within the province of the authority of the league president to express an official opinion in the matter." As he did three years later, he highlighted spring training and added a view held throughout his tenure: "The whole subject is a 'sociological problem,' something society, not the big leagues, must solve."[18] Like his later comments, Frick didn't blame owners or executives, denied any formal barrier, and offered other reasons why baseball wasn't integrated.

Both articles implied Frick was part of the problem. In a way, he was. After five years as president, none of the magnates had expressed interest in signing Blacks. He was quite aware of their power over him since they hired him, paid his salary, renewed his contract, and could terminate his employment. Even if the risk was minimal that his comments in a Black or Communist newspaper might be read, Frick was unwilling to take the risk. Further, his observations weren't incorrect. When Robinson debuted, he encountered problems with players, managers, and fans. There were also difficulties during spring training, when staying in hotels and eating with teammates. While those observations proved accurate, Frick's comments left the impression he was a barrier.

Historians were far from the first to offer that assessment, Bill Veeck making the allegation in 1962 in *Veeck as in Wreck*. He claimed Frick blocked him from acquiring the Phillies in 1943 due to his intent to staff it with Black players. The former owner of three American League clubs also claimed Frick bragged to others that he had stopped Veeck from "contaminating the league."[19] Still commissioner when Veeck's book came out, Frick never denied the claims publicly but didn't comment on other Veeck criticisms either. He also ignored other jabs at his leadership, so his lack of response was consistent. Interestingly, Veeck's Phillies claim remains an ongoing debate among baseball scholars. Jules Tygiel, in *Baseball's Great Experiment*, his classic study of Robinson and integration, affirmed Veeck. Other than citing Veeck's book, however, his only evidence was an interview with the maverick in 1980, when Veeck again owned the White Sox. As the definitive historical study, Tygiel's book furthered the perception of Frick as an ardent opponent of integration, strengthening Veeck's claim Frick was an obstacle.[20]

That interpretation of the Phillies' story has been mitigated since.[21] In 1998 three authors debunked the assertion, categorizing Veeck's claims as myth. That prompted Tygiel to revisit, adjusting his position considerably, as no records verify Veeck's claims and Veeck was off by a year. He added that evidence dated Veeck's interest in integration to 1946. Tygiel was critical of Frick for not responding and critical of the debunking article for relying solely on the absence of evidence.[22] In a new biography of Veeck, Paul Dickson, a noted baseball writer, reverted to the original story, devoting an appendix to it. He concluded Veeck's claims were valid because he made them many times before his 1962 book and wasn't known to lie.[23] A year later, another article denied Veeck's claim. The authors argued that although Veeck wasn't a fabricator, he did love "to tweak and nettle stodgy baseball officials." As for Frick's failure to rebut, the authors noted Frick had "adopted the diplomatic stance of silence, as people often do in refusing to dignify an unfounded accusation with a response."[24] In fact, Frick consistently behaved in that fashion throughout his career. Regardless, the Phillies myth continues to have life.

Yet, there is no primary evidence to support it, as Tygiel concluded in 2006. Veeck was interested in the Phillies. *The Sporting News* ran a short story in late October 1942 indicating Veeck had met with owner Gerald Nugent around the World Series. Veeck acknowledged the meeting with Nugent, who "quoted some large figures, of course, but that was all." He added that if he bought the club, he would stay in Milwaukee, sending Charlie Grimm to run the team.[25] That interest was brought up with the National League's Board of Directors on November 4, 1942. Nugent mentioned being approached by Veeck weeks earlier, adding he hadn't "heard back from him and that was three weeks ago." Later, Frick indicated Veeck approached him, before meeting with Nugent, with the discussion getting specific on financials. Veeck indicated he could meet the minimum amount asked by Phillies' shareholders, estimated at $154,000, but Frick added it was unclear if the total figure Veeck had in mind was $200,000 or $400,000 and acknowledged that neither was acceptable to Nugent. Frick hadn't heard from Veeck since.[26] In subsequent league meetings in 1942, a nameless potential buyer was mentioned, though it didn't appear to be Veeck. By February 9, 1943, a deal had been reached to sell to a partnership headed by William Cox. After November 4 Veeck was never mentioned again in the league minutes.

After *The Sporting News* ran its story about Veeck, there was no other mention.[27] Further, no evidence in any primary source indicates a formal offer. Nor is there evidence that Frick discussed the matter with Landis or that Frick bragged to others of blocking Veeck. Beyond the fact Veeck had conveyed interest in the Phillies, with no apparent follow-through, no source supports his allegations. Whatever Frick's views were on integration in 1942, he didn't block efforts to purchase the woebegone Phillies, which had become an albatross to the National League. Put another way, Robinson was the first serious effort to integrate baseball, and Frick definitely had a role. He was not a crusader, but his actions made him a facilitator of integration, even if Veeck later clouded the picture.

NOTHING COMES EASY

Actually, until Rickey signed Robinson with the Dodgers, Frick had no direct involvement. Frick was a pragmatist and politically savvy during his baseball career, demonstrated during the war by his efforts to keep baseball alive. Those lessons carried over to 1946 due to New York State's Ives-Quinn Act and the city's La Guardia Committee for Unity, which likely shaped his efforts behind the scenes. As baseball had no formal position on integration, Frick could do little else until Rickey brought Robinson to the Majors, which then required his signature. That occurred after a tumultuous series of events.

Although Rickey planned on Robinson in 1947, he hoped Dodgers players would initiate the request after watching him in spring training. That proved wishful thinking. Some were from southern states, raised in a segregated culture, and even regarded Blacks as less than human. Thus, dissention wasn't surprising. A few, led by Dixie Walker, petitioned to keep Robinson off the roster. Learning of it, Manager Leo Durocher called an impromptu midnight meeting and was succinct in his speech: "I'm the manager of this ball club and I'm interested in one thing. Winning . . . I'll play an elephant if he can do the job, and to make room for him, I'll send my own brother home. . . . He's going to win pennants for us. He's going to put money in your pockets and money in mine."[28] Rickey met the following day with the disgruntled players, nipping their petition effort in the bud. Tension remained, however. Even with Robinson's outstanding spring, there was still no groundswell of support weeks before the season when a crisis involving Durocher erupted.

That wasn't a surprise, as Durocher had a reputation as a hothead, earning the nickname "Leo the Lip." Starting his ninth year with the Dodgers, he had been fined more by Frick than other players or managers. He was hired by Larry MacPhail in 1938, and their relationship was rocky at best. MacPhail fired him at least thirty-five times over five years, quickly hiring him back. When MacPhail purchased the Yankees in 1945, he approached Durocher about managing the club, but friction developed when he declined. It came to a head during a spring training game in Havana, Cuba, between the teams in 1947. The issue involved gamblers, men with whom Durocher had been banned from associating but were present as MacPhail's guests. Durocher complained about their presence, upsetting MacPhail and causing him to protest to Chandler.[29] At MacPhail's insistence, a hearing with the commissioner was scheduled for late March in Sarasota, Florida.

Durocher's temper and gambling connections weren't his only problems leading into the hearing. Though raised Catholic, Durocher had divorced his first two wives and was now in a relationship with Laraine Day, a movie actress and divorcee. She had recently been granted that divorce and was required to wait a year before remarrying. Instead, she obtained another divorce decree in Mexico and married Durocher in Texas later the same day. That generated considerable controversy, especially with the Catholic Church. The Catholic Youth Organization of Brooklyn pulled out of the Dodgers' Knothole Club for youth, depleting half its membership.[30] Other church leaders called for Durocher's release, and Chandler received similar advice prior to the hearing from a Catholic Supreme Court justice.[31] That controversy, coupled with Durocher's past behavior and gambling ties, weighed on Chandler.

The first hearing on March 24 apparently went well, though two major participants didn't attend. Branch Rickey asked for a delay due to a family funeral, which was glossed over. Frick declined: "The Commissioner invited me to come, but I don't want to attend."[32] He did have breakfast that morning with Walter O'Malley, the Dodgers attorney representing Rickey at the meeting. The Chandler session centered around a rant by MacPhail, and little opportunity was provided for Durocher or the Dodgers to defend themselves, with a club official calling it a travesty. Durocher was puzzled, telling his new bride, "It went off as easy as pie. They hardly asked me anything. I can't figure it out."[33] A second meeting was scheduled four days later, and parties representing both Yankees and Dodgers were present this time, including MacPhail and Rickey. Frick again did not attend. After some discussion, Chandler asked the Yankees' group to leave the room, along with the stenographer. He then asked the Dodgers, "How much would it hurt you folks to have your fellow out of baseball?" Rickey, out of character, slammed the table with his fist, tears streaming down his cheeks, exclaiming, "Happy, what on earth is the matter with you?"[34] In spite of that, no decision was rendered. Almost two weeks passed, the new season now less than a week away, when Chandler announced his decision by phone to the Dodgers.

Durocher, who had played a key role in Robinson being accepted, was banned for the season. Rickey did not receive it well. Neither did others who hoped for baseball's integration, including Dan Dodson, chairman of the La Guardia Committee for Unity: "Many of us will always believe that it was Chandler's way of getting at Rickey, whom he could not touch personally but whose manager was vulnerable." Harold Parrott, a Dodger executive, believed the magnates had conspired to make Robinson's debut more difficult: "What the black man needed behind him was Durocher's bark and brass and bellow." Jules Tygiel disagreed with that assessment, instead ascribing it to "an insecure new commissioner."[35]

Perhaps Tygiel was correct, given the pressures on Chandler. However, the commissioner was aware by then of the Ives-Quinn Act, which made it difficult to use the best-interests-of-baseball clause to block Robinson. The changing attitudes following World War II also presented difficulties, as awareness of segregation's evils increased. Still, in spite of his efforts later to reinvent history, Chandler couldn't escape his Kentucky background and racial views. Those opinions were made clear when he later supported Strom Thurmond, a segregationist South Carolina governor running for president in 1948. While casting himself as Robinson's advocate decades later, his views seemingly hadn't changed when attempting to become George Wallace's running mate in 1968. Chandler was a segregationist throughout his life. He was handcuffed from blocking Robinson but apparently realized an opportunity to make his debut difficult.

Along with Durocher's suspension, fines were handed out to both the Yankees and Dodgers, the latter club informed when Chandler telephoned on April 9, as they prepared the news release announcing Robinson's signing. Rickey, not known for language worse than "Judas Priest," shouted, "You son of a bitch!" to the phone as the commissioner conveyed the suspension and fines. Chandler also prohibited all parties from publicly discussing his ruling, threatening additional fines. As they absorbed the decision, Rickey's son, director of Brooklyn's farm system, asked his father if he had informed Chandler about Robinson. Rickey thundered: "No! It's a league matter."[36] Shortly after, Ford Frick executed his duty, signing Robinson's contract. The rookie would make his debut in less than a week in spite of Chandler's obstacles.

While Frick, not Chandler, had the only formal role in Robinson's debut, the Kentuckian reinvented history later. In his memoir decades after, Chandler recalled Rickey visiting his home in Versailles, Kentucky, in January 1947 to ask permission to bring up Robinson. Over a roaring fire, Chandler supposedly told Rickey if Robinson could put his life on the line for his country, then he could certainly play baseball for the Dodgers.[37] The only problem with the story is it likely never happened. Such a meeting was unnecessary. As Rickey stated, it was a league matter. Only the league president could block a player, and Frick was ready to give his approval. With his signature, history was made.

However, the Durocher saga tarnishes the story. Why did Frick not participate in either meeting? Did he sense a negative ruling was a foregone conclusion? That's unlikely, since he would have made Rickey aware. Did he feel it was not his issue because the dispute involved teams from both leagues, thus in Chandler's domain? Perhaps he did not anticipate the ruling's severity. When Rickey contacted him later, Frick responded, "I wasn't present at the hearings and I don't think I can do anything about it."[38] Frick did join Rickey, O'Malley, and other Dodgers officials on April 21, however, to meet with Chandler to request Durocher's reinstatement. Chandler responded hours later, turning down the request, declaring the case closed.[39] There is no other evidence of Frick being involved. MacPhail did have to appear before the commissioner again after proclaiming Chandler had failed to develop enough evidence for a "5-minute suspension."[40] In spite of Frick's positive role, he seemed AWOL on this matter. Jackie Robinson would make his debut without a major supporter in the dugout with him.

THE DRAMA CONTINUES

In spite of losing Durocher, the Dodgers' clubhouse stayed peaceful, but the Phillies launched a major attack on Robinson a week into the season. The movie *42* depicts the harassment inflicted by Phillies players and manager Ben Chapman. Every racist term and stereotype was shouted at Robinson each time he came to bat. The rookie downplayed it, ignoring the epithets and acting unbothered, honoring his commitment to Rickey not to respond. Years later he admitted "that this day of all the unpleasant days of my life brought me nearer to cracking up than I had ever been."[41] As traumatic as that experience would later be depicted, *New York Times* coverage of the Phillies series did not mention it, generally reporting a normal three-game series. Both Roscoe McGowen and Joseph Sheehan covered it, and neither noted excessive behavior. Rather, Robinson was mentioned only for having scored the sole run in the first game. They noted that Chapman wasn't present at the third game, but the major story was the Dodgers sweeping the series.[42] Why was Chapman missing? Was he sick? Had Frick been at either of the first two games to observe his behavior? Had he been called to Frick's office on April 25 to discuss his antics? Those questions remain unanswered.

In fact, the first indication of something out of the ordinary occurring appeared two weeks later in *The Sporting News*, and even then, the story seemed positive. Chapman explained to a sportswriter why Robinson had been ridiculed so perversely: "We will treat Robinson the same as we do . . . any other man who is likely to step up to the plate and beat us." Chapman added, "We'll ride him. . . . There is not a man who has come to the big leagues since baseball had been played who has not been ridden, who has not had to prove he can take it." The writer agreed. Chapman concluded, "Baseball is big enough for everybody who has the stuff—but let's not carry anyone around on a cushion. And let's get the chips off our shoulders and play ball."[43] In essence, the Phillies' behavior was explained as a normal part of baseball.

Only when the next incident occurred, a threatened strike by Cardinals players, did the Phillies' behavior receive scrutiny. In a column about the strike threat, the Chapman incident was mentioned, asserting the manager had ridden Robinson "in a particularly vicious manner." The author added that "Frick took this matter up with the Philadelphia management and that Chapman had been advised to keep his bench comment above the belt."[44] Had that advice been given back in New York in April? The author didn't say. Other secondary sources instead infer Commissioner Chandler was the intervenor.[45] That was unlikely. The incident was a league matter, exclusively under the jurisdiction of its president, making Frick fully responsible. Further, he was in close proximity to address it.

If the Phillies' treatment of Robinson lacked media attention, such was not the case with the threatened Cardinals strike. The story was covered while the team was still in town, generating controversy immediately. It remains controversial, though basic facts are agreed upon. Sam Breadon, owner of the Cards, was worried some players might strike, flying to New York to meet with Frick prior to the series. From there, the stories vary, ranging from the potential strikers receiving an ultimatum from Frick to Breadon talking with the discontents, to the entire event never occurring. For those differences alone, the threat merits examination.

The initial story, by Stanley Woodward—sports editor of the *New York Herald Tribune*—came out on May 9, at the close of the series. Woodward claimed Frick met with the strikers, saying, "If you do this, you will be suspended from the league. . . . I don't care if it wrecks the National League for five years. This is the United States of America, and one citizen has as much right to play as another. The National League will go down the line with Robinson whatever the consequences."[46] The same day, the *New York Times* reported, its story differing substantially, that Frick acknowledged the threat but hadn't spoken to the players; instead, Breadon conducted the meeting. Frick added, "From what Breadon told me afterward the trouble was smoothed over. I don't know what he said to them, who the ringleader was, or any other details."[47] A reader of both newspapers would have concluded there was a strike threat but left unsure how it was resolved. The *Times* added confusion the next day, with Frick now referring to the strike as a dead issue: "A mountain had been made out of a mole hill anyway." In the same article, Breadon vehemently denied any threat and claimed he had not spoken to the players. Breadon admitted discussing the threat with Frick but stressed he came to Brooklyn to support his slumping club.[48] It seems clear in the aftermath that all involved parties intended to downplay the incident, with the Cardinals organization close to total denial.

That didn't prevent sportswriter Arthur Daley from offering some observations later. Certain the threat was real, Daley didn't mince words:

> This outbreak of Jim Crowism was as insane as it was ugly. Fortunately for the National League, however, it has an able, honest, sensible, just and forthright president in Ford Christopher Frick. His reaction to the plot was positively heartwarming. He didn't shilly-shally or equivocate. He leaped in and grasped the bull by the horns. . . . Frick knows the game from the inside out. . . . Hence, he was able to act intelligently and properly, decrying the scheme with such passionate indignation

> that the ring-leaders must be hanging their heads in shame. . . . It will serve to clear the air and let in wholesome breezes.[49]

Daley wasn't persuaded by the efforts to soft-pedal the issue.

The Sporting News also printed a follow-up by Stan Woodward to his *Herald Tribune* article. Woodward backed down slightly from his story while emphasizing the threat was real. He acknowledged Frick may not have delivered the ultimatum but stressed the story was "essentially right and factual." He added, "The denial by Sam Breadon, St. Louis owner, that a strike was or is threatened is so spurious as to be beneath notice. The admission by Ford C. Frick, National League president, that the strike was contemplated was above and beyond the rabbitry generally adhered to by the tycoons of our National Game. Such frankness, when compared to the furtiveness of other baseball barons, makes Frick the Mister Baseball of our time."[50] Although Frick downplayed the threat and the Cardinals' brass ignored it, sportswriters remained convinced it was real. In the decades since, the threat has been downplayed, due to a lack of hard evidence and efforts by the parties involved to minimize it. For those reasons, a recent study suggests the threat never occurred. Essentially, it suggests Breadon overreacted to the possibility and New York writers blew the story out of proportion. More particularly, since the Cardinals were on a long losing streak, it wasn't in the team's interest to forfeit any games. That conclusion also gives credence to the denials from Breadon, the club's manager, and the players.[51] Essentially, the strike threat was a "tempest in a teapot," as Frick claimed at the time.

However, three facts strongly substantiate both the strike and Frick's role in its prevention. First, in his memoir Frick considered the incident important, downplaying his own role but asserting that the threat was real.[52] Second, in 2007 Buzzie Bavasi was interviewed by me, focusing on Frick. The next year, I wrote a draft about Frick, mentioning that evidence of the strike threat was, at best, inconclusive and shared it with Bavasi. He offered limited comments, except for the strike. He was adamant Frick met directly with the strikers, threatening to remove them from baseball as long as he served as National League president. Bavasi added that he assisted in arranging the meeting.[53] Finally, sportswriters were convinced both of the event and Frick's involvement, in spite of efforts later to minimize the story. Although the extent remains unclear, Frick appeared to have a major role in supporting Robinson.

Frick's efforts overall explain why he was included with Robinson and Rickey as recipients of Thomas Jefferson Award in 1948, presented by the Council Against Intolerance in America. For his perseverance and success, Robinson received an award for "the advancement of democracy during 1947." Rickey and Frick received an award for having broken "the color barrier in American baseball." Both were decided by a nationwide poll of officials from one thousand civic organizations and editors of five hundred newspapers, with the baseball executives awarded in the public-service classification. The honors were presented at the annual banquet in New York on April 11, where 250 witnessed Frick accepting.[54] All were recognized for one of the most impactful events of 1947. It was Frick, not Chandler, who was the facilitator for integration and for protecting it against discontented players.[55]

MORE STRUGGLES

Robinson's first season was challenging, but it was successful for him, the Dodgers, and other clubs integrating soon after. The Dodgers and the Giants would win eight out of ten pennants through 1956. The Cleveland Indians, the first integrated American League club, won two pennants and finished in second six times over the same period. Still, most clubs were slow to follow, only half integrating by 1955. Only the segregated Yankees had consistent success, winning eight pennants and seven World Series. The other clubs that were slow to integrate regularly finished in the second division. Between 1947 and 1959, when the Red Sox became the final integrated club, no evidence suggests that league presidents or the commissioner applied pressure to integrate. Decisions were left to the clubs, and for all its successes, integration remained a slow process.

As for Robinson, challenges remained, though none as blatant as during his first season. Rickey released him from his commitment not to retaliate after two seasons, now being able to react to a brushback pitch or a purposeful collision. Over the next three years, any misbehavior from Robinson, known to have a temper, came under Frick's jurisdiction. At least two incidents occurred. Early in 1951 Robinson claimed some umpires were "on him," and he expected to hear from Frick about an incident with Babe Panelli.[56] Frick did react, saying he "was tired" of his "popping off, and all that business" and would control him if the Dodgers didn't. In the other case, his reaction stemmed from Robinson colliding with pitcher Sal Maglie after laying down a bunt, perhaps retaliating to the hurler's notorious beanballs. Walter O'Malley, now the Dodgers' majority owner, emphasized Robinson "has the full support of the Dodger organization."[57] No fines were forthcoming. Near the end of the 1951 season, however, Frick did fine Robinson. Roy Campanella, the Dodgers' catcher, was thrown out late in a game with the Braves. Robinson and Preacher Roe were fined "for the scenes they put on in the runways and in front of the umpires' dressing room in the presence of fans and opposing ballplayers," as they believed the ejection cost them a victory. Campanella was fined for his behavior that caused his ejection. Robinson may have damaged a dressing-room door, though he and Roe denied involvement.[58] The incident reflected the tight pennant race with the Giants, which may explain why no one was suspended. That was the only case of punishment by Frick.

Frick no longer had league authority once becoming commissioner. There was one matter, however, he couldn't avoid. On November 30, 1952, Robinson was a guest on a New York television show called *Youth Wants to Know*. Near its end, a teenager asked him if he thought the segregated Yankees were "prejudiced against Negro players." After a pause, Robinson responded: "I think the Yankee management is prejudiced. There isn't a single Negro on the team and very few in the entire Yankee farm system."[59] The Yankee front office took umbrage, filing a complaint with Frick and utilizing local media to have him censor Robinson. No condemnation was forthcoming, though Frick requested that Robinson "soft-pedal" such comments. At the same time, he stated a ballplayer "still has the right of free speech."[60] The issue passed, with Robinson apparently toning down comments though still expressing his views. Years later, Robinson claimed Frick's support was an important part of his success.[61]

While praising Frick for his support, Robinson also criticized him for his weak position on civil rights. In his book *Baseball Has Done It*, a series of stories contributed by Black players about their baseball experiences, especially in the South, Robinson focused largely on the harassment they encountered. A common theme was discrimination in spring training and when playing for southern Minor League clubs. Near the end, Robinson asserted, "Baseball, which has profited greatly both at the box office and in the quality of play from Negro participation, should stop ducking the broader issue of civil rights. . . . You, Mr. Commissioner, are a general who doesn't know he has an army or is in a war."[62] In essence, baseball should have applied more pressure to bring an end to discrimination and provide a safe environment for players.

Ironically, earlier in that book Frick explained why he didn't use his position to promote civil rights: "Baseball's function is not to lead crusades, not to settle sociological problems, not to become involved in any sort of controversial racial or religious question."[63] Although Frick's views were far from Robinson's, those early 1960s comments weren't far removed from those he made in the 1930s. Ford Frick was never a crusader. It was not his inclination to get too far in front of an issue, especially if it impacted owners. At the same time, his personal tendencies and beliefs leaned toward fairness. Even though in his life he rarely interacted with minorities, he wasn't hesitant to intervene out of fairness. Hence, if Rickey wanted to integrate, Frick supported it. Further, if others opposing integration behaved inappropriately, Frick responded. While not proactive in integration, he played an important role in enabling it. Thus, it wasn't surprising for Robinson both to praise and criticize Frick. Although not a crusader, he was consistent in his treatment of Robinson and other Black ballplayers, ensuring their opportunities in baseball. Frick was an integral component of Jackie's story, as Robinson himself acknowledged.

5

Second Time's a Charm

Kenesaw Mountain Landis, baseball's first commissioner, died after a long hospital stay in late 1944. The magnates created a triumvirate to run baseball while deliberating over a replacement. Frick, one of the three, emerged as a front-runner, simultaneously with his efforts to salvage 1945. The preference of some to hire an outsider doomed his candidacy, and Senator Albert Benjamin Chandler of Kentucky was selected instead. The magnates reduced the position's authority, including requiring a three-fourths rather than majority vote for selection and reelection. As the end of his first term approached, Chandler received nine votes, not the necessary twelve for reelection. After some delay, he agreed to vacate the office early. The magnates again debated over whether to look internally or externally, with Frick again a candidate. This time owners deadlocked on insiders, Frick and Warren Giles, Cincinnati's general manager. The standoff was broken with Frick's election in September 1951.

REPLACING A CZAR

While Kennesaw Mountain Landis had been hospitalized for over a month, his death wasn't anticipated, though his health had been declining for years.[1] Positive reports from the hospital fueled optimism until close to his passing.[2] Just before, in early November, the leagues' directors held a special meeting to discuss Landis, given his long hospital stay. They speculated he'd retire because he suggested doing so when his contract expired in January 1946.[3] Instead, the directors—four league executives from each league—renewed Landis's contract another seven years. The ailing commissioner was allegedly uplifted by their vote.[4] Whether the action was serious or merely intended to improve Landis's disposition, his death rendered it moot.

The directors took no further action, as the Winter Meetings were two weeks away. Sympathies poured in after Landis's death; Frick called it "a terrific loss to baseball. He contributed more to the game than any other man. I feel a deep personal loss, for through our years of close association, I developed for him an intense personal affection."[5] Frick also commented on a replacement: "I don't think that at this time the club owners have any one man in mind who would carry on the work that Landis did. I believe it may take some time before they would agree upon a choice. However, that is just my guess." He also suggested Harridge and he would constitute an advisory council with a third person until a replacement was chosen.[6] Soon after, Arch Ward, *Chicago Tribune* sports editor, speculated correctly that Leslie O'Connor would be the third person.[7] O'Connor, an attorney, was Landis's secretary all twenty-four years of his commissionership. Though generally behind the scenes, he often executed Landis's rulings, causing owners to view him skeptically. O'Connor would be the tiebreaker if the leagues failed to agree.

At the Winter Meetings, owners reassessed the commissioner's duties and powers; National League magnates foreshadowed the outcome. Some, including Branch Rickey, felt they should move quickly to replace Landis. Warren Giles was more cautious. He asserted that a new agreement on commissioner duties needed to be established for the triumvirate so it could readily be passed on to the replacement. He also stressed the agreement needs to "be trimmed some. I think that the conduct detrimental to baseball should be made a little bit more workable . . . and I think that in itself reduces some of the powers, . . . and I think it is desirable that that be done."[8] His comments reflected a consensus that commissioner powers needed scaling down.

In fact, the Winter Meetings designated a committee to revise the commissioner's powers, the same group that had renewed Landis's contract. Frick's league was represented by Rickey, Giles, Stoneham, and Phil Wrigley. Harridge's representatives included Alva Bradley of the Indians, Tom Yawkey of the Red Sox, Donald Barnes of the Browns, and John A. Zeller of the Tigers, along with Joseph Hostetler, the league's secretary and counsel. Their purpose was to review the commissioner's powers and duties, and they denied any intent to "clip the wings." The committee's recommendations were presented at the February meetings.[9] Its charge reflected concerns that the commissioner was too powerful.

Indeed, the committee report recommended some wing-clipping. It showed agreement on the commissioner's overall authority: "The Major Leagues and their constituent clubs severally agree to be bound by the decisions of the commissioner and the discipline imposed by him under the provisions of this agreement. . . . No diminution of the compensation of powers of the present or any succeeding commissioner shall be made during the term of his office." While that implied the status quo, the clipping came later, labeled as "one noted change to the previous agreement." It provided that "no Major League rule or other joint action of the two Major Leagues and no act or procedure taken in compliance with any such Major League rule or joint action of the two Major Leagues shall be considered or construed to be detrimental to baseball." Wrigley summarized what that meant: "If he [the commissioner] thinks something is bad, he has got to bring it back to the leagues. He has not got the final say."[10] Essentially, unlike Landis, the commissioner could no longer overrule magnates without consulting and obtaining their agreement. The owners had taken advantage of Landis's passing to constrain the replacement. As a long-time New York sportswriter summarized the changes, the new commissioner would have to rule "straight by the book" as the owners wrote it. He could only recommend, not make changes. Further, in case of disagreement, owners no longer waived their right to take a contested ruling to court. Finally, they changed the vote to hire or renew from a majority to three-quarters.[11] This would haunt Albert Benjamin "Happy" Chandler when it came time for contract renewal, also impacting Frick even earlier.

Frick was the front-runner before the February meetings, the obvious insider. Leslie O'Connor removed himself: "I have a short life to live, and I want none of that job. It's a killer." His withdrawal also stemmed from his conviction that the position should be shared. Earlier that year, Harridge also withdrew, expressing a preference to remain in his job.[12] Frick was the only one who didn't remove himself, though he indicated he was a reluctant candidate. He told a New York columnist, "If the newspaper boys think I'm campaigning for the Landis job, they have another think coming, I think . . . I agree with Leslie O'Connor. The Landis job is a man-killing job." But he straddled: "Still, a fellow can't live forever, can he?"[13] There is little evidence Frick campaigned openly. Not surprisingly, most of his support came from his league's owners. He had little need to promote his candidacy with them. There was reluctance from American League magnates, given league rivalries. He had some support from them, though, especially from Larry MacPhail, now part owner of the Yankees. At the same time, he didn't take advantage of his Washington work with

Clark Griffith in January 1945. Although Griffith indicated he leaned toward Frick, he hadn't been asked to support him.[14] Frick's preference for his current job was supported by that lack of campaigning.

Nonetheless, he remained the front-runner in February, and sportswriters regarded him the likely choice. In late January *The Sporting News* ran a major article on Frick, asserting in its headline, "He Isn't Trying on Landis' Toga for Size—Yet." The entire page of the weekly was devoted to Frick, saying he is viewed "as one of the outstanding prospects for the post of baseball commissioner" and calling him "one of the game's most capable executives." The article also highlighted past accomplishments, again implying front-runner status. It ended, however, by stating, "He is quite content with the job he has had for ten years, and is looking forward to four more years in the present office."[15] Various accounts speculated he had ten or eleven votes, suggesting one additional magnate would put him over the top. Going into the meetings, one sportswriter touted Frick as the likely choice, emphasizing that Frick had never removed his name from consideration.[16] A new commissioner appeared imminent.

For two reasons, the election of Frick didn't happen. One was a letter from Warren Giles to the owners, calling for someone outside baseball.[17] When the February meetings did not produce a commissioner, Giles offered his reasons publicly: "Frick has always been and still is one of my best friends and I consider he has done a wonderful job for us as league president. But I am opposed to him as a commissioner just as I would oppose anyone else in baseball, including myself, because I am convinced baseball must, in order to hold the confidence of the public, as well as the players, name someone outside the game."[18] That was at least one league vote lost, but contrary to expectations, no vote was taken. The other factor working against Frick was the parliamentary rules governing baseball meetings. Any agenda item had to be submitted to Leslie O'Connor fifteen days before. In this case, nothing had been submitted to allow for a vote. The article reported this to be "regarded by baseball observers as a neat parliamentary move aimed to deal a staggering blow to the candidacy of Frick."[19] It would have taken all sixteen clubs to agree to add an item and at least five clubs preferred to proceed slowly, preventing a vote. If Frick had eleven votes, they were irrelevant. He remained a candidate, having never removed his name, but others would now be considered from outside.

The February joint meeting verified that by appointing a four-man committee to consider candidates. Frick announced it. It hadn't been intended to be made public, but because the rumors were extensive, he decided with Harridge to acknowledge it to John Drebinger of the *New York Times*. Each league had appointed two members: Bradley, part owner of the Indians, and Donald Barnes, president of the Browns, representing the American League and Sam Breadon and Wrigley from the National League.[20] In announcing the committee, magnates suggested a more extensive search would occur. Coincidentally, another article in the same issue by Drebinger featured an announcement from Senator Albert Chandler that the War Office was not likely to block baseball in 1945, emphasizing that as a morale builder baseball has "earned its right to retain its place."[21] Serving on the Senate military committee, his remarks carried weight. Perhaps consequently, he would become a candidate.

DON'T WISH TOO HARD FOR SOMETHING

Frick had little concern about his changing status, being deeply engaged in more pressing matters. The upcoming season remained uncertain, and William Harridge and he were tasked to work out details in Washington on how it might be conducted. Satisfied with his current job and busy negotiating the game's status, becoming commissioner wasn't a priority. He didn't campaign for it and had little time to do so. Thus, Frick no longer appeared the front-runner.

In fact, no one was viewed as such, though a few were conjectured. Two were prominent figures—J. Edgar Hoover, head of the FBI and a known baseball fan, and James A. Farley, former postmaster general, now a Coca Cola executive. A third, John W. Bricker, former Ohio governor and 1944 Republican candidate for vice president, had removed his name. Attention focused more on the search committee, speculating on the members' preferences. Both Don Barnes and Alva Bradley leaned toward an outsider. Phil Wrigley, once considered in Frick's camp, was now also so inclined. Sam Breadon, a longtime friend of Frick's, had been solidly in his camp but was now more receptive to others.[22] Momentum had definitely shifted away from Frick. There was little speculation in the newspapers about candidates, suggesting the committee was deliberately working behind the scenes. It had already passed by a deadline to select a new commissioner by season's start, but expectations ran high when a meeting was announced for Cleveland on April 24. It looked as though their efforts, under wraps for almost three months, might finally bear fruit.

In reality, the committee hadn't made progress, made clear when the Cleveland session started. The committee proposed hiring an interim commissioner through 1945, putting off any decision until the Winter Meetings. Not known for subtleness, Larry MacPhail went on a tirade, shouting at Barnes, "Why, you will be the laughingstock of the country. . . . I never heard of anything so ridiculous. Why did you call us out here? Just to say we were boobs to come all the way to Cleveland?" He threatened to leave, remaining only due to other business items. Once those were completed, magnates focused that afternoon on how the search should proceed, the triumvirate running baseball not included in the process. Frick hung out with other National League executives not involved in the search, saying nothing about his prospects nor conveying interest: "I hope they elect someone. I don't care whom they choose. But we need a commissioner right now."[23] He didn't know it, but he would get his wish, with help from MacPhail.

He and others were upset over the lack of effort by the committee, though it had created a list of potential candidates and reduced it to six. The committee had also assembled biographies, though no interviews had been conducted, and little more was known about the candidates than two months before. MacPhail mockingly claimed the committee clipped the names from the sports pages and gotten the biographies from *Who's Who*.[24] At this point he took charge, getting magnates to rule out an interim commissioner and instead focus on someone among the finalists. With reluctance, those names were put forth. They included Frick and Farley, both already mentioned. The other four were new, including Judge Fred Vinson, a member of the War Mobilization Board; Robert P. Patterson, undersecretary of war; Robert Hannegan, head of the National Democratic Committee; and Frank Lausche, governor of Ohio. This brought a negative reaction from MacPhail, who had been an early supporter of Frick. Given the opposition from Giles and American League owners, he gravitated toward the unmentioned Chandler, highly critical of the six: "Gentlemen, I am astonished at the weakness of the list submitted to us, after months of research. Why, for example, is Judge Patterson submitted to us and Senator Chandler ignored? Why is Judge Vinson named, when he would not take the job if we offered it, and Senator Chandler, who is available, is snubbed altogether?"[25] Without objection, the senator was added.

The owners then agreed to narrow the list, given MacPhail's observation that neither Vinson nor Patterson would accept. They decided to rate the remaining five in the order of preference. Surprisingly, Chandler received five first-place votes, one more than Hannegan. Lausche received three, while Frick and Farley, once considered frontrunners, had two each.[26] Farley was ruled out because his salary with Coca Cola was considerably higher than the commissioner's compensation. Frick was also dropped, as the preference had gravitated heavily toward an outsider. They also dropped Lausche, limiting the discussion to the top-two vote recipients. Before taking a second vote, it was mentioned Truman might not release Hannegan as head of the Democratic Party. On the subsequent round, eleven ballots were cast for Chandler, five for Hannegan. Stoneham then switched, and with the twelve required votes, the owners then made it unanimous.[27] Albert Benjamin Chandler was baseball's second commissioner.

Chandler certainly had credentials. A native of western Kentucky, his parents separated when he was young. Raised by his father, a poor farmer, a larger influence was his grandfather, a Confederate veteran. In spite of his early hardships, Chandler was a good student, athlete, and class leader in high school. He attended Transylvania College, where he played football and baseball, sang in the glee club, and performed in theatrical productions. He was cheerful, buoyant, and self-assured, earning him the nickname "Happy," which stuck the remainder of his life. After receiving a law degree from The University of Kentucky, he entered politics and was elected governor and subsequently U.S. senator. In spite of his outgoing demeanor, he could be ruthless and vindictive toward those disagreeing with him.[28] He also didn't receive criticism well. Those characteristics became obvious later, but owners were pleased with their decision.

The only reservation, interestingly, was offered by Warren Giles, the leading advocate for an outsider. Residing in Cincinnati and aware of Kentucky politics, Giles was familiar with the senator. A native of Moline, Illinois, Giles may have looked negatively at Chandler's southern ways, mentioning his singing proclivities and a possible scandal related to one of the senator's campaigns. Samuel Breadon rebutted Giles's concerns, and the moguls finalized their selection. Giles got his outsider but may have wondered if he had pushed too hard. There was an additional irony. He had been chosen in part because Hannegan might not have been available immediately. When owners called Chandler to congratulate him, he initially refused the job, indicating he shouldn't leave the Senate while the war persisted. The magnates agreed he could keep both positions during the war, and with that, he accepted.[29] "Happy" Chandler became commissioner, though the transition wasn't easy.

THE LONG LEARNING CURVE

Although Chandler may have created doubts by not resigning, he had a good start with Frick. If the league president had any regrets at not being selected, they weren't demonstrated. The men met in Washington two days after Chandler was named, with the new commissioner requesting the session. He explained, "There was nothing along lines of official business about our talk. I merely invited Frick down to fill me in for personal guidance since he knows as much about baseball as anybody." Frick added that neither party had anything particular in mind.[30] They appeared to start on good terms.

The magnates may have had second thoughts, however, following their July meetings. Chandler rejected the magnates' curtailing of Landis's powers, the most significant the best-interests-of-baseball clause: "I was elected unanimously. When I accepted I assumed I would have full powers and I insist upon having full powers and nothing short of it." He added, "Gentlemen, I will state my case simply and very briefly. I will be the sole judge of 'conduct detrimental to baseball.' If any gentleman present takes it upon himself to challenge my rulings, then you must immediately seek a new commissioner."[31] Chandler also claimed Landis required owners to accept any decision he made, even if it was wrong. Leslie O'Connor corrected him, saying that request had come from the owners. Chandler responded, "I just read what the book said. . . . Mr. O'Connor will give advice . . . but will make no decisions. I will make the decisions."[32] No record shows that the magnates challenged him, but given Chandler's alterations, they likely weren't pleased. They were also perturbed he remained in the Senate rather than committing full-time.

The July confrontation was not to be his last. The next developed with the league presidents. As the World Series approached, Chandler joined them in a meeting with the designated umpires. The refs were under the jurisdiction of their leagues, but that didn't stop Chandler from suggesting, with umpires present, to double their salaries. Both presidents were angry at Chandler's presumptuousness and rejected his proposal. Harridge, more vocal, stated, "That the engaging and discharging of the umpires was wholly a league affair and none of the commissioner's business."[33] Rumors spread in October that owners were prepared to buy out Chandler's contract, though it was quicky denied. With Chandler's blessing, Frick spoke to reporters: "There is no basis of fact to the story." Frick had engineered the meeting, making clear he wasn't part of the ouster effort. He also stressed he had never declared himself a candidate, halting rumors that his supporters were behind the move. He added that his league remained unanimous for the commissioner.[34] That nipped the ouster rumors.

It is unclear how serious magnates were, but the rumors produced the desired result, with Chandler announcing he would resign his Senate seat on November 1. Some owners remained upset, but they were pleased he would now be full-time. Chandler pointed out he had yet to take a payment from baseball, which was five times his Senate salary. Not surprisingly, that same day Leslie O'Connor stepped down as secretary and was named general manager of the White Sox. Both Frick and Harridge emphasized that O'Connor's replacement would require their approval.[35] Chandler's first six months had been tenuous, but by the Winter Meetings he appeared secure.

More important, the next two years strengthened his status, with a series of events improving his prominence. The threat of the Mexican League, particularly his decision to ban any departed player for five years, provided Chandler a platform to demonstrate his authority. The reforms stemming from the MacPhail Report—the pension plan, a minimum wage, and an allowance for spring training expenses—endeared him to players. That gained him more credit than was due since he had no role in the recommendations though also no qualms about receiving the credit. Chandler was also assisted by soaring attendance after the war, with no apparent negative offset from both leagues integrating in 1947. Even his confrontation with Sam Breadon over the Mexican League and his suspension of Durocher appeared to be minor blips on his favorable reception.

However, two ominous problems appeared in October 1947 that would impact Chandler's tenure, who by then anticipated serving for life. First, Danny Gardella, one of the players who jumped to the Mexican League, sued baseball for $300,000. Claiming baseball had violated the Sherman and Clayton Antitrust Acts by suspending him, he said the rule "deprives him of his livelihood, destroys his ability as a professional baseball player, and has resulted in damages amounting to $100,000." The suit called for treble damages.[36] The case impacted baseball for the next year and a half, as other returning players sought reinstatement, compelling Chandler to end his ban. Gardella and other players would be compensated and have the opportunity to be reinstated. To avoid a court decision, baseball also settled with Gardella separately. The whole antitrust implication of the case, however, would pique Congress's interest. The second incident involved the commissioner's new nemesis—Leslie O'Connor. The White Sox had signed a seventeen-year-old pitcher out of high school, violating the rule prohibiting contracts until after graduation. The Sox contended the rule only applied to schools who were members of the National Federation of High School Athletics Association. The player's school was not. Chandler ignored the claim, rendered the player a free agent, fined the White Sox $500, removed O'Connor from the executive council, and threatened to remove the club from league meetings until it complied.[37] The matter was resolved, but it preluded other conflicts and left the Sox resentful.

Because those issues seemed resolved in late 1949, Chandler was emboldened to seek a new contract early, claiming he had other options and needed certainty to focus exclusively on baseball. It wasn't a good time. Baseball attendance declined in both leagues, and discontent persisted among executives over Mexican League issues. Even strong supporters, including Connie Mack and Clark Griffith, discouraged him from expediting the vote, but the Kentuckian insisted. Harridge pointed out Landis's contract had never been renewed early, arguing strongly against. Still, the renewal only fell short by one vote, 11–5. That would haunt Chandler later.[38]

During the following season, a confrontation between the commissioner and Fred Saigh, new owner of the Cardinals, may have made Saigh a ringleader against Chandler. During the 1950 season, Saigh had approval from the Dodgers and Frick to schedule a Sunday-night game against the Dodgers, but Chandler forbade it, claiming it "would cause us to forfeit the support and good will of thousands of the religious people of this country." *Chicago Tribune* sports editor Arch Ward weighed in: "Still we can't see why there is objection to Sunday night baseball and little or no fuss to other Sunday night sports activities."[39] Saigh dropped his plans after both Frick and league attorney Louis Carroll explained that league rules prohibited the game, allowing Chandler to overrule Frick.

Saigh stressed that was the only reason for dropping it, not Chandler's prohibition.[40] Chandler won the battle but cultivated an adversary.

Unknowingly, he cultivated another ringleader. Del Webb, a major developer from Phoenix, Arizona, had been recruited by Larry MacPhail along with Dan Topping to purchase the Yankees in 1945; they would remain the sole owners after MacPhail stepped down in 1947. Webb conducted considerable business in Las Vegas, including construction of the Flamingo Hotel, partly owned by mobster Benjamin "Bugsy" Siegel. Because gambling connections were involved, Chandler hired someone secretly to investigate Webb, and he also investigated Saigh due to federal tax issues.[41] Both men became aware and prepared for revenge at the 1950 Winter Meetings. They were good at maintaining silence, as Chandler was assured during the Minor League meetings, which always preceded the Winter Meetings, that his contract would be renewed. Though no formal vote was taken then, magnates told league presidents Chandler could expect another seven-year contract. They then told the commissioner "that his re-election . . . in St. Petersburg, Florida next month would be a mere formality." He was advised to have his lawyer draw up a new contract.[42] As the meetings in Florida began, everything appeared normal, but that proved to be the calm before the storm.

It is unclear if the rebel owners were organized in November, but they were well prepared by the December meetings, possessing the five votes necessary to end Chandler's tenure. Besides Saigh and Webb, the others included Lou Perini of the Braves, Bob Carpenter of the Phillies, and Bill DeWitt of the Browns. All five had grudges, usually involving player-signing conflicts, and were committed to the ouster. All but DeWitt were relatively new to baseball. They were joined by Charles Comiskey of the White Sox, likely due to Chandler's ruling earlier, and John Galbreath, new owner of the Pirates. Galbreath owned racehorses and may have been persuaded by Webb due to the gambling concerns. On one vote even Ellis Ryan—part owner of the Indians—appeared to join them.[43]

In part, the ouster was the old-time owners against the newcomers, lending support to the supposition that newer magnates, with careers outside of baseball, were more inclined to dislike Chandler's leadership. It was more than personality differences. Many owners thought his treatment of player signings was arbitrary, some a threat to their business interests. Many disapproved of his early renewal attempt. Other complaints included behaving as if he were already commissioner for life, taking credit for attendance increases, and resisting calls to lift the Mexican League five-year ban. Even worse, many resented that he claimed responsibility for the minimum wage and pension plan, which he had little to do with.[44] In essence, he failed to realize his position's limitations.

Rumors immediately surfaced about a replacement, but until Chandler's resignation six months later, a serious search wouldn't occur. A committee was created at the December meetings, with Ellis Ryan and Del Webb representing the American League and Lou Perini and Phil Wrigley the Senior Circuit. That didn't bode well for Chandler's reconsideration hopes because three of them were among his opponents. The replacement rumors included some repeats from 1945, including Vinson, Farley, and Lausche, along with the usual insiders—Harridge and George Trautman, head of the Minor Leagues. There were also newcomers, including Stuart Symington, Paul Douglass, and Milton Eisenhower. Frick's name was also mentioned, once again, but he was adamant he didn't want the job.[45] One New York sportswriter, Bill Corum, addressing Chandler's failed reelection, proved prophetic. Calling Frick "the most logical candidate," he added, "In additional to all other necessary qualifications, Frick is an experienced baseball man, which is the business that the commissioner runs. Or helps to run."[46] Nine months later, the magnates reached that conclusion in an unusual fashion.

A LATE-NIGHT CALL AND POLICE VISIT

Chandler stubbornly remained commissioner for seven months, rejecting offers to buy out his contract and delaying the search to replace him. First, he insisted on another vote, hoping to change some dissenters. The vote in March was again 9–7.[47] One anonymous executive suggested Chandler might have fared better had he stayed in his Cincinnati office "instead of making speeches over the country for his retention."[48] Some players considered hiring Chandler as their own commissioner. While the magnates rejected the idea, "Happy" embraced it: "It is wonderful to think the players still possess that confidence in me. They have always been my pals and this proves they are not going to forget me even if the club owners do."[49] As late as June, Chandler offered no indication he would leave before his contract expired in April 1952, even as owners pushed for an earlier date. He rationalized, "The majority are still supporting me. They have urged me to stay on until my contract runs out. I can't walk out until all my friends among the owners want me to go."[50] Shortly after, he announced he'd step down July 15, 1951, with full compensation. Finally, the magnates could focus on a replacement.

They quickly expressed their preferences. Del Webb wanted a big name in business, speculating on James Farley. Walter O'Malley, now full owner of the Dodgers, stated that Frick met his requirements: "a judicial temperament, administrative ability, an awareness of public relations, and a firm belief baseball is the national sport and must be sustained as such."[51] Clark Griffith opposed both: "Those who want Frick or a big businessman forget that the commissioner is not merely an employee of the major league club owners. The commissioner represents the fans, he represents the players, he represents the game. I want a strong national figure."[52] The owners were far from forming a consensus.

By August five remained in contention. Those included Frick and Warren Giles, both insiders, and Lausche, ousted General Douglas MacArthur, and Milton Eisenhower, president of Penn State University, from the outside. Ellis Ryan pushed for a decision before the World Series. Larry MacPhail, out of baseball, claimed that had Giles not strongly opposed, Frick would have already been commissioner.[53] The magnates had moved away from a businessman but still seemed far from a decision. Two events caused them to narrow their focus further.

The exact sequence is unclear, but both involved high-ranking military generals. The *Chicago Tribune* reported on its front page August 28 that three owners met with Douglass MacArthur, ready to offer him the position if he agreed to one item—that he not take public positions on military and political issues. He refused, removing himself from consideration. A day later, *The Sporting News* reported on its front page that magnates offered the job to Major General Emmett O'Donnell, commander of the Fifteenth Air Force Division based in California. Since the country was deeply involved in the Korean War, President Truman blocked his departure.[54] Baseball struck out on military officers and was down to four candidates. The owners agreed to meet in Chicago on September 20 to reach consensus.

The only remaining outsider was Governor Lausche, since Eisenhower hadn't been considered seriously. In early September, however, *The Sporting News* reported, "The Governor did not have an even money chance to be elected commissioner. . . . Lausche did not have the support of the Cleveland club and that the major leagues were not enamored of the idea of getting themselves into the complex political convolutions featuring the one-time mayor of Cleveland."[55] Since Ellis Ryan, Cleveland's primary owner, was on the committee, his views were a major stumbling block. Prior to the meeting, though, Lausche removed himself, rejecting a salary five times that as governor. He explained, "There are thousands of young men in the military forces who could make more money and enjoy greater comfort in civilian life, but to them an assignment has been made to serve their country. I, as a public official, cannot do less."[56] He may have also surmised he couldn't overcome Ryan's opposition. In any case, the magnates were down to two insiders as the meeting loomed.

When owners convened in Chicago, a local paper declared Giles the frontrunner, but short of the twelve votes.[57] Giles attended the meeting, representing owner Powel Crosley. Frick wasn't present. Unlike Giles, he had no vote and was in Miami the day before, attending the funeral of former umpire William Klem, returning home the day of the meeting.[58] A *New York Times* article on the nineteenth indicated Giles had the advantage, though a deadlock was possible. Contacted in Miami, Frick adamantly asserted he wasn't seeking the position: "I've never been a candidate for the job and I haven't talked to anyone about it." He'd accept "if they put the finger on me."[59] They would ultimately "put the finger" on him, only after a long and arduous session. Giles removed himself from the room when votes were conducted, with his club represented by Assistant General Manager Gabe Paul. It was reported that at least fifty ballots were held, Giles never receiving more than ten votes. That meant Frick only received six, enough to continue the stalemate. Those six mostly represented American League clubs, which were concerned they'd be required to take special trips to Cincinnati when they or players were called to the commissioner's office, as had occurred with Chandler. It was a major inconvenience. After they broke for dinner, Giles was summoned and asked by owners if he would withdraw. He did, with Frick elected 14–2 on the next ballot, and then unanimously. Ford Frick was baseball's third commissioner.[60]

It would take a while for Frick to learn about it. Giles was chosen to call Frick's home, but his numerous attempts produced no answer. Given the urgency to notify him before the news was made public, Charles Segar, National League director of publicity, called the Bronxville police department to locate him. When the police found him at home, it was 11:00 p.m., with Frick dressed for bed.[61] Whether the police provided official notification or had him return Giles's phone call wasn't stated, but either way he was informed. An anxious press spoke with him on the phone shortly after. In that initial "press conference," he admitted, "It came so sudden that I have not had a chance to think about the job. I will do the best I can, but it is a big one."[62] By the next morning Frick had time to reflect: "I can honestly say it came as a complete surprise. The screening committee had never even spoken to me about the commissionership. The first hint that I might be in the running was when I heard yesterday the vote was 10 for Warren [Giles] and six for me. And that was only scuttlebutt." He added, "Now that they've saddled me with it, I'm going to be the commissioner. Don't worry about that." He further announced headquarters would be in New York.[63] That gratified American League owners because both leagues had teams there.

In one regard, Frick followed suit with Chandler—he declined the position initially, announcing the World Series would be run by the committee that governed since Chandler resigned. In this case, magnates weren't concerned. His stated purpose for waiting until November was his desire to cheer one more time for his league's club. After that, he would stay "strictly neutral."[64] He would be disappointed once again, as the Yankees prevailed, but as he cheered for the Giants, he was contemplating his new challenges.

Among sportswriters his selection was well received. Arch Ward was delighted: "Congratulations to Ford Frick and a salute to baseball, too. . . . Selecting one of its own for commissioner is a wholesome trend. . . . No one could be better qualified to administer the affairs of the game's highest office than a man who, through long personal experience, is thoroughly familiar with its problems, needs and aims. . . . Frick's election marks the birth of a new and promising era in the history of baseball."[65] J. G. Taylor Spink, a Frick advocate, was equally pleased: "After several months of screening varied types of prospects—generals, judges, business leaders and politicians—the major leagues rightly came to the conclusion that their best choice as commissioner was a man from the game itself. In selecting Ford Frick, the magnates acted wisely, for they not only picked a leader thoroughly schooled in the administration of the game and acquainted with its problems, but one of high personal integrity."[66] Sportswriters in New York and around the country were also supportive.

Frick's predecessor, however, would become one of his biggest critics. Years later, in fact, Chandler claimed, "When the clubs pushed me out in 1951, they had a vacancy and they decided to keep it."[67] Chandler was convinced Frick resented him for winning in 1945, accusing him of making his job more difficult before the 1950 vote. Yet, Frick never campaigned for commissioner in 1945, as he was busy in Washington. Even when alone with Clark Griffith, he conveyed no interest. Nor was there any interest expressed in 1951, though he could have removed his name from consideration as had Harridge. Hence, he was interested in being considered, at the same time stressing his satisfaction in remaining league president. As one editorial put it, many challenges lay ahead: reuniting owners divided under Chandler, addressing congressional challenges to the reserve clause, dealing with the loss of players to the Korean War, and maintaining the integrity of the national pastime.[68] There would be other challenges. For now, if Frick had any interest in being commissioner—and he seemed to because he never withdrew from consideration—the second time was a charm.

Nationalizing the Game

After the National Agreement in 1903 brought peace between the new American League and the National League, the Major Leagues were static, in the same ten markets for the next fifty years. All were in the northeast quadrant, from Boston to St. Louis, east to west, and Detroit to Cincinnati, north to south. Following baseball's first antitrust hearings in 1951, Frick initiated a restructuring of relocation rules at the 1952 Winter Meetings. Now less restrictive, the floodgates were opened. During Frick's fourteen years as commissioner, six franchises relocated—one twice. Frick took a laissez-faire approach, considering relocations "league matters." Even when the National League vacated New York, he maintained that stance. He wasn't always consistent. In one situation, he blocked a move until the departing team could be replaced. As Frick was retiring, he faced perhaps the most controversial move during his tenure.

STABILITY OR STAGNATION?

Following the 1890 season, when three Major Leagues competed, the next two seasons witnessed the demise of the Players' League and the consolidation of the American Association into a twelve-team National League. None was west of St. Louis or south of Cincinnati. In 1899 the league eliminated four financially struggling franchises—Louisville, Washington, Baltimore, and Cleveland. A season later, the Western League, then a Minor League, claimed all but Louisville for franchises and negotiated a move to Chicago with the National League club's concurrence. A year later, the Western League renamed itself the American League, moving franchises into Detroit and Milwaukee and establishing teams in the National League cities of Boston and Philadelphia. It also signed players. For the next two years, the leagues battled for talent. The American League moved the Milwaukee franchise into St. Louis after the 1901 season, making it a two-team city. A year later, the league relocated a team from Baltimore to New York. Early in 1903, the leagues negotiated the National Agreement, respecting each other's reserve clause and securing peace and stability for franchises.

The stability was disrupted in 1914 with the emergence of the Federal League, which again raided the other leagues' players. They entered new cities, with franchises in Buffalo, Baltimore, Indianapolis, and Kansas City. Their other four locations competed directly with a team in the same city, and in three—St. Louis, Chicago, and New York—there were already at least two teams. The Federal League lasted only two years, marking the last fully executed attempt to establish a new league. When it folded, normalcy returned—sixteen clubs in ten cities, all in the northeastern quadrant. New York had three clubs and Boston, Philadelphia, Chicago, and St. Louis two. Five cities had one—Washington, Pittsburgh, Cleveland, Cincinnati, and Detroit, a configuration that continued through 1952.

While the population was expanding rapidly in other sections of the country, the Majors remained static.[1] There was a logistical reason. The ability of teams to reach other cities in less than a day was limited. The closest and largest concentration of major cities was in the northeast quadrant, reachable within twenty-four hours by railroads. Although clubs began using planes as early as 1936, it still took almost two decades for air travel to gain acceptability and normal utilization. By the early 1950s jet airplanes also substantially reduced the time between the coasts. Correspondingly, more cities lobbied for franchises. The West Coast pressured early. By 1940 Los Angeles had surpassed many Major League cities in population, becoming the fifth largest city in the United States. Baltimore was larger than five cities but trailed LA by more than half a million. Five other cities without Major League teams were larger than Cincinnati, the smallest market; four, like Baltimore, were in the northeast quadrant.

The potential of Los Angeles didn't go unnoticed. An interested LA group approached St. Louis Browns owners in 1941 to explore relocation. Donald Barnes, the Browns' president, presented the move at the Winter Meetings, though it was rejected unanimously, even Barnes voting against.[2] A number of issues complicated the effort. Foremost, Japan had just bombed Pearl Harbor. Further, scheduling would have been difficult if only one club was to move west. Additionally, jet travel was still in the future. Finally, all sixteen clubs had to approve. If any team in the other league had an interest in LA, it could block the move, a significant obstacle.

World War II was the biggest obstacle, but West Coast interest regenerated when it ended, with the Pacific Coast League taking the initiative. Two of its eight teams were in Los Angeles, and another in San Francisco, which was already larger than Cincinnati and growing rapidly. Three other markets—Seattle, Portland, and Oakland—were close to Cincinnati in size and also growing rapidly. Thus, the league believed it was in a strong position to propose becoming a third Major League. At the Minor League Winter Meetings in 1945, Clarence Rowland, the league's president, so proposed and "threw a blockbuster into a dull pre-convention session."[3] No response was given, but it became a topic at the Winter Meetings a week later.

To no one's surprise, the owners rejected the idea, perhaps unanimously. The reason given was the league's inability to pay the higher salaries afforded by the Majors, largely due to smaller ballparks—admission fees still being the primary revenue source. While not surprised, Rowland conveyed displeasure: "Millions of baseball-minded people in the states of California, Washington and Oregon want better than minor league baseball . . . but we cannot accomplish this ambition while burdened with the draft and faced by the forced sale of star players in order to avoid the draft." He added, "We will be back."[4] They were, driven by that loss of star players to the Majors. Rowland may have had other concerns, precipitated when Barnes expressed how easy a West Coast move would be if approved.[5] The Pacific Coast League clearly didn't want to lose its largest markets.

True to his promise, Rowland introduced the proposal again in 1946 and 1947, getting the Majors to agree to visit the West Coast in August 1947. This was no token visit because it included Chandler, Frick, and Harridge and three other officials, including Leslie O'Connor. When the group arrived, one member suggested owners had little interest in baseball on the coast since most "are still very much opposed to transporting teams in planes." When the executives convened, Rowland made clear that no Major League club was welcome on the West Coast. Further, he was more interested in protecting his players and receiving a higher status for his league than Minor League status. One reporter concluded, "So, outside of enjoying some California hospitality and trying some of its famous golf courses, the committee . . . just went along for the ride."[6] The two sides were no closer, with the Majors again rejecting special status at the Winter Meetings in December 1947.[7] The trip was for naught.

Nothing changed over the next two years, and both sides maintained their positions, though Frick attempted to calm concerns in 1948. Convinced no changes would occur soon, he offered, "As long as I have been in office, no owner or responsible executive has approached me with a plan to move to another city. I personally think the major leagues will expand; such a move will be needed to take in cities that have attained major league size since the present leagues were formed. Not just the west coast alone, but the entire country would have to be considered.... If the step is undertaken, it will be with the mutual consent of all parties concerned." Even in 1950, in spite of continuing Pacific Coast League demands, Frick did not consider the issue pressing and did not regard higher status for it as "being imminent."[8] The conflict persisted when Frick became commissioner.

Even without progress, Rowland wouldn't back down. In late August 1951, while the Majors were without a commissioner, he dropped a bombshell by threatening to remove his league from all Major League requirements. In essence, it would become an independent league with no obligation to have players drafted or purchased by Major or Minor League clubs. He also stated the San Francisco Seals, which was for sale, could not be acquired by any Major League club, adding that Phil Wrigley, owner of the LA franchise, supported the boycott.[9] While the Majors were leaderless, Rowland drew a line in the sand.

Frick got the message when named commissioner and addressed the issue during the joint meeting of the Major-Minor Advisory Committee following the World Series. The other two Triple-A Minor Leagues—the International and American Associations—questioned the Pacific Coast League demand for special treatment, and the discussion continued for hours before a compromise was reached "largely through the acumen of Ford Frick." The concept of an *open classification* was proposed for the Pacific Coast League, including requirements for attendance, stadium size, and approval of the majority of its members. A player could waive his right to be drafted by the Majors, and draft prices would be raised. The league accepted, naming a committee to meet with the Majors to finalize details.[10] Their secession threat was addressed, as the league was also assured no Major League club would relocate to its markets.

Frick quickly announced the plan: "The open classification would give a league the chance to build up its player personnel, parks and attendance figures preliminary to making the bigger step, into the major company."

Addressing the league, he added, "The Coast league does not now demand major recognition. But it wants the chance to keep its players and build up to major rating. I am very sympathetic toward that." He acknowledged that expanding either Major League to ten or twelve teams had been discussed and abandoned.[11] Rowland, who had been pursuing special status for years, was ecstatic: "Commissioner Ford Frick has been in office less than a month and this is the first recognition by the major leagues that the Coast League is faced with unusual and special problems."[12] Frick began his commissionership on a positive note with the fledging Minor League.

He didn't accept sole credit for the new posture. In his announcement of the arrangement, he recognized that it "has been contrived with an eye to Congress, the House Subcommittee on Monopolies, the Department of Justice and the Pacific Coast League."[13] By the time Frick announced the open-classification plan, both rounds of the 1951 Subcommittee on Antitrust and Monopoly hearings had occurred. Frick was called as a witness twice, first in July while still president, then in October in one of his first acts as commissioner. His announcement on the Pacific Coast League was not derived in a vacuum, instead a byproduct of the first congressional hearings on baseball. It wasn't the only aftereffect.

A CONGRESSIONAL NUDGE

Until 1951, baseball had never been called before Congress, even after the Black Sox scandal or during World War II. Two people provided the catalyst for the 1951 hearings: Danny Gardella, who in 1946 jumped to the newly created Mexican League, and Emmanuel Celler, chairman of the House Judiciary Committee and its Subcommittee on Antitrust and Monopoly. Gardella sued baseball when he was blocked from even playing semipro ball. As his case moved through the courts, Chandler settled, reinstating Gardella and other banned players.[14] That settlement piqued the interest of Celler as did actions from other congressional members. He decided to investigate baseball's antitrust exemption, established by the U.S. Supreme Court in 1922. His investigation covered the reserve clause, territorial rights, farm systems, geographical distribution of clubs, and broadcasting of games, with the Gardella case referenced specifically.[15] The hearings began in July, just as Chandler resigned and before a new commissioner was named. Frick was one of the first to testify.

He had only one foregoer—Ty Cobb—and was waiting his turn when questioning began. Franchise relocation was introduced, unsurprisingly, by Republican Patrick J. Hillings, who represented a Los Angeles county district. Although Cobb was not an expert, it didn't stop Hillings from asking him if baseball should expand or establish a third league. Unsatisfied with Cobb's answer, which was basically that the ballparks were insufficient, Hillings suggested baseball move a team from a city with two teams. Frick heard the comment. In his opening statement, he addressed baseball's two top concerns: "It is important to recognize two fundamental bases on which the structure is built and stands. The first of these is the recognition of territorial rights; the second is the right of player contract reserve." He added that new cities would obtain clubs, without stating how.[16]

Much of Frick's early questioning focused on the reserve clause, specifically the Gardella case—until Hillings took his turn. The congressman zeroed in on Major League baseball in Southern California. Frick pointed out that the Pacific Coast League agreed it was not yet ready, adding that the whole league would provide the quickest way to get Major League ball out west. He added that LA could already support two Major League clubs, and San Francisco, Oakland, and Seattle one each, though he expressed skepticism about San Diego, Portland, and Sacramento. When the struggling Browns were suggested, Frick stressed that two teams needed to move to make the West Coast viable and noted that the league requested that the Majors not consider moving franchises to the West Coast. At one point, Celler accused baseball of being stuck on the status quo, failing to recognize West Coast potential. Frick replied, "Within the foreseeable future . . . within a very limited length of time—you will see M.L.B. on the Pacific Coast or other cities if they so desire."[17] Near the end of his testimony, the discussion turned to the difficulty of relocation due to unanimous consent required from all owners. Expansion or franchise relocation clearly became a central topic during Frick's testimony. When he finished, Celler conveyed his gratitude: "Mr. Frick, I just wanted to express my appreciation for your coming here. . . . You have made a very valuable contribution to this inquiry. We are very grateful to you."[18] It was an early indication that the Majors would be pleased by the hearings' outcome, though not suggesting the longer-term relationship between Celler and Frick.

When Celler resumed the hearings in October, Frick returned in his new capacity. Again, Hillings's questions focused on the West Coast. Frick promised that meetings with the Pacific Coast League would be one of his first actions, which he soon kept: "I say this with all sincerity, that for the first time the members of baseball . . . were stirred to this by your subcommittee hearing." Hillings was pleased: "That certainly is the most encouraging news I have heard presented to this committee on this situation." When questioning ended, Frick volunteered, "I believe that baseball has profited very much from hearing this discussion from you gentlemen and from the witnesses on things we can correct . . . within our own organization . . . and I want you to know that I have gotten a great deal out of it."[19] On franchise transfers, he would soon deliver.

Although his Pacific Coast League proposal didn't immediately bring baseball west, it provided a structure within which that could occur. Changing the policy on relocations could not be addressed expeditiously due to the time required to place the issue on the Winter Meetings' agenda. Further, being new to the job, Frick needed time to discuss with owners the essence of the Celler subcommittee and view its final report to convince them relocation rules needed to be changed. A month before the Winter Meetings in 1952, Frick was ready to publicize potential relocation rule changes, making clear he was confident of support. Although the rules in each league might differ after the changes, Frick speculated that at least a majority vote in the affected league would be needed to approve a transfer. The other league's owners would have no voice. *The Sporting News* conjectured the Cardinals and Braves would be the teams taking advantage, the Cards courted by Houston and the Braves suffering from poor attendance. Frick indicated Houston was five years away from supporting a Major League club but had no comment concerning the Braves. He stressed the change was due to the Celler subcommittee. A week later, Frank Lane, general manager of the White Sox, suggested most cites with two clubs were destined to lose one.[20] Speculation now proliferated.

At the meetings in December, the leagues formally enacted the changes, the existing rule replaced by two parts. First, "the circuit of either league shall not be changed to include any city in the circuit of the other Major League except by the unanimous consent of the clubs constituting both major leagues." Second, "in the case of a Major League club transferring its franchise to a city not presently in the major leagues, approval for such a change shall be confined to the league of which the major league club is a member." Later, the National League approved an amendment that any franchise proposing a move must file between October 1 and November 25 of the year before the season, though the American League did not act on the time frame because it hadn't received proper notice.[21] That difference would haunt Frick later.

In the meantime, speculation intensified on which franchises would move and where they might go. One article had the Braves heading to Milwaukee and was equally convinced the Browns were heading to LA, reflecting the 1941 overtures. Another rumor, fueled by O'Malley, had the Browns moving to Milwaukee: "I wonder whether Houston and Montreal, as well as Milwaukee, may not be more solidly in the major league news. And how about the recurring story that Detroit will support two major league teams?"[22] What was certain with these postulations was that the door was now open to franchise moves, which addressed struggling franchises as well as Celler committee demands.

A THREE-YEAR TRIFECTA

Some team relocation speculations proved accurate, less so the locations.[23] Both Braves and Browns had financial difficulty, with Boston's travails occurring recently. Attendance boomed for the Braves and owner Lou Perini's syndicate after the war. The team drew over a million fans each year from 1947 through 1949, but turnout declined precipitously by 1952, when merely 281,000 attended. Only then did Perini grow concerned. Bill Veeck recently had acquired the Browns, purchasing a club historically fortunate to draw merely half a million fans per year. Even that was rare, explaining why the club entertained the LA move. Veeck had success in his first full season, doubling attendance and surpassing half a million. Much of that was due to promotions, including signing Satchel Paige and pinch-hitting a midget. That helped short-term, but his long-term goal was having St. Louis to himself by enticing the Cardinals to leave.[24] That wasn't unrealistic.

First, the Browns owned Sportsman Park, renting it to the Cardinals and imposing high rental charges. Second, Cards owner Fred Saigh was on trial for tax evasion and would be forced to sell if found guilty. Finally, strong interest was shown by groups in Houston and Detroit to purchase and relocate the club. Veeck appeared to be in the driver's seat, with prospects becoming even brighter in January 1953, when Saigh was found guilty and sentenced to fifteen months in jail. Saigh acknowledged, "I will have to dispose of the Cardinals. There is no way I can stay in baseball."[25] Although a Houston group pursued the Cards seriously, that was preempted by a local man with deep pockets—August A. Busch Jr., owner of Anheuser-Busch Brewery.[26] A month after Saigh was in jail, Veeck's dreams were shattered.

That wouldn't stop the maverick owner, who shifted his attention to Milwaukee. During World War II, Veeck owned and built the successful and profitable Minor League Brewers. Further, the city had since constructed a Major League–sized ballpark. Although Lou Perini's Braves owned the city's Minor League club, giving Perini the first right to relocate there, he was handcuffed. First, the league had adopted the rule limiting the time to declare relocations to the two months following the season, and it now was well past the deadline. Second, he doubted Milwaukee was large enough for the Majors. Unrestrained by that deadline, still popular in Milwaukee and apparently undeterred by Perini's Minor League rights, Veeck proposed moving his Browns there. Frick attempted to douse the fire: "I am not opposed to transferring of major league clubs to other cities or promoting a minor league city to major. But I think the idea of moving a major league franchise right now is perfectly nonsensical," adding he would not sanction any moves.[27] That wouldn't be the final word.

Veeck's interest in Milwaukee had fanned the flames. Before that interest was even announced, Frick received a telegram from Wisconsin's governor asking that he alter his position that it was too late to move. Perini was also urged to get out of the way.[28] Perini responded by requesting baseball's executive council to have the American League adopt the same rule as the National League, thus blocking Veeck. Though no immediate action was taken, Frick suggested such would be adopted within three weeks.[29] The next day, Baltimore complicated the situation further as Mayor Thomas D'Alesandro Jr. announced a bid for the Browns. Jack Dunn III, owner of the Minor League club in Baltimore, agreed to sell the club, and the International League offered cities where it could relocate.[30] Like Milwaukee's venue, Baltimore's ballpark met Major League standards, but the city was considerably larger. Veeck had an alternative if Perini still pursued Milwaukee.

With the situation growing fluid, Frick reconsidered, requesting a conference of the affected parties. They met in Tampa on March 15, where Frick gave Veeck and Perini approval to relocate to Baltimore and Milwaukee, respectively. He stressed they must follow the rules, including getting consent from their leagues and the affected Minor Leagues, both to be decided at league meetings the next two days. Though giving his blessing, Frick was not pleased: "The executive council is recommending at the July meeting . . . that they adopt a rule whereby the major leagues cannot draft any minor league territory at any time except between October 1 and December 1." These moves were no longer affected, but future relocations would be.[31] It looked like both clubs would be moving, breaking the fifty years of status quo.

The American League met the day after Frick's announcement, with indications Veeck would receive the six votes needed, Harridge having polled the owners before. Much to Veeck's shock, he was rejected by a vote of 5–2, the official explanation that it was too close to Opening Day along with the Browns' improved attendance in 1952. Harridge added that television commitments, schedules, ticket sales, and possible lawsuits also presented problems.[32] Veeck reflected a day later, "I'm a victim of duplicity and a lot of lying so and so's. The only reasons anyone can give for voting against me are either silly or malicious. I prefer to think they're malicious." A *New York Times* columnist concluded, "The other owners didn't like the idea of a precipitous last-minute change, they didn't like the way Veeck manipulated the scheme. They didn't like Veeck. All were important factors."[33] Frick was silent, consistent with it being a league matter. The biggest loser was Baltimore, still without Major League baseball.

By contrast, when the National League met the following day, Perini received unanimous approval, with the problems put forth by Harridge not of concern to its magnates. A month later, the Braves opened in Milwaukee to a sellout crowd, drawing over 1.8 million fans for the year, larger than any season in Boston and six and a half times as many as the previous year. Frick was present for opening day, as were the city's mayor and Wisconsin's governor.[34] Any doubts Perini had about fan support were alleviated.

Veeck had no choice but remain in St. Louis, focusing on ways to facilitate a move. Even before the season, he sold Sportsman Park to the Cardinals, which leased it back to the Browns for their duration. Busch hoped to rename the park Budweiser Stadium, but a phone call from a concerned Frick persuaded him to name it after his family instead. Veeck received $800,000 for the ballpark, negotiating a maximum five-year lease at $175,000 a year. He then sold six thousand shares of Browns stock to a Baltimore group, though he and associates retained 80 percent control. Veeck also made it known that interest in the Browns had declined badly, with season-ticket cancellations outweighing purchases by three to one.[35] The writing was on the wall for relocating, though where remained unclear.

Veeck was open to other cities, especially LA, by far the most attractive market without Major League baseball. At the July meeting, franchise relocation was a major topic. Still pushing the American league to move west, Del Webb, the Yankees' owner, suggested Veeck move to LA and the Mack family's Athletics to San Francisco or possibly Kansas City.[36] At the same meeting, it was conjectured the National League was encouraging Cincinnati and the Phillies to consider California, as both leagues realized that two teams from the same league needed to move. Clarence Rowland adamantly insisted his Pacific Coast League would fight any such efforts. Frick stayed positive: "There is no reason now why any club cannot move its franchise elsewhere if it so desires. It is my concern only that it is done legally and that all rules are observed."[37] More relocations seemed imminent, with Veeck leading the way.

Because Veeck was already intending to move, Frick's comments were encouraging. LA and Baltimore presented the best alternatives, and Veeck explored them. Coming back from a visit west in August, Veeck told *The Sporting News* that both LA and San Francisco were very attractive cities, though neither had a suitable ballpark. He ruled out Kansas City and remained noncommittal about Baltimore. A week later, Veeck expressed strong interest in LA, though the Mack family dashed his hopes, emphasizing they had no interest in San Francisco and no intent to sell.[38] Veeck thus had no partner for a West Coast move, leaving Baltimore the viable option. Matters came to a head in September, as both LA and Baltimore increased pressure and American League owners convened in New York to finalize a decision.

Veeck had three options—move to Baltimore, move to LA, or stay in St. Louis. Most of the opposition to Baltimore came from the A's and Senators, which opposed competition so close to their markets, especially coming from Veeck. Del Webb also dissented, insisting an American League club move west. Together, that was enough to block Baltimore. The first vote was 4–4, thus keeping the club in St. Louis. Webb wanted thirty more days to decide, but that wasn't an option because Veeck faced bankruptcy. The LA group backed off, lacking a stadium, while the Baltimore group, led by D'Alesandro, pursued the Browns diligently, appealing to Frick. Harridge demanded a resolution, perhaps with Frick's encouragement, and the Baltimore group increased its offer, causing Veeck to agree to sell, with the magnates supporting unanimously.[39] Major League baseball was finally back in Baltimore, and like Milwaukee, it would draw well over a million fans in its first season. Even though many believed that completed the first round of moves, difficulties in Philadelphia emerged to complete the relocation trifecta.

The Philadelphia Athletics were one of two American League clubs still owned by the same family from its creation, in this case the same person—Connie Mack (born Cornelius McGillicuddy), who managed the club until 1951. By 1954 his sons—Roy and Earle—controlled most stock. Connie had created dynasties in the early 1910s and immediately before the Depression, and for their first forty-five years, the A's were the premier Philadelphia franchise. That changed when the Carpenter family purchased the Phillies, their deeper pockets bringing success to the previously dismal club, including a 1950 pennant. When the A's finished last in 1954, drawing just over three hundred thousand fans, relocation pressure grew. Though still alive, Connie Mack was now a figurehead, and his sons' financial difficulties caused them to contemplate selling.[40] The A's had clearly changed their thoughts from months earlier.

However, they had to pursue a sale quietly, especially if it involved a move, due to Frick's declaration in May. Disturbed by the speculation of franchise moves during the season and its impact on ticket sales, the commissioner had banned such talk. "I told them any comment of that type was detrimental to the minor league involved and harmful to the game. I said I would consider any comments of that type detrimental to baseball." Interestingly, in the same column Wrigley and Veeck denied involvement in moving the Athletics to LA.[41] Three months later, Chicago businessman Arnold Johnson announced intent to purchase the Athletics, moving them to Kansas City. While acknowledging Frick's gag rule, Johnson softened negative reactions, asserting that Dan Topping and Del Webb would work closely with him, as they owned the Kansas City farm club.[42] That hinted at Johnson's deep connection to the Yankees.

It was deep, indeed. Johnson was vice chairman of Automatic Canteen Corporation of America, a major provider of vending machines. Topping and Webb were investors. In late 1953 they sold Yankee Stadium and the Kansas City ballpark to a group headed by Johnson, claiming it was cheaper to lease the stadiums back. When that deal was announced, the Yankees' owners noted Johnson was interested in bringing the Majors to Kansas City and, as owners of the farm club, they supported him doing so. All those relationships with Johnson complicated matters, though Frick initially didn't see a problem with Johnson owning Yankee Stadium if he had nothing to do with the team and the rental fee wasn't related to operations.[43] The other league owners strongly differed, with Johnson's ownership of Yankee Stadium being the major drawback, even more than Kansas City having a lower population than Cincinnati. A few owners still wanted LA, though Webb was satisfied with Kansas City, and Frick remained adamant that LA wasn't ready without a sufficient stadium. Some magnates preferred that the club remain in Philadelphia, especially when the Macks received a local offer apparently more lucrative than Johnson's. It took four different meetings over two months before owners voted 8–0 for Johnson's purchase and 6–2—the minimum needed—to allow the move. It marked the beginning of problems caused by Johnson's relationships with the Yankees.[44] Nevertheless, the A's opened in Kansas City in 1955 and, like the others, would draw over a million fans their first season.

Frick seemed pleased. Three more cities now had Major League baseball, addressing a top issue from the congressional hearings. However, all moves were to metropolises within a reasonable train ride, and Major League baseball was still played only in the northeast quadrant. It required another three years for that to change.

CALIFORNIA DREAMING BECOMES A REALITY

The Athletics' relocation, along with Frick's comments, clarified what was necessary for a West Coast move. First, cities desiring a Major League franchise needed a stadium with sufficient capacity or a financial commitment to construct one. All three cities obtaining teams had met that requirement. Second, a West Coast move required two teams—one for LA, the other San Francisco, both from the same league—to facilitate schedules and travel. Finally, though unstated, no city should be vacated by relocations, leaving only two possibilities—Chicago or New York. They were the only markets left with two or more teams.

Although Celler's antitrust hearings helped to precipitate the initial moves, other postwar developments also contributed. One was the growth of television. Why bother going to a game if one could watch it from the comfort of home? Other factors enhanced television's attraction. Many ballparks were decades old and deteriorating, often along abandoned trolley or train routes. More families owned cars, preferring to drive to games, where parking was limited and surrounding neighborhoods deteriorating as families moved to the suburbs. That created challenges for weaker clubs, helping explain why the Braves, Browns, and A's departed. Many of those conditions were also realities for the Dodgers and Giants, though both still attracted over a million fans. For them, attendance was static or declining, clarifying to both Walter O'Malley and Horace Stoneham that new ballparks with ample parking were necessities.

Both owners explored New York City alternatives. O'Malley identified Brooklyn property with sufficient space for parking close to public transportation and expressways, offering to build the ballpark if provided the land. Stoneham was less aggressive, considering Minneapolis, where he owned the farm club, an alternative. The market, which included Saint Paul, had a population larger than Milwaukee, Cincinnati, or Kansas City. O'Malley disregarded a relocation, but his efforts locally ran into obstacles. The largest was Robert Moses, perhaps the most powerful man in New York City or state. He nixed the Brooklyn site, proposing a location in Queens where the World's Fair was held and where Shea Stadium would be built. It presented a major problem—it wasn't in Brooklyn. O'Malley also received little help from Robert Wagner, New York's mayor, who supported new ballparks for both clubs but offered only lip service. There was little sense of urgency to construct new ballparks.[45]

It wasn't for lack of trying, especially by O'Malley. He identified a location while also beginning to explore other options. He arranged to play seven of his eighty-one home games in Jersey City during the 1957 season. He also sold Ebbets Field, with a leaseback for two seasons. Both actions demonstrated his need for a new ballpark along with a preference to remain in Brooklyn, though neither caused Moses to move off the Queens site or gained greater support from the mayor.[46] Before the 1957 season, a California move began to look realistic, which garnered Stoneham's attention, their joint interest enhanced by the success of the relocating clubs. By the end of 1956 the Braves had drawn over two million fans in Milwaukee each of the last three seasons. Whereas the Orioles had only drawn a million their first year, the next two seasons produced similar results with a second-division team. The A's surpassed a million fans during their first two seasons, also with second-division finishes. Essentially, O'Malley and Stoneham observed three clubs equaling or outperforming their attendance while the Dodgers and Giants consistently finished near the top. That made relocation enticing.

That was certainly true for O'Malley. He became more open with reporters in early 1957, suggesting if stadium issues weren't resolved favorably in six months he would need to look elsewhere. He was also open about LA, backing talk with his own money. At the New York Baseball Writers' Association dinner in February, he asked Phil Wrigley, owner of the Los Angeles Angels—the Cubs' farm club—the price for his ballpark and club. Wrigley put forth $3 million and reached a deal immediately.[47] The Dodgers now owned the LA Minor League club, increasing the likelihood of a cross-country relocation.

This wasn't due solely to New York's lack of cooperation, as California cities were increasingly more proactive. Losing both the Browns and A's produced a flurry of LA actions in 1954. When the A's announced they were for sale and Frick prevented LA from consideration, West Coast strategies changed. A San Francisco alderman met with the LA mayor to coordinate efforts for two Major League clubs. They met with Frick soon after, the commissioner stressing he'd "talk turkey" when they had ballpark commitments and also suggesting the teams should be existing clubs. A San Francisco bond issue, with $5 million committed for a ballpark once there was a team, passed overwhelmingly soon after. Frick said, "I am amazed, happy, pleased." After that passage, LA announced a sixty-thousand-seat ballpark would be presented in a bond issue. Clarence Rowland announced his retirement as Pacific Coast League president and asked Major League Baseball for clarification on its West Coast plans.[48] By the end of 1954 it appeared California's two largest cities would soon have Major League baseball, with New York's National League clubs the targets.

However, the cities then received a dose of cold water. Horace Stoneham backed off first, saying he was 100 percent New York with "no chance for shift." A week later, O'Malley followed. While confident California would be represented in the Majors within five years, he stressed, "It will not be the Dodgers." He remained committed to Brooklyn. Even Frick seemed unenthusiastic, perhaps due to Rowland's protests. He now suggested a third league may be the best solution to meet California's desire for Major League baseball.[49] As the 1955 season began, California baseball seemed years away. In fact, for all of 1955 and most of 1956, the prospect of either New York club departing seemed unlikely. Most efforts to keep them in New York remained out of the news, and neither O'Malley nor Stoneham said much, both stressing they remained committed to New York. Even the California cities were silent. The only story involving California and Major League Baseball in late 1956 was a denial from Calvin Griffith, owner of the Senators, that he was moving to the West Coast in 1957. As for 1958, Griffith was circumspect: "We don't look that far ahead. We'll take one year at a time."[50] Nothing appeared imminent for California.

O'Malley reversed that scenario in 1957, bringing Horace Stoneham into a discussion of relocating together. O'Malley was aware of Stoneham's interest in Minnesota, but what differed now was the Dodgers' lack of progress with New York officials. Both also realized the benefits of continuing their rivalry. By the time they met, O'Malley had purchased the Minor League Angels and was exploring stadium locations. He even took his picture with the mayor of LA, who had visited him at the Dodgers' spring training site in Vero Beach, Florida. He publicly encouraged Stoneham to look at San Francisco, which the Giants' mogul was probably already pursuing.[51] In any case, their joint efforts were official by March 1957.

The speculation became so rampant by May that Frick reminded owners and executives of the gag rule imposed years earlier: "No change can be made during the playing season and any publicity relative to future action is to be avoided by all clubs."[52] That didn't help. A day later the mayor of San Francisco—George Christopher—announced that preliminary terms were established with Stoneham, "under which the New York Giants may shift to San Francisco next season with the Brooklyn Dodgers moving to Los Angeles." Stoneham refused to verify that. O'Malley commented, "I'm not going to dignify that by any reply at this time." Frick again stressed, "This Roman Holiday of speculation is harmful to both teams."[53] The commissioner may have hoped to stop speculation, but matters had now gone too far.

If any doubts remained, even while the owners still denied the rumors, they were removed after the National League meeting in late May when owners voted unanimously to allow the clubs to move together but also could opt to remain in New York. The Dodgers already had franchise rights in LA, while the Giants needed to acquire them in San Francisco. Further, both had to decide by October 1. This time Frick was supportive, calling the procedure proper: "My order was to do something or say nothing at all. I was against the constant flow of rumors and gossip." When a reporter asked if the Pacific Coast League might sue, Frick acknowledged, "If that is true, the moves might wind up in the courts. If that happens, the shifts might take years to materialize."[54] The clubs' moves were ratified if done in tandem, but obstacles still remained.

One was another hearing of Celler's subcommittee in June, and the Brooklyn chairman wasn't pleased with baseball. While satisfied with the franchise relocations to date, he certainly wasn't regarding the Dodgers. As a lifelong resident of Brooklyn and its congressman for over thirty years, he found the loss of his team troubling. Conversely, Congressman Hillings, a strong advocate for California baseball, felt rewarded. Recognizing this, Frick treaded cautiously in his testimony, stressing nothing was finalized, and added, "The transfer of the franchise of a Major League Club presents many difficult problems." The commissioner clouded the issue further by suggesting a third league. He was concerned Congress might diminish baseball's antitrust exemption, saying it "would seriously injure professional baseball with no offsetting benefit to the public."[55] In essence, Frick straddled in an effort to protect the antitrust exemption.

When O'Malley and Stoneham testified later, they were more direct. O'Malley didn't mince words, asserting that New York City officials had twice "sabotaged" his efforts to stay in Brooklyn. He stressed that no final commitment had been made to move, but time was running out, adding that LA's inducements "are difficult to overlook."[56] Stoneham was more direct in July. Citing the deterioration of the Polo Grounds and the neighborhood around it, coupled with declining attendance, he admitted he was leaning toward moving, clarifying that it wasn't predicated on the Dodgers moving. In essence, Stoneham strongly implied his move was imminent.[57] Celler may not have liked what he heard, but he could do little.[58]

Based on Stoneham's testimony, it was not surprising the Giants would announce first. They did so in late August, well before the October 1 deadline, its board voting in favor, 8–1. Stoneham cited lack of attendance as the main factor. He regretted leaving New York, where the Giants had played since 1883, adding, "We're sorry to disappoint the kids of New York, but we didn't see many of their parents out there at the Polo Grounds in recent years." He also emphasized they were moving regardless of what the Dodgers would do, though he had yet to address a final detail: swapping his Minneapolis Minor League franchise for Yawkey's in San Francisco.[59] That was resolved in mid-October, when O'Malley finalized his move.

The Dodgers went past the October 1 deadline, still awaiting a positive decision on Chavez Ravine, where they hoped to build its ballpark. When the Los Angeles City Council approved it on October 7, the Dodgers announced the next day. Unlike Stoneham, O'Malley expressed no regret, only indicating he would work out territorial-rights issues with the two Minor League clubs in the area. There had been brief apprehension in LA in September when Nelson Rockefeller, then a private citizen, met with

Frick, Giles, and O'Malley to explore purchasing land in Brooklyn using family money to invest in the Dodgers. Although the news precipitated concern, it came to naught. Consequently, New York City would no longer be part of the National League, a reality bemoaned by a *New York Times* columnist who wished Frick had dictatorial powers to block the moves and who added prophetically that only with expansion would New York again join the Senior Circuit.[60]

Frick was less philosophical. He was thrilled to move into major untapped markets but regretted seeing two clubs he had worked with since 1934 leave the Big Apple. He was also concerned about franchise issues caused by the loss of three Pacific Coast League markets, though he had plans to address the situation. In spite of all the remorse in Brooklyn and Manhattan, Frick didn't regret his support. Speaking to over one thousand people at a luncheon before the opening game in San Francisco, he noted that as a New Yorker, he was sad but added, "As Commissioner of Baseball I believe this to be the finest move ever made. The progress baseball will make in the next five to ten years will overshadow all past developments."[61] Whether Frick had authority to block the moves was debatable, but he left no doubt of his support for them.

FILIBUSTERING THE SENATORS

Frick approached the first five relocations in a laissez-faire fashion; his philosophy as commissioner to stay out of league matters. With the change in Major League rules in 1952, that's what franchise relocations became. His only intervention, in 1953, was to block a move past the deadline, only to back away after realizing the challenges of stopping it. Even then, he let the leagues decide. The same held true for the Browns and A's, with his only public position being that a move to California had to involve two teams in the same league. He also did not initially have difficulty with Arnold Johnson owning Yankee Stadium, though American League owners changed his thinking. He also let the Dodgers and Giants moves take their course. Living in New York, he was certainly aware of their local difficulties, but his only intervention was emphasizing the gag order. Any move was beyond his authority to interfere. That would change, however, when Senators owner Calvin Griffith considered relocation.

The Griffith family had owned the Senators for over four decades. Clark Griffith initially acquired a 40 percent interest in the club while still manager, soon gaining concessions from other investors to garner control.

He had successes, winning three pennants in the 1920s and 1930s and the World Series in 1924. Yet, he never profited much, even being unable to invest in a farm system. By the 1950s, while still marginally profitable, the club was performing poorly and consistently one of the worst teams. Many regarded Washington as "first in war, first in peace, and last in the American League."[62] While his teams struggled, Griffith was a valuable asset due to Washington connections, formally presenting season tickets yearly to the president. More important, he was instrumental with Frick in keeping baseball alive during World War II, thanks to his relationships. His 1955 death left a serious vacuum.

His nephew Calvin and his sister, whom the childless Griffiths had raised, inherited the club. The sister deferred to her brother, and the younger Griffith was more attuned to gate receipts than political matters. From 1954 to 1958, the club surpassed five hundred thousand fans only once, with four hundred thousand the norm otherwise. As was the case of many Major League cities, the ballpark was old and deteriorating, as was the neighborhood. Washington had agreed to construct a new stadium for both baseball and football, though Griffith disliked the location. Further, the relocation of the Browns to nearby Baltimore had drawn away fans. Griffith briefly flirted with LA in 1956, and while ruling out any move in 1957, he kept that option until the Dodgers moved there. By then the House and Senate subcommittees had conducted baseball antitrust hearings most years since 1951. Baseball's antitrust exemptions were created by two Supreme Court decisions, though the later ruling in 1953 emphasized revisions should be made by Congress. In 1957 Congress seemed prepared to do so, and the threat of losing the reserve clause was baseball's greatest worry. The departure of Washington's only franchise wouldn't be helpful.

The relocation issue grew serious in 1958. Griffith was more public about Minneapolis–Saint Paul now that LA was off the table, though he declined offering a proposal at the July meeting.[63] He may have delayed action because the Estes Kefauver Senate Subcommittee antitrust hearings were still occurring. When Frick testified, he didn't mince words when asked about the Senators relocating: "Removal of the club from Washington would be catastrophic. Baseball cannot afford not to be in the nation's capital." A day later, Senator Karl Mundt of North Dakota took Frick seriously, proposing an amendment allowing baseball its antitrust exemption as long as Washington had a Major League club.[64] The position of Frick and numerous senators was clear—baseball jeopardized its exemption if Washington was to be vacated.

A month and a half later, however, Griffith hadn't changed, as it was expected he would propose moving at the next meeting, in spite of opposition from his top minority partner—Gabriel Murphy—who owned 40 percent. Murphy announced in late August he was working to prevent any move. Two weeks later, anticipating Griffith's request, Frick conveyed his desire to expand to ten teams in each league, rather than relocations. When asked about Washington, he stressed it wasn't progress if a team left a city without Major League ball. In his sports column the next day, Arthur Daley expounded, "If the baseball Senators ever move their franchise, . . . the legislative Senators won't have a compunction or a fond feeling left. . . . An evacuation of the capitol by the sport would leave it friendless in the one spot where it most needs friends. . . . It would be insane to jeopardize this relationship."[65] Griffith wasn't deterred.

The situation did, however, affect the other American League owners as they considered the move, voting it down, 5–3. The magnates claimed the only reason relocation was requested was because Griffith disagreed with the location of the new Washington stadium.[66] After the vote, Griffith emphasized the stadium issue would continue to drive his relocation plans, though the frustrated city of Minneapolis withdrew its offer. It appeared Frick had counseled league magnates against the proposed move before the meeting, which likely helped produce the rejection.[67] Although the club would remain in Washington in 1959, relocation definitely wasn't dead for Griffith.

Indeed, it reappeared the following year. Griffith was vague, though Minnesota remained the likely target. Frick, as expected, remained outspoken against it, this time bringing in Joe Cronin, the new American League president, to strengthen the opposition. That didn't sit well with Griffith, as Cronin was a relative: "Frick doesn't have a vote. We don't have to pay any attention to him." He did acknowledge, though, needing a favorable vote from league owners. Frick responded, "If Griffith can't operate successfully in Washington, a fine baseball town, how can we assume he can operate in Minneapolis after the novelty wears off?" He added that the club was not in financial distress: "The Washington club always shows a profit, even when it finishes in eighth place. Simply because a club owner wants to make more money than he is making is no cause to move a franchise."[68] Frick again prevailed by the identical 5–3 margin.

Griffith expected to have the support, but a reporter summarized it succinctly: "Moguls took Frick's cue." Griffith was placated by the prospect that expansion might provide his club the opportunity to move.[69] In the meantime, the nation's capital still had Major League baseball.

The prospect of expansion seemed to quiet Griffith because there was no further talk of relocation until October 1960 when both leagues agreed to expand. His silence suggested that a new franchise in Washington might be created, freeing his move to Minnesota. He may have been equally confident the Continental League, which had a Minneapolis franchise, would never materialize. In any case, he never threatened relocation during the 1960 season. In turn, his move was approved when owners met in October to ratify adding two teams in 1961. It took three years, but Griffith finally obtained his goal.[70]

So did Frick. He may have claimed no authority to block a relocation, but his vocal position against the Senators affected American League owners. Those who supported Frick were generally invested in baseball longer and had worked more regularly with him. Only Baltimore and Kansas City, with newer owners, supported Griffith. Due to the congressional hearings, it was easier for Frick to make his case that relocating out of Washington would be detrimental, also allowing him to convey that no Major League city should face losing a team. Three years later, that would come back to haunt him.

A BRAVE REDUNDANCY

As he prepared for the 1963 All-Star Game in Cleveland, Frick felt comfortable there wouldn't be further relocations during his tenure. Six teams had moved to new cities; expansion had filled the National League's New York vacancy and kept a team in Washington. Seven new cities now experienced Major League baseball, with the game now played in different sections of the country. Another expansion was in the planning stages, though unlikely to occur during his commissionership, as he contemplated retirement after the 1965 World Series. Though challenges remained, relocations weren't among them.

William Bartholomay, a Chicago insurance executive, was also at the All-Star Game. His syndicate had purchased the Braves in late 1962, so this was his first game as an owner. He had always planned to attend, but he and other syndicate investors were also scheduled to meet with a delegation from Atlanta. The Georgia group included the city's mayor, the top executive of Coca Cola, and Andrew Young, then a leader in the Southern Christian Leadership Conference and close to Martin Luther King Jr. The group came to Cleveland to approach the Indians' owners about relocating to Atlanta but had also requested an audience with Bartholomay. Young was included to convey that Atlanta was different from other Southern cities—forward thinking, especially regarding race relations. The syndicate was impressed.[71] Even though Atlanta sought no commitment and Bartholomay's group had not purchased with intent to relocate, Atlanta's delegation had provided reasons to ponder.

That definitely wasn't the original plan. Bartholomay and some partners were from Chicago, where he grew up a baseball fan. In 1961 his group purchased the 46 percent interest in the White Sox owned by Charles Comiskey.[72] The intent was to buy out Arthur Allen, who had purchased the other 54 percent from Bill Veeck, and thus own a team in his hometown. When Allen made clear he had no interest in selling, the syndicate looked north, approaching Lou Perini twice before convincing him to sell the Braves. Perini, fifty-nine and feeling too old to own a team, maintained a 10 percent interest, with the syndicate promising to remain in Milwaukee. That commitment was reported locally, noting that the syndicate included some local, civic-minded members.[73] Nothing suggested there would be any risk to Milwaukee's team.

There were reasons, however, to consider Atlanta's overture, many known when the syndicate had purchased the Braves. Milwaukee wasn't growing as rapidly as it had previously, and attendance was declining. In the two years before Bartholomay's group purchased the club, it had dropped by almost 750,000 although it remained stable the first year the group operated in Milwaukee. Although the Braves were no longer pennant contenders, the team was still a first-division club. The greatest concern, however, also known when purchased, was a significant decline in the broadcast market. When Perini moved to Milwaukee, there was no western competition, with the Braves having broadcasting rights in Minnesota and the Dakotas. When Washington moved in 1961, however, the Braves were now boxed in on all sides, their broadcasting market declining significantly. By comparison Atlanta offered a seven-state region, with rapid growth in the metropolitan area—a 50 percent increase from 1950 to 1960.[74] All of those factors weighed on the syndicate.

The Braves weren't the first to propose moving in 1964. Charlie Finley purchased the Kansas City Athletics after Johnson's death in 1960. An innovative maverick, he quickly conflicted with city officials and local sportswriters and even was at odds with baseball leadership, including fellow owners. His differences culminated in January 1964 when he announced relocation of the A's, who had been in Kansas City less than a decade, to Louisville, an even smaller market. The controversy stemmed from a stadium dispute, prompting Finley to take the Louisville proposal to American League owners. They rejected him, 9–1, instructing Finley to reach agreement with Kansas City by February 1 or face forfeiture of his franchise. Finley, with encouragement from Emanual Celler, threatened to sue the league for antitrust violations. That went nowhere. Two weeks later, in testimony before the Senate Antitrust Subcommittee, Frick stated he had no doubt the courts would reject Finley's case, adding it was "a league matter."[75] The Louisville move was stopped, though Finley would vacate Kansas City four years later.

The Finley controversy may have produced some hesitation for Bartholomay because nothing transpired for another five months. Indeed, the season was well along when rumors materialized in July. Joseph Durso of the *New York Times* broke the story, claiming the Braves were heading to Atlanta for the 1965 season. The article mentioned numerous inducements, including a new stadium and the seven-state television market. John McHale, president of the Braves, denied the report but acknowledged attendance was declining and the club was boxed in on all sides from broadcast growth. Frick asserted he would only become involved to address compensation for the Minor League club in Atlanta. Warren Giles, National League president, emphasized that a request should be made by October 1. Concerned, Congressman Henry Reuss of Wisconsin suggested baseball create a pooling of revenues for smaller-market teams. Giles called it "impractical" and also stressed that no move was on the upcoming meeting's agenda.[76] The move remained a rumor.

It stayed that way for the remainder of the season, reemerging in October with comments from Congressman Reuss. He asserted that Milwaukee County was ready to bring a lawsuit against the Braves and any National League club supporting relocation. He also indicated the club's contract with the county required playing all home games in Milwaukee in 1965 and suggested that depriving the city of a Major League team would constitute an antitrust violation.[77] Part of Reuss's prediction proved true. The Milwaukee County Board obtained a restraining order from the Wisconsin Circuit Court, based on the agreement to play at County

Stadium in 1965. The team thus postponed its relocation request, though it had unanimous support from league owners to relocate. One county board member accused Braves' owners of being attracted to the lure of "fast money," to which Bartholomay replied, "Economic considerations are always the big ones, whether you're getting married or running a baseball club."[78] While the Braves remained in Wisconsin for 1965, the future was far less clear.

The league held a special meeting in November, voting unanimously to prohibit the Braves from moving to Atlanta—in 1965. Owners also voted unanimously to allow the move in 1966 when the stadium agreement transpired. Bartholomay's syndicate was now assured of the move, announcing later that month the purchase of Atlanta's Minor League club and relocating it to Richmond, Virginia, at Frick's suggestion.[79] Those actions, however, did not stop Wisconsin officials from further efforts to keep the team. Battle lines were drawn when Congressman Reuss conducted a radio interview with Emanuel Celler, still chair of the House Judiciary Committee. Celler supported Wisconsin's plan to sue the Braves, bemoaning that baseball had become far more of a business than a sport, with total focus on profits. He also called Frick a "puppet in the hands of the owners."[80] As had been the case throughout Frick's tenure, it appeared the antitrust issue would again loom large, with a Milwaukee judge filing a restraining order to keep the Braves in Wisconsin in 1966. Atlanta also did so because the Braves had signed an agreement for 1966. In effect, each state filed antitrust claims against the other.[81]

The Wisconsin case came before the Milwaukee court in March 1966, and a favorable ruling was reached to prohibit the Braves from playing in Atlanta. A quick appeal to the state's supreme court, however, reversed that decision by a 4–3 margin. By the time an appeal was made to the U.S. Supreme Court, the season was underway, the Braves were playing in Atlanta, and nothing altered that situation because the Supreme Court refused to hear the case. By early 1967 the Milwaukee County Board dropped its litigation.[82] The club was cleared to stay in Atlanta, Milwaukee was without Major League baseball, and Ford Frick was retired.

Frick's last involvement was a deposition in November 1965, shortly before retiring. It provided an excellent summary of his thoughts and the difficulty he had in contradicting his previous position that no Major League city should be vacated. He acknowledged meeting in July with Bartholomay, probably when the relocation rumor started, telling him the move was a league matter but indicating he "felt that leaving a city without a major league baseball club was a very serious matter and that they should consider it carefully and then restudy the situation before presenting the matter to the National League." Stressing that his only tool in such an issue was persuasion, Frick added, "The No. 1 responsibility of the owners is to themselves, their stockholders and their partners as investors. Their responsibility to the community is to put on the best show they can." He acknowledged that the major justification "is a matter of sheer economics and business judgment."[83] While stressing that Milwaukee deserved consideration in any expansion, he offered no promises. Cutting to the chase, Frick acknowledged Major League Baseball was, indeed, a business.

The Braves' relocation was not the kind of note on which Frick intended to end his career, though it encompassed issues similar to other relocations. A city without a club presented an attractive offer, either with a new ballpark, a larger population, a growing market, or greater broadcast potential. In all cases, the city losing the club attempted to retain it, sometimes reverting to legal action. None succeeded. In all cases, the moves initially proved successful, though many clubs who moved had problems and some relocated again. Through all the moves Frick was involved, though, he always declared that any relocation was a league matter. He was technically correct, but that didn't stop him when a move threatened the "best interests of baseball," as was the case with Calvin Griffith. Frick never referenced his best-interests power, but there were other means at his disposal. It only took three owners, many of whom he had worked with for years, to stop a relocation in the American League. Whatever the pluses and minuses of the seven relocations, Major League baseball was now a national game, with clubs in all four quadrants. One of the complaints registered at the 1951 antitrust hearings had been fully addressed.

1. Ford and sister Clara. Ford is thirteen or fourteen years old, and his sister is five and a half years younger. Courtesy of Kelly Frick Richards.

2. DePauw chapter of Sigma Delta Chi in 1914–15 yearbook. Frick is first row, second from left. Later known as the Society for Professional Journalists, the organization was founded at DePauw in 1909, which is a reason he attended. DePauw University Archives and Special Collections.

3. Frick during his years as a sportswriter in New York City. National Baseball Hall of Fame and Museum, Cooperstown, New York.

4. With son, Fred, at DePauw's campus newspaper office in May 1935. Elder Frick was an editor his last three years. The picture was taken the day before Frick presided at the Majors' first night game in Cincinnati. DePauw University Archives and Special Collections.

5. Frick is across from Stan Musial and beside a picture of the latter's portrayal on the cover of the *Saturday Evening Post* in 1954. Frick later wrote the "Gallant Knight" tribute on Musial's plaque outside Busch Stadium. National Baseball Hall of Fame and Museum, Cooperstown, New York.

6. At Los Angeles Coliseum with Warren Giles, National League president, and Dodgers Wally Moon and Gil Hodges. The Dodgers' move from Brooklyn was a major component of franchise transfers and expansion. National Baseball Hall of Fame and Museum, Cooperstown, New York.

7. With three of his fraternity brothers in front of Phi Kappa Psi's chapter house at the fiftieth reunion in 1965. It was the DePauw chapter's one hundredth anniversary celebration, and Frick was the keynote speaker. Baseball's first draft, which he helped establish, also occurred at about that time. DePauw University Archives and Special Collections.

8. With Commissioner Bowie Kuhn at his Hall of Fame induction in 1971. Frick set the precedent for commissioners to preside at induction ceremonies. National Baseball Hall of Fame and Museum, Cooperstown, New York.

9. With his family at his induction (*left to right*): grandson Ford, granddaughter Kelly, Frick, wife Eleanor, son Fred, and daughter-in-law Jere. National Baseball Hall of Fame and Museum, Cooperstown, New York.

7

Not a Minor Problem

From the start of the twentieth century, Minor Leagues had gone through periods of boom and bust. Frick witnessed both as league president, the downside during the Great Depression and World War II, the boom after. As commissioner, he had limited authority over the Minors, as the various leagues were run independently with their own organizations. That started to change during his tenure. The biggest challenge was declining attendance, causing teams and leagues to fold. Because the attendance decline corresponded with the growth of television and broadcasting Major League games, television and radio were considered culprits. Efforts were made to limit broadcasts in Minor League markets, but antitrust rules and Major League owners seeking new revenue sources were deterrents. Finally, with Frick's encouragement, the Majors set aside funds to help struggling Minor League teams, with oversight established for allocations. Those efforts were helpful but didn't resolve the problem. Instead, when baseball expanded, the Minors were reorganized. With considerable involvement from the commissioner, a streamlined and more profitable Minor League organization was achieved by the time Frick retired.

A RICH, UNSTABLE HISTORY

When the National League was created in 1876, lower-level leagues soon followed the model established by its founder, William Hulbert. Teams were owned by private investors, and the leagues followed set schedules, with no deviations. When a second Major League began and the reserve clause was established, Minor League organizations entered into agreements with the Majors to protect players and ensure compensation when their players were signed. Twice, Minor Leagues emerged to challenge the Majors, starting with the Western League, headed by Ban Johnson, which changed to the American League in 1900. A year later, it declared war with the National League, raiding players and attracting much of its talent. The other was the Federal League in 1914, growing out of a Minor League created the year before. On both occasions, player control was contested, and Minor Leagues struggled financially. Unlike the American League, though, the Federal League only lasted two years. World War I disrupted baseball at all levels, but when the war ended the Minors returned to ongoing agreements that determined when players could be signed and the amount of compensation. A player could opt to remain in the Minors, though the higher compensation made that rare. A level of stability was achieved by 1920.

That status quo meant Minors at all levels were ultimately feeders for the Majors, and their relationship generally wasn't harmonious. Major League clubs had no control over Minor League teams. Although set rates to sign players existed, a Minor League team's owner could negotiate a higher price. The arrangement saved money on player development and scouting, but no authority existed for the Major League team, and too much dependence was on the Minor League team. Whereas Minor League clubs relied heavily upon payments for players to be profitable, they could reject offers. It was a relationship begging for change.

As with integration, Branch Rickey was the change agent. In the aftermath of the Federal League's demise, Rickey joined the Cardinals, at the time the weakest team in the Majors. Rickey intended to change that, first as manager and then general manager in the early 1920s. He decided that the Cardinals could improve more rapidly if they acquired and operated their own Minor League clubs, which would provide full control over player signings and development. It worked. By the mid-1920s the Cards were one of the best National League teams.[1] They were so successful other clubs soon copied, though that proved somewhat unstable because Commissioner Landis disliked the control it produced and attempted to disrupt it in the late 1930s.[2] In spite of that, the farm system persisted. Major League club ownership was a major reason the Minors survived during the Depression.[3]

By the late 1930s the situation improved, with attendance increasing for both entities. Unfortunately, that didn't last. The outbreak of World War II diminished the availability of Minor League talent, thus reducing the number of teams. Even the Majors had difficulty staying alive, and many Minor Leagues shut down completely. Most healthy baseball talent was conscripted, and those remaining were Major League prospects. For both farm clubs and independently owned teams, it was often easier to shut down. That changed when the war ended.

From 1946 through 1949, Minor Leagues grew exponentially. By the second postwar season, there were 368 teams and fifty-two leagues. Sixty percent of the clubs were owned by or affiliated with Major League clubs, generally at the higher levels. Perhaps due to the Cardinals, almost twice as many affiliates were in the National League than the American League.[4] Minor Leagues expanded for the next three years, and in 1949, 448 teams were playing in fifty-nine leagues, attracting almost forty million fans to their games.[5] All Minor League teams were part of the National Association of Professional Baseball Leagues, the Minors' umbrella organization. It was a prosperous time, but the decline was already beginning.

BETWEEN A ROCK AND A HARD PLACE

There were signs of trouble before 1949. Phillies owner Robert Carpenter, Jr. also owned the Triple-A affiliate in Wilmington, Delaware. He noted a significant drop in attendance in 1948, from 124,000 to 102,000, occurring while the team had improved. Curious, Carpenter conversed with fans; many responded that they watched the Phillies on television instead. Carpenter concluded that, unlike radio, television might be deterring Minor League attendance.[6] He was the canary in the coal mine, though that didn't stop expansion from continuing in 1950. After 1950, though, retrenchment started, mostly among lower-level affiliated clubs. Fifty-five teams were eliminated, almost all affiliates, the number of teams falling below four hundred. As one sportswriter described it, "The kindergarten and lower grade teaching departments of the talent development system are suffering badly."[7] As the 1951 season began, there was little reason for optimism, as attendance declined by a million in the first month. By this point consensus coalesced on the culprit—Major League telecasts—the same problem Carpenter observed earlier.[8] Baseball executives acknowledged the problem and were confident of the cause, but they were uncertain how to solve it.

The huge drop in attendance, roughly 25 percent, was noted by George Trautman, president of the National Association of Professional Baseball Leagues since 1946. Headquartered in Columbus, Ohio, with a Cardinals-affiliated club, up to that point Trautman had only experienced the good times since taking office. When attendance dropped, he was convinced television broadcast of Major League games was the cause. As the Winter

Meetings loomed in 1950, his focus was on unrestricted telecasts of Major League games in a Minor League club's territory, concluding that without modification, the Minors would be destroyed. At the Winter Meetings, he met with Chandler, formally requesting Major League clubs curtail such telecasts.[9] Chandler never conveyed Trautman's request because he was also informed then that his contract wouldn't be renewed. It did gain Frick's attention, though he initially believed the decline was caused more by radio. He didn't hold back: "I don't mind saying it's a terrific problem. We're going to get together to outline a program with every intention of protecting the minors as much as we can. We've got to help minor league baseball. We'd be silly if we didn't. However, I frankly don't know just how much we can do." Frick did suggest other causes, including decreasing consumer purchasing power, the troubled world situation, and unusually bad weather. He also noted radio was here to stay, providing an important income source.[10] The most accurate part of his observations, though, was his skepticism. Nothing came out of the meetings.

The attendance decline wasn't limited to the Minors, as Major League attendance declined in 1951 by over a million. Television manufacturers had their own view, noting attendance increased for clubs televising all home games, while dropping a million and a half for those that didn't.[11] Obviously, there was a lack of consensus on the problem going into the 1952 season.

By the end of 1952 the picture seemed clearer. Now commissioner, Frick was convinced that both television and radio were culprits. At the Winter Meetings he declared, "The most pressing problem now has to do with television and radio, especially as regards impacts on the minors." He named a group to investigate.[12] Frick selected general managers George Weiss of the Yankees and Frank Lane of the White Sox, for the American League, and Bill Walsingham of the Cardinals and Chub Feeney of the Giants, for the National League. He also included Frank Shaughnessy, International League president, and Edwin Johnson, Western League president and also U.S. senator from Colorado, to represent the Minors. Frick, Trautman, and Tommy Richardson, president of the Eastern League, were unofficial members. Frick summarized the issue facing the group: "The biggest problem before the committee will be the impact of major league telecasts on minor league games." The committee was to issue a report by July 7.[13] It appeared baseball understood the problem and was attempting to address it.

Senator Johnson was an interesting, controversial choice. A Democrat, he was one of the biggest critics of the New Deal. As the keynote speaker at the annual Baseball Writers' Association of America meeting in February, he lambasted Major League Baseball, saying that though he had supported it in the Celler hearings, he could no longer do so. Instead, he declared, "Baseball is a cruel and heartless monopoly, motivated by avarice and greed." He noted the Minors since 1948 had declined 40 percent in attendance. Arthur Daley, *New York Times* columnist, agreed, asserting Major League televised games were "proving absolutely ruinous and Senator Johnson was completely justified in his attack." George Weiss took exception, claiming the Majors operated with concern for the Minors and noting the Minor Leagues would suffer without that help.[14] There were clearly significant differences within the committee.

Those differences proved irrelevant, as Johnson seized the initiative by scheduling a subcommittee hearing of the Committee on Interstate and Foreign Commerce. The senator offered a bill allowing Minor League clubs to prohibit telecasts in their territory of any Major League game without permission. Subcommittee members included Warren Magnuson of Washington, John Bricker of Ohio, and Andrew Schoeppel of Kansas. In opening comments, Johnson noted baseball had been restricted by the Justice Department in 1949 from blocking telecasts due to antitrust laws, and Minor League baseball had been on the decline since, with most clubs operating at a loss. Most participants in the hearing represented professional baseball, though Gordon McLendon of Liberty Broadcasting System, who had a $12 million lawsuit against Major League Baseball, also testified. The Justice Department and the National Association of Broadcasters (NAB) declined to participate.[15]

Frick was the main witness after a Johnson introduction that highlighted the commissioner's Colorado years. Frick outlined the history of clause 1(d), which baseball adopted in 1946 to protect a club's territorial rights, intending to protect teams from another's broadcasts. Frick stressed, "We eliminated them [1(d)] because we were high-pressured by the Department of Justice at a time when we were already faced with 5 or 6 litigations, . . . and not because at any time we had the slightest doubt as to the legality of our position." Called back later, he added, "I want to make it clear that a restriction that makes it necessary for us to permit television or radio to come into a town at the hour and the time that the club in town is playing a ball game, . . . is forcing us to eat our young."

Over the four days of hearings, Frick's comments stood out, but Trautman had impact, emphasizing Minor League attendance had decreased more than sixteen million since 1949.[16] Branch Rickey and "Happy" Chandler also affirmed Frick in testimony.

Passage of broadcast protection, which was Johnson's intention, was unlikely. Although the Justice Department declined to testify, its position on restoring 1(d) was well known—it opposed it on antitrust considerations. The broadcasters' association didn't testify but instead submitted a letter opposing the restoration, claiming passage would legalize antitrust, deprive fans of baseball games, and stymy television's technological progress.[17] Even then, the legislation was unlikely to reach the Senate floor. Lyndon Johnson, majority leader, was a member of the full committee and owned radio stations in Texas, and no legislation would reach the floor without his approval. Thus, baseball couldn't expect congressional help.

That didn't affect Edwin Johnson's optimism. Following the hearings, he promised to spearhead passage: "I haven't counted noses, but I have every confidence the bill will pass." *The Sporting News* stressed, "The Johnson bill deserves the support of every Congressman interested in the maintenance of the grassroots of the National Pastime and concerned with the development of free enterprise."[18] A month later, Frick again emphasized the importance of legislation and the modesty of baseball's request: "We are not fighting radio and television. . . . What we ask for is limited control. We ask for permission to make arrangements protecting our minor league clubs against the constant, perpetual encroachment of major league radio and TV. . . . Without the minors, the majors could not exist five years . . . and the minors are the most important section of the whole baseball structure."[19] Johnson's confidence and pleas from baseball's top brass would go for naught.

There were further efforts to address the issue. Early in 1954 Frank Shaughnessy suggested Frick require clubs to pay Minor League teams for broadcasts in their territory. Frick rejected the idea, indicating the sixteen clubs would have to enter into an agreement the Justice Department considered illegal.[20] A few months later, the commissioner suggested placing the Minors under his control: "I am not looking for powers, but the day must come when all of baseball pulls together. One man should be in full control to serve the best interests of all."[21] The Minors weren't interested. Clark Griffith suggested that baseball limit radio and television and require all clubs to relinquish their farm teams.[22] Because Griffith's

Senators owned no Minor League clubs, other magnates were unreceptive. Some lower-classification Minor League clubs combined to sue Major League Baseball and Frick for $50 million. Frick noted, "Baseball is in a strange situation with people suing you on one side for restraint and on the other for lack of restraint."[23] Through it all, one effort would have impact, thanks to a September meeting between Trautman and Major League farm directors. It paid dividends that year.[24]

The core financial problem with Minor League clubs was largely at the lower levels. Triple-A and Double-A clubs generally did well, but the A, B, C, and D loops—in smaller markets—were struggling or folding. The Majors addressed the problem at the 1954 Winter Meetings, agreeing to cover some of their expenses. Major League Baseball would assume some operating costs, including spring training, transportation expenses, and part of the manager's salary. It also would pay more for players transferred to higher levels. Frick considered it a lifeline: "This is by far the most important piece of legislation passed at these meetings. It can well be the means of survival for many clubs in the lower minor league categories." The Minors again proposed prohibiting Major League broadcasts, but the Majors rejected it, citing antitrust.[25] It was, however, a significant step to take on some fiscal responsibility. The extent of Frick's role is unclear, but it began a process to aid the Minors.

Frick hadn't given up on Congress. Although television caused problems for the Minors, it provided a growing revenue source for Major League clubs, one they weren't inclined to relinquish. Finding a solution required threading a tiny needle, and the commissioner remained convinced legislation was the solution, even after Johnson's bill failed. In late 1955 Frick announced baseball would set up a collective test-case arrangement on game broadcasts, addressing the collusion issue by absolving individual owners of liability as the case moved through the court system. He hoped that would provide the road map for a legislative solution. Attorney General Herbert Brownwell Jr. rejected it, which maintained the status quo, requiring each club to make its own broadcast arrangements.[26] As the Minor League season started in 1956, it was reduced to twenty-seven leagues and 209 clubs, the lowest number since 1945.[27] The subsidies stopped the bleeding, but Frick's other efforts went for naught.

The situation grew worse late in 1957, especially when the CBS network announced an agreement with five clubs to broadcast a Sunday-afternoon game weekly. Even though the network promised to black out games in

Minor League markets where games were transpiring, Minor League officials panicked and threatened to block it. Frick responded positively: "Good, I hope they can get Congress to pass legislation making it possible for us to put restrictions on television. I'm heartily in favor of the minors' stand on this." Both ranking members of the House antitrust subcommittee, Emanuel Celler and Kenneth Keating, requested that Frick block the telecasts. The three met in January, with the legislators offering help, "within the law," on television issues. Celler, demonstrating his frustration with baseball, claimed the Majors "created this themselves," adding that they should address it on their own rather than seek legislation. Frick, facing Celler's efforts to place baseball under antitrust laws, relinquished the broadcast issue: "We've given up trying to tackle the minor league problem from the legal end. . . . Now, if we had legislation, we could simply forbid the majors to telecast into minor league territory on the day of a game there, and our problem would be solved. But we can't get that legislation."[28] There appeared to be no public-policy resolution.

The commissioner continued to influence Congress, though, while blaming broadcasters for the stalemate. At a hearing before Celler's subcommittee in summer 1959, Frick accused the National Association of Broadcasters of having "a very short-sighted and destructive viewpoint" and was critical of its assertion that limiting Major League game coverage during Minor League games would black out half the markets. He proffered a seventy-five-mile-radius blackout in affected areas, emphasizing his clubs were willing to forego revenue.[29] At the hearing, Chairman Celler claimed the decline in Minor League attendance was due to diverse causes, not just broadcasting.[30] On that point, the congressman was likely more accurate than Frick.

WHERE ARE THE FANS?

In reality, the Minors were not alone in losing fans—the Majors did as well. Like the Minors, attendance boomed after World War II, almost doubling to twenty-one million between 1945 and 1948. There was a slight decline in 1949, more significant ones subsequently. By 1953 attendance was just over fourteen million, almost one-third of the fans gone. After that, attendance increased slowly; only in 1962 did it exceed 1948 attendance. More noteworthy, mean attendance didn't surpass 1948 until 1977.[31] Much of the increase in the late 1950s resulted from relocations. New locations outdrew previous ones, largely due to the novelty. Growth was also facilitated by expansion in 1961 and 1962. Without relocation and expansion, attendance in Major League parks was static or declining through the 1950s, as even the successful Dodgers and Yankees experienced declines.

A number of demographic trends explain parts of the decline. Although the postwar era was prosperous, it also witnessed movement to the suburbs. Many ballparks lacked parking, and many fans preferred driving rather than public transportation. That led to construction of new ballparks in the 1960s, built with ample parking. There were also population shifts to other sections of the country, much of the postwar growth in the South and the West—hence, the reason for relocations and expansion. Television was also a distraction because most clubs telecast some home games, providing fans a cheaper and more convenient option than attending. The era saw other professional sports grow in popularity as well.

Minor League towns had additional challenges. Some were declining as people moved from metropolitan areas, mostly to suburbs, and especially to the South and West. Likewise, television provided an entertainment alternative well beyond baseball games. Finally, the 1950s were an anomaly for the United States, as other countries slowly recovered from World War II damages. Families could afford entertainment alternatives to baseball and took advantage of them. In effect, many Minor League clubs were facing greater competition while also located in declining markets.

Another problem was the lack of ability to offer fans roster consistency. That had always affected the Minors, but it had increased with farm-system expansion and affiliate relationships. The Minors lost independence and were at the mercy of the Majors for how and when their players were moved. A standout player was unlikely to spend much time at any level, not long enough to develop a loyal following. If a Minor League club remained independent, however, it was difficult to recruit players. In 1956 the owner of the Triple-A club in Buffalo, New York, then unaffiliated, determined the Majors controlled over 90 percent of players, rendering it difficult for the club to field a team. Frick addressed that problem, though it remained a deterrent against remaining independent.[32] An effort was made to address the issue before the 1957 season by limiting Opening Day rosters to twenty-eight players, down from forty for the first month, making more players available to the Minors when their seasons started. That limit of twenty-eight also applied to all Minor League levels.[33] Those roster limitations foreshadowed forthcoming help.

Relocation and expansion also created problems. Every time a Major League team relocated, it forced a Minor League club to move. During Frick's commissionership, Minor League clubs were shut out of nine cities and usually moved to smaller markets. The three Triple-A leagues had no alternative but to adapt. Although compensation was provided if the club was independently owned, the reality was the same, as any such move had ripple effects on lower clubs. It was not surprising the commissioner became involved to resolve these situations.

Major League expansion created another problem. Over the course of two seasons, in 1961 and 1962, four new teams were established, with both leagues developing procedures for them to draft their players—not only twenty-five players to fill each team's roster but also players to staff their Minor League affiliates. Much of the talent pool came from existing clubs, and although there were procedures to compensate teams, the changes were disruptive throughout to existing Minor League clubs. The usual churning of players at various levels already contributed to instability; expansion exacerbated the problem. In that regard, expansion was the last catalyst to precipitate major changes.

The combination of deteriorating fan base and loss of larger markets even before expansion highlighted the need for an overhaul. By 1958, after the California moves, restructuring seemed obvious, even though the Majors were already subsidizing the Minors. Trautman called a meeting of the various leagues to develop a realignment that would prove beneficial by reducing travel and operating expenses. It presented a significant opportunity, but the Minors' clubs and leagues rejected it. A veteran writer summarized the situation: "Until now, the minors have been laying virtually all the blame for their troubles on their big brothers. At their special two-day meeting here, they had a chance to do something by themselves, without interference or pressure from the majors—and ingloriously muffed the ball. This they cannot place blame on the big fellows; the fault lies with their own greediness."[34] When it came to accepting change, the Minors were their own worst enemy. Frick would salvage the situation, though that would require another five years.

AN EVOLVING SOLUTION

The 1954 attempt to help with lower Minor League expenses proved inadequate because attendance continued to decline. Frick grew concerned as the 1955 season began, and to convey his thoughts, he utilized the meeting between Major and Minor League executives that extended operating agreements. Emphasizing the need for further assistance from the Majors, he reiterated the dilemma: "We are in the position of being sued on one hand for restricting broadcasts and on the other for not restricting them." He added, "It's important to us and to the minor leagues that we get this problem cleared up as quickly as possible."[35] While Frick believed the current subsidies were a step forward, he felt they were insufficient.

Earlier, at the 1955 Winter Meetings, Walter O'Malley offered a suggestion to help the Minors—that Major League Baseball enter into a broadcast agreement with a network for a game of the week in 1957. He estimated revenue generated would be roughly $3 million and proposed that half go to the Minors and the remainder be split between Major League clubs. Without commenting on the merits, Frick acknowledged no action could be taken because it wasn't on the agenda thirty days prior.[36] During the same session, a rumor floated around the meeting that baseball would cancel the 1956 season in protest of the Justice Department's ruling against baseball's attempts to restrict broadcasts. Frick called it "utterly preposterous and nonsensical. I can assure you that nothing like this ever has been contemplated by the major leagues." He stressed that whatever the differences, he was confident they could be worked out.[37] Unfortunately, that would not prove true with the broadcast controversy because the Minors continued to suffer.

As the problem continued through 1955, the commissioner announced after the season that Major League Baseball would set aside $500,000 for the aid and betterment of the lower-level Minors, administered by a six-man committee reporting to him. Two weeks later, he named the six, two each from the American, National, and Minor Leagues. In December Frick announced Bill DeWitt, assistant general manager of the Yankees and formerly with the Browns, would administer the funds from St. Louis.[38] DeWitt had been in baseball for decades and was highly regarded by his peers. The bigger story was that the Majors finally committed a considerable sum and the apparatus to administer it, rather than attempting to gain help from Congress. For the next four years, that would prove to be a work in progress.

The funding was obviously important to Frick, who stressed at every stage that the committee and administrator would report to him. The concept was well received by the Minors, producing the most harmonious Major and Minor League meetings in recent memory. Trautman was optimistic, feeling certain the twenty-eight leagues starting the 1956 season would be around in 1957, thanks to the subsidy. One reporter observed, "The entire week of meetings was on a highly optimistic note, climaxed by a resolution adopted on the final day that commended the majors for their action in setting up the half-million-dollar stabilization fund."[39] In his editorial a week later, Spink credited Frick. He added that the new cooperation between the organizations "may be remembered as the finest accomplishment of Frick's and Trautman's regime."[40] Although the fund was a major step forward, it was not the panacea anticipated.

In reality, Frick faced new challenges following the 1957 and 1958 seasons. Perhaps the biggest were the Dodgers' and Giants' moves, the displacement of three Pacific Coast League clubs, and issues concerning their relocation and compensation. Frick was involved personally, along with Dodgers and Giants executives, Trautman, Leslie O'Connor of the Pacific Coast League, two club executives from that league, heads of two other Minor Leagues, and Lou Carroll, a Major League Baseball attorney. Discussions focused on the cities gaining clubs—Phoenix, Salt Lake City, and Spokane—as well as payments to the relocating clubs. O'Malley and Stoneham agreed to make two of them their Triple-A affiliates and pay the Pacific Coast League $900,000 for the franchise preemptions.[41] While that issue was resolved, the CBS network clouded matters by announcing plans to televise Sunday games of five Major League teams into Minor League markets. That became the hot topic at the Minor League meetings in late 1957, with Frank Shaughnessy threatening to take the issue to Congress. Frick was supportive.[42] Though the Minor League fund stabilized the situation, the growth and lucrativeness of Major League broadcasts assured challenges would continue.

The broadcasts triggered the discussed ill-fated effort at the 1958 Minor League Winter Meetings to realign and restructure, which broke down until Frick intervened. The breakdown occurred when the renewal of the $500,000 Minor League fund was also announced. The committee continued its policy of not publicizing fund distribution, concluding there wasn't "anything to be gained by publicizing the financial difficulties of some clubs and it was felt that civic pride of the communities involved could be seriously damaged by divulging such information."[43] The failure to achieve league realignment offset that funding news until Frick reconvened the parties in December, though he downplayed his role: "I didn't want coercion on anybody. . . . I wanted them to handle the matter in a fair and sensible manner." It worked. The lower-level organizations met again "with a renewed spirit of cooperation" and were able to reach agreement on restructuring two leagues.[44] That did not resolve overall realignment needs, but it did show progress for the 1959 season, thanks to Frick's intervention.

The Minors still struggled, losing seven additional leagues by the end of 1959. Earlier that year, they had received some good news, as Major League Baseball's radio and television committee announced that all Minor League levels would be recipients of a million-dollar fund. The allocation was doubled, in effect, though Frick and league presidents stipulated two requirements. First, a team had to complete the season. Second, none of the money would be allocated to clubs wholly owned by the Majors. Shaughnessy was elated: "We've become very happy with our treatment by the major league committeemen. I know they're going to help keep us alive in any way they can." His enthusiasm was diminished later when he realized that to receive funds, clubs had to agree not to take legal action against Major League clubs due to telecasts.[45] That additional condition did not sit well, but Minor League owners were reconciled with the Majors at the December meetings, appeased by the larger sum. Frick emphasized, "I believe this action by the majors will have a stimulating effect on any minor league clubs which might have been on the fence. There is no doubt but that the player development fund has helped many leagues and clubs to survive." Trautman called it the "forerunner of a long era of peace and understanding."[46] Holding Major League clubs harmless seemed a reasonable trade for keeping Minor clubs alive.

After the 1960 season, two hundred Minor League clubs were recipients of $800,000, with seventeen Triple-A clubs getting $20,000 and lower-level teams between $12,000 and $3,000. The funds were a big lift. Even with subsidies, though, many clubs still were "deep in the red," leaving their future in doubt.[47] Although subsidies were helping, especially after the increase, they remained insufficient. It was obvious by late 1960 that more was needed, leaving additional realignment of the leagues on the table.

REALIGNMENT FEELS SO GOOD

Dealing with the Minor Leagues was not an easy task for the commissioner. First, he wasn't officially in control—the Minors had their own head, Trautman, who also had limited authority. Like the two Major Leagues, individual Minor Leagues had their own presidents, at any classification, responsible for their operations. Further, the various levels added challenges. The Minors consisted of Triple-A, the highest level, then Double-A and Single-A. Further down were B, C, and D leagues, based on the caliber of play; they were generally located in small towns. Whereas the majority of clubs were wholly owned by Major League teams, many remained independent. Regardless, all were essential, as there was no other system to develop talent. The main alternative, colleges, had never been a direct feeder, so it was understandable that owners felt the game couldn't survive without the Minors. The challenge was keeping them viable operationally and financially, which was what Frick was facing. The most sensible solution appeared to be both consolidation and realignment, as there were too many leagues, too many levels, and too much independence. It was truly a jigsaw puzzle, exacerbated by Major League broadcasts and the lack of government willingness to help. The Majors and the Minors would have to solve it together.

A solution was proposed early in Frick's tenure. Near the end of the 1954 season, Frank Shaughnessy suggested replacing lower-level classifications, especially C and D, with industrial-league teams. Essentially, local companies or corporations would employ players in those leagues, paying them salaries for work and supporting them during the season. Such organizations existed outside the parameters of professional baseball. The largest benefit from such leagues would be compensating players who were unable to support themselves on the salary paid by lower Minor Leagues.[48] Trautman was assured the idea would be studied, but he remained skeptical. Articles in an issue of *The Sporting News* debated industrial-league pros and cons, while Spink, the weekly's editor, suggested alternatively that lower leagues should be shut down with dependence placed on colleges.[49] Given the friction between colleges and Major League Baseball at the time, that didn't seem viable. While following this debate closely, Frick offered no comments.

It wasn't until 1957 that realignment and consolidation received serious consideration, a year after funding was developed. By then obviously neither industrial leagues nor colleges provided solutions. Frick advocated both consolidation and realignment, hoping the subsidy program would facilitate his objectives. By mid-1957 he also anticipated the West Coast moves and met with all three Triple-A league presidents and representatives from four lower leagues to discuss franchise shifts. Frick downplayed the session, calling it "totally exploratory," though the timing, given the progression of the Dodgers and Giants plans, wasn't coincidental. When the moves were finalized, they met again to establish the new Pacific Coast League cities, though the national broadcasts on CBS stymied other proposals.[50] That didn't prevent further discussion.

Frick had hoped for significant consolidation, but it didn't happen. No progress was made on keeping broadcasts out of Minor League markets, and the Minors, while appreciating the subsidies, were not receptive to change. The key to realignment was for the American Association to expand from eight to ten teams, taking three clubs from the Texas League's largest cities with compensation for them. The expectation was that the openings in the Texas League would stimulate other lower leagues to expand or consolidate, but that failed when the American Association balked, with its owners reluctant to add teams. Frick intervened, convincing the American Association to expand and accept all three Texas League teams; that left the Texas league with six clubs.[51] Though that segment was completed, there were still too many teams, levels, and leagues.

Although disappointed, the commissioner searched for something dramatic to help, which proved to be expansion. That was already being considered, as Bill DeWitt recognized in 1959, acknowledging that the ten-team American Association, with five clubs competing in each division, was an experiment to determine if it could work for the Majors. He credited Frick for the concept.[52] At the same time, Frick didn't want to wait to see how expansion in the Majors would work and still pushed for additional consolidation, realignment, and reclassification. However, while many teams and leagues continued to struggle, even with subsidies, no agreement could be reached on any of the three.[53] Though change didn't come easy, Frick continued pursuing his goals.

His perseverance succeeded in 1962, when he achieved all three objectives. He arranged a meeting in mid-May to consider restructuring. In the announcement, Frick emphasized that the current structure, from Triple-A down to D classifications, was unwieldy and unrealistic. He stressed there should be an equivalent number of Triple-A clubs as was in the Majors. At the time, there were two extra Triple-A teams. He was optimistic: "I have great hopes that we'll be able to put the program into effect in '63. . . . This is a package plan that will cover financial commitments as well as reclassification and realignment of the minors."[54] The commissioner offered no further details, remaining coy while optimistic. Before the meeting, an article discussed potential Minor League alignments, though it devoted more space to efforts considered to speed up games. It mentioned plans to consolidate to three classifications and create a businesslike system for support. Beyond that, the article was vague, only mentioning that the committee was chaired by John Galbreath, owner of the Pirates, who had become one the more influential and effective magnates. The proposed changes remained so confidential, however, that the editorial in the same issue of *The Sporting News* pleaded for Major League Baseball to go slowly and not take steps that were too drastic.[55]

Indeed, the meeting achieved his objectives. The various levels of the Minors were consolidated into Triple-A, Double-A, and Single-A. There would be twenty Triple-A clubs, twenty Double-A clubs, and sixty Single-A clubs. Each of the Major League clubs would be responsible for a team at each of the two top levels and for three clubs at A level. All B, C, and D clubs and leagues would be consolidated into the A level. Each Major League club would thus be responsible for a minimum of five Minor League teams. In effect, the twenty Major League clubs were now responsible for the financial well-being of one hundred farm clubs. A club could control more than five teams, and Galbreath indicated his Pirates would be responsible for seven clubs and also expected others would do so. Frick said, "We approved a broad, general plan to stabilize a sound minor league system, adequate to take care of our player development program. . . . But this is just the beginning. There is still a lot of work ahead because we would like to have the new plan in operation for the 1963 season. We want it completed for formal passage at the winter meetings." This time, Spink approved the consolidation and reorganization, though still many details needed to be resolved.[56]

Some proved challenging, though the structure for the 1963 season was finalized by the new year. As late as October, some Minor League operators were struggling with the outline, even suggesting the overhaul had "flopped."[57] By the Winter Meetings, though, Frick's confidence of approval proved prescient. There were now three classifications. The 1963 season would start with 104 clubs in fifteen leagues, down slightly from the 116 clubs in seventeen leagues the year before. Frick's intervention resolved uncertainty from the meetings in November.[58] The commissioner was confident of success: "If a minor league operator can't make a go of it under this plan, his city doesn't deserve to have baseball. . . . The majors will give him the players, train them and pay part or all of their salaries. All the minor club will be responsible for is providing the park, travel, food and lodging when the team is on the road during the league season, promotion and things like that."[59] There were downsides. In particular, one established league—the American Association—was eliminated, a byproduct of only twenty Triple-A clubs and the requirement for at least eight teams in a league.[60] Frick's goal of a new structure by the 1963 season was accomplished, though two challenges remained.

Neither was major but both required Frick's involvement. The first was dissatisfaction with the Triple-A alignment. Neither league liked the ten-team configurations they were left with from the restructuring. Each preferred an eight-team format, which would have produced less travel expense. With each of the twenty Major League teams responsible for a Triple-A club, that wasn't possible. The American Association had been eliminated, and no one wanted six-team leagues, so Frick insisted one of the leagues go to twelve clubs.[61] Both leagues balked, necessitating the commissioner's intervention. During the Minor League meetings, the Pacific Coast League agreed to twelve teams for 1964, adding both Little Rock and Indianapolis. In doing so, it divided into East and West Divisions, each playing more games within their region. Still, the league ranged from Indianapolis to Honolulu, though divisions reduced the travel costs.[62] Peace was restored, with both leagues satisfied.

The second challenge was actually resolved sooner, though it needed Frick to formalize it. With realignment, all Minor Leagues were more closely tied to the Majors than at any time in their history. That was intentional. Whether Frick planned to gain full control of the Minors ultimately or merely wanted better coordination is unclear. It is clear Frick intended the two entities to work more closely. When Trautman died in 1963, it was even questioned whether the Minors should remain independent.[63] Frick never answered that directly, but simultaneously with his retirement announcement, he did note the two organizations would locate their offices in the same building within two years, meaning he would experience no benefit.[64] Soon after, Phil Piton was named the new Minor League association president, having worked for years in Trautman's office in Columbus and before that for Commissioner Landis. Piton endorsed Frick's concept, stressing the Minors would remain independent.[65] Though it was unclear how far they might be consolidated, it did ensure more cooperation.

Overall, the realignment was successful. It lasted for almost sixty years until Major League Baseball affected another reorganization in 2021. By then the Minor Leagues were more directly under the Major's auspices. By the 1965 season *The Sporting News* was convinced the Minor Leagues were on a much stronger footing.[66] Frick had resolved a pressing problem that persisted through most of his tenure.

ANOTHER SIGNIFICANT CHANGE

Frick wasn't a crusader. He did not believe baseball should lead on social issues, articulating that the sport shouldn't be in the forefront of civil rights. Generally, that was the case, but he made an exception when Little Rock, Arkansas, petitioned to obtain a Triple-A franchise. It happened in 1962 when the Minors were going through reorganization. Frick was aware of past history with Southern baseball clubs—segregation, separate seating arrangements, separate hotels and restaurants for Blacks and whites. The plight of African American players in the South after 1947 was well documented by those experiencing it.[67] In part, it was why Little Rock had no franchise. Frick approved its petition—with conditions. The new club was required to allow Black players. Further, all players on home or visiting teams would share the same hotel and eating accommodations. All seats at the ballpark would be available to any paying customer, regardless of race, with Black people having full and equal access. Little Rock accepted. On Opening Day 1963, Governor Orval Faubus threw out the first pitch—the same governor who had blocked the entrance to Central High School in Little Rock six years earlier.[68] How much Ford Frick's demands helped is unknown, but Little Rock wouldn't have obtained a Triple-A club had it not agreed.

The Minor Leagues had struggled through most of Frick's tenure. Attendance declined, the number of leagues and teams decreased, and efforts failed to help. After numerous unsuccessful attempts to control broadcasts in Minor League markets, Frick realized different actions were necessary. Starting in 1956, owners agreed to a program subsidizing the weakest teams at lower levels. Although that helped and the amount later increased, teams still struggled, making it clear more was needed. In 1958 Frick proposed a major realignment of the Minors but encountered a typical roadblock—resistance to change. With additional efforts, dealing with owners and executives from both the Majors and Minors, the commissioner achieved significant restructuring, which remained intact for almost sixty years. Largely due to Frick's efforts, the Minor Leagues were stabilized, ultimately growing and expanding. Even in the South, baseball was becoming integrated. Frick played a major role in spearheading the much-needed changes, establishing a closer relationship between the organizations.

8

The Hardball Politics of Expansion

Talk of expansion began shortly after World War II and initially focused on the Pacific Coast League's demands. Ford Frick spoke positively though alternated on the process—more teams or a new league. Franchise relocations in the 1950s diminished talk of expansion, but the Giants' and Dodgers' moves soon reinvigorated discussion. New York politicians were concerned about losing their National League presence and created a committee to procure a team. Without progress, the chairman, William Shea, undertook a different approach by forming a new Major—the Continental League. With Branch Rickey as its commissioner, it procured investors from eight cities, all without a Major League team, except New York. The largest roadblock was player procurement; when legislation couldn't facilitate that process, the league folded. The Majors did expand into three of the Continental League's cities, including New York. However, when the two leagues finalized their cities, the Yankees and Dodgers balked at a second team in their cities. Only Frick's involvement enabled the American League to expand in 1961, and the National League a year later.

MUCH TALK, LITTLE ACTION

To many, expansion talk only surfaced in the late 1950s when the Continental League emerged. In fact, discussions had already taken place for over a decade. When World War II ended, the Pacific Coast League moved quickly to position itself as a third Major League. Having lost many superstars in the past, like Joe DiMaggio and Ted Williams, the league hoped players could be protected by evolving into a Major League. With rapidly growing cities—LA and San Francisco were already larger than many Major League cities—it felt it had a case. Major League owners disagreed, rejecting its proposal unanimously in late 1945 and citing inadequately sized ballparks and inability to afford competitive salaries.

The magnates did agree there was long-term potential and established a committee. Unsatisfied, Clarence Rowland, Pacific Coast League president, continued to pursue parallel status, rejecting the status quo.[1]

Rowland's insistence achieved a visit from baseball's top brass in August 1947. Chandler, Frick, and Harridge, along with a club official from each league, traveled to California to assess the situation. They visited cities of five clubs—LA, San Francisco, Oakland, and San Diego. Harridge left due to illness, but the others viewed sites firsthand, though Rowland rendered the trip moot by abandoning his Major League request. Instead, he recommended the league be granted a higher classification, exempting their players from being drafted. One reporter observed, "So, outside of enjoying some California hospitality and trying some of its famous golf courses, the committee . . . just went for the ride."[2] That closely reflected its accomplishments, as Rowland's proposal was rejected. Frick's league did vote to expand to ten teams, but the American League voted 5–2 against doing so. Even with the National League action, "the whole thing is some way off in the distance," according to *The Sporting News*.[3] Other than laying groundwork, the league was no closer to its objective.

Although Rowland persisted, visiting both league presidents and Chandler, he wasn't making progress. Frick favored expansion rather than franchise relocation. Indicating there was no expressed interest in any existing club moving, he added, "I personally think the major leagues will expand. Such a move will be needed to take in cities that have attained major league size since the present leagues were formed. Not just the West Coast alone, but the entire country would have to be considered."[4] His key point was that Pacific Coast League cities weren't alone in deserving consideration, and he also stressed expansion wasn't likely in the near future. A year after his league had voted to expand, Frick cooled expectations.

He remained consistent in May 1950 when speaking in Toronto, predicting both it and Montreal would eventually receive franchises. He also suggested a third league, but only after existing leagues both expanded to twelve.[5] He offered no specifics though made clear California cities were not the only candidates. His speech generated new interest, which caused him to add a cautionary note. Making headlines in *The Sporting News*, Frick emphasized that he "does believe we are on the verge of recasting the major league map, and he does not regard recognition for the Pacific Coast League as being imminent." In part, Frick was downplaying expectations. He claimed, "The Pacific Coast League does not hope for third major recognition. It wants to be made free of the draft."[6]

Rowland, however, refused to relinquish his efforts, even as the Majors remained unreceptive; he received a boost from the 1951 Subcommittee on Antitrust and Monopoly hearing in the House of Representatives. In particular, comments from Congressman Patrick Hillings of LA provided encouragement. Hillings berated baseball for maintaining its locations for almost fifty years, with two or more clubs in five cities, and was especially perplexed that his booming metropolis couldn't obtain a franchise. Rowland seized the opportunity. He threatened to boycott baseball unless his league was granted relief from drafting players and gained status above other Minors. The ultimate goal was becoming a Major League.[7] Rowland timed his declaration nicely—when Frick was named commissioner. Threats of a renegade Minor League and of baseball losing its antitrust exemption assured Frick's attention.

In his first major decision, the commissioner largely granted Rowland's demands, offering the league open status, a step up from Triple-A, including the opportunity to become a third Major League. Six of its eight teams needed to approve the status and meet guidelines in aggregate for stadium capacity, season attendance, and population. There would be no limits on player salaries, and proof of financial stability would be provided.[8] Rowland was elated, confident his league could meet the requirements. Addressing the capacity issue, he said, "At present our physical plants are not adequate to handle major league crowds. Granted five years to build them up, we could get ready to step into the major league family." He also expressed optimism, which proved unfounded: "We feel it is a great point in our favor to have the commissioner and his committee recognize the fact that for either league to expand to ten or 12 clubs by invading another league's territory is not feasible."[9] Frick affirmed Rowland's confidence and asserted that the Majors had abandoned expansion as impractical.[10] It appeared the only option for growth, then, would be annexing another league.

Frick's proposal was modified by baseball's executive committee before it was finalized. The population requirement was increased, a minimum capacity was set for each ballpark, the aggregate size required for the eight cities was established, a balanced schedule of at least 154 games was stipulated, a pension plan was required, and all Major and Minor League agreements were to be accepted. Frick announced those requirements with Rowland's support. In particular, Rowland was pleased the Majors "cannot kidnap a P.C.L. city without entailing tremendous cost and red tape."[11] The new guidelines were well received. Speaking to the LA Rotary Club in March 1952, Frick left "no doubt about his willingness to meet the issue head-on. . . . His frank remarks were in striking contrast to the answers given a year ago by Frick's predecessor, A. B. ['Happy'] Chandler, who seemed to see the cue for a funny story in every query."[12] Some local sportswriters were less impressed, believing Frick was having it both ways and noting that including the entire league would slow the process for California's two largest cities.[13] The writers had a better take on the significance of the change.

In fact, even the new National League president did not agree with Frick on encompassing the league as a whole. While Frick was convinced Pacific Coast League cities would be ready in five to ten years, Warren Giles remained skeptical: "Los Angeles and San Francisco are big league cities now—much more so than some cities in the American and National leagues today. The fans out here deserve big league ball. Asking them to wait until the other Pacific Coast cities can qualify is like telling two fellows in a block they can't buy a Cadillac until all their neighbors can afford one." Giles qualified his comments by noting that no current owner showed interest in moving to the West Coast.[14] He even joined Will Harridge in asserting there were no plans for any relocations there, assuring Rowland his larger cities were safe.[15] While both league presidents seemed to fall in line, the West Coast wasn't off the table.

Even Frick vacillated. A year after proclaiming a third league was the only way to expand, he spoke differently. In a speech in Honolulu while traveling to Japan in October 1953, he stated expansion was certain when two requirements were met—a city had to have a ballpark of sufficient size, and its players were of Major League caliber. He maintained that the West Coast was logical for expansion, while not mentioning a third league.[16] Returning from Japan, Frick was even clearer: "Conditions have changed all over the country and there are many cities that want and can support major league baseball. Our problem is how to work out a way to meet the demand. . . . I am convinced the demand for a change . . . is so urgent that I'd welcome any serious discussion on any proposal." He added that two twelve-team leagues, with geographic divisions and a playoff for the World Series, was the best format. He left little room for uncertainty: "I doubt whether a third major league would solve the problem."[17] The door was open to consider expansion markets, apparently not for a third league.

A year later, one American League executive took the initiative to gain his league an advantage. Hank Greenberg, general manager of the Indians, advocated expansion to ten clubs. He explained that his opposition to the Baltimore and Kansas City relocations was their small size compared to other options, adding the league had to be proactive to stay ahead of its rival.[18] Greenberg appeared to have the two largest California cities in mind. A month later, his league established a committee, chaired by Frank Lane of the White Sox, to examine expansion opportunities, only to learn the Senior Circuit had already taken similar action shortly after Greenberg's proclamation.[19] By the end of 1954 expansion appeared eminent.

Then, almost as quickly, the inevitability was gone. At the scheduling meetings in late January 1955, the National League voted not to entertain applications for new franchises. The owners rejected a ten-team league and couldn't perceive any advantages with expansion. While the American League didn't take similar action, Lane's committee announced no plans for action on Greenberg's proposal. Both leagues explored adding two clubs and considered the two California cities, Montreal, Toronto, Minneapolis–Saint Paul, and Dallas, but both postponed action for at least a year.[20] Frick brought finality when he placed a gag rule on any expansion discussion: "While everyone in baseball recognizes that expansion is inevitable as a long-range program, no purpose is served by continued interviews, publicity and discussion on this subject. Quite the contrary, minor-league cities are being definitely harmed by this loose talk on the part of their major league brothers. . . . Such talk, if persisted in, must be considered by the commissioner to be detrimental to baseball."[21] There was little expansion talk over the next two years.

It was Frick who reopened discussion at a Houston speech in May 1957, by then aware the Giants and Dodgers were serious about relocating to California and Houston was clamoring for a franchise. He proclaimed the Majors "must be extended from coast to coast, north to south. . . . I don't know when it will be or what form it will take but I have a hunch we will see three major leagues. . . . I believe in a fundamental theory that baseball cannot sit tight. Baseball has sat tight for about fifty years. The time has come when serious thought must be given to a change."[22] The logjam appeared broken, with expansion again a topic of discussion.

The pending California moves would break the logjam, largely due to New York losing two of its three ball clubs. Spink played off Frick's Houston speech and the pending moves: "Ford Frick never spoke with greater wisdom than when he told *The Sporting News* recently that Organized Ball must look at the entire picture of possible expansion. It is high time the game's top brass worked out a long-range program which will pinpoint its plans for the future, instead of leaving them to chance." Spink added it was "inconceivable that New York, with ten times the population of some other big league cities, should be reduced to one big league club."[23] His comments, coupled with another round of antitrust hearings, got Frick's attention, and he organized a meeting with Minor League presidents to consider the effects of the California moves.[24] The ongoing speculation on expansion would take a new turn, eventually producing more serious consideration.

NEW YORK'S SINGING THE BLUES

New York officials certainly shared Spink's opinion about their city being left with one team. They had been aware the Giants might move, with Minneapolis–Saint Paul the likely location. That was fine if the Dodgers stayed. After all, New York was by far the largest city in the United States, and while Boston, St. Louis, and Philadelphia had lost teams, they were far smaller than the Big Apple. So was Chicago, which still had two clubs. Many politicians, including Mayor Robert Wagner, were so confident of not losing both that they ignored warning signals, including the Dodgers' purchase of the LA farm club and sale of Ebbets Field. Surely, O'Malley wouldn't depart from his roots. After he moved and Wagner won reelection, the mayor became focused.[25] New York, in his mind, could not be a one-league city.

The demeanor of Warren Giles, National League president, didn't provide comfort. As *New York Times* sportswriter Arthur Daley noted, Giles conveyed "total unconcern over the disappearance of his circuit from New York and patted himself on the back for being so progressive as to have franchises in California. That's pure hogwash. It was surprising that a man in his position could mouth such empty words. . . . What baseball needs right now is a dictator. . . . Commissioner Ford Frick has no powers to remake the baseball map and it's a shame he couldn't be granted such Hitlerian privileges." Prophetically, Daley claimed that only with expansion could New York obtain a National League club.[26] His comments didn't stop Wagner from pursuing options.

With the official departure of the Dodgers, the mayor announced a committee to bring a team back in November, naming four prominent New York business leaders. James Farley, an executive with Coca Cola, had served as postmaster general under FDR and was twice considered for baseball commissioner. Bernard Gimbel was chief executive of the New York department store bearing his name. Clinton W. Blume was a real estate executive and once a Major League player. William Shea was a New York lawyer with strong Democratic connections and a reputation for getting things accomplished.[27] When it became clear no National League team was likely to relocate, the committee requested a meeting with Frick.

As the committee met during the December holidays, a possibility came up that the vacancy might be filled—Powel Crosley indicated his Cincinnati Redlegs were interested. He was having difficulties negotiating a new stadium agreement, especially over additional parking spaces. During the meeting, Frick suggested the move could receive quick approval, though there was disagreement on whether the Yankees could block it.[28] The possibility was rendered moot when it became clear Crosley used the potential relocation as a bargaining ploy for Cincinnati concessions. The committee, headed by Shea, was back to square one.

Even before the Dodgers' move was finalized, the issue of territorial rights had percolated. The American League claimed that if the Dodgers joined the Giants, then after fifteen days the other league relinquished any claim to bring in another club. The National League, supported by Frick, insisted those rights were maintained.[29] In effect, if the commissioner was correct, then New York would become an open market for an existing or new National League franchise. The issue remained a topic of debate for the next nine months, though Rule 1(c) made clear the Yankees, starting fifteen days after the clubs departed, could block any move. Frick thus was overly optimistic, though he was confident the open-market concept would be adopted by both leagues. Territorial rights dated to the National League's founding in 1876, when the eight members were granted exclusive rights in their cities. It was reestablished when the two leagues signed the National Agreement in 1903 and strengthened with the 1922 Supreme Court *Federal Baseball* decision, exempting the sport from antitrust laws. As interpreted, a team was able to use territorial rights to prevent another club from moving there. By making a city an open market, a second team was permitted under negotiated guidelines.

The problem with the open-market concept was that it didn't exist in actuality. Frick acknowledged such in October when the Dodgers departed, putting territorial issues on hold until the Giants and Dodgers reached deals with the Pacific Coast League. Then there would be a fifteen-day waiting period until New York would "become American League territory under terms of the present rule. It would then take the consent of the American League clubs to permit a team from another league to invade their territory."[30] At that point, both leagues, under current guidelines, were required to consent to allow a National League club to move to New York. Frick believed he could get the rule changed. That wasn't easily done. Territorial rights were discussed extensively at the Winter Meetings, but at Frick's request, the leagues took no action, allowing him to maintain the open-market concept. He appointed a four-man committee, chaired by Frank Lane, to establish a policy for larger cities, with the leagues represented equally.[31] The committee offered a proposal that Frick supported enthusiastically: any city with a population over two million should be declared open. By 1957 standards, that included New York, LA, Philadelphia, and Detroit. Before a second club could locate there, an appropriate ballpark was required, and both leagues had to approve, with the commissioner breaking a tie vote. The new club's ballpark had to be more than five miles from the existing club, and if another team moved to LA in the next five years, the Dodgers would be compensated in part.[32] It appeared Frick had an operative policy.

In fact, he suggested modifications. He felt three million might be a better standard but added that, regardless, New York was already open territory. He added that a new ballpark would need to be constructed in New York, acknowledging Ebbets Field and the Polo Grounds were too antiquated. He added that the city needed to aid construction: "It must be accepted that private capital can no longer build a modern stadium." Instead, cities must have a "municipally owned and operated year-round recreation stadium."[33] Essentially, Frick was promoting all-purpose stadiums, financed primarily by government. Further, such a stadium was the only way New York could gain a second club.

Unfortunately for the commissioner, neither requirement—a new ballpark nor territorial rights—was easy to achieve. Shea's committee was clear on the stadium and was beginning the process of financing and constructing only when a franchise commitment was received. The issue of territorial rights—what constituted an open market and whether any compensation for the existing club was included—remained contested. Both came to the forefront at the February meeting in 1958. The focus was Lane's proposal, which reiterated the committee's December proposal while glossing over Frick's suggestions.[34] Unsurprisingly, the Yankees resisted. So did the Tigers. With Detroit approaching the two-million population mark, the team demanded a higher minimum. The Tigers also wanted both leagues to approve without the commissioner being able to break a tie. Finally, the owner demanded compensation if the other league moved there. Detroit also argued that Lane's committee lacked representation, since none of the members was an owner.[35] Both leagues rejected the proposal but invited Shea's committee to attend the Summer Meetings.[36] Disappointed, Frick remained optimistic about resolving the open-city issue.

Frick incorporated the Tigers' suggestions, adding two owners to Lane's committee, resulting in alterations to the proposal. The new policy addressed relocation to a city with an existing franchise, raising the population level to exclude all cities except New York, LA, and San Francisco. It addressed relocations specifically. Only the league of the relocating team, along with the commissioner, needed to approve the move. The existing team in that city and its league would have no say. The proposal further stipulated the following: "Such approval by the commissioner shall be withheld until after hearings have been held and necessary investigations conducted." Shea considered it a good step but also expected an expression of "an active interest in moving a team" from the National League.[37] Both leagues had to approve the proposal.

Neither did. The American League discussed franchise relocations, while stressing that no club, even the Senators, was requesting permission to relocate. Expansion wasn't on the league's agenda. The National League entertained William Shea and Mayor Robert Wagner's proposal for a new stadium, located in Flushing Meadows, a location the Dodgers had rejected. Although Wagner made it clear that no funding would be committed until a franchise was assured, the league gave Shea's committee an audience and also created a committee to study expansion.[38] It appeared Wagner and Shea had made some progress, but that soon changed. When the leagues convened for a special meeting in September, both voted to remain at eight teams through 1959, putting expansion off the table. Frick also indicated such: "I favor expansion and . . . it is bound to come, but at this time I have no program and therefore no recommendations to make."[39] What prompted Frick is unclear, but he may have realized he lacked sufficient support in either league. Arthur Daley called the meeting a waste of time, referring to Frick as "a sound-thinking but powerless man. He wants an orderly process on expansion to ten teams, but he's getting nowhere." He concluded the only place owners had sensitivity was their pocketbooks.[40] Needless to say, Shea and Wagner felt the rug had been pulled out from under them.

During the meeting, Frick articulated a vision of how expansion should occur. It proved prophetic, projecting what would actually occur over the next twelve years, though rejected in 1958: "I formerly talked about a third major league. I have changed. To my way of thinking, the answer now would be two twelve-club leagues. Each league would have two six-team sections. The clubs would play all the teams in their own sections, plus a limited number of games with the teams in the other section of the same league. At the end of the season, the two winners would meet in a special playoff. . . . Most certainly, within ten years, I expect to see twenty-four major league clubs in this country."[41] He was slightly off on timing, but on target with the format. For the next two years, though, he vacillated due to Shea's new strategy.

THINKING CONTINENTALLY

Shea made the bombshell announcement on November 13, 1958: his committee would establish a new eight-team league, starting with New York. He proposed a stadium at Flushing Meadows and new investors from seven cities without Major League clubs. He added that the league would raid the Majors and Minors for players if necessary.[42] Effectively, Shea proposed an outlaw league, one engaging in salary wars and talent bidding. The concept wasn't new. The American League started as an outlaw league in 1901, competing for players until the National Agreement. The Federal League emerged in the same fashion in 1914; though only lasting two years, the league left legacies, including baseball's antitrust exemption and Wrigley Field. Both the pre-1903 American League and the Federal League had been Minor Leagues with established organizations, whereas Shea's would start from scratch.

The reaction from baseball was unfavorable. Frick was outspoken: "Everyone knows I am in favor of the New York territory being kept open for a major league club. The threat to raid the National and American Leagues for players is a serious issue. . . . I cannot conceive of players joining a third league and forfeiting their pension rights." Other officials echoed him. Not surprisingly, Emanuel Celler strongly endorsed the idea: "It would inject some competition into baseball's present monopoly."[43] Branch Rickey echoed him. Still associated with the Pirates but largely retired, he emphasized, "'America is ready for a third league,' although adding that the raiding of players would be 'most unfortunate.'" In an attempt to avoid confrontation, he continued, "The cities are there, the population is there, but I think it should be organized by the two present major leagues." He disavowed any involvement. However, Shea was unfamiliar with baseball's structure and politics. Rickey's later role suggests he was already a resource.[44]

In any case, Rickey wasn't the only cautious one. The day after his announcement, Shea promised to "consult Frick when the proposal for the new league is ready." He added the league would only operate independently if the Majors rejected them. Frick responded that a new league would "require a lot of work and planning and how all of this can be done without the help and advice of the commissioner I wouldn't know." J. Norman Lewis, attorney for the Major League Baseball Players' Association, speculated players wouldn't consider jumping, as the new league would have an acute challenge starting, given the reserve clause.[45] Regardless, the league had no investors or cities lined up other than New York.

Baseball's reaction wasn't totally in concert with Frick. Giles remained adamant that his league had no desire to expand. He was dead set against a new league, fearing a loss of quality: "We must keep a small structure rather than enlarging it and diluting it. If enlargement means a dilution of our product, we are not keeping faith with the people." Instead, he proposed strengthening the Minors.[46] Frick kept his distance: "I believe thoroughly in expansion, and I believe expansion is inevitable. I am for it and I am for another team in New York. It is not that I am in opposition to Warren [Giles] or am trying to find fault with him. It is simply that we do not agree on this matter."[47] Clearly, the top brass wasn't on the same page in reacting to a potential renegade league.

Much of that was rectified at the 1958 Winter Meetings. Giles again expressed his opposition to expansion, whether through additional teams or a new league. Two days later, however, his league directed two owners to hire a national research agency to investigate expansion and realignment along with changes in policy and procedure. The American League concurred, and the leagues named Phil Wrigley, Walter O'Malley, Arnold Johnson of the Athletics, and George Medinger of the Indians to the committee. It was hoped this might encourage Shea to work with Frick.[48] Expansion was back on baseball's agenda.

As a result, matters appeared nebulous as the expansion committee began and Shea continued efforts to find investors. In mid-April Shea announced progress, mentioning that six cities—New York, Houston, Toronto, Montreal, Dallas, and Minneapolis–Saint Paul—were lined up: "We have made progress, but we do not think it is in the best interests to issue any statement at this time." Frick responded, "I don't know anything about a third major league. I don't know who the people are. Apparently, they are not working within organized baseball." Shea ignored the suggestion to work jointly with Frick. "It's our firm opinion that the only way by which New York would obtain another major league franchise would be through the formation of a third major league," said Shea.[49] Shea's committee appeared uninterested in working with baseball, even as it expressed renewed interest in expansion.

Frick, perhaps prompted by the Senate Subcommittee on Antitrust and Monopoly having scheduled hearings in late July on baseball's antitrust exemption, decided on a new approach. Frick had gone through a tumultuous hearing before Celler's subcommittee the previous year, and the friction between the Majors and the upstart league weighed on him, especially the attention the new league received from Congress. Hence, he called for a special meeting of owners and executives at the estate of Pirates owner John Galbreath, near Columbus, Ohio. The focus was on how the Majors should approach Shea's league, given the upcoming hearings. The outcome startled the sports world as baseball announced it was open to a new league. Frick said, "The major leagues recognize the desire of certain groups to obtain major league franchises. Since there is no existing plan to expand the present major leagues, the two Major Leagues declare they will favorably consider an application for major league status within the present baseball structure by an acceptable group of eight clubs that would qualify."[50] No specifics were mentioned, though he was clearly referring to Shea's organization.

The Galbreath meeting established ten conditions a new league had to meet: (1) The eight clubs are responsible for all territorial provisions and financial obligations in constructing their organizations. (2) Full and complete data will be provided on financial structure. (3) All eight cities must be larger than the smallest in the Majors. (4) All ballparks must accommodate a minimum of twenty-five thousand people. (5) The league should have a balanced schedule of at least 154 games. (6) The league should have the same minimum salary as the Majors, with no maximum limitations. (7) It will become party to the Major League agreement and professional baseball agreement. (8) The league must accept the uniform Major League player's contract and its provisions. (9) It will join the players' pension plan or adopt one comparable. (10) It should file the application for approval six months prior to consideration. Frick added, "I have always thought that such expansion is inevitable. I firmly believe we will have a third major league within five years. That, of course, is a personal opinion."[51] One condition not mentioned, which later would become an obstacle, was incurring the costs for dislocating Minor League clubs, which was already done by both Major Leagues. Still, the Majors had laid out conditions by which it would accept a league, seemingly a dramatic shift.

Shea initially did not respond, though he likely was aware of sportswriters' speculations on why Major League Baseball had shifted. In a *Chicago Tribune* column, David Conlin posited three reasons: First, pending legislation was in Congress. Second, he pointed to Branch Rickey's past baseball success, implying his involvement. Third, he surmised Frick believed many cities were large enough to support Major League baseball, while most owners opposed expansion. Conlin also interpreted the guidelines as saying, "You're welcome, but you'll have to do all the work—including finding the players—by yourselves."[52] In that regard, Conlin was on target. Also notable was his anticipation that Rickey would have a role. Arthur Daley was even more cynical: "That was a mighty noble and unselfish gesture the big-league owners made last week in unexpectedly deciding to welcome the formation of a third major league. If they continue to let themselves be carried away by such generosity, they next will announce that there will be no charge for the air that fans breathe at the ball parks. . . . Except for an empty permission, they offer nothing." Daley concluded the only workable approach was expansion.[53] He wasn't alone.

Before the Senate hearings in late July, Burton Hawkins, sportswriter for the *Washington Star*, obtained viewpoints anonymously of "two highly-respected major league officials" concerning the third league. Both considered it pure politics: "Ford Frick's talk in Columbus recently about smoothing the path for a third major league was a gesture. The man is scared to death of Celler and Kefauver, but let's face it—baseball is a monopoly and the present 16 major league owners aren't going to dilute their holdings." Further, the new league would "have to get up to $15,000,000 to match what's in the players' pension fund. Augmenting stadiums already existing and building new stadiums will cost each city $8,000,000 to $12,000,000. Then they need players, farm systems, officials and so forth." In conclusion, the sources asserted, "For political purposes, a third major league is good for lowering wool over innocent eyes. Such talk may win votes in New York, proposed hub of the new wheel. It may delay anti-monopoly legislation being authored by Rep. Celler or Sen. Kefauver, but a third major league figures to be strangled slowly, surviving only on paper as long as it will serve a purpose."[54] Although their comments proved prophetic, they didn't impact the Senate hearings.

Frick and Shea were the ones who did have an impact on the hearings. By conducting the Galbreath meeting and announcing support for a third league, Frick reduced any desire from Shea for legislation. Thus, when Shea met with Chairman Estes Kefauver first, he requested no action that would affect baseball's support until after his meeting with Frick in August. That achieved Frick's objective, stopping Kefauver's proposal to limit the number of players a Major League team controlled to eighty. Most clubs had hundreds under contract, and needless to say, Frick opposed the limit: "No, it doesn't abolish the reserve clause, but it does impair it. I'm absolutely opposed to the whole bill. If it should become law, I can't see how anyone could be interested in operating a ball club, much less new people coming in." He was pleased Shea interceded, as Frick believed any player restrictions would harm the efforts of the new league.[55] Shea's request also guaranteed nothing would come from the hearings, though the player-limit threat remained.

Perhaps the biggest news at the hearings was from William Shea's testimony. He named his league the Continental and announced the first five cities—New York, Toronto, Houston, Denver, and Minneapolis–Saint Paul. He was certain the others would soon follow, promising each ballpark would seat at least thirty-five thousand fans. All clubs' investors would provide an initial $2.5 million, and the league would begin in 1961.[56] The following day, before Frick testified, Shea criticized Giles and Joe Cronin, the new American League president, for their comments. Giles asserted that five teams did not constitute a league, and Cronin suggested the league would hurt the Minors and have difficulty acquiring talent. Shea replied,

"I wish these league presidents would talk with Ford C. Frick before they go popping off with statements like that." By then it was rumored Rickey might be named the league's commissioner.[57] Giles and Cronin made clear that regardless of Rickey's involvement, the Continental League didn't have full support from baseball's top brass.

Frick did damage control during his testimony. He promised baseball was "on the level" in helping the new league, convinced Shea was making a "bona fide effort." He also stressed that limiting each club to eighty players would not only hurt the new league but also "tend to wreck both the major and minor leagues and lower the quality of professional baseball play."[58] Although the committee took no action, the comments by the league presidents generated a response from Kefauver. Using pointed language, he advised baseball to aid the third league.[59] Implicit was unwanted legislation if it did not. With the end of the hearings and the announcement from Shea of the Continental League, the stage was set for the league's meeting with Frick. Two days before, however, Frick dampened expectations: "I can't see how this meeting can possibly be anything more than an exploratory one with many more to follow before we can get anywhere. . . . I am going to the meeting prepared to help in any way possible." Shea countered, "The expansion to a third league in inevitable. Let's get on with it while we have the men and money to promote it." Shea said he was seeking clarification on four points: players, territorial rights, pensions, and additional cities.[60] Frick's dampening of expectations was closer to reality.

In fact, the biggest story at the meeting was Branch Rickey, seventy-seven, being named commissioner. Rickey resigned from his titular position with Pittsburgh to devote full time to the endeavor, thus avoiding any conflict of interest. Shea indicated, "We felt he was the only man who could conclude the operation we have undertaken. He didn't want the job. We had to plead with him." Frick didn't comment on Rickey but noted afterward, "It was a very friendly and cooperative meeting. The baseball committee has given its unanimous support of the new league provided it meets with of baseball's rules and regulations." With that comment, Frick reiterated that the ten requirements listed in May remained. He added that they would meet again as soon as the Continental League secured its last three cities.[61] Frick made no indication that anything would be expedited by baseball, even with the intent to commence the Continental League in 1961.

Two weeks later, testifying before Celler's subcommittee, Frick questioned the 1961 timeline. Most of Celler's hearing focused on televising Major League games in Minor League markets, coupled with concern baseball might switch to pay television in the future. The Continental League wasn't discussed until the third day. Frick reiterated what he told the Kefauver committee in July, that ending the reserve clause or limiting the number of players controlled would not help the new league. He also emphasized, "I have been on record that my personal feeling has always been that the proper procedure would be to expand. I think it would be easier." He added that since Major League owners got behind the new league, he supported it. However, its biggest problems were obtaining players and developing a farm system, which he believed would be doable in six years.[62] His comments received mixed reaction from committee members, but no legislative action was taken.

Shea did pick up on Frick's comments in the hearings, responding a month later. He criticized Frick for not supporting the league's start in 1961, claiming the date was realistic if baseball cooperated. Shea also said that Frick's comments were not in keeping with his promise of cooperation, though he also stressed that he didn't want the Continental League to be an outlaw league or to violate the reserve clause.[63] Still, his comments suggested considerable friction existed. Later that month, Shea received additional cause for concern. The American League appointed a committee of three—George Weiss, Hank Greenberg, and Bill DeWitt of Detroit—to study expansion and suggested it could expand into LA and the Twin Cities and their counterpart league could expand into New York and Houston. Joe Cronin clarified there was no intent to add clubs in 1960, but the following year was a possibility. Shea claimed the committee was set up "for propaganda purposes and to hurt the Continental League." Rickey accused Frick of reneging on his promise to support the new league rather than expand. Frick responded, "At no time was a commitment made that we would sit still and wait for a new league to be formed. I am saying now what I have always said. I am not an advocate of a third league but of expansion."[64] The battle lines were again drawn.

SHOWDOWN IN THE SENATE

Predictably, William Shea accused Frick of blocking the Continental League; he thus threatened to go outlaw to acquire players.[65] Frick then stressed that the league had to conform to standards: "From the beginning

I've declared for expansion of major league baseball, whether it is done by expanding the two major leagues or by establishing a third one. But taking sides in this is not my job. My job is simply to see that whatever is done is accomplished according to baseball law. Certainly Mr. Rickey knows this and what the laws are." Covering that response, sportswriter John Drebinger considered Frick "a mild-mannered fellow who doesn't lose his temper easily. But, he's certainly getting close."[66] Frick's long-term friendship with Rickey was tested.

The Continental League was pleased, however, at the Winter Meetings' outcome. The National League rejected the other league's proposal that they each add one club and begin interleague play, and the American League consequently ended expansion efforts. Following those decisions, Frick announced, "Now that the American and National Leagues have reinstated their positions announced last May, the Continental League continues to have the opportunity to proceed with its announced program."[67] The new league had further reason for optimism, as it gained the final commitments—Atlanta, Dallas–Fort Worth, and Buffalo—at the end of January 1960.

Both sides had additional reasons for reconciling when Senator Kenneth Keating of New York offered to mediate to achieve accommodation before Kefauver's committee reconvened to consider legislation restricting Major League Baseball. As a congressman, Keating had worked closely with Frick and was largely favorable to baseball. Because he represented New York state, he had a vested interest in seeing a National League franchise return to the Big Apple. Both sides accepted mediation after each met with Keating independently. Frick noted that Keating's involvement wouldn't be necessary if the new league met baseball's conditions, adding if the new league developed its own talent, it would likely take four years to achieve Major League status.[68] It appeared progress was possible, though Frick still didn't share Rickey's optimism on the starting date. Rickey remained determined, announcing after the last cities were finalized that his league would definitely start in 1961.[69] The sides were still far apart.

That became clear in April, when the Continental League attempted to establish its first Minor League in eight North Carolina towns. The Western Carolina League, one of those that folded during the 1950s, was attempting a return. Rickey was a friend of John Moss, who had been involved with the earlier league; Moss agreed to establish the Continental

League's first Minor League. Its structure, however, would be different than that of the Majors—the players wouldn't be assigned to specific clubs in the new league. Frick nixed it. First, baseball's rules prohibited such pooling. Second, Major League Baseball did not recognize the Continental League yet because it hadn't achieved indemnifications with Minor League clubs in its cities. The new Minor League could exist, but it could not function under the auspices proposed.[70] That ruling would stand, though it generated backlash.

That came not only from Shea and Rickey, as expected, but also from Congress. Irked by Frick's opposition to the Western Carolina League structure, Shea exclaimed that baseball should "help us or suffer the consequences."[71] Emanuel Celler, now clearly an adversary, agreed: "They keep Shea and Branch Rickey on tender hooks with nice promises of help, but no performance." Celler further suggested that Shea bring an antitrust lawsuit against baseball and even encouraged the Continental League to raid its players.[72] Encouraged, Rickey threatened to go outlaw yet stressed he preferred not going outside "the canopy of baseball." Frick responded, "I wonder if it wouldn't help a bit if we had fewer complaints, less alibiing, and a little more positive action."[73] The friction escalated as the Kefauver hearings loomed.

When the proposed legislation was announced, it was clear Frick wouldn't view it favorably because it limited the control of players by every Major League ball club to one hundred. Further, sixty of those exempted could be made available each year, and indemnification to displaced Minor League clubs would be limited. In essence, the legislation was highly favorable for the Continental League because, on average, the sixteen Major League teams each controlled 193 players, with the bill reducing that by half and even availing most of them for the new league.[74] Rickey and Shea were pleased, as it addressed two major concerns—obtaining players and the expense of compensating relocated Minor League clubs. Frick minced few words in opposition, calling the legislation "vicious, discriminatory, badly written and disastrous." Elaboration wasn't necessary, but he expanded on his comment anyway: "This bill is absolutely unacceptable because it goes beyond antitrust exemptions and attempts to spell out the operating rules for baseball."[75] Further, he said, "Anybody who knows anything about baseball realizes that if this became federal law, the minors would be put out of business. . . . Scouting staffs would be disbanded. Bonuses to young players would be eliminated. Farm systems would be broken up. Subsidies to minor league clubs would be done away with. . . . Does the Congress want this? I know it doesn't."[76]

As the hearings approached, Shea conveyed what his league would do if the legislation failed—"fight or quit"—adding the latter was not an option. Instead, he claimed, "I don't believe they'd dare sue us if we raided them for players. They know they wouldn't have a leg to stand on. The reserve clause in a player's contract isn't worth the paper it's written on, but I hope it doesn't come to this."[77] He seemed prepared to go to court if legislation failed. Arthur Daley was skeptical. Calling the legislation confiscatory for setting a limited price on the sixty players subject to the draft, he claimed, "The Continental cannot go outlaw . . . because no player will walk out on the pension plan. If the third league can only gain a foothold through government intercession, its plight is more desperate than most folks suppose."[78] Essentially, he believed Shea's threats were hollow, even as the two sides grew increasingly polarized.

The hearings were limited to five witnesses, three for the Continental League and two for organized baseball. Shea, Rickey, and former Senator Edwin Johnson testified for the Continental League, and Frick and George M. Trautman spoke for baseball. Their testimony was predictable, offering little new. There were, however, some insightful and prophetic tidbits. Shea made known his major objective: "I have a job to do. We want a second team in New York." Johnson stressed that unless the bill was enacted, "the Continental League will be a dead duck and it isn't likely that anyone again will try to organize another major league." Rickey attempted to justify why he opposed expansion seven years earlier when he claimed there wasn't enough talent. Frick reminded the committee of the Celler committee's conclusion eight years prior: "Congress cannot properly, nor should it enact a comprehensive code to govern every detail of baseball's business." Trautman summarized, "I would be unforgivingly remiss in my obligation to those who elected me president were I not to oppose it [the legislation] most vigorously."[79] The testimony from the five was not surprising nor impactful.

What did have an impact was baseball's lobbying effort. Baseball developed an extensive grassroots structure, discussed later, built on personal contacts with members of both houses. Congressional relationships of those involved with Major and Minor League teams were identified and utilized when legislation affecting baseball was proposed. Contacts were made in person, by telephone, or by telegram. In this hearing, contacts came from those personally acquainted with the senators. It helped that key committee members, especially Keating and Philip Hart, were strongly supportive of baseball and represented both political parties. Both served baseball well in the Senate.

Such proved true here as the Judiciary Committee sent the bill to the Senate floor without recommendation, basically guaranteeing defeat. It lacked recommendation due to strong opposition, especially from Keating, Hart, and Senator Alexander Wiley of Wisconsin. Kefauver still pushed it forward.[80] It was rejected by a 73–12 margin on the floor and sent back for reconsideration, meaning that with little time left on the Senate calendar the bill was dead. The Continental League would have to struggle to obtain players and faced substantial costs for indemnification, certainly delaying its start. Rickey still insisted it wouldn't be halted, while Frick countered that the league would have to pay indemnifications to even be recognized.[81]

Though Rickey wasn't ready to acknowledge it, the writing was on the wall and became clearer after the Majors' Summer Meetings. The National League voted to expand to ten teams in response the bill's defeat. The Junior Circuit also indicated its readiness to expand, and both leagues established committees to prepare for the Continental League's demise. Frick stressed he could not perceive of any expansion plans without New York, complicating the Continental League's problems further because William Shea considered the action "a hopeful sign."[82] It seemed Major League expansion was imminent and a third league dead.

A meeting was held in early August between Rickey, Shea, and Continental League investors on one hand and Frick, Giles, Cronin, and representatives from some clubs on the other hand. It made the end of the third league official. All parties agreed both Major Leagues would expand into markets identified by the Continental League, with priority given to its investors.[83] In the Sports of the Times column, John Drebinger summarized Frick's achievement: "Needless to say, the commissioner is highly pleased with the turn developments have taken. He had recommended more than 5 years ago that the majors had better lend a serious eye to expansion by taking in the more prosperous minor league cities. However, to gain his end he had to play a shrewd, cool hand." Acknowledging the commissioner was aware considerable work lay ahead, Drebinger added that Frick "has no intention of letting them [the owners] slip back into their former snug complacency now that the Continentals are safely out of their hair." He also speculated that New York, Houston, and Minneapolis–Saint Paul were certain choices.[84] It appeared Frick achieved his expansion goal.

Some scholars have viewed the demise of the Continental League with remorse. Russell D. Buhite noted its many positive innovations. A high percentage of the television revenue and gate receipts were to be shared equally among the eight clubs, with the larger markets not benefiting from greater television revenue, as existed with the Majors. Minor League talent would be controlled and developed by the league rather than individual teams, facilitating development, directed and funded by Continental League's central office.[85] That helped ensure parity. It is questionable, however, whether those policies would have been executed had they joined the Majors. Baseball had its own rules and was unlikely to alter them to accommodate the new entry. In any case, expansion would occur without incorporating the Continental League's innovations. And, though expansion was now certain, Frick would wonder in the coming months whether the trials he faced made it worthwhile.

A "LEAGUE MATTER"?

It didn't take long after the August meeting for doubts to surface. At a banquet the same month before a Yankee old-timers game, Dan Topping pressured Frick on whether he would declare LA an open city like New York, thus meriting a second ball club. Frick responded, "I don't think this is the time or place, but I will accept the challenge." He acknowledged that any city reaching LA's size should be a candidate for a second club.[86] Days later, in his Sports of the Times column, Drebinger supported Frick: "The Continental may moan a bit at having only three instead of four of their cities accepted in a new amalgamation. But then that Chicago meeting, it's been carefully pointed out, was only a committee, not a major league level. . . . Besides, the Continentals are no longer in a position to wage much of a fight anyway."[87] Drebinger anticipated the developing controversy.

Still, until the leagues met in October, speculation on prospective cities was subdued. Limited reporting suggested the process would be peaceful and the new clubs wouldn't begin until 1962. Del Webb, chair of the American League expansion committee, met with Frick to discuss options, with both indicating afterward that the process would be achieved peacefully before the 1962 season. It was also conjectured that

LA wouldn't be included. Frick elaborated, "As a result, four Continental League areas will come into the majors in time to play in 1962, and Los Angeles will come into the American League with the second draft, before 1965, if it does not get a franchise sooner, by transfer."[88] Essentially, O'Malley could still expect to have LA to himself, and additional expansion seemed imminent by 1965, when each league would add two more clubs. Expansion so far appeared harmonious.

The separate October meetings changed that dramatically and reignited controversy. The process started calmly. During the World Series, the cities of New York and Houston, along with their ownership groups, applied for National League franchises. Houston representatives had held discussions with the Junior Circuit but concluded the National League made more sense. Both anticipated acceptance the following week when the National League officials met. Frick was pleased: "I think this is the first concrete step in the right direction. I have always talked expansion. I have always favored expansion. Expansion is the answer to baseball's problems. I think it is just great if we should now get our expansion program underway."[89] The commissioner spoke cautiously, though, not wanting to get ahead of the official meetings. Del Webb, spearheading the American League's expansion, was coy, saying only his league was ready, but adding it was not limited to Continental League cities. Although he didn't counter speculation that the league would select Dallas–Fort Worth and Minneapolis–Saint Paul, it was public knowledge that Hank Greenberg was assembling a group to consider LA.[90] The American League offered no reaction, however, regarding the cities requesting National League franchises.

The National League meeting in Chicago proceeded as expected. Both New York and Houston were accepted, starting in 1962. Giles added that he anticipated two additional clubs within four years. He recognized the other league had to approve the New York club but added that Frick held the tie-breaking vote and favored two teams in both New York and LA. As for the American League moving into LA, O'Malley provided a ready answer: "I don't think that would be very smart. I believe they will go to the coast eventually. San Diego and Seattle are wonderful cities."[91] Again, the Junior Circuit didn't suggest any controversy, as Cronin approved the two selections, agreeing New York was an open city and announcing their meeting on October 26.[92] For Frick, the process was proceeding as expected.

Until the American League dropped a bombshell, that is. First, it allowed Cal Griffith to relocate to Minneapolis–Saint Paul, with Washington—in line with Frick's wishes—receiving an expansion club. The other new franchise would be in LA. The biggest surprise was that the new clubs would start in 1961, merely months away. Further, no Continental League investors were involved. Frick was surprised, though ambiguous in his initial response: "I haven't seen anything official yet. There are so many things to be considered, such as ball parks and what to do regarding players, that I cannot make any comment until I have talked to the people involved officially." The Junior Circuit approved the new franchises unanimously, while Griffith's move to Minnesota barely succeeded, 6–2.[93] The actions obviously caught many off guard, William Shea and Walter O'Malley among them. Shea called it "one of the lowest blows beneath the belt in the history of sports." O'Malley suggested the decision would "wreak havoc" on LA's sports scene and added his hope to get his own ballpark built before another team arrived. Celler expressed satisfaction with both leagues, to which Shea responded, "He's been fooled because the N.L. put a team in New York."[94] The American League decisions had clearly generated controversy.

A day later, having absorbed the actions, Frick clarified his response. He approved the American League decisions with caveats: "I do think the A.L. would have used better judgment were it to delay its expansion plans until 1962. . . . There is a tremendous lot of work to be done if they are going to do this next spring and frankly it looks to me like a mighty tough assignment." He acknowledged he would have to get involved if either league balked about New York or LA. He also indicated no concern about Continental League reaction because the promise to locate in their cities with their investors was not at an official meeting. Shea was now more accepting, pleased his main mission—a National League team in New York—had been accomplished, though he still regarded the action "a low blow." The American League announced that Elwood Quesada, a former director of the Federal Aviation Administration, would head a group purchasing the new Washington franchise.[95] There was no announcement for LA, which, coupled with the 1961 start, guaranteed serious problems lay ahead.

A column by Shirley Povich in *The Sporting News* provided a partial explanation for the seemingly rash actions. Essentially, Junior Circuit owners felt double-crossed by the National League. Del Webb stressed that the two leagues were supposed to have acted in concert for their decisions, but instead "they pulled a fast one on us before the World's Series and held a hurry-up meeting to take in New York and Houston." Webb believed it was O'Malley's doing. Povich contended that Webb took pleasure in invading O'Malley's domain, especially while his stadium was still under construction, and noted Webb believed his league would become a "bush league" if not positioned on the West Coast.[96] Basically, his league's decisions appeared to stem from revenge and inferiority.

Frick was now concerned about how expansion had been handled, calling Cronin and Giles to his office and leaving little doubt of his dissatisfaction. Pointedly, he outlined how expansion would be handled going forward: "Any further expansion steps should be taken jointly following executive sessions for the leagues in which the league presidents and the commissioner should be present." He emphasized that expansion could no longer be a league matter: "We must avoid going off on tangents and getting at dagger point on issues of mutual concern. When we take new clubs into the majors, we must be sure they go in under a strong program."[97] Frick implied a minor step toward consolidation under the commissioner, noting the leagues could no longer act independently on some issues.

In the meantime, steps were undertaken to clarify the still undefined franchise awarded to LA. Coming out of the meeting where it was chosen, Hank Greenberg, president and part owner of Bill Veeck's White Sox, was the frontrunner. Responding to O'Malley's comments that another team in LA "would wreak havoc," he asserted, "I'm not interested in O'Malley's opinions, but only those of the people of Los Angeles." O'Malley maintained his position, citing problems with leasing the Coliseum, given the other sports venues utilizing it. He said that "we had hoped to get our own problems in pioneering the territory and building our stadium behind us before the relatives moved in." Greenberg was nonplussed.[98] He exulted confidence while visiting his potential market. O'Malley had reason for concern. The White Sox president had been not only a Hall of Fame star but also a successful executive. Hired by Veeck for the Indians in 1948, he soon became general manager, remaining until 1957. During that period, the Indians were consistently a premier team, winning the pennant in 1954 and finishing second otherwise. The White Sox also won a pennant for Greenberg in his first year. Essentially, he had a proven track record. Moreover, he was closely tied to Veeck, who had been interested in Southern California since surveying for Wrigley in 1954. Sources speculated Veeck might sell the Sox with intent to run the LA franchise later.[99] If nothing else, Veeck's promotional successes concerned O'Malley, as he was still getting established and had invested heavily in the move and the ballpark.

O'Malley had other reasons. Greenberg indicated a desire to play in the Coliseum, creating substantial challenges for usage. O'Malley feared his Dodgers could be excluded from many good game dates. Further, Greenberg had also announced C. Arnholt Smith, owner of the Minor League San Diego Padres, as his major investor, who had ardently opposed O'Malley in his efforts to obtain Chavez Ravine for his ballpark.[100] The Dodgers' owner likely conveyed his concerns to Frick.

Whatever was conveyed, Frick made his position clear in mid-November—both leagues must address the territorial issues for New York and LA before teams could move there. He referenced Rule 1(c), which read, "The circuit of either major league shall not be changed to include any city in the circuit of the other major league except by unanimous consent of both major leagues."[101] Although Frick had consistently declared both as open cities, neither league had revised the rules. The commissioner emphasized, "Rule one must be amended. Both leagues must get together and amend the rule.... Until that this done, I will not permit a second team to go into L.A. or into N.Y. for that matter."[102] That was unlikely to be addressed before the Winter Meetings. Though some sportswriters believed Frick was backtracking, he was consistent in insisting both leagues act on Rule 1(c) before enacting his open-city declaration.

The following day, November 16, Frick went further, indicating O'Malley would also need indemnification for some of the expenses he incurred in relocating the Dodgers. Otherwise, he would block the new club: "This is not a personal matter with me and I would take the same position if Greenberg were now in L.A. and O'Malley were trying to get in. It just isn't fair. O'Malley has spent about a million dollars setting up his Dodgers in Los Angeles and therefore is entitled to get some of it back from any A.L. club that wishes to share the territory. So far the new syndicate wants to pay nothing and I won't stand for that."[103] Again, Frick was consistent, having stated two years earlier that any LA move within five years required indemnification.

Whether intended or not, Frick's comments generated major reactions. Greenberg indicated he was dropping out, with the major reason being required to pay O'Malley anything. Veeck also reacted, having just rejected an offer of $4 million from Charles Finley for his 54 percent stake in the White Sox, which had apparently been entertained until Frick clarified the indemnification controversy. The following day, Greenberg withdrew, and Veeck announced he was remaining with the White Sox while accusing Frick of being partial to the National League and, in particular, to O'Malley.[104] On the same day the Washington ownership was announced, the status of the new LA club remained uncertain. Two new teams—Houston and Washington—were solidified. So was New York, except for lacking official clearance.

As the Winter Meetings approached, baseball's top brass was deeply engaged to resolve the dilemma. Frick traveled to LA to meet O'Malley. Shortly thereafter, so did Del Webb. The two owners then returned to New York for further meetings with Frick, including the two leagues' attorneys. Although Frick insisted that 1(c) had to be redressed, not just for present circumstances but also for the future, indemnification to both Dodgers and Yankees remained a stumbling block. Consequently, American League owners put forth a plan postponing resolution for a year. It was certainly a creative proposal and, if approved, would have provided an interesting 1961 season. Both LA and New York franchises would be postponed for a year due to Rule 1(c). Houston and Washington would begin in 1961 because neither was contested. Each league would become a nine-team circuit, thus requiring interleague play. The season would be 166 games, with each team playing two three-game series with the nine clubs in the other league, hence fifty-four games against the opposing league. Frick endorsed it: "It isn't the best answer in the world, but it is a solution to their [American League] problem. If the two leagues can get together on it, I will approve it."[105] All Junior Circuit owners supported the plan, giving the National League until the start of the Winter Meetings to approve it. At least one magnate—O'Malley—endorsed it, having favored interleague play already. Advantageously for him, it also postponed an American League franchise in LA for a year.[106] In many ways, it was a revolutionary solution to baseball's dilemma and generated considerable interest.

It proved short-lived. Initially, the Senior Circuit offered no reaction, with its magnates waiting until the deadline. Meanwhile, meetings between the commissioner, the league presidents, and their lawyers grew intense. At one point, it was rumored the American League would put a team in Houston for the 1961 season instead of LA, thus competing and gaining a year on the National League entry. Frick quickly extinguished that idea, stating he wouldn't tolerate it.[107] The meetings continued the following day, November 30, at the Minor League meetings. With no resolution again, Frick demanded "a rule that baseball can live with for years to come."[108] That appeared out of reach as the Senior Circuit left interleague play hanging.

Talks continued without resolution on 1(c) or a National League decision on interleague play. In a meeting with Webb, Frick, and the league presidents, O'Malley laid out the conditions required for him to accept an American League team. First, the team would not start until 1962 and wouldn't play in the Coliseum. Second, a yet-to-be-determined payment was required to offset some of his costs in moving. Third, the ultimate location of the new club would be at least fifteen miles from Chavez Ravine. Finally, the owners had to be generally interested in baseball and not just publicity seekers.[109] The last point reflected O'Malley's view of Veeck's baseball promotions. Shortly before, Arthur Daley concluded that the American League had discovered "to its dismay that it has painted itself into a corner of the room." He added that allowing the move to Minnesota compounded the problem, because Frick was adamant Washington must have a Major League club.[110] With nothing worked out during the Minor League sessions, it appeared the two Majors were heading into volatile Winter Meetings.

RESOLUTION

It remained volatile until the meetings. The new LA club still had no owner and no place to play and was uncertain it would even be permitted in 1961. Neither had the Senior Circuit decided on interleague play. The night before the meetings, there was an indication the dilemma would be resolved, based on a series of amendments to alter Rule 1(c). Still not publicized, they would formally be presented when the meetings started. Though Frick did not guarantee the amendments would be approved, he indicated there was support, adding that the nine-team proposal with interleague play would be rejected.[111] The commissioner's thoughts proved accurate, as the National League did reject nine-team leagues and interleague play, but Rule 1(c) remained unresolved. In fact, Frick held a meeting of owners from each league, including Webb but not O'Malley. Horace Stoneham was included, as was John Galbreath of the Pirates, who had played a key role resolving a pension dispute in 1954. The assignment for the committee was to hash out a solution to both Rule 1(c) and the new LA club.[112] The prospect of any resolution remained uncertain.

The following day, though, the pieces came together. First, the LA Angels finally had an owner—Gene Autry. Autry was well known to the general public as a movie star and country and western singer, most famous for "Rudolph the Red-Nosed Reindeer." Although his performing career was long past, he was a major owner of radio and television stations in California.[113] Charlie Finley, whose offer had been rejected by Veeck, then bid on the LA franchise, losing out again but soon purchasing the Athletics. With Autry, O'Malley now had someone with whom he could negotiate. In particular, Autry agreed to play initially in Wrigley Field in LA, now owned by the City of Los Angeles, and when Chavez Ravine was completed, he would play home games there until his stadium was built.[114] The picture on 1(c) still remained blurry.

That would change the next day. First, the remaining questions about the Angels were resolved. They would start in 1961 and not play at the Coliseum, as O'Malley had demanded. There were no limits on radio telecasts, but only eleven Angels games were allowed on television during their first year. The more significant resolution was changes made to Rule 1(c). For a second team to move into a city, it had to have a population of at least 2.4 million. Second, any new ballpark had to be at least five miles away from the existing stadium. Third, although both leagues would approve the new team, it would only require three-quarters support in each. Finally, the new club was required to pay the existing one $100,000, plus some indemnification to the first club moving there. Both the Yankees and Dodgers would receive the one hundred grand, but the latter would also be compensated for some relocation costs. Frick was ecstatic: "I can tell you without the cooperation of O'Malley and his Dodger associates, as well as the new owners of the Los Angeles club, we definitely would have been in the damnedest mess we've have known in baseball." On the new territorial rule, he added, "With conditions changing and populations increasing in cities all over the country, it was imperative that the old rule had to be amended. I consider the rule as adopted today an excellent one, a rule all baseball can live with no matter who sits as commissioner."[115] One could sense the relief in his comments because both leagues' owners agreed unanimously, with no need for him to break a tie.

Frick acknowledged such the following day. Although he could have broken any ties, "it would have left nothing but bitterness and offered no solution at all to similar problems in the future." He was sure both leagues would expand to twelve teams in a few years.[116] After the resolution, Arthur Daley noted, "When O'Malley capitulated and permitted the other circuit to enter his grand duchy, he rescued the Americans from the straight-jacket into which they had unthinkably and impetuously climbed. . . . The big surrender not only got the Americans off the hook, but also freed Commissioner Ford Frick from a sticky wicket. He might have had to decide between the warring factions and take sides. When it was all over, he was the most relieved man at the meeting." Daley also emphasized that when the Senior Circuit took New York and Houston first, American League owners "acted like petulant children."[117] The largest baseball drama in 1960, and perhaps of many years, had come to an end amicably. After a decade and a half of discussion, the majors had added four clubs.

The last two months hadn't been easy. Sportswriter Bob Burnes, who reported on the Winter Meetings' showdown for *The Sporting News*, noted that the final deal was completed in John Galbreath's hotel suite between 9:00 p.m. on December 6 and 4:00 a.m. on December 7. Autry and O'Malley were both there, and Frick was in and out. At least two other owners were always present. It was truly give-and-take. Burnes said, "During all the negotiations, misinformed members of the press took pot shots at Frick. The commissioner ignored the shafts and stood steadfast for the objective he had set out from the very beginning—a settlement that would benefit everyone in baseball. Just how Frick would have voted if he had been required to break a tie between the leagues on the expansion problem, will probably never be known, but Frick's determination to make the leagues settle the issue between themselves was a credit to the commissioner's judgment." O'Malley asserted, "The commissioner steered a straight course. If he had lost his sense of direction, we would have wound up in an awful mess."[118] Still, in baseball historiography, Frick rarely receives any credit.

It was, truly, a hardball political game Frick played. He needed to convince magnates who believed additional teams would encroach on their profits. He had to deal with a persistent upstart league, headed by a legendary baseball executive and a tenacious New York lawyer, who took the matter to Congress. There, Frick took advantage of his lobbying organization to defeat Kefauver's legislation. He then helped negotiate a settlement after the Continental League folded and agreements with the Yankees' and Dodgers' owners, who remained recalcitrant on territorial rights. Yet, as recently as 2018 an article contended that Frick was ineffective on expansion. In his article written for a SABR publication, Warren Corbett made four points critical of Frick, similar to those made by Veeck decades earlier. First, he claimed Frick delayed expansion for years, "on instruction from his masters, the owners." Second, he gave Frick no credit for defeating Kefauver's bill restricting the number of players a club controlled. Third, he claimed that when the leagues met to expand, the owners took matters into their own hands, walking over a docile Frick. Finally, Corbett asserted O'Malley pushed Frick to order compensation for the Dodgers if an American League team came.[119] Frick received no credit.

In fact, Frick consistently played a lead role in bringing about expansion. He spoke in favor of it even before being named commissioner, though he vacillated on whether it should be via a new league or additions to existing ones. Part of that reflected circumstances, like the early efforts of the Pacific Coast League. It was owners who usually offered resistance. The Continental League that brought more recalcitrant owners around, coupled with baseball's lobbying efforts, defeated the Kefauver bill. Frick let the leagues make their own expansion decisions and subsequently realized the commissioner needed to be involved directly. Going forward, it would no longer be a league matter. Finally, Frick stated that any relocating team that compensated the displaced Minor League club was entitled to compensation for a period of five years if another club later located there. The deal with O'Malley reflected that declaration. Though expansion would certainly have occurred, its ultimate form reflected Frick's major role.

When the leagues voted to expand in 1960, Ford Frick believed the next expansion was imminent—at most five years away. It proved longer, not occurring until 1969. At that point, both leagues did what Frick had projected more than a decade earlier—split into two divisions, with the champions meeting for the World Series. That year was magical for three of the initial expansion clubs. The Astros and Senators both completed that season at a .500 or better percentage for the first time. The Mets also did so, along with winning both the pennant and the World Series. In one way, the Angels outdid the other three. They finished in third place with a won-lost record far above .500 in 1962, only their second year.

9

A Popular '60s Draft

In 1935 Bert Bell, co-owner of the Philadelphia Eagles and later commissioner of the National Football League, proposed a player draft. Teams would select in order, from weakest to strongest in the standings, with players only negotiating with the club drafting them. It was adopted unanimously. It worked well and still does, but while Landis was commissioner baseball never considered it. After the war, magnates were focused on the large pool of talent and concerned about high bonus payments by wealthier clubs. To counter the perceived overpayments, owners imposed a bonus limit—with loopholes. Those pitfalls led to its termination in 1950, resulting in even higher bonuses. Deeply concerned about money paid to unproven talent, owners imposed a limit of $4,000 for bonuses in 1953; any higher amount required the player to spend two full seasons in the Majors. That proved unworkable and was discontinued after 1957. New restrictions were attempted with limited success, including a first-year draft of Minor League players. Antitrust concerns prevented the football-style draft from consideration until Frick was assured by Senator Kefauver that it wasn't an issue. Soon after, Frick proposed the football-style draft, adopted in 1964. It remains today.

POSTWAR FITS AND STARTS

The 1945 Winter Meetings presented owners with many challenges. They were upset with Happy Chandler, given his delay in becoming full-time commissioner until November, along with some of his decisions. Another challenge stemmed from the large quantity of unsigned talent, many believing high bonuses would be paid by wealthier clubs to sign players. Prior to the war, high bonuses were rare compared to those projected for 1945. Due to both distrust of Chandler and of each other, owners placed bonus payments on the agenda. They had other concerns as well.[1] Only after the Pacific Coast League's initial move to achieve Major League status and Chandler were discussed did owners turn to bonuses. One proposed eliminating such payments. Much of their discussion was off the record, and a decision was put off a day.[2] Even then, discussion was delayed until the end of their session. Once again, after numerous options were considered, there was no resolution.[3] Bonus payments proved too contentious and thus were assigned to a joint committee to present in February.

The committee had two representatives from each league, along with attorneys from both. Louis Carroll, long-serving lawyer for the National League, drafted and presented the recommendations, emphasizing the substantial risk if bonuses were prohibited. Instead, he considered it more effective to add restrictions, making bonuses less attractive. For bonuses exceeding $6,000, players would be required to be on the Major League roster after one year. Further, that player could not be optioned again unless he went through the waiver process and was unclaimed by other clubs. There were also penalties for failing to file the contract with the league office or for not disclosing the full amount; these penalties were intended to prevent loopholes that had circumvented bonus limits. The restrictions were adopted unanimously.[4] *New York Times* sportswriter John Drebinger noted the $6,000 limit even included indirect benefits like payments to family members.[5] Although bonus concerns were apparently addressed, that didn't end future discussions. At the 1946 Winter Meetings, it was argued that $6,000 was too limited. Rickey proposed $7,500 but was quickly voted down.[6] Frick suggested an amendment to remove training, medical, and moving expenses from the calculation, recommending it be established formally at near year's Winter Meetings.[7] Once approved, the policy lasted two years.[8] Although the National League minutes are nebulous, problems clearly remained with the bonus policy and were addressed directly at the 1949 Winter Meetings.

By then the difficulties had escalated, as the player representatives from each league indicated in July 1949 that they had reservations. The reps—Dixie Walker and Fred Hutchinson—claimed the "bonus baby" rule that put inexperienced players on Major League rosters after one year took spots from veterans with more experience and talent. Hence, fans witnessed an inferior brand of baseball.[9] Beyond their complaints, many executives were also expressing misgivings. In November the Major League Baseball Council, consisting of Chandler, Frick, Harridge, William DeWitt of the Browns, and Frank McKinney of the Pirates, met to reconsider the bonus plan and proposed elimination at the Winter Meetings.[10] That foreshadowed additional struggles.

When owners convened in December, the Majors acted to change the bonus rule—sort of. The National League voted 5–3 in favor of keeping it, while the American League voted 8–0 to eliminate. Not reluctant to break ties, Chandler sided with the Junior Circuit. However, his action didn't end the bonus rule. At the Minor League meetings before, its owners maintained the rule, failing by a small margin to eliminate it. Although Chandler's vote decided the issue for the Majors, the Minors also had to act for it to take effect.[11] They didn't until the following year, thus maintaining the bonus policy for 1950 and generating more player complaints. Marty Marion, now National League player rep, circulated a petition to prohibit all bonuses, asserting, "Every time a kid gets a big wad of dough for signing, he reaches into the pockets of the veterans of that club, and it must be stopped." Frick wasn't receptive: "There is no doubt what Marion says about bonuses is correct, but he is moving into a department of baseball which is not exactly his business. It is not the province of the players to interfere with the magnates' financial practices and business policies."[12] While chastising Marion, Frick signaled the bonus rule may be doomed.

Once the Minor Leagues ratified its elimination at their 1950 meetings, the Majors followed suit. They were venturing into the Wild West on signings, as there were now no rules or restrictions. In his column, Arthur Daley offered a requiem. "[Baseball has] rid itself of the pernicious and crippling bonus rule, . . . unworkable and as obnoxious as prohibition." He added that it was "conceived along idealistic lines that held no consideration for practicality." He further stressed that it created morale problems, causing friction between veterans and bonus babies, just as Frick recognized. He concluded, "The bonus rule never did achieve its purpose. It didn't halt extravagant spending, it retarded development of kids it was supposed to help and in some instances ruined them."[13] Unfortunately, two years later the magnates failed to heed his assessment.

For 1951 and 1952, Major League clubs were free to offer any amount they chose. During the 1951 season, there were few comments about bonuses, but by mid-1952 major concerns were expressed, led by Browns owner Bill Veeck. Emphasizing that the lack of a bonus rule gave advantages to richer clubs, Veeck argued it destroyed competition. He mentioned three teams, all with wealthy owners, and noted one of them, the Red Sox, had recently signed two players for over $75,000. Clubs in smaller markets like Veeck's couldn't compete. Now commissioner, Frick acknowledged Veeck's concerns, placing it on the agenda at the Summer Meetings.[14] Veeck had gained the commissioner's attention.

Though no decisions were made, a committee chaired by Branch Rickey was established to offer recommendations at the 1952 Winter Meetings. Rickey was reluctant but was joined by Frick, George Trautman, Frank Lane of the White Sox, and two Minor League owners. More notable was the presence of owners of two clubs Veeck had singled out for their extravagance—Joe Cronin of the Red Sox and Bob Carpenter of the Phillies. Rickey stressed it was an initial meeting and that more work lay ahead. He also mentioned his preference was for a draft similar to football's and said, "The bonus will ruin baseball if it isn't curtailed."[15] The groundwork was laid for a new plan, but it would not be what Rickey had in mind.

THE COMMISSIONER "MEETS" AN EARLY BONUS BABY

Eddie Mathews grew up in Santa Barbara, California, excelling in both baseball and football in high school. He received many scholarship offers for football, but in the late 1940s baseball was more popular with better monetary prospects. Being a left-handed, power-hitting third baseman offered substantial bonus opportunities. His father, both an athlete and sports fan, took considerable interest as baseball scouts pursued Eddie. Though bonus rules limited his Minor League experience to one year if he signed for over $6,000, the monetary amount was less important than how quickly he could reach the Majors. Mathews and his father focused on the Boston Braves, with third basemen Bob Elliott's age suggesting an early opportunity. Mathews signed after graduation in 1949 for $6,000, lower than other offers. It was a fortuitous decision, since it allowed Mathews additional time to develop in the Minors. He spent the second half of the 1949 season at the A level and was promoted to Double-A the following year. By that time he was considered a top prospect. A short stint in the Korean War interrupted the early 1951 season, but he was discharged due to his father's illness and status as sole supporter. He returned to the Minors, finishing the season at the Triple-A level with the Milwaukee Brewers, the top farm club. He was invited to spring training in 1952.[16]

As he had done when National League president, Ford Frick visited all spring training camps. While attending the Braves camp during a practice session, Frick stood in foul territory beyond third base, away from the foul line and engaged in conversation with two club executives. That day, manager Tommy Holmes decided to experiment with Mathews in left field, exploring an alternative for getting his bat in the lineup quickly. A foul ball was hit toward Mathews. He charged it, hoping to make a good impression on Holmes. Oblivious to the three gentlemen standing there, Mathews ran into them, knocking all three over. Frick was taken aback, shaken but unharmed. In fact, Mathews incurred the only injury—a broken nose.[17] It is unknown if words were exchanged, but the young prospect likely experienced considerable ribbing from teammates for the impression he had left with the new commissioner.

Frick never commented about the chance meeting, even though he served as commissioner for most of Mathews's career. Mathews achieved the distinction as the only player ever to play for the same ball club in three different cities, with Frick playing a minor role in that achievement. The bigger distinction, though obviously unknown to them when they met as rookies, was their later inductions to the Hall of Fame.

HOPING FOR DIFFERENT RESULTS

Rickey was not alone in favoring a football-style draft. At least one other committee member—Phillies owner Robert Carpenter Jr., who had opposed the first bonus plan—also supported it. In subsequent meetings, however, the draft idea was abandoned. A year earlier it might have been possible, but the 1951 Celler hearings had raised antitrust concerns, putting baseball in a defensive mode. Years later, Frick offered a rationale when addressing the Chicago Executive Club. He portrayed the football draft "as an undemocratic process depriving college players of their bargaining rights."[18] Perhaps the commissioner had feared adoption would produce further antitrust investigations, threatening baseball's exemption and rendering vulnerable both the reserve clause and territorial rights. In any case, the draft idea was eliminated.

Instead, the committee proposed at the Winter Meetings to reestablish the bonus restriction with harsher enforcement, including heavy fines and suspensions for those in violation.[19] The restriction would be even tighter than 1946—$4,000 rather than $6,000.[20] By then Rickey had departed the Dodgers, replaced by Walter O'Malley. Frank Lane was named chair. Frick clarified that the new rule was not a restriction because clubs could spend any amount for signings. However, if it exceeded $4,000, the signee was required to spend two seasons on the Major League roster, occupying one of twenty-five spots. Further, the commissioner would enforce the policy with heavy fines, including terminating the player's contract. Frick explained, "I'm convinced some form of bonus legislation is necessary in order to stop the ridiculously huge sum of money being spent on untried youngsters who have never swung a bat or thrown a ball in organized baseball."[21]

Not surprisingly, sportswriters viewed the new bonus rule with skepticism. Writing for *The Sporting News*, Edgar Brands suggested the plan had loopholes, explaining why the first bonus plan had failed: "First, it did not stop what it was intended to stop—the payment of huge amounts to untried youngsters. Second, it was winked at so frequently it became a farce." Addressing the new plan, he said, "The ultimate success of the bonus rule, however amended, depends upon the self-restraint of the club owners, enforcement and the elimination of 'under-table' dealing. Ford Frick has promised that he will not hesitate to act if he finds evidence of skullduggery."[22] Given the previous failure, there was reason for skepticism.

Nonetheless, Frick fully intended to enforce the plan, even with early evidence that it wouldn't restrict spending. Frank Leja, a seventeen-year-old first baseman at Holyoke High School in Massachusetts, was labeled the "next Lou Gehrig" by one scout. He attracted interest from numerous clubs, three of which were reprimanded by Frick for attempting to sign him prior to the end of summer leagues. The commissioner even interrogated Leja before punishing those clubs. The Yankees signed him when Leja was a guest of Dan Topping at the World Series, for an amount reported to be $100,000 (more than $1 million in 2025) spread over a few years. It was later reported as $45,000 and may have been even lower, but it was still well over the limit. Leja was stuck on the Yankees' roster for two years, during which he batted seven times with one hit. Although he later demonstrated his power in the Minors, the Yankees never recalled him. He played for the expansion LA Angels in 1962, where he batted sixteen more times but never safely.[23] His signing, however, suggested the new bonus rule was ineffective in controlling bonus payments. Further, Leja's performance suggested the challenges players faced if unable to develop in the Minors. That proved a common outcome for many bonus babies.

Fifty-eight players were signed for more than $4,000, most spending two years in the Majors before being optioned. The last twenty, who signed after the start of the 1956 season, did not spend all two years with the parent club because baseball ended the bonus rule at the Winter Meetings in 1957. There were notable successes. Roughly one-third of the group had playing careers exceeding three seasons on a Major League roster, a few ten years or longer. Since those receiving large bonuses were allegedly the cream of the crop, that success rate wasn't impressive. For most, the two years were lost time, producing unimpressive careers.[24]

There were notable exceptions, as four bonus babies have been inducted into the Hall of Fame—Al Kaline, Roberto Clemente, Sandy Koufax, and Harmon Killebrew. Their success stories vary. Kaline was signed at nineteen by the Tigers in June 1953. He joined the club for the rest of the season, playing in only thirty games with thirty plate appearances. A year later he was a regular and the following season had the highest batting average in the league. He spent more than twenty seasons with the Tigers, hitting 399 home runs and batting .297; he was inducted into the Hall of Fame after the five-year minimum wait time for eligibility. Sandy Koufax signed with the Dodgers during college and struggled for many seasons, though remaining on the roster. After learning how to utilize his talents, he became baseball's most dominant pitcher for six seasons. Killebrew had similar struggles, but after his two years in the Majors he spent time in the Minors during the next three. When he returned with the Senators and Twins, he became one of the game's most dominant power hitters.[25] Of them, only Kaline succeeded from the start.

Roberto Clemente, the other bonus baby in the Hall, followed a different route, playing a full season in the Minors before being called up. Although he spent his entire career with the Pirates until his tragic death, Clemente actually signed with the Brooklyn Dodgers in April 1954 for $10,000. The Dodgers took their chances, optioning him to their Montreal Triple-A farm club. He played in half the games, batting .257, but was noticed by the Pirates, who had the first pick in the Rule 5 Draft. The Dodgers lost him for having optioned him against the rules. Ford Frick was present at the draft and witnessed the Pirates claim Clemente.[26] In effect, Frick observed the bonus rule being enforced and the price paid for not following the rules.

It was evident quickly that few bonus babies other than Kaline experienced much playing time. As expected, that raised concerns, including from Frick, though less regarding their struggles than the excessive dollar amounts paid. He was equally concerned with players languishing five years or more in the Minors, which laid the groundwork if the bonus rules were terminated. Addressing a committee of Major and Minor League executives charged with examining operations, controlling players, and procedures for drafting, he offered two criticisms: "Something is wrong with a system which permits a club to keep a player down in the minors for five years without ever getting a shot at a major league job." It was likely he was referring to the Yankees, Dodgers, Red Sox, and Cardinals, all considered "talent misers." About the bonus problems, he said, "We need to establish legislation which will discourage the present high payment of bonuses to untried youngsters and which will instead permit reasonable compensation for them based on improvement, effort and ability."[27] Essentially, Frick implied the bonus rule wasn't working and changes were needed. However, he avoided specifics on both problems.

Throughout 1954 and into 1955, Frick clarified the $4,000 bonus figure, reminding clubs he intended to enforce it strongly. Following the 1954 Summer Meetings, he notified clubs: "The commissioner's office will interpret the bonus rule stringently. If you have any doubt in your own mind, don't do it, that's the safest way." In early 1955 he added, "Any promise or commitment to any free agent, as a condition of his signing, which offers to him any privilege that is not commonly accorded to all players of the classification to which he is signed, must be construed as a thing of value and added inducement."[28] Lack of discussion at the 1954 Winter Meetings for changes and no reaction to Frick's clarifications implied there was general acceptance.

By summer 1955, though, dissention developed. In June, Gabe Paul, Cincinnati's general manager, requested a vote for an unrestricted draft at the Winter Meetings, all but forty players on a club's roster made available if adopted. Paul suggested it would end the bonus program, implying that Frick favored it. In July, Del Webb, Frank Lane, and Spike Briggs, part owner of the Tigers, jointly proposed eliminating the bonus rule, letting the market dictate the value of a new player. Briggs objected to "putting so much money into the hands of fuzzy-cheeked youngsters who seldom make the grade."[29] Yet he favored eliminating the rule restricting such payments. Their suggestion echoed comments prior to ending the first bonus rule in 1950, which recognized many bonus babies were struggling. It appeared momentum was growing to end the program.

During that period, Frick disciplined a club for a serious violation—the Baltimore Orioles. Initially, the situation appeared minor. The problem stemmed from placing a bonus player on the disabled list (DL) for an injury, which entailed removing him from the roster and replacing him with a more experienced player. Frick blocked the move, stressing a doctor's certificate was required before such action was approved. However, there was more to the Orioles situation than was first apparent. Frick made one player a free agent, and Baltimore released another due to what general manager Paul Richards called "a signing error."[30] No further details were provided, with the matter apparently resolved.

It wasn't. A month later Frick made another player a free agent and this time assessed substantial fines. The player was Thomas Borland, a pitcher signed by Baltimore out of Oklahoma A&M (now Oklahoma State) for $40,000, spread over three years. However, the contract wasn't submitted to the office of the league president as required. After he was signed, Baltimore had Borland pitch in an exhibition game in which he performed poorly. Concluding he needed Minor League experience, the club announced his signing for $4,000. Frick came down hard when he became aware. He fined Richards $2,500 (close to $30,000 in 2025) and the organization $2,000. The club's owner, unaware of the cover-up, escaped penalty. Frick acknowledged that he didn't suspend Richards due to the team's newness in Baltimore but emphasized a suspension greater than a year would occur with another violation. Borland was declared a free agent, allowing him to sign elsewhere, with Baltimore losing its $40,000 investment.[31] It was Frick's most severe penalty during the five years of the bonus rule.

Borland, the beneficiary, had a rather typical career for a bonus baby. He signed with the Boston Red Sox in 1955 but spent two years in the military before playing in the Minors in 1958, spending two years there before being called up in 1960. He appeared in twenty-six games that year and one game in 1961, with an earned run average of almost 7.00 and without a win. The Red Sox traded him to the Houston Colt .45s, though he never again appeared in the Majors.[32] Borland is better remembered for the largest bonus-violation fine than for his baseball career. In spite of that scandal, clubs continued to offer excessive bonuses, yet the rule still wasn't brought up for discussion at the Winter Meetings in 1955 or 1956. Although no Borland-like incident occurred then, players were still signing for large amounts, which suggests the bonus rule faced little opposition. That would change during 1957, as discontent grew over players losing two years of development while occupying roster spots of veterans. The same complaints that existed during the first bonus program surfaced again.

Frick took the initiative, though only tangentially. He proposed an unrestricted draft for Minor League players with over four years of experience. Frick long favored extending opportunities for players having little hope for advancement, recommending they should be subject to an "unrestricted draft" to provide opportunity for advancement.[33] His concern dated back to the Supreme Court *Toolson v. New York Yankees* decision in 1953, discussed later. Frick's recommendation for such a draft also laid groundwork for ending the bonus rule. The four-year player draft would actually have little impact on controlling bonuses, but a similar draft for first-year players, also on the table, clearly would. Momentum for both concepts materialized rapidly. Although there is no evidence Frick introduced the subject at the July meetings, he focused on both when meeting with George Trautman in September. They offered little information on either draft proposal, but they stressed the bonus rule would be a top item at the Winter Meetings. Frick indicated that baseball's executive committee had already approved ending it and suggested the four-year draft was imminent. Despite fear of excessive spending once again surfacing, committee members agreed elimination of the bonus rule was necessary. As for the unrestricted four-year draft, Frick considered it "far and away the most important piece of legislation with which baseball is currently confronted."[34] Most important, the Majors and Minors were in concert.

The push grew stronger during the World Series, with Auggie Busch leading the effort to end the bonus rule. While some owners remained reticent, most felt the bonus was either "1) bad; 2) unenforceable; 3) a handicap to the boy; or 4) a combination of all three." Most concurred with Roy Hamey, general manager of the Phillies: "The bonus rule is bad, we've got to get rid of it and I'll go along with anybody who wants to scrap the whole thing." Although the commissioner and league presidents remained circumspect, none spoke in favor of keeping or fine-tuning the bonus rule. Two weeks later, J. G. Taylor Spink weighed in, stating that the draft of four-year Minor Leaguers and ending of the bonus rule were certain outcomes at the meetings.[35]

The Minors were the first to approve both, and the Majors followed suit. One reporter referred to the sessions as "the most important and bombastic meetings." The biggest sticking point was what to do with the twenty-one players who remained under the two-year bonus rule. Should they be allowed to be optioned or required to serve their entire two-years in the Majors? The leagues had agreed on both the draft and ending the bonus rule, but they differed on servitude. The American League owners wanted to send the twenty-one affected players to the Minors immediately, and the National League owners preferred that they remain the entire two years. Frick supported the National League position, though based on a technicality. The Minors had already adjourned, having removed any restrictions on the affected players. The Players' Association also supported sending them to the Minors immediately, as it was primarily concerned with losing veteran spots on the roster. As one observer concluded, "I'm sure that with the added pressure of the American League and some of the National League teams, Frick will cast his vote to clear bonus players off cluttered major league rosters."[36] The issue was addressed a month later, with both the Minors and Majors agreeing to allow all remaining bonus babies to be optioned. The second effort at bonus restrictions was ended, having created similar problems and controversies as did the first. The new program to draft players with more than four years in the Minors was also established, and there were no longer any restrictions on amounts paid to sign players.

A BONUS STORY

Twenty-year-old Jay Hook was one of those caught in limbo by the initial failure to agree on the remaining bonus babies. He wondered for over a month if he would be optioned or return to Cincinnati. Hook had signed a contract with the Redlegs for $65,000 on September 3, 1957, immediately appearing for one inning in a game that night. That was a rarity. For the remainder of the season, he appeared in only two more games, both as a starter. The second was notable. In a meaningless game in Milwaukee, the last of the season, Hook, for five innings, allowed no hits, though two men had reached base. When he returned to the dugout after the fifth, Manager Birdie Tebbetts told him he was finished, that he was too young to even think about a no-hitter. The bonus baby's season was over, and so was his immediate future with the club. Once agreement was reached, Hook was optioned.[37]

He had been an outstanding pitcher for his high school in Grayslake, Illinois, and he earned a scholarship at Northwestern University, where the young hurler pursued an engineering degree. During the 1957 summer season following his first college year, he was scouted. A Redlegs scout took notice, approaching Hook after a game and flying him to Cincinnati for a tryout. That led to a meeting with general manager Gabe Paul, who expressed more than a casual interest, intending to sign Hook on the spot until realizing he wasn't of legal age. To close the deal, Paul flew Hook's father from Chicago. Fortunately, his dad was able to get away from managing his drugstore in Grayslake and closed the deal.

Hook was offered a bonus of $65,000, on the higher side during the bonus-baby era, and worth more than $740,000 in 2025. It was clearly too substantial to turn down. As they negotiated, Hook also planned to continue his engineering degree at Northwestern. With the excitement of starting a baseball career, he almost missed what Paul added. In essence, of the $65,000, $21,000 would be taken out to pay his salary for the next three years, equating to the $7,000 minimum wage then in place. In effect, the bonus was reduced to $44,000. There was little either Hook or his father could do since the contract was signed. Still, it was a healthy bonus.

Hook wasn't surprised at being optioned once the bonus rule was eliminated. He was sent to Nashville in 1958, a Double-A affiliate. He pitched well and was called up in September, starting one game. It did not match his Milwaukee start a year earlier, as he yielded four runs in three innings and was credited with the loss. His Nashville season achieved a promotion to Seattle, the Red's Triple-A affiliate, and his performances there had him called up halfway through the season. He started fifteen games in 1959, winning five, the first against his hometown Cubs. He remained with the Reds in 1960. Hook acknowledged he benefitted from the bonus rule being eliminated, as that provided him a year and a half of development. He was thus better prepared.[38]

From then on, though, his career didn't proceed as expected. He was a solid and consistent starter in 1960, better than his 11-18 record indicated. The Reds had high expectations for 1961, but a severe case of the mumps kept him on the DL for over a month. When he returned, he was weak from being quarantined, with little time provided to regain strength. It was a lost season. The Reds had future expectations but failed to protect him during the expansion draft in 1962, and the Mets made him their first pick. Playing on a team that lost a record 120 games in 1962 was not easy, as Hook won only 8 games while losing 19. He did gain one major distinction—the first pitcher to win a game for the lowly Mets. The next season fared no better, and Hook was traded to the Braves. Whatever Mets manager Casey Stengel thought about Hook's pitching talent, he was impressed with his hitting. Hook threw right-handed but batted left and was speedy. Stengel thought he could use him as a pinch-hitter and had him take batting practice with other hitters. The opportunity soon came for him to pinch-hit—he struck out. As he walked in the dugout, Stengel assured him he no longer needed to take batting practice.

With the trade, he no longer had to play for a last-place team. However, he didn't stay with Milwaukee and was instead optioned to Denver, its Triple-A affiliate. He pitched decently, and general manager John McHale promised to bring Hook up in September when clubs increased their rosters. Shortly before the call-up, though, Hook was injured sliding into second base and unable to pitch. Nonetheless, McHale delivered on his promise, putting Hook on the forty-man roster. That was all he needed to qualify for the pension plan.

Hook's experience was a fair representation of many bonus babies. They didn't have the careers of a Kaline or Koufax. A few never played in the Majors past the required two years. Overall, the bonus rule was detrimental to player development because it restricted important development time in the Minors. The magnates now realized they needed a different direction.

STILL SEARCHING

Jay Hook didn't interact much with Ford Frick, though he did serve as player rep for the Mets. Frick didn't need much contact to be aware that most bonus babies struggled and bonus rules were difficult to enforce. Likewise, he knew ending bonus restrictions would escalate spending for unproven players, while also realizing the draft for long-term Minor League players wouldn't address that excess. Still, it was difficult to focus on bonuses problems in 1958 with the National League vacating New York and antitrust hearings occurring in both chambers. In addition, the Minors continued to struggle financially, even after the Majors set up a program supporting the weakest clubs. Frick had much to deal with beyond excessive bonuses.

Frick was pleased with the unrestricted draft for long-term players in the Minors. Geared to provide opportunities for such players, it was influenced largely by the *Toolson* decision. Earl Toolson had languished for years in the Yankee system, with no opportunity to advance. To change that, he sued for antitrust violations. Although his efforts failed, the four-year draft was meant to mitigate such experiences. There was concern the signing price of $25,000 might be too high for those spending so much time in the Minors, but twelve players were drafted, surprising many. Also unexpected, eight had already experienced some playing time in the Majors.[39] Frick was pleased they would have another opportunity.

The commissioner also remained interested in finding a way to control bonuses paid to unproven talent. Frick was empathic when talking with a reporter during the Kefauver Subcommittee on Antitrust and Monopoly hearings in mid-July. He emphasized that any bonus had to have a maximum and also said, "The other approach is a suggestion for an unrestricted draft of first-year players. I'd call it somewhat socialistic but I don't doubt that it would be an effective curb. A club isn't going to put out $100,000 or more for a boy if it stands a chance of losing him after a year. There's no question we made a mistake by scrapping the old bonus rule, but that's the way baseball works. It's a trial and error system, much like our own government."[40] Essentially, Frick was laying groundwork to address the recurring bonus dilemma.

At a special meeting of owners in early September, Frick addressed the challenge in typical style—creating a committee to report at the Winter Meetings. He named three representatives from each league: Chub Feeney of the Giants, Bing Devine of the Cardinals, and Joe Brown of the Pirates for the National League, and Park Carroll of the A's, Bill Walsingham of the Orioles, and Frank Lane of the Indians for the American League. Lane was chairman again. Their sole focus was bonuses, as teams had already spent over $6 million to that point signing amateurs.[41] Sportswriters were skeptical. Arthur Daley asked if the committee was even necessary, since owners had done nothing to confront bonus problems. He added, "Commissioner Ford Frick, a sound-thinking but powerless man, makes Cassandra-like prophecies and offers suggestions that are ignored."[42] It seemed questionable the committee could accomplish anything.

Contrary to Daley's skepticism, Lane's committee developed a proposal, providing Frick an outline well ahead of the deadline for the Winter Meetings agenda. It would not affect bonuses already granted or even limit them going forward. Frick's assistant, Charlie Segar, explained: "It will bring with it unrestricted draft of minor league players. Such a draft, which would place all minor league players on the selection list after one season, would mean tremendous reductions in bonus moneys." Segar served for Frick at the meetings, and Trautman represented the Minors. It was noted that the concept—bonuses would go down because the player might be lost in a year—was basically the same Frick had advocated since becoming commissioner.[43] Frick didn't take credit, likely satisfied with the progress.

The proposal would not survive unchanged, however, as George Weiss quickly announced his opposition.[44] Other free-spending teams, including the Dodgers, also raised concerns. The proposal was modified during the Minor League sessions in that a team could protect a player three additional years if not selected in the unrestricted draft, providing more player stability for the Minors. It also limited the drafting price at $15,000, anticipating a club would hesitate to offer large bonuses if it lost the player a year later at that amount.[45] The most important change was allowing protection of some first-year players by allowing their inclusion on the forty-man roster. Those revisions, adopted in December, defined the first unrestricted draft held in December 1959. The plan was a one-year trial, to be reviewed following the first draft.

That review came at the 1960 Winter Meetings. Surprisingly, the draft of four-year players proved more popular than the one-year draft because only one player, Mike Lee, was selected in the newer draft. The Giants had signed him for $70,000; the Indians, seeing him unprotected, selected him for $15,000. The Giants lost both a prospect and $55,000.[46] A similar pattern occurred at the 1960 drafts. This time, six players were selected from the first-year group, for $12,000 each, while seventeen were chosen from the four-year draft.[47] If the purpose was to control bonuses to amateur players, the new rule was ineffective—bonus costs continued to escalate, and few were selected in the first-year draft. The Minors voted to continue it in 1961 but didn't make it permanent.[48] That suggested further changes were forthcoming.

Those efforts were already underway, as interest in a draft similar to professional football and basketball was percolating. Early in 1959 Parke Carroll, general manager of the A's, supported it. Noting the imbalance of clubs, especially in the American League, Carroll claimed such a selection process would give weaker teams an opportunity to get stronger.[49] Later that year, before the Minor League meetings, Bob Howsam, president and general manager of the Denver Bears, proposed a similar draft, citing pro basketball's success. He stressed that such a draft would help equalize talent distribution and end wild bonus bidding. Unlike Carroll, Howsam had the benefit of knowing that the Kefauver subcommittee had already granted antitrust protection for professional football, allowing it to maintain its draft.[50] Although the first-year draft would be conducted in 1961, sentiment was growing for a football-style draft at the same time opposition to the first-year draft was increasing.

Fear of baseball losing its antitrust exemption remained the largest obstacle to such a draft. James Gallagher, supervisor of scouts for the Phillies and long-serving chair of baseball's rules committee, questioned those fears. Strongly advocating that a free-agent draft would solve exorbitant bonuses, he suggested baseball was listening too closely to lawyers. He pointed out that when "the Justice Dept. people told the late Bert Bell, the National Football League commissioner, that they did not like the draft . . . he replied: 'Gentlemen, we need it to conduct our business, and while we are sorry you don't like it, we will have to continue despite your displeasure.' Bell had guts. We, on the other hand, go right on running scared, and for what? Why? What harm would be done to anybody if we had a free-agent draft?" He added that killing such a draft at the Winter Meetings was a serious mistake; the Majors realized such within a year.[51] Galbreath's comments suggested momentum was growing. However, unforeseen events and opposition continued to block what increasingly seemed a solution to excessive bonuses.

The football draft was definitely explored and discussed. In June 1961 the American League came out in favor of such a draft, generating a front-page story in *The Sporting News*. The article stimulated cautious acknowledgement from Frick: "Do not ask this question now. In short, the draft is being studied."[52] The commissioner planned to confer with Senators Phil Hart of Michigan and Kenneth Keating of New York, both Kefauver subcommittee members and strong supporters of baseball, to work through legal and political aspects. House support was more questionable, with an Emanuel Celler aide stating, "Mr. Celler is against any regulation that would give baseball owners more control over the players." The signals were mixed at best. When Frick met with Kefauver in July, a leading adversary, he was given assurance the senator wouldn't oppose a free-agent draft.[53] In spite of that message, reticence remained.

The most obvious reason for it was Celler's opposition, but it wasn't the only concern. Conceptually, similarities and differences existed between a baseball draft and football's. Both drafted amateur players and were intended to create balance—the weaker teams drafting first, the stronger teams last. With basketball having instituted it as well, there was reason to believe baseball wouldn't be challenged, as Kefauver had indicated.

Still, there were troublesome differences. Football chose their players from a single source—college. Baseball drew players from high schools, colleges, and American Legion leagues. Further, almost all of football's players drafted were twenty-one or older. Many in baseball would be under twenty-one and thus minors by law in 1961, like Jay Hook when he signed. Finally, baseball had a reserve clause perceived to give a club control of a player for his entire career, which was regarded as a sacred cow. Football didn't have such a clause; players were free to sign with another team after two years.[54] Baseball's attorneys had valid reasons to advise proceeding slowly.

For those reasons, Frick shifted away from a free-agent draft, instead attempting to toughen the first-year draft. As was typical, he created a committee rather than deciding unilaterally, selecting three from each league, one owner and two general managers. John Fetzer of the Tigers was the American League owner, with Lee MacPhail of the Orioles and Roy Hamey of the Yankees the general managers. Their National League counterparts were Bob Carpenter, Phillies owner, along with Joe Brown of the Pirates and Bing Devine of the Cardinals. Their mission was to formulate a stronger plan for the first-year draft, thus discouraging clubs from paying outlandish bonuses.[55] MacPhail became chairman, with recommendations timed for the 1961 Winter Meetings.

What they proposed certainly made the existing rules tougher. Announcing in November and predicting passage, Frick asserted, "It will make the lavish spending for untried players so impractical that clubs for their own protection will abandon this silly practice, which in recent years has gotten completely out of hand."[56] His details two days later made clear what he meant. A team could only protect one first-year player, also placed on the twenty-five-man roster. After one year in the Minors, all other players could be drafted for $8,000, placement on the forty-man roster no longer assuring protection. Thus, any bonus greater than $8,000 could be a loss. What Frick liked most was that the policy was "self-enforcing." He wouldn't have to be a policeman searching for violations. The policy was anticipated to reduce bonus expenditures in half from the $6 million in 1961.[57] Though formal approval was necessary, Frick was confident of adoption.

Indeed, it was passed with little opposition. Most of that occurred during the Minor League meetings, primarily from the Dodgers. In fact, it was rumored Frick gave Dodgers president Buzzie Bavasi a tongue-lashing for his efforts to defeat it at the Minor's confab.[58] During the Minor League sessions, the largest number of players in forty-seven years was selected, including fifteen from the first-year group at the current bonus rule price of $12,000.[59] It signaled that interest in first-year players was growing. It then passed at the Majors' meetings, the only opposition again from the Dodgers. Frick was pleased: "I'm more delighted over this year's progress than with anything we've done in a long time." He had achieved his top reform.[60] When asked why he had ended the bonus-baby program, he replied, "It wasn't the violations of the old bonus rules that I found most objectionable. It was the mistrust in the minds of everyone. It created a bad atmosphere of suspicion and doubt." Dodgers owner Walter O'Malley wasn't shy in explaining his opposition: "This rule is socialistic. It encourages the indolent, lazy clubs, while it restricts those who hustle and work hard to find the top prospects."[61] In any case, its success in holding down bonuses wouldn't be demonstrated until 1962, though all clubs besides the Dodgers accepted the tougher rule.

Early on, it appeared to be working. Frick praised it as the 1962 season began: "The new bonus rule has proved itself to be air-tight, foolproof, firm against the loophole seeker who made a mockery of such regulations in the past, and a reproach to us because we took so long to discover the remedy." As for adopting a draft like football, he said, "It may be there will come a time when we will take up this form of draft. But at this time our owners are not so sure it is entirely legal."[62] A month later, Spink praised the new rule, noting it limited amounts offered in bonus payments. Within another month, he changed his tune: "Some of the most extravagant bonuses in history have been paid out this year." He estimated that bonuses may have reached $3 million halfway into 1962.[63] In the same issue of *The Sporting News*, it was noted the expansion Houston Colt .45s had found a loophole by signing their new players to 1963 contracts and waiting until winter ball to start them in the Minors. Paul Richards, the club's general manager, was again finding ways around the rules.[64] Essentially, the new rule's success was, at best, ambiguous.

By year's end the results remained mixed. The new first-year draft did make more players available. Overall, forty-five were selected, up from sixteen in 1961, with over $400,000 paid to the clubs who initially signed them. Those teams, of course, were out whatever they had paid in bonuses, often substantially more than they received back.[65] There was concern, however, that it still hadn't controlled bonuses paid to amateurs. Further, many executives didn't perceive it as a long-term solution. Instead, a growing thought was that the only solution was adopting the football-style draft with assurances Congress and the Justice Department wouldn't act.[66] Obviously, antitrust fears remained. Momentum was still lacking to move beyond the current bonus rule, and thus no action occurred at the 1962 Winter Meetings.

The following year likewise saw no momentum, as no one challenged the current bonus rule, and thus it wasn't on the agenda. Further, whereas many clubs were dissatisfied with the one-year bonus rule, the leagues were divided on a free-agent draft. Roughly half of the ten National League clubs held negative opinions about it, while the Junior Circuit supported it; thus, sufficient consensus was lacking to alter the rule. The four new franchises also created a problem. Because they were only one or two years old, with weaker players, they had far greater need to develop young talent, yet they weren't allowed to protect additional players. An amendment was offered belatedly, with Frick's approval, to allow the new clubs to protect four players rather than one.[67] Otherwise, the status quo remained, with the bonus rule the same for 1965 as 1964. Behind the scenes, though, forces were percolating to produce major changes.

AN ENDURING SOLUTION

Exactly when Frick formally decided on the free-agent draft is unclear, but he was gravitating there by the 1963 Winter Meetings. The free-agent draft, after being discussed for years, now appeared the most logical way for controlling bonuses. For both football and basketball, it had produced greater parity. Further, the current bonus rule hadn't limited bonuses and had created problems for the expansion clubs. Other factors also influenced Frick. He was sixty-nine years old and had decided to retire in late 1965. His 1962 meeting with Kefauver offered encouragement that the Senate would not intervene if baseball adopted the draft. Additionally, the antitrust picture now seemed clear; other sports were not likely to receive exemption, but it was even less likely baseball would lose it.[68] Both past history and the advice of baseball's attorneys gave Frick confidence to proceed with the free-agent draft. Thus, it wasn't surprising when it was announced at a meeting of baseball executives on January 15, 1964. Frick called the meeting, limiting attendance to only the top executive of each club, the league presidents, and Charles Segar. The outcome was authorization for Frick, along with Giles and Cronin, to formulate a proposal to be presented to club owners at a future meeting.[69] Baseball now appeared serious about a football-style draft.

Although there is no documentation of the meeting, what is known is that the three men appeared to promote it during spring training. Frick personally traveled to Arizona and Florida to meet with the general managers, emphasizing that he was seeking suggestions: "There are many bugs that must be cleared up, such as in what order the clubs should pick . . . and what players should be eligible. There are other questions, such as how long a club may take before signing a drafted player and how many times the player, after being drafted, can be optioned out." He committed to presenting an outline at the Summer Meetings: "If things go as I hope, we'll have the thing in effect for the spring of 1965."[70] Little opposition was conveyed.

Sportswriters and some executives dissented. Joe King, with the *New York World-Telegram*, sounded skeptical in his *Sporting News* column: "Why doesn't Ford Frick let a lawyer find a legal means, if any, of establishing a pro-type draft of baseball prospects and devote the prestige of the commissionership to a more positive and inspiring propagation of baseball? Who says the kids are going to accept a draft, anyway, if the price is not right?"[71] Leslie O'Connor went further, opposing the draft publicly. Having been Landis's assistant, an executive with the White Sox, and president of the Pacific Coast League, O'Connor had credibility. Claiming the draft would deprive a player of his constitutional rights, he sent a thirty-page pamphlet to congressmen arguing against any legislation granting antitrust exemption.[72] Fortunately for baseball, O'Connor undertook the wrong strategy. Baseball was moving forward regardless of congressional antitrust action, and its grassroots organization provided the sport protection, even if it hadn't succeeded in exempting other sports. In spite of O'Connor's past, it's doubtful Frick found his opposition concerning.

The proposal wasn't finalized by July, and opposition developed by then from a potentially concerning source. Walter Byers, executive director of the NCAA (National College Athletic Association), announced his qualified opposition. Focusing on the Phillip Hart legislation exempting all major pro sports from antitrust laws, Byers asserted, "The Hart bill . . . would eliminate any bargaining by the individual. He could deal only with the club that selected him. We have reservations about such a free-agent draft on moral grounds. Denying the prospective athlete any right of choice before he is able to play is bad in principle." He then qualified his stance: "If Congress is going to legalize the free-agent draft, we think it's only fair to provide that a boy can't be drafted until he completes his education."[73] In other words, Byers's "moral" ground centered on guaranteeing that colleges could keep their players all four years, hardly a position lacking self-interest. As with O'Connor, his opposition wouldn't prove troublesome, partly due to its self-interest, but also because Frick had a separate deal with the NCAA to support college summer baseball, as will be discussed in chapter 12. So far, the free-agent draft was progressing.

At least it was until the special meeting of owners in August to discuss details and timing. Only half offered support, forcing the proposal to be tabled. Those in opposition suggested maintaining the existing first-year draft with alterations, feeling it could be effective in curtailing bonuses and distributing talent equitably. They also expressed concern the free-agent draft would bring attention from the Justice Department and the House Judiciary Committee.[74] The meeting appeared to delay Frick's plans by at least a year—if not stop it altogether. C. C. Johnson Spink called it "a sharp rebuff to and a major defeat for Commissioner Ford Frick as well as the committee which had worked for a long time to effect such legislation. Frick had said accomplishment of this was his No. 1 goal prior to retirement." He added, "It is difficult to justify the [current] first-year rule along financial lines. The bonus system today has to cost the major leagues upwards of $5,000,000 a year with no guarantee they will get a good return on their money." He urged owners to go back to work on the free-agent draft.[75] In spite of that encouragement, it no longer seemed likely in 1965.

Frick hadn't conceded, however, as he convened a three-day meeting of the general managers in early November. Its outcome was a recommendation to owners that they adopt the free-agent draft as proposed, including provisions that no high school player be drafted until his class graduated and no college player be taken until his sophomore year ended. The owners met in Phoenix immediately afterward and adopted the proposal.[76] Since this was not a formal meeting, it still required enactment at the Winter Meetings, including Minor League approval. Nonetheless, in the two-plus months since rejection, Frick had brought the draft back on track.

That rendered the Winter Meetings outcome a foregone conclusion. The Minor Leagues voted unanimously, and the Majors voted the following day, with only one opposing vote in each league. Not surprisingly, O'Malley spoke in opposition at the Minor League session, warning it would leave baseball open to restraint of trade charges or antitrust legislation. Contradicting the Dodgers' magnate, Frick, Louis Carroll, and Benjamin Fiery, the leagues' attorneys, were confident the draft wouldn't produce federal action. Gabe Paul, general manager of the Indians and strong supporter, exclaimed, "This could be the greatest development since night baseball."[77] *New York Times* reporter Joseph Durso called it a "revolutionary change." He continued, "They were approved after months of politicking and palace intrigue among the big league teams."[78] The baseball magnates had indeed enacted a dramatic change.

Although Frick left little documentation beyond his quotes, it was apparent the draft became personal as he approached retirement. He personally met with the general managers in 1964 and remained a strong advocate leading into the ill-fated August meeting; its backlash was a surprise. The quick turnaround by November typified Frick's management style. Few public comments were provided before the general managers and owners met, but the rapid turnaround suggests many behind the scenes conversations. How much of it was arm-twisting is unknown, but there is little doubt adoption would not have occurred without his involvement. One can only speculate on how much time would have elapsed before the draft was started if it had not been completed by his retirement.

The assessment by *The Sporting News* shortly after passage provides a serious postmortem. Frick was credited with a major role, although a report that he "swung some of the opposition into line" was denied. Baseball's executives were aware of his strong support, some indicating it was effective. By the time the Majors voted, even the Dodgers were reluctantly in line. The American League favored unanimously, and the only negative in the Senior Circuit came from the Cardinals, with Auggie Busch fearing judicial repercussions. Frick summarized his feelings prophetically: "I think we came out of these meetings with a more positive and definitive program than we've ever had. Baseball has finally gotten off dead center."[79] Success could be fleeting, however, if the first draft went poorly.

Frick was aware of that, so he was very particular in selecting the committee that developed its format. Both league presidents were on it, along with Phil Piton, the new president of the Minor's National Association of Professional Baseball Leagues. Two general managers were also selected—Lee MacPhail of the Orioles and Joe Brown of the Pirates, both highly regarded by peers. Frick was also a member. He presided over the meeting in Tampa during spring training, where numerous club officials were invited to discuss problems and pose questions about structure and implementation. Frick, in turn, committed to keep those officials informed of any changes after the committee met to formulize plans.[80] Although plans were developed carefully, most details were finalized in less than a month. The draft would take place in New York City on June 8. Rather than separate drafts for high school, college, and American Legion players, all would be drafted together. It would proceed in reverse order, the weakest clubs having the first choices. The leagues would annually alternate which would begin, with this year's top pick belonging to the American League. Teams would have six months to negotiate. If a deal could not be reached, the player would be drafted again the following year.[81] The deliberations and preparations had proceeded carefully.

As draft day approached, there were still considerable differences concerning its merits. On one side, Johnny Johnson, Yankees' farm system director, called it "communistic." Consistent with past opposition, O'Malley questioned its legality. Wealthier clubs, who could afford extravagant bonuses, tended to be more negative. On the other hand, most executives agreed with its goals: to save money on bonuses and to provide more even distribution of talent. Many also liked the six-month period to negotiate.[82] Spink was optimistic: "One of the most momentous events in modern baseball was scheduled to take place on June 8–9 in New York—the first free-agent draft. . . . If this draft is only half as successful as the proponents of the legislation have forecast it will be a tremendous step forward."[83]

By all accounts there was good reason for optimism. Clifford Kachline, covering the draft process for years, was impressed: "Like the Gemini space program, Organized Baseball's first venture into the free-agent player draft got away to a remarkably smooth start. The blastoff was perfect and all of the technicians behind the great innovation, from Commissioner Ford Frick on down, expressed satisfaction with the launch." John McHale, the Braves' president, said, "I think the commissioner and his staff should be congratulated for the manner in which the meetings were conducted." Other clubs echoed that sentiment. As expected, Rick Monday, a sophomore at Arizona State University, was selected first by the A's. Frick opened the affair, then turned the process over to Charles Segar, and even critics were impressed with how smoothly it was conducted.[84] Baseball began an enduring venture.

Even parents and players drafted were impressed with the smoothness of the implementation. Frick was certainly pleased. "The reaction from the boys and their families has been very good. There are bound to be some bugs in the machinery because this is the first time we've tried it. We have been working over two years on this plan with the hope of letting the clubs which finish down in the leagues get a better chance at the talent," he said. A *Chicago Tribune* sports columnist agreed: "The recent major league talent draft, though it showed some imperfections, is a progressive step in baseball. Now the clubs are operating sensibly and will equalize competition the way it is equalized in professional football."[85] By most standards the draft has helped bring parity to the Majors. Neither Frick nor the columnist mentioned the other motive—controlling bonus payouts. The lack of complaints about amounts paid draftees suggests it also accomplished that objective. It was an enduring success.

Another action at the 1964 Winter Meetings received major attention—providing additional power to baseball's commissioner. When Landis died, magnates placed limitations on the position (see chapter 5). The changes were subtle, intended to prevent overstepping of authority, as many felt Landis had done. Before Chandler's selection, owners inserted a right to take to court any disagreement with a commissioner's ruling. They also established that no action they took complying with existing baseball rules could be construed by the commissioner as "detrimental to baseball."[86] That clause seemed to usurp what had been interpreted to provide the commissioner with total authority over the magnates. Sportswriters concluded commissioner powers had been reduced substantially, that both Chandler and Frick had become mere administrators with limited powers. The reality was different. As long as the commissioner acknowledged that owners hired him, paid his salary, and could thus fire him, he could accomplish much—not by decree, but by persuasion. Frick understood this and knew how to work around restrictions, though he was concerned his replacement might not. Frick probably pushed to reestablish Landis's alleged powers to facilitate matters for his successor. In effect, with or without the constraints, an understanding of the internal politics and knowing how to work through them was the only way any commissioner could manage. Essentially, a commissioner could be effective if he cared less about image and more about how to work through internal and external politics for accomplishments. Hence, Frick was successful with the draft.

10

Preserving the "Exemption"

A top priority when Ford Frick was named commissioner was maintaining baseball's exemption from the Sherman Antitrust Act, granted by the U.S. Supreme Court in 1922 in *Federal Baseball Club v. National League*. Since its creation, professional baseball experienced tumultuous periods, but that decision stabilized it, with no competition coming from new leagues and confidence the reserve clause was secure. That changed in 1951. Emanuel Celler's Antitrust Subcommittee in the U.S. House of Representatives decided to examine the game's exemption then, responding in part to the *Gardella v. Chandler* decision in 1949. Ultimately, no action was recommended by the subcommittee, but the Supreme Court soon after reviewed its 1922 decision. In *Toolson v. New York Yankees*, the court produced a positive result for baseball, reaffirming its 1922 ruling, while stressing it was Congress's job to place baseball under antitrust. Numerous congressional hearings followed, with Frick testifying almost once a year. Throughout those hearings, baseball maintained its exemption, even after the Supreme Court placed other major sports under antitrust in 1957. It was a major achievement.

DECADES OF TURMOIL STABILIZED

The creation of the National League by William Hulbert in 1876 was a concerted effort to bring stability to the professional game that the first association failed to achieve. Hulbert superseded it, establishing eight teams in major markets, all within a twenty-four-hour train ride. Each club committed to a set schedule against others, and all guaranteed exclusive territorial rights in their cities. Three years later, with cities dropping out and being replaced, the league adopted the reserve clause, which guaranteed that the best players would remain with the same club. A second Major League—the American Association—emerged in the early

1880s, respecting the territorial rights and reserve clause Hulbert helped establish. That changed after the 1889 season.

Players in both leagues were dissatisfied with salaries and convinced the reserve clause kept them at their club's mercy. Led by John Montgomery Ward, a star pitcher and also a lawyer, many of the better players established the Players' League in 1890. Eight new teams were created, almost all in cities with existing Major League clubs. The new league often outdrew the other two leagues, though the competition reduced attendance for teams overall. When the season ended, Players' League investors were persuaded they couldn't survive and sold their interests to the other leagues' owners, eliminating the league. The American Association folded a year later, with four of its teams joining the eight National League clubs. Territorial rights and the reserve clause were again secure.

The league's size proved problematic. Too many teams were eliminated early from contention, losing fan interest. By 1899 it had become so severe that four teams were abolished—Cleveland, Louisville, Washington, and Baltimore. Baltimore had been one of the better-performing clubs on the field but struggled at the box office. Three markets didn't go for long without baseball. The Western League, a strong Minor League organization headed by Byron Bancroft "Ban" Johnson, jumped at the opportunity provided by the void. In 1900 Johnson changed the name to the American League and moved into Washington, Baltimore, Cleveland, and Chicago. A year later, it surprised the National League by declaring itself a Major League, moving teams into Boston and Philadelphia to compete head-on. The American League also established franchises in Detroit and Milwaukee. Chaos returned.

Not only were territorial rights disregarded, but so was the reserve clause. The American League didn't hesitate to raid the other league for players, succeeding more often than not. It ignored territorial rights again by moving its Milwaukee club to St. Louis in 1902 and Baltimore to New York a year later. Player salaries increased considerably. The Senior Circuit sued for peace before the 1903 season, resulting in the National Agreement. With it, the reserve clause was restored, player salaries decreased, and territorial rights were respected—though four cities out of the ten now had two clubs and New York three. The agreement also established an after-season series between the leagues' winners, soon labeled the World Series.

Once again, peace didn't last. In 1913 James Gilmore organized a new Minor League, the Federal League. Duplicating Ban Johnson's actions, Gilmore declared his organization a Major League a year later, established clubs in three new cities, filled the Baltimore vacancy, and competed head-to-head with existing clubs in Pittsburgh, Brooklyn, Chicago, and St. Louis. New York City now had four teams, Chicago and St. Louis three. Once again, the reserve clause was rendered moot, though the Federal League had less success than the American had in attracting players. After its initial season, the Federal League owners were convinced the other leagues had colluded, and they filed an antitrust suit with a Chicago federal court early in 1915. The judge was Kenesaw Mountain Landis, a noted trustbuster notorious for his quick rulings. This time, Landis delayed, refusing to act during the season. When it ended, the Federal League had suffered severe financial losses and reached out to settle.[1] That rendered its antitrust case moot, and settlements were quickly reached with most clubs. Only the Baltimore Terrapins held out, due in part to its numerous shareholders and to also wanting a Major League team, with Baltimore having lost two already. They rejected a deal while hoping to gain a relocating franchise or threatening to take its case to court if they couldn't.[2] Since Judge Landis hadn't ruled on the earlier case, the investors were convinced they had an antitrust case against baseball.

They filed in a Philadelphia court in 1917, though the investors dropped it four days later in hope of a settlement. When that failed, the shareholders brought suit again, this time in Washington, though the hearing was delayed until spring 1919. Judge Wendell Stafford heard the case for the DC federal court, and after both sides presented, he instructed the jury that organized baseball had attempted to "monopolize commerce between the states." In effect, Stafford decided the case, leaving the jury only to determine the award. The amount decided, $80,000 with treble damages, was sufficient to have the Majors appeal. The Washington Court of Appeals overturned the decision, with the chief judge ruling that playing of baseball games was not a form of "trade or commerce," and thus the Sherman Act wasn't applicable.[3] The Terrapins' owners appealed to the Supreme Court because the two rulings differed so markedly. Baseball's status under the Sherman Act was obviously open to interpretation in the courts.

Baseball was not the first antitrust issue heard by the Supreme Court. It had reviewed one involving the insurance industry, concluding it did not engage in interstate commerce. Similarly, in a case involving the

Sugar Trust, which controlled 98 percent of the nation's refinement, it ruled the Sherman Act didn't apply because production was different from commerce. Conversely, it ruled that the Sherman Act applied to both Standard Oil and the American Tobacco Company because both shipped interstate. Likewise, the court declared it applicable to a correspondence school that sent books and papers from one state to another.[4] Given that track record, the appeal by the Terrapins was a gamble. Due to a swelling caseload, caused in part by the Sherman Act, the court had lobbied Congress for years to have discretion on hearing cases, and in 1925 Congress passed the Judiciary Act, providing such discretion.[5] That was not the case in 1922, however, so the court was required to hear and render a decision.

Like the cases mentioned, the 1890 Sherman Act was the focus, which had prohibited any restraint of trade or commerce crossing state lines. Three elements had to be proven: First was proof of a conspiracy, a collaboration of parties. Second was the actual restraint of commerce or trade. Third, such restraint had to involve interstate commerce. Justice Oliver Wendell Holmes Jr. authored the court's decision: "As put by the defendants, personal effort, not related to production, is not a subject of commerce." The transportation of players across state lines was merely incidental. In effect, Holmes, author of a 9–0 decision, reflected comments made by baseball's chief attorney, George Wharton Pepper, that "labor . . . is not a commodity or article of commerce."[6] The playing of baseball games, though crossing state lines, did not meet the definition of commerce in the Sherman Act. The law didn't apply.

The Sherman Act wasn't exclusive in shaping Holmes' opinion; the Clayton Act of 1914, in particular section 6, also played a role. It was adopted to keep labor contracts out of consideration regarding interstate commerce or antitrust: "The labor of a human being is not a commodity or article of commerce." This had been the core of George Wharton Pepper's argument, along with being the basis for the earlier Court of Appeals' ruling.[7] Thus, similar language in Holmes's opinion wasn't surprising. The playing of baseball, a labor rather than a commodity, was not commerce.

While the *Federal Baseball Club v. National League* decision was subsequently interpreted as granting baseball an antitrust exemption, such wasn't the intent. The ruling merely stated that given the definition of commerce, the Sherman Act wasn't applicable. It didn't exempt the sport from anything.[8] Nonetheless, both territorial rights and the reserve clause were interpreted to be covered by the decision, which helped provide baseball with decades of stability. From 1922 until 1946, baseball wasn't impacted by court rulings. Most important, there were no threats from new leagues to challenge the reserve clause or territorial rights. It was logical for baseball's executives to conclude that the 1922 decision provided them protection that hadn't previously existed. While suffering through the Great Depression and World War II, baseball was not threatened with challenges to territory or player control. That started to change in 1946.

OH, DANNY BOY

As baseball executives prepared for the first season in five without war, it's doubtful Jorge Pasquel was a concern to them. For that matter, they unlikely gave any regard to the Mexican League, of which he was president. That soon changed. Pasquel entertained no thoughts of moving into American cities to compete, but he was interested in attracting Major League talent. Territorial rights weren't threatened, but the reserve clause was. Pasquel began a concerted effort to sign players, attracting them to Mexico with the promise of larger salaries. Along with his brothers, Pasquel was an owner of the Veracruz club when named president. As far back as 1943, he had attracted players from the Negro Leagues, and their success convinced him to pursue the Majors' talent. He anticipated that higher salaries would attract players, their skills drawing more fans, and thus the money to pay them. He had some success, as over twenty players signed contracts.[9] A couple soon returned, because they were unaccustomed to the different culture and playing environment. Most stayed through 1946, though many regretted their decision and hoped to return to their clubs.

Unfortunately, they could not. Before the 1946 season, Happy Chandler, still a rookie commissioner, banned any player who had jumped unless they returned before the season. Otherwise, they were banned from baseball for five years. No one opposed Chandler's ruling; its timing was likely deterring some players from jumping. Ford Frick appeared supportive of Chandler, suggesting others might return: "The Mexican climate and living conditions south of the border are not suitable to United States ballplayers."[10] His comment proved prophetic. Many of those who jumped were ready to come back after one season but blocked by the ruling.

One was Danny Gardella, who had played for the New York Giants in 1944 and 1945. Short—only 5 feet 7—and left-handed, he could only play outfield. He had spent time in the Minors in the late 1930s, but with limited prospects, he returned home in New York City, holding numerous jobs. He continued to play baseball during the summer, and his success, especially in 1943, caught the attention of Giants manager Mel Ott, who was losing players to the war. Gardella was classified 4-F due to a punctured eardrum, sent to the Minors after signing, and called up in May 1944. While adequate at the plate, he struggled in the field and was returned to the Minors. He was with the Giants for all of 1945, appearing in 121 games.[11]

With the large number of returning players at war's end, Gardella realized he was unlikely to make the roster. Nonetheless, the Giants offered him $5,000, larger than what he had earned until late the previous season. Expecting more, Gardella left spring training and threatened to jump to the Mexican League. Instead, he reported to the Giants, but Ott was tired of his antics and sent him to the Minors. Offended, Gardella contacted Pasquel and was offered a contract with Veracruz for $8,000 with a $5,000 signing bonus. Although he played well, he and his spouse missed the United States and returned after the season.

Gardella was aware of the ban.[12] He played winter ball in Cuba and then signed for the summer with the Gulf Oilers, a semipro team on Staten Island. When his club was scheduled to play the Cleveland Buckeyes, a Negro League team, Chandler sent a telegram. It stated that anyone who participated against Gardella or any other former Mexican League player would be banned for life from baseball. In essence, Chandler, who had already blacklisted Mexican League players, was now penalizing those who competed against them after they returned. The loss of his baseball livelihood prompted Gardella to explore legal action. A friend sent him to Frederic Johnson, a lawyer familiar with antitrust law.[13] Johnson filed a lawsuit, naming baseball's top four executives—Chandler, Frick, Harridge, and Trautman—as defendants, along with the National Exhibition Company, the parent company of the Giants. He sued for $100,000, subject to treble damages, claiming baseball's reserve clause "is monopolistic and tends to restrain trade and commerce in violation of the Sherman and Clayton anti-trust laws." Johnson added that the ban "deprives him [Gardella] of his livelihood, destroys his ability as a professional baseball player, and has resulted in damages amounting to $100,000."[14] Baseball faced its first antitrust case since *Federal Baseball Club v. National League*.

It was filed with the Second Circuit Court in New York before Judge Henry Goddard, who served on the bench for thirty years.[15] In late January 1948 Johnson argued that *Federal Baseball Club v. National League* was no longer relevant, citing the establishment of Minor League farm systems and the advent of both radio and television broadcasts crossing state lines. Both had occurred since 1922.[16] Essentially, changing conditions dictated that baseball was engaged in interstate commerce. At the same time, negotiations were transpiring between Chandler and Pasquel that could have rendered the case irrelevant. Pasquel was seeking a place for his struggling league within organized baseball but failing due to his own intransigence and National League opposition, the latter perhaps due to Frick being excluded from negotiations. Had a deal been reached, the ban on players could have ended and the case been rendered moot.[17] Instead, Gardella's suit continued.

Judge Goddard rendered his decision in July 1948, seeking a middle ground. He dismissed the Gardella suit, citing *Federal Baseball Club v. National League*, while suggesting a Supreme Court reversal was possible. Goddard believed the decisions the Supreme Court relied upon were "substantially lessened if not completely overruled by a later decision." Fredric Johnson made clear he would take the case to the Court of Appeals in New York. Noting the appeals court recently cited *Federal Baseball Club v. National League* in a case arguing whether opera was interstate commerce, Goddard concluded it was well positioned to review Gardella's case.[18] In effect, he kicked the can down the road.

Goodard was correct concerning the Court of Appeals. In a split decision, rendered in early February 1949, it ruled, 2–1, that baseball was involved in interstate commerce by current definitions. Judges Jerome N. Frank and Learned Hand agreed that radio and television broadcasts changed the nature of baseball, bringing the game under the Sherman and Clayton Acts. Frank also believed the reserve clause was illegal, in violation of the Thirteenth Amendment because it created "involuntary servitude." Hand was more moderate but felt the reserve needed elimination if baseball was ruled a monopoly. The third judge on the panel, Harrie B. Chase, countered the others. He didn't believe the reserve clause violated the Sherman Antitrust Act and felt broadcasting of games was no different than sending a game's progress over telegraph, as was done in 1922. It was a ruling that, without appeal to a higher court, might threaten the game's antitrust protection. Frick was cautious: "If we are in violation of any rule, we will first have to determine which rule it is we are violating. I'm not a lawyer, however, and can't say too much about these decisions." It was suggested Chandler end the ban on Mexican League jumpers, thus reinstating them, though the commissioner felt that would show weakness.[19] It was clear baseball would need to appeal to the Supreme Court or reach a deal with Gardella.

The Second Circuit Court decision initiated a series of actions over the next seven months. First, other banned players threatened to sue baseball. Two did, requesting far more than was at stake in the Gardella case.[20] In late April baseball attorneys asked a federal court to dismiss *Gardella v. Chandler*, denying baseball was interstate commerce, contending its broadcasts were incidental to the game, and stressing the importance of the reserve clause. Frick explained the reserve clause was "to prevent the more powerful clubs in the major leagues from signing the star players of their less prosperous rivals at the end of each year and to equalize the opportunities of each team to win the pennant."[21] By June Chandler lifted his ban, allowing all players to return at the same salary received when they departed during a thirty-day tryout period. All but Gardella accepted and dropped their lawsuits. In announcing Gardella wouldn't apply for reinstatement, Johnson conveyed confidence he had baseball "on the run."[22] Now the contested issue only involved one player, though it remained a major threat.

That threat precipitated interest from Congress. In early April 1949 a bill was introduced in the House of Representatives prohibiting any antitrust prosecution of sports. Specifically, it protected all sports from being classified as interstate commerce because they broadcast games. The bill was introduced by Wilbur Mills of Arkansas and Albert Sydney Herlong of Florida, both Democrats. Herlong had an interest because he was formerly president of the Florida State Baseball League. The legislation clarified that it did not affect the *Gardella* case, but it clearly aimed to protect all sports from antitrust. The two congressmen promised major hearings with witnesses, including Joe DiMaggio, Ted Williams, Jackie Robinson, Satchel Paige, Bob Feller, and Stan Musial. Baseball may have discouraged the hearings because its lead attorney on the *Gardella* case advised Chandler not to pursue legislation.[23] Although nothing materialized, the bill helped stimulate the Celler hearings in 1951.

The *Gardella* suit was resolved in the fall 1949. By dropping the suit, Gardella received a $60,000 payment, half going to Johnson. He was also granted a 1950 tryout with the Cardinals and was quickly optioned, ending his career.[24] Baseball had dodged the challenge to its exemption, though the New York Court of Appeals decision remained unresolved, providing fodder for the next round of cases. Those, along with Gardella's, were noted by Emanuel Celler as he contemplated baseball hearings in 1951.

BASEBALL COMES TO CONGRESS

Emanuel Celler chaired both the Antitrust Subcommittee and the Judiciary Committee to which it reported. After becoming chair in 1949, he likely put off hearings on the Mills and Herlong bills. With a new Congress in 1951 and baseball facing antitrust lawsuits, Celler decided it was a good time to examine baseball's operations and procedures. His congressional career had demonstrated strong support for the underdog. Celler grew up in Brooklyn, a son of Jewish immigrants, and since his election in 1922, he was a strong advocate of civil rights and was involved in all such legislation after World War II. He was also a supporter of immigration and an advocate for open-border laws. Consistent with his support of the underdog, he was also antimonopoly, believing government had a role to protect and maintain competition.[25] Nonetheless, he appeared to approach the baseball hearings with an open mind.

When the hearings commenced, baseball had no commissioner. Chandler's contract was not renewed at the 1950 Winter Meetings, and the owners had yet to decide on a replacement. Frick was still National League president, representing baseball at the hearings in that capacity. Days after Chandler resigned, Frick learned he would be the second witness, following lead-off hitter Ty Cobb. The publicly stated purpose of the hearings was to determine if legislation was necessary to exempt baseball from antitrust laws.[26] If Frick was nervous or concerned, it wasn't evident. He offered an optimistic tone at the Hall of Fame induction in July: "I believe a better game will come out of the hearings. I believe the committee will throw away the mists and open a new highway for baseball through the years ahead."[27] Although baseball was entering unchartered territory, Frick remained positive.

The witness net was cast widely. It included current and former players; current and former executives, including Chandler and Leslie O'Connor (who had to be subpoenaed); a former umpire fired by Harridge for allegedly spying for Chandler; Frederic Johnson; numerous sportswriters, including J. G. Taylor Spink; and Minor League owners and players.

Not all witnesses were favorable because Celler didn't want the hearing to appear to be a whitewash. Indeed, many blemishes were highlighted. Chandler's ban of Mexican ballplayers was criticized, as was the allegedly destroyed 1946 MacPhail Report. The deal in which Walter O'Malley acquired Branch Rickey's interest in the Dodgers was also questioned. Baseball's warts, including the reserve clause, were fair game during two weeks in late July and August and another two in October.[28] Frederic Johnson was able to express his criticism of the reserve clause, calling it both "illegal and inequitable" and adding that it "hinders both free labor and free competition."[29] Frick was a featured witness, testifying for much of the first two days and returning on its last day in late October, this time as commissioner. He was the second witness when president and the second-to-last witness when commissioner.

Chairman Celler set the tone in his opening statement. He mentioned that the legislation proposed by Mills and Herlong intended to protect all major sports, exempting them from antitrust laws as they were at the time. He referred to the *Gardella* case and its threat of treble damages; addressed current cases in federal courts, such as the *Toolson* suit; and outlined areas of discontent, including the reserve clause, the farm system, the commissioner's powers, the geographical distribution of Major League clubs, and challenges involving the broadcasting and televising of games. Celler emphasized the intent was to help baseball, setting a tone that wasn't adversarial.[30]

Though he had expressed optimism, Frick was prepared for the worst and accompanied by two attorneys—Paul Porter and Louis Carroll—to assist him with the questions. Carroll had been the National League attorney for at least a decade, advising Frick during much of his tenure as president. Porter was relatively new to baseball, having worked in the Roosevelt and Truman administrations, with his last position as chairman of the Federal Communications Commission. More recently, he had partnered with Thurmond Arnold, notorious during FDR's presidency for his trust-busting efforts.[31] Porter may have been hired by Chandler, who became acquainted with him while serving in the Senate. In any case, his antitrust expertise proved helpful in guiding Frick through the intensive questioning.

Frick began with prepared remarks, portraying himself as "fundamentally a lucky fan . . . who by good luck has been permitted to live a little closer to the game." He embellished parts of his past history, calling himself "a farm lad, . . . playing the game of the pasture land" and "rushing to scan the sports pages in Chicago papers every morning." He also claimed to play baseball in college, "rather poorly, I guess—but with a great deal of enthusiasm." He also referred to his background as sportswriter and pioneer broadcaster in New York. He finished by noting some feared the hearings would tear away the "very foundations of the game" and "disrupt a typically American institution." Celler denied any such intention, for which Frick thanked him.[32] The commissioner utilized myths about his past to create a country-boy-made-good image, softening the perception of a stiff, privileged baseball executive.

He then turned to core issues: "Organized baseball today is something more than a consolidated balance sheet and bank account. . . . It is important to recognize two fundamental bases on which the structure is built and stands. The first of these is the recognition of territorial rights; the second is the right of player contract reserve." In that statement, he summarized seventy-five years of baseball history. He went on to explain how baseball clubs were both competitors and partners, needing to compete on the field but also work together enforcing the rules and establishing schedules. He ended by stressing there were only two alternatives to the reserve clause—eliminate it or establish a long-term contract. He emphasized neither was viable, having produced chaos in early baseball. Resuming the next morning, he added, "The reserve clause is the foundation of professional baseball." Frick also summarized ways baseball supported World War II efforts, establishing its significance beyond the game itself.[33] He then received questions, which occupied a good portion of the day.

The questioning encompassed many topics. When discussing players banned for jumping to the Mexican League, Frick cautiously conceded that labeling it as "blacklisting" was appropriate. He elaborated further on how the reserve applied to all players signed by a club, even at the Minors' lower levels. As for allowing players to have a say in selecting a commissioner, he conceded, after being pushed, "I would personally have no objection whatsoever to the players of baseball having a voice in the election of the commissioner." When pressured by Celler and Congressman Hillings from LA on franchise transfers, in particular being accused by Celler of being stuck in the status quo, Frick predicted that "within the foreseeable future, within a very limited length of time—you will see major league baseball on the Pacific Coast or other cities if they so desire." Frick answered questions to the subcommittee's satisfaction, conveyed when Frick's testimony ended on July 31. Celler, not one to compliment witnesses, made an exception by expressing his appreciation for the testimony.[34] Frick was likely smiling as he left the hearing, though it would prove to be a rare compliment from Celler.

Frick returned at the hearings' close in October. Not much new was covered, though he was questioned on the recent deal in which Walter O'Malley bought out Rickey's one-quarter ownership of the Dodgers. Since Chandler had approved it, Frick stressed there was no reason for him as a league president to be involved. He added that were he commissioner, he wouldn't have allowed the deal. That produced another Celler compliment: "I appreciate your candor. That indicates that you are going to make a good commissioner. That is courageous and I complement you on that answer."[35] That was a nice boost for Frick so early in his tenure.

There were other interesting exchanges at the hearings' close. The assistant counsel to the subcommittee, John Paul Stevens, later a Supreme Court justice, pushed Frick hard concerning poor relations between players and owners. Frick responded, "My dear Mr. Stevens . . . as commissioner of baseball I would again reiterate . . . that the player relationship between the club owners . . . to me has been one of the most pleasant things I have seen develop in baseball." He then added that the commissioner should represent, in order, the "players, the public and the owners."[36] Regardless of whether those comments reflected reality, they conveyed what the subcommittee wanted to hear.

Frick again addressed the primary concern of Congressman Hillings and his desire for Major League baseball in LA, stressing that meeting with the Pacific Coast League would be one of his first duties as commissioner. Hillings, in turn, expressed satisfaction with baseball's renewed West Coast interest.[37] From all sides, the hearings ended positively.

When the hearings' report was published the following May, baseball and its commissioner received additional satisfaction—the subcommittee recommended no action. On the reserve clause, it concluded, "If the reserve clause is merely used for the purpose of promoting competition among the various clubs in organized baseball and is necessary for the successful operation of the game, it would seem unlikely that its use would be regarded as an abuse of monopoly power."[38] It also addressed territorial rights, mostly in the context of the control of club transfers. At present, any club in either league could veto another's decision. The report noted that Frick emphasized a complete review of the baseball map was needed. It further indicated that Frick "is the first commissioner whose background and experience is most intimately connected with organized major league baseball."[39] Overall, the comments were favorable.

The conclusions of the subcommittee were that (1) the reserve clause should not be restricted, (2) baseball should not be granted full antitrust exemption because it would give too much freedom for bad practices—hence bills giving sports full antitrust exemptions should be rejected, (3) baseball should not be saddled with any government regulatory agency, and (4) the findings do favor some kind of legislation protecting the reserve clause, "provided that such rules guarantee players a reasonable opportunity to advance in their profession and to be paid at a rate commensurate with their ability. At the same time, baseball should not be protected from any geographical realignment of franchises or arbitrary blacklisting."[40] Essentially, the status quo was ratified.

Frick was satisfied: "Baseball can find much of benefit in the expressed opinions and suggestions of Mr. Celler and his associates. That baseball faces many problems is self-evident. That these problems as they arise can best be handled within the organization itself is apparently the unanimous opinion of the committee." In his weekly editorial, J. G. Taylor Spink noted, "The committee's basic conclusions—that baseball cannot profitably exist without some form of reserve clause, but that it would be unwise to exempt the sport from the provisions of the anti-trust laws—should fill every executive, from the commissioner himself to the humblest franchise in the minors, with a deep sense of responsibility. For while the report in general displays understanding of and sympathy with the game's many problems, it places responsibility for the solution of those problems squarely in the hands of the game's officials."[41]

In that regard, the report was mixed because baseball didn't receive legislative protection. At the same time, there were no restrictions on the reserve clause. It encouraged baseball to consider franchise relocations, which Frick quickly moved to do by changing relocation rules. While little was gained, nothing was lost. Baseball could operate as it had. There was a lesson in that for Frick, reinforcing what he learned during World War II while protecting the 1945 season—it was easier to maintain the status quo than pass legislation. Put another way, it was easier to play defense than offense with Congress, a lesson Ford Frick recalled well during future dealings. That was reinforced when the Supreme Court ruled again on baseball and antitrust in 1953.

DEJA VU ALL OVER AGAIN (SORT OF)

The pending court cases regarding baseball's antitrust status were no surprise to executives. One involved a Dodger ballplayer stuck in the lower Minors and the other a disgruntled Minor League club owner in El Paso, Texas. Both argued baseball was violating antitrust laws, requested a review of the *Federal Baseball* case, and were represented by Frederic Johnson. Johnson lost both, the judge ruling that due to *Federal Baseball*, the plaintiffs had no standing. That reflected a similar ruling in another court concerning Earl Toolson, a pitcher in the Yankees farm system who felt stifled in the Minors. *Federal Baseball* again preempted. Although Johnson indicated an appeal, Frick and Trautman issued a positive joint statement on the rulings: "It confirms the belief held all along by all baseball administrators that we have been and are operating within the law."[42] Their comfort would prove short-lived, for Johnson succeeded in his Supreme Court appeal.

That was less likely to happen in 1953 because the court wasn't required to hear every case. At the very least, stare decisis—let the earlier decision stand—suggested it wouldn't accept the appeal given *Federal Baseball*. However, Johnson incorporated the *Gardella* ruling from the New York Court of Appeals that indicated antitrust laws applied to baseball. This discrepancy was enough for the Supreme Court to accept the case, combining Johnson's two cases with Toolson's. Baseball was represented by the leagues' attorneys—Benjamin Fiery from the American League and Louis Carroll from the National League. They had two major contentions supporting the status quo—the 1922 decision and the threat of retroactivity. If the court overturned *Federal Baseball*, it could open the door for all players current and past to sue for damages caused by antitrust violations, an outcome potentially disastrous financially. By contrast there would be no retroactivity if Congress was to enact legislation.[43] Further, Congress had just conducted extensive hearings, deciding that no action was necessary. Those issues would weigh heavily with the court.

Their decision was quick, rendered a month later. By a 7–2 vote the justices upheld *Federal Baseball*. There was a twist, however, as stated in the short brief written by new Chief Justice Earl Warren: "Congress . . .

has not seen fit to bring such business [baseball] under these laws by legislation having prospective effect. The business has been left for thirty years to develop, on the understanding that it was not subject to existing antitrust legislation. The present case asks us to overrule the prior decision and, with retrospective effect, hold the legislation applicable. We think that if there are evils in this field which now warrant application to it of the antitrust laws it should be by legislation." In essence, past inaction by Congress did not excuse it from acting, if necessary, given potential retroactivity from a court decision. Unlike *Federal Baseball*, there were two dissenting justices. Most of that stemmed from the argument that any antitrust exemption should come from Congress: "Congress, however, has enacted no express exemption of organized baseball from the Sherman Act, and no court has demonstrated the existence of an implied exemption from that Act of any sport that is so highly organized as to amount to an interstate monopoly or which restrains interstate trade or commerce. . . . It is interstate trade or commerce and, as such, it is subject to the Sherman Act until exempted."[44] Although the two dissenters felt baseball shouldn't be exempt, all agreed it was Congress's responsibility.

Clearly, the concern of retroactivity prevailed, for the justices voted in the affirmative and referenced that in their brief. Yet, it wasn't a necessary byproduct. Frederic Johnson attempted to make this point in statements before the hearing, stressing the intent was not to make all players free agents with compensation for past damages. Rather, "all we are asking for is a reasonable interpretation of the Reserve Clause so that the 16 major league clubs do not monopolize the player market."[45] For whatever reason, his point didn't resonate, and the outcome left baseball with the perceived exemption it hadn't actually received thirty years earlier.

More important, as legal scholar Ed Edmonds has noted, the *Toolson* case accomplished what *Federal Baseball* had not—solidifying the antitrust exemption.[46] The *Federal Baseball* case, was merely an opinion that baseball wasn't included in the Sherman Act's definitions of trade or commerce; it had never ruled baseball to be exempt. This time, the court's majority didn't rely on the commerce rationale, muting the argument accepted in the *Gardella* appeal. As far as the Supreme Court was concerned, baseball was now exempted. At the same time, the court made clear Congress was free to act at any time to bring the sport under antitrust laws without retroactivity. Frick's focus now turned fully to Congress.

Whereas most baseball executives were elated with *Toolson*, Frick was cautious: "It does not mean that baseball is granted a license to do as it pleases. . . . From now on, the responsibility is ours of modernizing baseball; of meeting the challenge of changing conditions; of stepping from the past into the changing present and making sure always that our decisions and our policies are based on honesty, on fairness, on true sportsmanship and with every consideration to the best interests of the fans and the players and those who have made baseball our National Game." In *The Sporting News*, J. G. Taylor Spink suggested the dissenting opinion "should serve as a warning that baseball has no unchallenged authority to serve its own ends without regard for the common good."[47]

Spink continued his caution soon after, focusing on the reserve clause:

> Contrary to popular belief, the Supreme Court decision did not legalize the reserve clause. . . . It did not in any sense determine the equity or lack thereof in an arrangement which gives the club indefinite control of the player's services, while guaranteeing the player no more security than a 30-day notice of dismissal. . . . For these reasons, it is important that the reserve clause—recognized by practically everyone, including the players, as the foundation of baseball as we know it—be liberalized in favor of the hired hands. Such a course would go far toward justifying the clause in the minds of the public, the courts and the Congress.[48]

Basically, more flexibility on the reserve clause, with more benefits to players, would improve baseball's status with Congress. Unfortunately, many team owners didn't take Spink's suggestions seriously, which would produce ramifications after Frick had retired. Frick, however, was establishing groundwork that anticipated congressional interest in the near term.

"AS GREAT A LOBBY THAT DESCENDED UPON THE HOUSE"

It is difficult to determine when Frick assembled a powerful grassroots lobbying organization. He realized the importance of involvement in government affairs during World War II, when work with both the War Department and Congress, discussed in chapter 3, was instrumental in saving the 1945 season. He strongly conveyed the need to be involved in government issues to the league magnates. As league president, however, he wasn't in a position to organize all baseball. That changed after he was named commissioner. There was still no evidence of an organization when the *Toolson* decision was reached, which may have provided the impetus to create one.

A key component of the court's ruling was that Congress, not the courts, had the responsibility to place baseball under antitrust laws, due to retroactivity. Logically, baseball's focus switched fully to Congress. The most effective way to lobby elected officials at any level is personal contact. Past or current relationships were, and remain, the most effective way to convey positions to elected officials, especially if the individual is a constituent. The contact could be direct, either in person or by phone, or indirect, through someone else's connection. The political process still functions this way, though a grassroots organization is utilized differently today than in the 1950s.

There is evidence a grassroots organization was in place by 1956, certainly when Celler resumed his sports hearings in 1957.[49] The structure included every owner and executive working for every Major and Minor League club. Magnates were matched with representatives, senators, or both, from their states with whom they had personal relationships. All states with Major League teams had matches with most of their federal legislators. Only four states—Maine, Vermont, West Virginia, and Wyoming—had no matches. Out of ninety-six senators, there were contacts with seventy-nine—over 80 percent. For the House, the percentage was smaller, but 218 congressmen had baseball contacts. Not surprisingly, states having the most contacts were those with Major League clubs, including Illinois, New York, Massachusetts, Ohio, Maryland, Michigan, Pennsylvania, and Wisconsin. Only Missouri had less than half its delegation covered. In nine Major League states, all of the senators and over 65 percent of the congressmen had officials assigned to them.

There were some interesting designations or lack thereof. Commissioner Frick had no one assigned specifically, suggesting all congressmen were contacts for him. Similarly, no executive was assigned to Celler, suggesting he was Frick's responsibility. Many executives had numerous contacts. Calvin Griffith, Washington's owner, had many senators and congressmen, likely due to proximity and familiarity. So did Hal Totten, president of the Three-I Minor League from 1951 to 1960, encompassing Indiana, Illinois, and Iowa.[50] George Medinger, part owner of Cleveland, was involved with most of the Ohio delegation. At the same time, while the Illinois delegation was well covered, neither Phil Wrigley nor Charles Comiskey Jr. had specific legislators assigned to them.

The Minors were deeply involved, with George Trautman coordinating their efforts. Trautman collected responses and reported them to Frick's office. Records were kept of responses from senators and congressmen on antitrust issues. In cases where there were no direct contacts with a delegation, such as Kansas, the governor of the state, George Docking, was utilized to encourage his federal legislators to work against bills placing baseball under antitrust laws. Myron V. George was one Kansas congressman receiving a letter from Docking, stating that baseball should regulate its own affairs, stressing, "To do anything to threaten the fundamental structure of the sport at this time would be a marked disservice to all our people." Similar efforts were executed from the league offices in Chicago and Cincinnati. Even though this organization appeared to be well established before, it was utilized most heavily between late April and early June 1958 when Celler's bill placing baseball's operations under antitrust laws when "reasonably necessary" passed out of committee and reached the House floor. The bill, discussed later, generated major apprehension among baseball executives. By succeeding in blocking passage by the full House, it demonstrated baseball's most concerted effort to maintain its antitrust exemption.

Emanuel Celler was shocked by the defeat and demonstrated his discontent that summer during hearings before Senator Estes Kefauver's Subcommittee on Antitrust and Monopoly. Still scathing two months after that defeat, the Brooklyn congressman didn't parse words: "I want to say parenthetically that I have never known, in my 35 years of experience, of as great a lobby that descended upon the House than that organized by baseball and football, that waylaid . . . Congress, during the days this bill was considered. They came upon Washington like locusts. They were in every nook and cranny." He further described the effort as "the like of which I have never seen in my life."[51] Those comments, coming from someone who had served in Congress since 1923, were powerful testimony about the effectiveness of baseball's grassroots efforts. It is difficult to gauge football's role then, but the sport wasn't yet close to baseball in popularity or strength. It was apparently the organization assembled and coordinated out of Frick's office that succeeded in overturning Celler's legislation. Though that lobbying effort produced a less sympathetic

Celler, it proved powerful enough that Congress never again threatened baseball's antitrust status during Frick's tenure.

CELLER'S LAST EFFORTS

That was certainly not for lack of effort between 1957 and 1960. The most concerted was by the House in 1957, previously mentioned, initiated by the *Radovich v. National Football League* decision from the Supreme Court in February. While pertaining to football, the decision was perceived by pro basketball and hockey to place them under antitrust laws as well, prompting numerous bills in the House that ran the gamut on sports antitrust. Some exempted all sports from the Sherman and Clayton Acts, including baseball. Others pursued compromise between the *Toolson* and *Radovich* decisions. Emanuel Celler clearly viewed the *Radovich* decision as an opportunity to end baseball's exemption.

The Radovich case had persisted for over a half decade when reviewed by the Supreme Court, its decision creating a shock wave throughout professional sports. Bill Radovich played football for the Detroit Lions in the 1940s. He requested to be traded to the LA Rams to be close to his ailing father, but the Lions refused. When Radovich then jumped to the Los Angeles Dons of the new All-America Football Conference in 1946, the NFL blacklisted him. That cost him another opportunity later with an NFL team, and he sued for damages in 1949. The suit languished until 1957, when it was rejected due to the *Toolson* decision. In 1955, however, the Supreme Court ruled that boxing fell under antitrust laws, disregarding *Toolson* in doing so. When the Justice Department joined the *Radovich* case, requesting a Supreme Court hearing, the court complied.[52] Its February decision came as a surprise. Three of the four major professional sports—football, basketball, and hockey—were now perceived to be covered by antitrust laws. Baseball maintained its exemption because the court had upheld it recently, though in his majority opinion, Justice Tom Clark wrote that baseball's exemption was of "dubious validity" at that point. If this had been the first time baseball was reviewed, it would no doubt be subjected to antitrust. However, given the precedents of *Federal Baseball* and *Toolson*, the court adhered to its rulings "as long as Congress continues to acquiesce." Congressman Celler quickly responded, introducing antitrust legislation, including baseball, when the session was only a month old.[53]

Frick's reaction was to suggest baseball people refrain from commenting on *Radovich* because it didn't apply to baseball. That produced a blast from Celler: "Frick wants to gag everyone. Hasn't he heard of the First Amendment?" Frick refused to respond, although committee member Kenneth Keating—a New York Republican—did. He opined that Congress "ought not to be telling the leaders of Organized Ball how to conduct themselves." His criticism actually represented a bigger difference with Celler. The chair preferred a shorter hearing, whereas Keating pushed for a more extensive probe.[54] Though representing the minority party, his suggestion won the day and also defined the battlelines. Frick called a special meeting in late March to begin preparations, conveying confidence afterward: "I believe every time our game has come before the courts, Congress or congressional committees, we have fared well. . . . I do not claim we are perfect, but I think we have done pretty well as stewards for a game that has come to be regarded as a national institution, even one of our ways of life. And, in our small way, we have contributed to the American way of life." He added that while professional baseball was a business, it didn't violate antitrust laws. He also concluded that, while sympathetic to football, "we are in no position to fight football's battles. If they can become exempt from the provision of the anti-trust act, we are all for it."[55] The commissioner seemed prepared, perhaps reflecting the power of his lobbying organization.

Keating certainly succeeded regarding the extensiveness of the hearings, which began on June 17 and ran through August 8. They were conducted over fifteen days with over fifty witnesses, the minutes over three thousand pages, more extensive than the 1951 hearings. Although the Kefauver Senate hearings the following year are more notorious, due to the ballplayers testifying, five recent or current stars were witnesses during Celler's hearings, including Stan Musial and Bob Feller. Even football provided celebrities, including George Halas and Red Grange. Celler had assembled a serious effort to achieve antitrust legislation for baseball while also investigating the impact of *Radovich*, and numerous bills were proposed. Celler's bill would bring baseball under all antitrust laws like other major sports. It provided certain exemptions, but even territorial rights and the reserve clause could be included. Congressman Patrick Hillings offered a permutation on the reserve clause, proposing it expire after five years, the last two with salary increases of at least 15 percent. One bill maintained baseball's exemptions and removed the other sports from antitrust.[56]

As extensive as the hearings were, most of the testimony was predictable, varying little from 1951. Frick was true to form. His opening statement was similar to 1951: "Any legislation which would place professional baseball completely under the antitrust laws would seriously injure professional baseball with no offsetting benefit to the public."[57] The most notable change in circumstances was the National League's unanimous approval a month before to allow the New York clubs to relocate to California. The beloved Dodgers from Celler's district might well be departing. That set off a lively discussion between Frick and Celler, especially since no announcement of the move had been made. Frick emphasized the move wasn't associated with antitrust laws and, further, no announcement was made because no decision was reached. Celler countered that baseball was subject to antitrust due to television rights and territorial issues. He sarcastically questioned Frick's leadership skills if he was actually unaware the two clubs might relocate. Frick responded that the commissioner didn't weigh in until it was time to approve the moves. At this point, Kenneth Keating asked Frick if the clubs might remain in New York if Celler weren't pushing for the legislation. Frick answered that it hadn't helped. Celler advised Frick, "I suggest you invoke the Fifth Amendment."

The commissioner responded, "I'm saving that for some other questions, Mr. Chairman."[58]

While that appeared to be the extent of their hostilities, the commissioner scored later. Somewhat tongue-in-cheek, Keating asked Frick why the Antitrust Subcommittee couldn't protect franchises like Brooklyn and Cincinnati. Frick's response wasn't surprising: "Well, your committee put a lot of pressure on us to move, and we moved."[59] Celler remained silent. At the end of his testimony, Frick stressed that losing the antitrust exemption would produce numerous litigations, making it difficult for baseball to operate. Unmoved, Celler did commend the commissioner on his testimony: "It has been a rather hard cross-examination to which you have been put and I do want to compliment you. You have been very fair."[60] It's doubtful that put Frick at ease this time.

Much of the remaining testimony was predictable. J. Norman Lewis, attorney for the Players' Association, expressed concern that any legislation would give too much power to owners but was vague when asked what he considered a "reasonable reserve clause."[61] That would cause him problems later. Bob Feller, just retired but still involved with the association, felt baseball should be under antitrust laws except for the reserve and territorial rights, believed players should have equal input on selecting the commissioner, and expressed a need for arbitration.[62] Congressman Patrick Hillings, previously a huge critic of baseball, now credited the sport for enabling the relocation of many franchises. He further complimented baseball for having acted in good faith pursuing the West Coast, adding that it should qualify them for some antitrust exemptions.[63]

Perhaps the most interesting testimony came from Walter O'Malley. When sworn in, Celler asked where the Dodgers would be playing baseball next year. O'Malley replied that he didn't know. He and Celler agreed that moving to a new ballpark at Flushing Meadow, located in Queens, wasn't a solution. He also reminded Celler and Keating that, at the 1951 hearings, both had supported a team moving to LA. O'Malley stressed that the only thing that could keep the Dodgers in Brooklyn was a new stadium at a site he selected. By the end of his testimony, O'Malley had gained sympathy from Keating but accomplished little with Celler.[64]

When the hearings ended, there was no immediate action. In fact, Celler waited until the following year to mark up a bill, intending to present it to the whole Judiciary. It was clear the hearings hadn't changed anyone. However, only one bill could be presented to the entire committee, which would then have to amend it or approve it to be moved to the full House, with enough modifications to pass it to the Senate. It remained a threat to baseball's exemption. As 1958 began, there was still no bill when Frick and Paul Porter met with Celler and Keating on a different matter, the Minor Leagues' plight with Major League broadcasts and efforts to black out all telecasts during its games. Nothing productive came from the meetings, indicating no legislation was likely. At the same time, there was no discussion of Celler's pending bill. It was still speculated that it would exempt all sports features from antitrust but make all business aspects subject to it.[65]

Celler introduced the bill in late January—H.R. 10378. To baseball's surprise, the bill didn't exempt it from either territorial rights or the reserve clause. Instead, it would exempt from antitrust coverage those procedures and structural features "reasonably necessary." Keating noted such legislation would cause unlimited legal actions if passed. The bill did mention that activities like player contracts, territorial rights, and rules of the game could fall under the "reasonably necessary" category, thus exempting them, but there was no certainty. Baseball's lawyers objected strongly, and Keating promised to get it removed. Frick was succinct: "No more effective way to destroy organized baseball could be devised."[66] Battle lines were drawn.

Celler thought he had a trump card because J. Norman Lewis indicated that the Players' Association supported it: "The Major League Baseball Players' Association, representing all major league players in America, has strongly endorsed this bill and has stated that 'deletion or elimination of the term "reasonably necessary" could be most detrimental to the interests and welfare of the players.'"[67] Lewis was correct—the association had endorsed it. A few weeks into spring training, though, it had second thoughts and scheduled another meeting with Lewis. The day before, Carl Erskine, the Dodgers' player rep, suggested the clause "reasonably necessary" threatened the reserve clause, which players supported. When they met the following day, with eleven of sixteen player reps present, all withdrew their support without providing reasons.[68] The actual reason for the change came out later, but it took Lewis by surprise. It also presented Celler with an unexpected obstacle.

The chairman surmised, "Their switch of position under pressure from the owners and from the commissioner of baseball proves conclusively that any legislation for sports must prohibit unreasonable action by the owners." Essentially, Celler insinuated improper tactics were employed on player reps by baseball executives. Keating viewed it differently: "It is apparent the players were misled in their original endorsement of the bill."[69] Evidence suggests Keating was closer to the truth. In later hearings, both Robin Roberts, a rep leader, and Ford Frick testified that Roberts initiated a meeting with Frick after realizing the association was at odds with baseball. There is also circumstantial evidence Lewis personally objected to the reserve clause and thus was attempting to steer the association away from it.[70] In any case, the players would terminate his contract in 1959.

While Lewis was a belated casualty, the battle was raging in the House in early 1958. The Judiciary Committee had to decide which bill to send to the floor—Celler's, with the "reasonably necessary" clause, or Keating's, which essentially provided antitrust exemptions for all sports in the significant areas. Celler prevailed, but only by a precarious 17–15 margin, sending his bill to the House, its outcome uncertain. Celler stressed his bill still allowed for the reserve clause, the farm system, and territorial rights but added, "They cannot have a blank check to do whatever they want." Frick claimed the bill "threatens the destruction of organized baseball requiring rules and agreements to be defended in court whenever challenged."[71] His comments foreshadowed the lobbying effort that was now unleashed.

As Celler later asserted, his bill was overturned by baseball's grassroots efforts, along with assistance from Kenneth Keating and other members. Keating had an alternative bill ready to offer and was joined by three other subcommittee members, fellow Republican William Miller and two Democrats. The alternative exempted major sports from most antitrust laws; in particular, that affected the reserve clause, territorial rights, and football's draft. It also protected Minor League clubs from telecasts.[72] It thus had the support of all sports, most importantly the powerful baseball lobby. Celler faced a serious threat to his efforts.

It succeeded. By an overwhelming voice vote on the House floor, the Keating bill replaced Celler's and passed, sending it to the Senate. While Keating was elated, he was guarded, calling his legislation a "middle-of-the-road approach." Celler was bitter, blaming Walter O'Malley for the defeat. He also blamed baseball owners in general, stating that with few exceptions "they're just after all the dough they can amass." Although baseball had succeeded, there was no assurance they could get the legislation through the Senate. Estes Kefauver had already scheduled hearings in July, anticipating Celler's bill, and he was "personally disinclined toward a complete exemption" as had passed the House.[73] Because the Senate had to act before the session's end, passage was unsure at best. Regardless, baseball's exemption would remain secure. In the end, Celler's defeat shifted efforts to the Senate and Kefauver going forward, since Celler's other hearings rendered no threat to baseball's exemption.

The first of Celler's remaining hearings came in 1959, which was a renewed effort by major sports to exempt all of them from antitrust after the Senate failed to act on Keating's bill. Celler's hearings followed Kefauver's hearings on his bill a month earlier that year, which also focused on exemptions for all sports. Baseball was largely on defense because it already had an exemption, and the efforts proved a huge challenge, as both committee chairs were unsupportive. Frick considered it an uphill battle but was supportive because it would provide baseball additional protection. The hearings were much shorter. Although Keating was no longer there as a counter, William Miller, later Barry Goldwater's running mate, proved a capable replacement. Celler attempted to open on a positive note, referencing the *Radovich* decision's conclusion that "congressional processes are more accommodative, affording the whole industry hearings and an opportunity to assist in the formulation of new legislation."[74] Frick testified exclusively for baseball, and Celler's bitterness was notable as he did. He asked if Frick reviewed the television contracts of the sixteen clubs. Frick said, "No, sir, I do not. The Justice Department told me if I get into that picture . . . I am going to be sued individually for violation." He asked why the Minors don't get some television revenues, to which Frick noted baseball was providing a million dollars a year. Celler asked if Frick would support legislation prohibiting pay television. Frick emphatically replied he "is not willing to accept anything in the way of legislation at this time which concerns something in the far distant future."[75] Their relationship was now clearly adversarial.

During Frick's testimony there were two interesting probes—why the Players' Association had changed its position on the Celler Bill and the possibility of a third Major League. Frick explained that Robin Roberts had approached him, and he conveyed baseball's objections to the "reasonable and necessary" clause. Lewis had told player reps baseball supported the bill, and Frick explained to Roberts that was false.[76] A longer discussion on the third league was held, with Frick offering two observations. First, he thought a 1961 start was unrealistic; acquiring and developing players could take up to six years. When it was suggested that legislation limiting player control might facilitate the process, Frick countered, "You cannot develop twenty-five major leaguers if you are limiting the number of players a club can control."[77] He would later make that point at a Kefauver hearing. Nothing resulted from Celler's hearing.

The final Frick appearance before Celler's subcommittee did prove productive. The proposed legislation would allow sports, especially pro football, to package telecast rights to networks, stemming from a federal court ruling prohibiting such. The issue emerged due to the new American Football League but also had ramifications for baseball. Frick had already met with Celler, testifying to formalize baseball's position. Appearing with Paul Porter, Frick expressed support, "provided baseball was accorded a similar permissive right to deal with its television problems on the same basis."[78] Whatever animosity remained did not prohibit passing beneficial legislation, in this case paving the way for future sports telecasting.

MIXED OUTCOMES IN THE SENATE

The 1958 hearings for Kefauver's Senate subcommittee had expected to consider the Celler antitrust bill but were instead presented with the baseball-favored Keating version. From this point on, the Senate would become baseball's primary focus. The 1958 hearings were especially important because the subcommittee had House legislation to act upon. The Senate counterpart of the Keating bill was similar to the House version, with forty-four sponsors, including John Kennedy, Hubert Humphrey, and Barry Goldwater.[79] The first day also became the most recalled of baseball's congressional hearings due to the players and managers Kefauver lined up to testify, thanks to the All-Star Game being played in Baltimore. A showman, Kefauver scheduled its start for the following day. It proved historic.

That was largely due to Casey Stengel. The manager of the New York Yankees was the lead witness, saying much without saying anything. It was true Stengelese. At one point, Senator Kefauver interrupted him: "Mr. Stengel, I am not sure I made my question clear."

Stengel replied, "Yes sir. Well that is all right. I am not sure I am going to answer yours perfectly either."

After considerable rambling, Senator Joseph C. O'Mahoney of Wyoming was frustrated: "Mr. Chairman, I think the witness is the best entertainment we have had around here in a long time, and it is a great temptation to keep asking him questions, but I think I had better desist."

Still seeking clarity, Senator John Carroll of Colorado asked, "Then what is the need of legislation, if they are getting along all right?"

Stengel said, "I didn't ask for the legislation."[80]

Mickey Mantle followed Stengel on the stand, and Kefauver asked his thoughts on antitrust laws.

Mantle said, "My views are just about the same as Casey's."

"If you will redefine just what Casey's views were, we would be very happy."[81]

Fortunately for Kefauver, more substantive comments would follow. Four other players testified—Ted Williams, Stan Musial, Robin Roberts, and Eddie Yost, all but Williams player reps. They supported the reserve, with Williams saying, "I personally don't see how baseball could operate without the reserve clause and still maintain the integrity of the game."

Roberts was asked about the Players' Association's reversal on the Celler bill. The Phillies pitcher explained that Lewis had indicated the owners wanted it, but he learned later that wasn't the case. He met with both Robert Carpenter Jr. and Ford Frick and subsequently withdrew the association's support. Eddie Yost also mentioned having met with Frick on the legislation.[82]

Two recently retired players also testified—Jackie Robinson and Bob Feller. Both supported the reserve clause, but Robinson felt it should only last five or six years. Feller was less concerned about the reserve clause but favored neutral arbitration for players, also stressing he saw no advantage to limiting the number of players a team controlled.[83] Overall, senators heard a message similar to that presented to Celler's subcommittee.

Tougher questions were asked of baseball executives, especially those from Senator O'Mahoney. Calvin Griffith, having inherited the Washington club from his uncle, was drilled about rumors he was considering relocating to Minnesota. Griffith was evasive, finally acknowledging it had been discussed in board meetings. At the end of the testimony, O'Mahoney, who adamantly opposed the Keating bill, asked another question: "What are you going to be able to do if this bill is enacted to strengthen the Washington team which you cannot do now?" When Griffith offered no answer, the senator had achieved his objective.[84]

Since Ford Frick testified longer, O'Mahoney had greater opportunity to score points. When Frick mentioned territorial rights as a reason for antitrust exemption, O'Mahoney questioned whether the Justice Department would challenge those rights. He accused baseball of wanting blank-check control over radio and television while lacking a plan to support the Minors. Frick responded that he only wanted limited, reasonable control. O'Mahoney then questioned how problematic antitrust matters really were. When Frick explained that such cases took longer, cost more, and carried treble damages, O'Mahoney countered that it hadn't broken baseball. Frick shot back: "Well, by George, it had got us pretty badly bent, I will tell you that." The senator criticized baseball for not expanding, putting Frick on the defensive. Frick replied, "Senator, I recognize your standpoint but I would have to disagree with you very, very thoroughly, an honest disagreement on what you have said . . . baseball has expanded geographically. It has not expanded numerically. That it will expand numerically, I think, is inevitable." The commissioner added he favored an expansion of existing leagues rather than a third league. When pushed on Washington's club departing, Frick asserted, "I think the removal of a club from Washington would be catastrophic." Finally, the two went back and forth on the reserve clause, with Frick claiming that it created equity and O'Mahoney countering that Yankees dominance proved otherwise.[85] It was the most intense drilling the commissioner would experience.

There were also forceful witnesses against baseball. Government officials representing the Justice Department, the Federal Trade Commission, and the Federal Communications Commission generally spoke favorably about antitrust oversight and opposed blackouts of telecasts in designated areas. Harold Fellows, president of the broadcasters association, appeared later, stating pointedly, "I do not believe that this Congress should operate on the assumption that the public interest will be protected because professional sports people are supposedly reasonable men." Perhaps the most damning comment came inadvertently from Bert Bell, football's commissioner. After tough questioning from O'Mahoney on football's need for exemption, Bell admitted it could live without it.[86] The case against the Keating bill grew stronger.

Emanuel Celler, appearing as a witness, summarized the case against Keating's bill. Noting that New York City had lost its National League teams, he suggested it would allow the Yankees to block another club. He added that Frick "cannot control the baseball owners. He admitted it to the committee. His office is too frail a reed for us to rely upon." Offering details on how baseball had abused its power, Celler concluded, "It would be better . . . to have no sports legislation, whatsoever, even though the Supreme Court has rendered contradictory decisions, than to enact these bills." Not surprisingly, O'Mahoney praised him. From the tone, it was clear the Keating bill wouldn't progress. Indeed, the subcommittee didn't act on it.[87]

The status quo was not secure for long, however. The following July, Kefauver introduced a bill that brought all four sports under antitrust. While baseball's reserve clause would remain, no Major League team could protect more than eighty players. Territorial rights were upheld, except in cities over two million. The Federal Communications Commission (FCC) would be given oversight on radio and television broadcasts, with no restrictions allowed.[88] This time, the subcommittee had a new member—Democrat Philip Hart of Michigan. With family connections to the Tigers, who once employed him, Hart proved a strong baseball ally. Kenneth Keating had also joined the Senate and, though not a subcommittee member, he did serve on the full Judiciary Committee. He introduced his own bill, identical to his previous legislation, again supported by the major sports.[89] The positions of football and baseball, while predictable, highlighted subtle differences. Baseball favored the Keating bill and opposed Kefauver's legislation. Football supported both, although it had reservations about language in Kefauver's. A new factor was the Continental League. As discussed in chapter 8, much of the hearing focused on it and, as mentioned then, Kefauver agreed to postpone any action because it was meeting with Frick in August and the league still lacked some investors.

As was the case with previous hearings, Frick received more questions. He began by explaining his support for Keating's bill for protecting the reserve clause and territorial rights and providing protection against a Supreme Court reversal. He also liked that it eliminated the need for future congressional hearings and enabled baseball to protect the Minors.[90] As for the proposed FCC oversight of broadcasts into Minor League territory in Kefauver's bill, Frick had concerns: "From the standpoint of baseball, . . . I am afraid of any sort of legislation that leaves to an outside body a determination of right and wrong. That could lead to extensive questions and regulation. Frankly, I would rather have no regulation at all, much as the minor leagues need it." He later emphasized his opposition to clubs being limited to eighty players.[91] Overall, the questioning was more focused and less hostile than the previous hearing, but legislation was on hold pending the Continental League's meetings with the Majors.

When it became clear that league would have considerable trouble acquiring players expeditiously, Kefauver introduced new legislation in May 1960 and scheduled hearings later that month. Although at first glance the bill appeared more conciliatory to baseball, it wasn't. It brought all sports under antitrust laws, excepting free-agent drafts, territorial rights, and the reserve clause—with limitations. It also made provision for blackouts for some Minor League games. While the legislation pertained to all four major sports, this particular hearing focused only on baseball, due to the Continental League's urgency.[92] There were only five witnesses, including Frick. Both William Shea and Branch Rickey testified for the Continental League. The testimony was already discussed in the previous chapter, but some interesting antitrust comments were offered and are worth noting here. Shea summarized his frustration with baseball owners and their antitrust exemption: "This small group represents at the same time one of the most potent monopolies and one of the most select private clubs in the country. . . . They control absolutely the two indispensable ingredients of their business: Players and territories." Rickey quoted Frick's admonition to owners after the *Toolson* decision: "Baseball must immediately outline plans and procedures for expansion and realignment."[93] The Continental League existed because baseball ignored that advice.

Frick had counters. Addressing player control limits that dealt only with baseball, he claimed, "The bill will discriminate unfairly against baseball by regulations and restrictions imposed on no other sport or business. I do not make this statement recklessly or as an exaggeration." If this bill passed, he emphasized, "Over 2000 players will lose their baseball jobs along with scores of managers, trainers, scouts and other necessary personnel." He favored the Continental League succeeding, but not "at the expense of the structures we have built up and at the expense of the reputation we have built up and at the expense of the tradition we have built up through 100 years of operation." Frick showed his frustration.

When his testimony ended, Senator Hart offered, "It must have been a long day, commissioner."

Frick replied, "It's been fun."[94]

As mentioned in chapter 9, baseball killed the legislation.

However, Frick wasn't finished with testifying before the Senate Antitrust Subcommittee. New hearings were conducted in late January and mid-February 1964, as other major sports continued to pursue exemptions. Their efforts may have been spurred because Kefauver was no longer chair, replaced by a more supportive Hart. Since most subcommittee members cosponsored the bill, there was additional reason for optimism. The hearings afforded Frick an opportunity to address two matters before retiring. First, he outlined the new player draft planned for 1965, along with how positive relations were with players. That was confirmed by Bob Friend, the Pirates' player rep since 1954, who noted, "Our relationship with the management of baseball has certainly been the best I have ever seen. . . . At this moment we don't have any pressing problem."[95] The commissioner was pleased, having apparently achieved peace with the Players' Association.

He was also optimistic about the legislation—until it was announced during the hearings that CBS was purchasing 80 percent of the Yankees. Dan Topping would remain president, and the ball club would be operated independently. Frick initially denied any knowledge of the deal. Congress was in an uproar, with many House members threatening antitrust legislation. With the Braves moving to Atlanta, Wisconsin Congressman Henry Reuss suggested baseball would lose its exemption. Celler echoed him, with even Hart expressing concerns. Frick later acknowledged his awareness, including the 8–2 approval from American League owners, but emphasized his concerns were addressed: (1) The Yankees would maintain their identity. (2) The was no conflict of interest. (3) There would be no discount provided to CBS for broadcasting baseball games.[96] Frick may have pacified the subcommittee, but the CBS deal ended any efforts in Congress to exempt sports from antitrust.

In fact, it precipitated the opposite. The House started the new session in 1965 with a bill ending baseball's antitrust exemption, introduced, unsurprisingly, by a Wisconsin congressman. Expecting it, Frick stated, "It doesn't upset me."[97] A month later, Senator Hart's subcommittee scheduled hearings not only focusing on the CBS deal but also examining antitrust implications from the Braves' move. By then the Justice Department had found no objections to the CBS deal. The largest concern expressed at Hart's hearing was that some baseball magnates held stock in CBS. Frick suggested that a blind trust might provide a solution. He also noted, "I don't believe the commissioner has—or should have—the power to halt an otherwise legitimate transfer of a club." At the same time, Hart reminded baseball, "You've been given a preferred status and so we expect responsible behavior." Even then, Hart was only proposing what Keating had earlier—placing the business side under antitrust.[98] The Justice Department's ruling on CBS had moderated opposition.

Frick discussed the Braves' situation during the hearing, but only indirectly. The commissioner contended that a community losing a ball club wasn't a sound reason to subject the sport to antitrust. Indeed, he stressed again that franchise relocations were solely a league matter. Nevertheless, though he was retiring, he was required to testify in the Wisconsin antitrust case against the Braves, which was basically an effort by Milwaukee to acquire a club if the Braves left. When the National League rejected adding clubs at the Winter Meetings, local officials moved forward to apply state antitrust laws. More stringent than federal laws, the case provided a serious threat to force the Braves to return, but for a 4–3 decision against it by the state supreme court.[99] By then Frick had retired. His career-long saga with antitrust ended before that resolution.

The commissioner achieved his goal—baseball remained exempt. He had survived a second and even a third review (*Radovich*) by the Supreme Court and numerous attempts in Congress. That wasn't by accident. Frick assembled an extensive lobbying organization that succeeded in blocking negative legislation, a notable achievement since he dealt with judiciary chairmen who advocated bringing baseball under antitrust during most of his tenure. Beyond the lobbying, Frick cultivated supporters in both branches to advocate baseball's position. In effect, he had allies carry the water within Congress. Men like Kenneth Keating and later Philip Hart and William Miller played instrumental roles in aiding baseball. Baseball was also helped by not requiring legislation and by participating largely to help the other sports. Frick understood it was easier to play defense than offense in Congress.

Was the effort worth it? The goal remained consistent: the antitrust exemption was necessary to protect the reserve clause and territorial rights. Two Supreme Court cases and the failure of Congress to pass legislation maintained that goal during Frick's tenure. However, the harmony between owners and players ended after Marvin Miller became head of the Players' Association. Although Miller never eliminated the reserve clause, he established neutral and binding grievance arbitration in 1970, ultimately producing free agency. The reserve clause was thus rendered moot, though players are still controlled for roughly a decade after being drafted. Territorial rights remain, but their importance is questionable. They were used by the Giants to block the A's from moving to San Jose, so they're heading to Las Vegas instead. Whereas New York, Los Angeles, Chicago, and the Baltimore and Washington area all support two teams, it seems unlikely a second club or new franchise would be established in Cleveland, Denver, or most other Major League cities today. Nonetheless, both issues were believed critical while Frick was commissioner. By any standard his efforts with Congress and the courts were instrumental in protecting those areas.

11

Changes Good, Bad, and Ugly

In addition to the changes discussed previously, Frick was responsible for many others. Though not at the same level, perhaps, they have reshaped the game. The best-known is the alleged asterisk, stemming from his declaration that any home run record needed to be achieved in 154 games, otherwise it would be considered a separate record. That association remains, even though eliminated by a later commissioner. An asterisk was never used. Even Frick's biography featured an "*" in its title, and he discussed the decision in the very first chapter. A far more impactful decision was made in 1962: with Frick's encouragement, the strike zone enlarged for 1963, a ruling that facilitated a major change later. Among the other important rulings, some remain, and others have been altered. All have impacted the game today.

DIPLOMACY ISN'T EASY

Frick hadn't begun his commissionership intending to promote baseball internationally, though pressure already existed to do so. Toronto and Montreal expressed interest in becoming Major League cities as he assumed his duties. A few Latin American players had already had their cup of coffee in the Majors, and some, like Minnie Miñoso, demonstrated considerable talent. Japan, the one Asian country that had adopted baseball until relations with the United States grew strained in the 1930s, saw renewed interest after the war.

In the aftermath of its surrender, Japan became an occupied country under U.S. oversight. General Douglas MacArthur, the commander, encouraged reestablishing baseball. To promote it, in 1949 he coordinated with Lefty O'Doul of the Pacific Coast League's San Francisco Seals to play exhibition games with reorganized professional clubs. As in the prewar era, the games were sponsored by Japanese newspaper companies. Though well-received, the Minor League club didn't generate the interest that

Major Leaguers had in the early 1930s. Further, when MacArthur was dismissed by President Truman in 1951, baseball interest diminished.[1]

It was soon regenerated. In June 1953 Shodi Yasuda, president of a Japanese newspaper, extended an invitation to Giants owner Horace Stoneham to bring his team to Japan at season's end. Stoneham was enthusiastic. He was granted permission from the State Department, its expeditiousness partly due to Japanese unrest with U.S. occupation. Ford Frick also offered Stoneham support, as he recognized the political and social benefits. However, he cautioned that existing rules prohibited more than three players on any team from barnstorming in the postseason, thus requiring endorsement from the other owners. Further, at least fifteen players were needed to make the trip. Approval was obtained in July with Frick's strong support, and Stoneham convinced sufficient players to go.[2] Frick announced he and spouse Eleanor would accompany them as goodwill ambassadors.

Somewhat ironically, the Giants weren't the only American team heading to Japan. Ed Lopat, a Yankees pitcher, assembled a team under existing rules and received financial backing from another Japanese newspaper conglomerate to tour and play exhibition games. Players on both squads had agreed to participate because travel costs were covered and they were promised $3,000. Lopat's players would receive the stipend while the Giants, to their chagrin, were only paid $1,000 due to poor ticket sales in smaller cities.[3] Nonetheless, the Giants' trip was regarded a success. Capacity crowds attended the opening ceremonies and the first four games. Frick performed an ambassadorial role, reading President Eisenhower's goodwill message at the beginning.[4] Frick and Eleanor departed early to continue their travels, and the Giants returned bearing a goodwill gift for Eisenhower, the armor outfit of a samurai warrior, formally presented to the president by Frick and Stoneham in February 1954. Frick assessed, "The Giants' trip to Japan was the best people-to-people goodwill gesture that the United States has made since the war, in my opinion." He added that the State Department was encouraging another such trip, perhaps annually.[5] It would take longer, with the next trip occurring in 1955.

This time, the Yankees were the representative. Owner Del Webb, general manager George Weiss, and Commissioner Frick headed the delegation, along with their spouses, players, and manager Casey Stengel. Japan was better prepared this time. The nation's prime minister,

Ichiro Hatoyma, held a reception, and the entourage was resoundingly welcomed by over one hundred thousand people lining the Tokyo streets as the team paraded through downtown. Frick was overwhelmed: "We've come here in the spirit of good will and in our small way to try to bring people closer together. I think that this demonstration today proves that it's working." As the trip ended, the commissioner offered an assessment of Japanese talent, stating they were not ready for the Majors but two or three could play in the higher-class Minors.[6] This time, players were compensated the promised amount, and it was agreed Japan's newspapers would sponsor a team every year. The Dodgers would go in 1956, but both countries then decided on every other year, which remained the procedure until 1964. Frick would return one more time before retiring.

The State Department sent the appropriate league president to replace Frick on the Japanese trips, but his presence was specifically requested for a different excursion in 1958. In April, Vice President Richard Nixon had undertaken a goodwill tour of South American countries. He was well received in many countries with only minor demonstrations. Venezuela was an exception. The country was conducting a heated election campaign, with anti-American sentiment running strong. Nixon's motorcade was attacked by a mob, his car badly damaged and almost turned over before the driver was able to escape. Nixon and his wife were unhurt, but two secret service agents were injured. It was heavily covered by American media, and the State Department was concerned about damaged relations. It utilized baseball's popularity in Venezuela to smooth tensions.

Frick was asked to recruit well-known players to accompany him to conduct baseball clinics and visit hospitals and other organizations. Six were recruited, including Bob Friend and Dick Groat of the Pirates, Elston Howard of the Yankees, Gus Triandos of the Orioles, Richie Ashburn of the Phillies, and Pete Runnels of the Red Sox. The trip began in early November and lasted ten days. Also joining the tour were Hall of Famer Frank Frisch and American League Chief of Umpires Cal Hubbard. During the ten days, the players conducted baseball clinics and civic and charity events in seven cities, including the capitol, Caracas. They were a big hit everywhere. One reporter concluded, "The expedition accomplished more in good will than a thousand politicians and government policy interpreters would have achieved." Frick predicted the program would be extended on a larger scale.[7] Regardless, the tour had done much to smooth relations. As with Japan, Frick's baseball diplomacy proved successful.

Back home, however, Frick could no longer rely on past successes. Although the problem was caused by pitcher Joe Stanka, the real dilemma was the reserve clause. At twenty-seven, after shuffling around the Minors, Stanka was signed with the White Sox late in 1959. While his performances were solid, he wasn't placed on the club's World Series roster. Over the winter, Stanka surmised his 1960 prospects were limited and requested placement on the voluntary retirement list. He then signed a lucrative contract with the Nankai Hawks in Japan, winning seventeen games and helping the club finish second. The White Sox noted his success and claimed they were owed $30,000, asserting that he hadn't retired. Frick agreed, using the reserve clause to claim Stanka was still property of the Sox, adding that "unless satisfaction was received, Japan tours by U.S. teams might be banned." The State Department grew concerned, and money was apparently paid.[8] Since other American players were considering Japanese baseball, however, further action was needed, prompting Frick to accompany Detroit to Japan in 1962.

That trip was successful. Specifically, the commissioner stated that one reason for going was that "we hope to agree on a definite set of rules under which American players may come to Japan." After meeting with Japanese Commissioner Yushi Uchimura, the two sides agreed on a trading pact between the countries' leagues, involving only players placed on their trading lists, with the agreement a byproduct of the Stanka issue. Along with that, the tour was a success. A Japanese journalist proclaimed it "cemented strong bonds between west and far east."[9] Frick returned home satisfied the problem with players jumping and threatening the reserve clause was resolved.

Such was not to be, however, after the Giants signed Japanese pitcher Masanori Murakami to a contract. What started as a positive move for both countries soon turned into a debacle with international implications. It started innocently enough. The Nankai Hawks, the same club that had signed Stanka, asked the Giants to allow three of the Hawks' players to be in the Giants' lower Minors for training and development in 1964. While there, nineteen-year-old Murakami stood out. The Giants were in a pennant race, needed a left-handed relief pitcher, and called up Murakami, who appeared in relief nine times, becoming the first Japanese player to appear in the Majors. His stats were impressive—fifteen innings pitched, one win, only three earned runs, and a walk. Because the Giants signed him to a 1964 contract, the reserve clause automatically kicked in for 1965, and the Giants expected him to return. That's when difficulties developed.

Murakami's performance for the Giants had made him a celebrity at home. He was a national hero—one the Nankai Hawks wanted back as a box-office attraction. They claimed Murakami was signed illegally because under Japanese law only the parent of a player under twenty-one could sign a valid contract. The Giants countered that their contract was legal. The Hawks prevented Murakami from returning, claiming he was homesick and wished to remain in Japan and asserting his contract wasn't valid, as the $10,000 paid was a bonus for the previous season. Frick, faced again with a challenge to the reserve clause, threatened to drop all agreements with Japan unless the contract was honored.[10] The Giants' season started without Murakami, as the controversy remained unresolved. Wanted on both sides of the Pacific, he was prevented from playing on either.

Two months later, with both sides realizing they needed to reduce tension, a diplomatic compromise was reached by the commissioners and clubs. The Hawks released Murakami from his 1965 contract, allowing him to play for the Giants. At season's end, he would request voluntary retirement, which enabled him to play for the Hawks in 1966. Essentially, he was treated similarly as Stanka, though Murakami was also prohibited from returning to the Majors after 1965. Frick was thus able to protect the reserve clause. Murakami had another good season for the Giants, one that would have returned him under normal circumstances. Instead, the young pitcher was a victim of cultural misunderstandings and American baseball politics—its reserve clause and antitrust exemption. Murakami had a decent career in Japan, but the incident set back the appearance of the next Japanese player for decades.[11]

Overall, Frick's diplomatic efforts succeeded. The Japanese tours went well until 1964, when the Pirates were canceled, an aftermath of the Murakami affair. However, they resumed in 1966 and lasted for more than a decade. When the State Department most needed baseball's help with Japan, Frick was cooperative. The same was true with Venezuela. Given cultural differences, coupled with complications caused by the reserve clause, the Murakami situation perhaps was inevitable. In the long run, though, Frick's policies provided opportunities for Latin American and Asian players in spite of stumbling blocks along the way.

A "PROPER TRYOUT"

For as long as professional baseball existed, players left gloves on the field when taking their turn at bat. Pitchers and catchers would bring in their gear, but other players retrieved gloves when they returned to the field. For over seventy-five years, incidents in which a glove impeded a batted ball or caused a fielder to trip were very rare. Nonetheless, when the Rules Committee met in November 1953, it voted unanimously to require that all gloves be removed.

The driving force behind the change was Hank Greenberg, the Indians' general manager. He felt leaving gloves on the field was unseemly, a "sloppy procedure." Further, he felt it improper to have a "game being affected by a ball being deflected by a glove." He was persuasive. The other committee members—Chairman Jim Gallagher of the Cubs; George Fletcher of the Phillies; Fresco Thompson of the Dodgers; Joe Cronin of the Red Sox; Bill DeWitt of the Browns (becoming the Orioles); Frank Shaughnessy, International League president; and two other Minor League representatives—all voted in favor.[12] When the decision was announced, there was little response from sportswriters, who were more interested in its other decisions.

Most focused on how a fly ball scoring a run was treated—now a sacrifice out rather than a time at bat—and on revising the balk rule so if a batter hit the pitch, the team could take either the hit or the balk. None mentioned the glove rule, and one merely offered a collective reference, calling every change "a wise one." Ford Frick was interviewed on his return from his world trip. He endorsed the sacrifice rule change but never referenced the glove rule, using the interview to advocate for the spit ball, as he often did. The only direct reference to the glove rule was a *The Sporting News* editorial endorsing the change, recognizing that "barring equipment from the field has been considered by previous rules bodies, going all the way back to the organization of the American League in 1901. But it was left to the Gallagher group to show the necessary initiative to put it in the rule book."[13] Given the lack of negative reaction, the glove rule appeared to be accepted.

That changed dramatically when enforcement began during spring training in 1954. Suddenly, Gallagher and Frick were inundated with telegrams, exclusively from the American League. Paul Richards, manager of the Orioles, perhaps the most vocal opponent, telegraphed, "Respectfully submit strong protest of new glove rule. Believe it will tend to slow up games, create considerable confusion and expend needlessly the energy of players. I personally do not recall any incident of a glove on the field effecting [*sic*] the outcome of a game. The new rule bans a custom of almost 100 years duration and the benefits, if any, to be derived do not by any means justify the presence of the rule in my personal opinion." Others rendered similar views, some claiming the gloves never caused problems, others citing the inconvenience of baserunners having to return to the dugout to retrieve their gloves. Many thought it would delay the game. The league's reaction was not unanimous. Manager Al López of the Indians telegraphed his support to Will Harridge: "We are perfectly happy with new playing rule 3.16 regarding players' gloves and have had no problems with it. Players have made no complaints and I hope we can keep rule."[14] It is possible López sincerely believed what he conveyed, but it may not have been coincidental that Greenberg was his boss.

López's support wasn't sufficient to reduce Gallagher's concerns. While an executive with the Cubs, in a league that had conveyed no opposition, Gallagher still found the Junior Circuit's reactions disturbing. He proposed that Frick allow him to conduct a mail survey of committee members, offering them an opportunity to reconsider. He was convinced that was the only way to temper their protests.

Frick disagreed. His written response offered insight into his management style under pressure:

> I hold no brief for or against this rule. However, I do feel that the Rules Committee is a regularly constituted standing committee with full authority to act—and once action is taken such rules become officially a part of the baseball code and are so adopted. Three members of each Major League were on the committee. The vote, I understand, was unanimous. Under such circumstances I do not believe any club or any league has the authority to vote a rule out of operation. . . . In fairness to the committee it should be given full and proper trial and the committee should not be subjected to pressure because a few individuals are unhappy over the rule.

He belittled some of the complaints, rejecting Gallagher's suggestion.[15]

Further, he sent a memorandum to owners threatening repercussions if the rule wasn't followed, delivered under his office's auspices to all Major League clubs and Minor League presidents:

> This rule is a part of the Official Baseball Rules. It cannot be changed by League or Individual Club action and League or Club officials who attempt to make their own determination as to the non-enforcement of the rule will be subject to such penalties as applied to other sections of the playing code. This may include reprimand, fine or forfeiture of the game, as the situation may indicate. . . . If a rule has been proved through experience to be not satisfactory, proper provisions are made for changing that rule. There is no provision nor should there be any provision for Clubs or individuals to change rules as they see fit simply because they do not happen to like them and before they have given the rule the proper tryout.[16]

His letter was succinct and successful, as leagues at all levels enforced it throughout 1954. When the Rules Committee reconvened, there was no effort to return to the old tradition. The idea for the change wasn't Frick's, but it wouldn't have been implemented without his support and insistence.

PENSION TENSIONS

The adoption of the MacPhail Report and creation of a pension plan in 1946 improved player-owner relations, though tensions remained. When Frick was named commissioner, some players felt they should have had input on his selection. More significant, after becoming commissioner there was growing confusion about how much of the World Series and All-Star Game monies were actually going to the pension plan. Player frustration came to a head in the summer of 1953 when players felt they were ignored at the July meetings.[17]

The player representatives—Allie Reynolds and Ralph Kiner—expressed their frustration by announcing they had retained the legal services of J. Norman Lewis to represent their interests. One player explained, "We don't get anywhere in those conferences. . . . The owners have facts, figures, lawyers and statements on all questions. We don't have anyone who can take time to look up those things and find out what's going on. . . . We're ballplayers." Lewis had sports-world experience. His law firm worked with the New York Giants, and he personally represented concessionaires at many ballparks. In reality, he was better prepared to represent the interests of the owners.[18]

Despite that, neither owners nor even some players were receptive to his hiring. Warren Giles spoke for magnates: "If the players delegate to anyone outside their own ranks any of their rights to discuss and negotiate individually, they are surrendering a privilege that has been very valuable to them." Frick remained quiet, though he acknowledged having had numerous conversations with Lewis.[19] Carl Erskine, player rep for the Dodgers, was mildly supportive: "I think it's a good thing to have hired such a man, although I don't think there is anything pressing at this time that we need him for." Hank Bauer of the Yankees, a teammate of Reynolds, claimed, "I have never been asked if I was in favor of hiring a lawyer. . . . I believe baseball has done very well by me." Bob Friend, Kiner's teammate, asserted, "It isn't very nice to have to call on some outsider to handle our business. It doesn't make us look good."[20] In spite of opposition, Lewis now officially represented players in their negotiations.

By October some player requests were achieved, while others—especially regarding the pension—were postponed. Improvements included increases in the moving allowance for traded players; spring training living expenses; coverage for surgery, illness, or injuries, even if not caused while playing; meal money on the road; and a decrease to eight from ten years for a player to achieve veteran status. Unresolved issues included increasing the minimum wage and changes to the pension plan. Regarding the pension, players had requested doubling monthly payments for both five- and ten-year players, along with reducing their annual payments.[21] Its postponement, coupled with a misunderstanding by Lewis and player reps on the amounts allocated from the World Series and All-Star Games, led to a major debacle at a planned meeting in Atlanta between Frick and the sixteen player reps at the Minor League meetings in late November.

Lewis laid the groundwork by criticizing the pension plan earlier that month. He outlined player demands for changes and claimed all receipts from the Series and All-Star Games were intended for the pension, not for the central fund—which also paid the commissioner's office administrative expenses. He was upset at not being invited either to the Atlanta meeting with player reps or to the Winter Meetings with owners.

Frick responded, "There is no reason for him to attend."[22]

The drama leading up to the meeting was further complicated by the rumor, later verified, that owners planned to terminate the pension due to the new demands. Former commissioner Chandler threw gasoline on the fire when reps contacted him; he advised them they shouldn't attend the Minor League meetings without their lawyer and claimed, incorrectly, that all money from the Series and All-Star Games was intended to fund the pension.[23]

The exclusion of Lewis, coupled with Chandler's advice, precipitated a boycott by the reps, refusing to attend even though Frick had paid their travel expenses. The commissioner indicated he hadn't been informed of Lewis's attendance until fifteen minutes before, after making it clear no lawyers were invited. The meeting was merely intended to clarify pension misunderstandings and emphasize that their demands would overspend the current program. Their boycott prevented him from doing so. As one reporter observed, "A bombshell in Major League player-owner relations exploded today with a detonation that just about reduced to a whisper everything else that happened on this third day of the annual minor league convention."[24] The aftermath of the debacle wasn't surprising.

Against Frick's wishes, owners in both leagues voted to end the Players' Pension Plan when it terminated in 1955, though Frick stressed that wouldn't happen: "I am thoroughly convinced this is an admirable pension plan. I will use every effort at my command to see that the plan is maintained but officially my position is only that of an administrator." In their joint session, owners rectified the situation somewhat by establishing a committee to review the current plan and address the misunderstandings. John Galbreath, owner of the Pirates, and Hank Greenberg were named to meet with Reynolds and Kiner to clarify the plan and conceptualize ways it could be improved when a new television contract was negotiated.[25] They weren't random selections. Galbreath was the owner of Kiner's ball club, and Greenberg had been his teammate. Whereas the December sessions and the nonmeeting in Atlanta appeared to threaten the pension, the committee selection offered reason for optimism.

That optimism proved valid, although that wasn't clear initially. Chandler continued his sniping: "I know I would be fighting for the players' side on this."[26] Two days later, Frick refused to acknowledge Chandler's comment, though it had precipitated his press conference. The commissioner clarified that from its conception, the pension plan received its funding only after front office administrative costs were covered from the Series' and All-Star Games' funds.[27] A week later, Greenberg offered hope for a resolution, emphasizing how unfortunate it was that "termination" of the plan had ever been mentioned. He stressed that the issue boiled down to one point—a new television contract. Said Greenberg, "If the new contract . . . brings much higher income, they'd [the players] like to study the possibility of getting higher benefits. I would think the owners would like to do the same thing."[28] Greenberg was hopeful.

His optimism was rewarded less than a month later. In mid-February Greenberg and Galbreath held a press conference that included Lewis and player reps. The new pension plan would start in 1957, after new broadcast contracts were negotiated. The commissioner would be responsible for those negotiations but would no longer have pension oversight duties. Instead, it would be governed by two owners and two player reps, with no arbitrator. Sixty percent of all revenues from both the World Series and the All-Star Game would be committed to it, and all five men present agreed this was a positive step in owner-player relations.[29] It suggested baseball was moving toward a more harmonious era.

The players, however, couldn't overlook the struggles and uncertainties they had experienced. Most notable, they began the process of establishing a more formal association than that set up in 1946, announcing at a meeting in July 1954 they had reestablished the Major League Baseball Players' Association, including the adoption of bylaws and a constitution drafted by Lewis. Along with Kiner and Reynolds, standouts at the meeting included Warren Spahn, Robin Roberts, Stan Musial, and Carl Erskine. Lewis would receive a $30,000 annual retainer from baseball's central fund to represent them, and all were adamant that the association wouldn't operate like union.[30] Interestingly, the actual organization wasn't finalized for another two years when Bob Feller was elected president and Musial vice president.[31] Once completed, the association remained a loose confederation during Frick's tenure, though the groundwork had been laid for greater power under Marvin Miller's leadership. Its creation was largely caused by the pension issue, born from the failed meeting with Frick.

Its creation, coupled with Greenberg's and Galbreath's efforts, didn't ease the unrest between owners and players. At the 1955 Winter Meetings, players again pushed to increase the minimum wage to $7,200, noting the cost of living had risen 44 percent since the $5,000 minimum was established. The minimum had been increased to $6,000 the year before, but reps remained unsatisfied. Players also had second thoughts about being excluded from the broadcast contract negotiations and demanded representation alongside the commissioner. Owners rejected both requests, though Frick assured them their demands would be considered. The matters came up again at the February meetings, but the magnates declined to address them, establishing a study committee instead. Frick promised to keep the pension committee informed during the negotiation process.[32] Clearly, there was still considerable distrust.

That tension would diminish later in 1956, however, when Frick announced the broadcast agreement with Gillette and NBC before the All-Star Game. The contract would pay $3,250,000 a year through 1961 for broadcasting both the World Series and the All-Star Game, roughly tripling money available for the pension plan. A *New York Times* columnist noted the new agreement even caused Lewis to sing Frick's praises: "I think the Commissioner did a great job. We have no kicks." It didn't change Chandler's attitude. En route to his seat at the All-Star Game in Washington, the previous commissioner happened to pass the current one. A reporter noted, "It was the only refreshing chill on a muggy day."[33] While the minimum wage remained an issue of contention, the pension plan and broadcast contract did not.

Lewis did feel important issues remained. At the 1958 Winter Meetings, he took a new approach to the minimum wage, proposing a guaranteed amount set aside instead—20 percent of a club's gross revenue. Not surprisingly, the magnates didn't receive it well. One quipped, "The players are moving closer and closer to a union." Tom Yawkey went further. He denounced "efforts of the players to interfere with the internal affairs and general conduct of major clubs." He threatened to sell his club if players persisted. Taken aback, Robin Roberts backed away from the demand while denying any element of coercion.[34] The severe reaction from the magnates may have been part of the reason for the association's 1959 termination of Lewis, though his antitrust efforts a year earlier were likely more impactful. Both times, Lewis overplayed his hand.

He wasn't replaced until the end of 1959. In conjunction with the Winter Meetings, the Players' Association announced hiring Robert C. Cannon, a former Wisconsin Circuit Court judge, as their legal adviser. In doing so, players declared there were "no serious controversial matters coming up with the owners." Robin Roberts added that when the next broadcast negotiations occurred, they had complete confidence Frick would make the best deal.[35] Cannon would prove the appropriate choice given those views, as he was favorable to owners and not confrontational. Partly for that reason, there was little friction until Frick retired in 1965.

While Frick's relationship with players remained peaceful, they weren't always harmonious. He was cautious in pushing owners on player requests;

thus, players perceived him as not always supportive. The reps' walkout had been a huge embarrassment, though Frick recovered, thanks to Galbreath and Greenburg, along with the new broadcast contract that enriched the pension substantially. With Cannon's hire and the players' conviction that the reserve was essential, Frick experienced years of labor peace. However, the boycott in 1953 directly led to strengthening the Players' Association, which would afford Marvin Miller the ability to build an exceptionally powerful labor union. Frick had achieved a peaceful coexistence, but his stubbornness over a meeting laid the groundwork for a major power shift in baseball.[36]

PITCHERS GET THEIR DUE

Frick was consistently a pitchers' advocate, believing they were disadvantaged by rules and rarely received due recognition. Since becoming commissioner, he looked for ways to provide them advantages. He had long been an advocate for a "clean" spit ball—a spitter without using other substances. He also suggested enlarging the strike zone, though he understood such changes were difficult.[37] He thus pursued other ways to acknowledge pitchers.

The death of Denton "Cy" Young—baseball's all-time winningest pitcher—in November 1955 provided an idea. A month later, Frick conducted an informal discussion with baseball writers, during which he suggested a new award named for the hurler. At the time, all players competed for each league's Most Valuable Player Award. Frick noted, "The present system in which all players are grouped in the Most Valuable Player award is unfair to pitchers because they appear in less games than players in other positions." He suggested the award be decided by sportswriters, just as the Most Valuable Player (MVP) and Rookie of the Year Awards already were.[38] The historical evidence certainly supported his claim that hurlers had less chance for recognition, as pitchers received the MVP Award less than 15 percent of the time. At the February meeting of the leagues in 1956, the award was approved.

J. G. Taylor Spink was quick to praise Frick. In his weekly editorial, he acknowledged, "Any school kid knows you can't . . . compare batting averages with earned-run averages. The new Cy Young Award remedies the long-standing injustice to the hurlers."[39] Many sportswriters were convinced a pitcher in each league should be recipients, but Frick was adamant that only one be awarded. While never clarifying why, it may have been because a pitcher was still eligible for the MVP. For the remainder of his tenure his wishes were honored, but a year after he retired a pitcher from each league was chosen. Though pleased with the award, Frick didn't abandon his mission to pursue other advantages for the pitcher.

ALL-STAR BLUES

The All-Star Game began in 1933, a creation of the *Chicago Tribune* and Major League Baseball. For the first few years, players were selected by fans, with the *Tribune* monitoring the vote. Landis felt the game became too much a popularity contest rather than selecting the best players and turned the vote over to players and managers in the respective leagues in 1938. That remained the mode until 1947, when Chandler returned selection to the fans and the *Tribune* again undertook ballot compilation. Frick, a vocal supporter of fan participation, was content with the process until 1956, when holes were developing.

The problem started when the *Tribune* announced in May it would no longer conduct the poll, perhaps due to the death a month earlier of Arch Ward, the game's creator. Regardless, Frick remained committed, stating baseball was "anxious to continue selection of teams by popular vote." He began soliciting other newspapers to conduct the polling.[40] A week later, he announced his office would coordinate it, noting agreement from over five hundred newspapers and radio and television stations to conduct it locally. He said, "The response was magnificent. This is still the fans' game." Mostly midwestern fans participated, though, and the ballots were down significantly, from 6.5 million to only 300,000. Although no Chicago or New York newspaper conducted a poll, a Cincinnati radio station undertook a huge campaign, selecting five starters from the Redlegs. Frick was defensive: "Everybody had the chance to vote, no matter where they lived, so there should be no squawk if somebody doesn't like the tea. What's more, the counting was done accurately with checks and double checks. I think we came up with a representative team. . . . Don't forget, Cincinnati has a good ball club."[41] In spite of his claims, there was disappointment in both the lower voter participation and the overrepresentation from one club.

In fact, *The Sporting News* recommended ending the fan vote. Addressing both low participation and the skewed vote, Spink concluded, "When the commissioner's office has no control over special drives which result in the preponderance of one city on a team, as in the case of Cincinnati, it becomes obvious something must be done. . . . There can be no question but that the managers in each league have a better opportunity than any fan to judge the comparative abilities of the players to be selected. . . . The time has come to restore the responsibility of player choices to the pilots in the best interest of the event itself." Will Harridge agreed, but Warren Giles was adamant about continuing the fan vote, perhaps due to his Cincinnati connections. Both leagues' managers supported Harridge, but Frick preferred to continue the poll.[42] Because his vote broke any tie, the fans had the vote for 1957.

If Frick thought the situation couldn't get worse, he was wrong. Cincinnati players were voted for seven of the eight positions, with Stan Musial the only non-Redleg by a narrow margin. The commissioner had rationalized five players, but not seven. He replaced the chosen center and right fielders with Willie Mays and Hank Aaron, and both league presidents concurred. Frick explained, "I took this step in an effort to be entirely fair to all fans and with no reflection on the sincerity or honesty of the Cincy poll." He said the outcome "has resulted in the selection of a team that would not be typical of the league."[43] Although most managers, players, and fans agreed, his ruling wasn't received well in Cincinnati. One fan hung Frick in effigy, placed it on a truck, and drove it around the city. Another, who had voted eight hundred times, proclaimed, "If it's the wrong way to choose a team, let them choose it next year." Another asserted, "This isn't Russia and no one man like Frick should make the decisions." Many accused the commissioner of changing the rules after the game began, and one threatened to sue.[44] Regardless, Frick's decision stood.

It altered the selection process for All-Star players for over a decade. Giles still preferred a vote by the fans and Harridge the managers, but Frick established the procedure used until 1970: "I would vote to have all the players in the Major Leagues do the picking. I would send out ballots to all 16 clubs and bar the players from voting for anyone on their own club." He rejected Giles idea of punch cards for fan voting as too expensive. In January 1958 Frick officially announced his procedure: the managers, coaches, and players in each league choosing the starters but unable to vote for teammates. The All-Star managers selected the pitchers. Frick said, "The fan poll idea was abandoned only after long consideration and with a great deal of regret. . . . I have been in favor of the fan vote but I'm not in favor of the way it turned out. It's been a joke in recent years." Following the 1958 game, Spink believed the player selections were good, but the lack of controversy from the fans' vote took away some drama and interest. Changing his tune, Spink hoped for a quick return to a fan poll.[45]

It was not to be for another twelve years, long after Frick retired. Even though technology to tabulate votes improved, the 1957 travesty likely remained with Frick, explaining his hesitancy to change back.

If the commissioner thought All-Star Game issues would diminish after selections went smoothly in 1958, he was soon corrected. After selections seemed resolved, the idea for a second game replaced it. Early in 1959, Robin Roberts presented the benefits of such a game to Frick, the league presidents, and the executive committee. They quickly accepted. The game would not be played during the same break but would consist of the same players. The remaining owners and players had yet to approve it, but Frick was optimistic, believing the game could be implemented quickly. He indicated proceeds would not go to the player pension but rather to the Old Timers Association pension and amateur baseball. Formal approval came three weeks later, but proceeds now would go to the players' pension, which now also included umpires and trainers. Sportswriters weren't receptive. Arthur Daley thought it one game too many, accusing the ballplayers of being greedy.[46] Others echoed him.

Whatever the perceptions, the players strongly favored a second game again in 1960. Robin Roberts and Harvey Kuenn, representing the leagues, appeared before the executive council to state their case in October. Their only alteration was that the games must be played within a four-day period. Frick promised to present it at the Winter Meetings. There, Roberts and Kuenn were informed the games would be played two days apart. Appreciative of two games, the reps indicated there were no pending issues with owners.[47] If sportswriters were opposed to the second game, their coverage didn't indicate it this time.

Attitudes began to shift after that second game, though. Kuenn, disappointed by poor attendance at Yankee Stadium, recommended returning to one game. The *New York Times* indicated that, other than the players, most baseball men felt the second game was "too much of a money-grab engineered by the players to butter their already substantial pension sources." More cautious, Frick indicated he would be guided by players' wishes. Within weeks, he was supportive, announcing there would be two games a month apart in 1961, and thereafter it would revert to one. His statement followed a poll of players indicating they still favored two games by a six-to-one margin, which explained Frick's continued support. However, his proclamation of only one game in 1962 proved premature as a rep sharply took issue: "We have voted only on the All-Star program for 1961. Frick cannot speak for 1962. That is an open matter. It has not yet come up."[48] It appeared the commissioner had gotten too far ahead this time.

Indeed, he had. Following the second game in 1961, ending in a nine-inning tie, the sixteen players' reps voted for a second game in 1962, claiming fan support showed both games were popular. Robert Cannon, as the association's attorney, requested Frick create a joint committee of player reps and owners to discuss details for the two games, making clear the association believed it was a "done deal." At the Winter Meetings, the magnates approved both, though American League owners adamantly opposed a second game in 1963. Frick backed down somewhat, indicating a second game would be played in 1962 only if the broadcaster was willing to pay $250,000.[49] Baseball was destined for two games again.

That marked its end. During the first All-Star break, the reps requested a reduction of games for 1963, from 162 to 153 or 156. They also wanted night games to be prohibited on departure days, offering elimination of the second game in return. The reps met with Frick during the World Series and were informed the executive council had already voted down the second game and would consider their concerns at the Winter Meetings, and Frick suggested there was a plan to offset the pension contribution. When they met in December, owners approved eliminating the second game but not the shorter season. They did raise the percentage from All-Star Game receipts for the pension from 60 to 95 percent, with Frick estimating it would cover most losses from a second game.[50] The two All-Star Game saga was over.

Because the fan vote was restored in 1970 and a second All-Star Game remains an anomaly, this doesn't seem to be a legacy. His decision on the selection process didn't last, and Frick never made efforts to return the vote to the fans. His reasons are unknown, though the extreme reactions from Cincinnati may have made him reticent while believing correctly that players were better judges. But so was J. G. Taylor Spink correct in acknowledging the interest generated when fans voted. As for the second game, Frick never seemed enthusiastic. However, the pension-plan contributions satisfied players and helped maintain labor peace. The second-game motive may have been a richer pension plan, as sportswriters suggested, but it also reduced tensions, helping to maintain peace until Marvin Miller became director.

NEW DIMENSIONS

Major League parks have always had quirks. Many were built in urban areas, along or at the end of trolley lines, their dimensions reflecting neighborhood contours, including short foul poles, high fences, deep straight-aways, or hanging decks. None of these idiosyncrasies caused concern until the Dodgers moved to LA and played temporarily in the Coliseum. Converting a stadium built for track and football presented a problem, as the left-field foul pole was only 250 feet from home plate. That had been overlooked at the Polo Grounds, which had a similarly short right-field foul pole, perhaps because most hitters were right-handed. The issue became more salient when new ballparks were in the planning stages, as franchises relocated and older parks grew obsolete.

Frick initially was concerned when the Dodgers considered playing their first season at Wrigley Field, LA's small Minor League ballpark. Appearing on a television program, he speculated Walter O'Malley might have some regrets with the move, calling it a "cow pasture" and expressing concerns that Ruth's home run record might be threatened. His reaction changed with the Coliseum, even with its left field foul pole: "I do not think Babe Ruth's record is in particular danger." League pitchers had a different perspective, convinced the home run potential would give the Dodgers an unfair advantage. Warren Spahn, ace pitcher for the Braves, reflected, "I'd like to see the day when the baseball people pass a rule making it mandatory for a ball to travel at least 300 feet to become a home run."[51] He didn't know it, but his comments resonated with the commissioner.

So would sportswriter observations after witnessing baseball at the Coliseum. In a poll of almost two hundred sportswriters, the majority felt any home run record helped by the left-field fence should be invalid, one suggesting such a record should be treated with a footnote. Another criticized Frick for not declaring that Coliseum home runs shouldn't be counted against Ruth's mark. If pitchers' concerns hadn't gained the commissioner's attention, sportswriters' comments did. While making no ruling on home runs, he requested the Rules Committee establish contour guidelines for all new or revamped ballparks constructed after June 1. The foul poles would be a minimum of 325 feet, and straight-away center field at least 400 feet. Frick said, "There is no question but what we are going to have more clubs and many new stadiums. Now is the time to plan for standardization. . . . I hope Babe Ruth's home run record won't be broken. I don't think it will be." The rules committee met in July, unanimously approving Frick's guidelines.[52] Existing ballparks were grandfathered, but the rule applied to all built in the future. It still does.

There was one challenge during Frick's tenure on the issue, coming, not surprisingly, from Charles Finley. He reconfigured his right-field fence in Kansas City to resemble Yankee stadium. Feeling the short fence in right gave the Yankees a distinct advantage, Finley announced he was reducing his distance to the same length—290 feet—calling it his "pennant porch." The extended deck was already constructed when he announced it, bringing an immediate reaction from Joe Cronin and Frick for its removal before the season began. If not, Frick promised that every game at the ballpark would be forfeited: "There's only one interpretation and I make that. There's no appeal in this. I've ruled on it and that's that. There is no hearing, no appeal, no nothing." Finley was adamant the "porch" would be there on Opening Day. Just two days later, he changed his mind, adding tongue-in-cheek that he was doing so out of the "great respect and admiration I've always had for the offices of the commissioner of baseball and the president of the American League." He accused them of allowing the Yankees to dominate because of their short fence.[53] Finley's posture was in character, but Frick made clear the dimension rule would be enforced.

Unlike Frick's All-Star Game policies, the dimension guidelines remain in place today. Only the Cubs' Wrigley Field and the Red Sox's Fenway Park have exemptions. Although the goal of the guidelines was standardization, it has allowed ballparks considerable creativity while remaining in compliance. There are other reasons to be concerned about cheap home runs, but not ballpark configuration.

THAT DAMNED ASTERISK

Unfortunately for Frick, he is best remembered for placing an asterisk beside Roger Maris's sixty-one home runs in 1961. Frick never stipulated use of an asterisk for records broken during the longer season. Rather, he stated that sixty-one home runs would have to be achieved in 154 games for it to surpass Ruth. Otherwise, done in the remaining eight games, "there would have to be some distinctive mark in the record books." It would be a separate record.[54] Nevertheless, the myth persists—even his 2016 biography is titled *Frick**. It remains the one decision eclipsing all others over his long career. Some scholars have considered it one of the most shameful acts in baseball history.[55] It wasn't regarded that way when announced, but the perspective has definitely changed since.

As suggested by his biographer, Frick did seem to be "haunted by the Babe." There were reasons. As a sportswriter for the *New York Evening Journal,* he knew Ruth well, the relationship growing when he became Ruth's primary ghostwriter. When the Yankees released Ruth in 1934, Frick arranged for him to play for the Braves. That didn't last long, but their relationship did. They golfed together often and, with spouses, regularly played bridge. As Ruth lay dying in 1948, only family and close friends were allowed to visit, with Frick one of the last. When Ruth died three days later, Frick noted, "I never saw a man with more heart and you can interpret that as meaning both courage on the field and consideration for others."[56] Without question, their relationship colored his perspective, which is a valid criticism of his ruling during the 1961 home run chase.

A more valid criticism when Frick announced the ruling in mid-July was that it wasn't his decision to make; that belonged instead to the Major Leagues' Records Committee. Made up of four sportswriters, the leagues' directors of public relations, and the head of the Elias Statistical Bureau, the group was established in 1958 to act officially, as authorized by Frick and the league presidents. Not meeting until December, it was intended to be the final authority on any record.[57] Frick unquestionably jumped the gun by not consulting the group before his announcement, and one member noted such at the time. John Drebinger, in a *New York Times* column, disagreed strongly with Frick's decision: "To this observer . . . a season is a season. . . . Ruling otherwise would set a precedent affecting a mass of statistics. . . . Baseball's top brass should have thought of that last January. . . . Ruth needs no asterisks to protect his place in baseball."[58] Although his comments did not reflect most reactions, they provided fodder for later criticism.

Many early criticisms suggested a ruling should have been established before the 1961 season, though Frick wasn't concerned earlier. In an interview with Arthur Daley in late 1960, he asserted, "I don't think the Babe's record is vulnerable. I'll grant you that Hank Greenberg and Jimmy Foxx came reasonably close. . . . Could they have gone the rest of the way if each had eight more games? I'm not too sure." He did assure Daley the Records Committee would study the issue, even hinting at two separate records if the record was broken in the last eight games. Frick wasn't alone in his confidence, as other sportswriters agreed. One claimed, "To put the matter conservatively, this particular record . . . which becomes all the more awe-inspiring as time marches on . . . is certainly in no immediate danger. And probably won't be at all until the majors start drafting players from outer space."[59] Neither Maris nor Mantle came from another planet, but the comments illustrate the confidence in the safety of Ruth's record, helping explain why the Records Committee hadn't acted.

There were other reasons, including the understanding that the 162-game season was temporary. Most believed further expansion was imminent, at most five years away. In the same issue of *The Sporting News* that suggested only an alien could break Ruth's record, Frick stated that additional teams could occur soon, as early as 1962. Two years later he was less optimistic but remained confident the next expansion would happen in the near term, the season reverting to 154 games. If records weren't treated separately, that could add confusion later.[60] When the next expansion occurred in 1969 and the 162-game schedule was maintained, Frick had been retired for years.

Another reason the Records Committee failed to consider the longer schedule was the extensive time spent negotiating problems created by the American League's unexpected early expansion. It was originally anticipated both leagues would expand in 1962. Instead, the Junior Circuit expanded a year earlier and moved into LA. Frick was heavily engaged in persuading O'Malley to accept a second franchise and Del Webb to allow a National League club in New York. That absorbed much of his time and attention. When combined with his confidence in Ruth's record and that the 162-game season was an anomaly, his failure to address the issue in advance was understandable.

Notably, the reaction following his July ruling was largely positive. In a survey done of Baseball Writers' Association of America members, Frick's ruling was supported by a two-to-one margin. Shirley Povich, sportswriter for the *Washington Post*, articulated the issue: "The slugger who equaled or surpassed Ruth's record with the help of a 162-game schedule should not be allowed to inherit Ruth's crown. . . . At best it would be artificial or synthetic." Hy Hurwitz of the *Boston Globe* offered a counter: "I don't think a rule should have been made in midseason, when it seemed possible that Babe Ruth's record may be broken." Others emphasized the "season is a season" argument in opposing the majority.[61] Though most comments were supportive, opponents provided fuel for later criticisms.

In the same *Sporting News* issue that presented Povich's and Hurwitz's views, ballplayers were interviewed, and again a strong majority were supportive of Frick. The most interesting comment came from Mickey

Mantle: "If I should break it in the one hundred and fifty-fifth game, I wouldn't want the record." Whitey Ford, teammate of both, stated, "It's got to be done within 154 games or it won't mean anything." Jim Gentile, whose grand slam record would be affected, also supported Frick. Perhaps the strongest opposing statement came from Al Kaline: "Whoever hits 61 home runs is entitled to the record, no matter how many games it would take. The owners and leagues made out the schedules and told us how many games we would have to play. So, if a record is broken in the official number of games scheduled, it should be a record." Maris was less assertive though not in concert with Mantle: "I think the commissioner shouldn't have made any 154-game ruling when he did." As usual, Yogi Berra was concise: "I can't comment on the subject."[62]

Frick seemed unmoved by any criticism until later in September, when he appeared sympathetic to Maris, perhaps affected by the criticism. Meaningfully, he was questioned by Joe Cronin, the new American League president and a former player: "I do not wish to become involved in a dispute with Ford. But I can see no logic in the ruling that if Ruth's record is to be topped it must be excelled inside 154 decisions." Frick appeared unmoved. It was clear by then that Mantle couldn't break it and Maris would have difficulty in 154 games, thus moderating Frick. Upset about the use of an asterisk in discussing the record, the commissioner stressed, "As for that star or asterisk business, I don't know how that cropped up or was attributed to me because I never said it. I certainly never meant to belittle Maris' feat should he wind up with more than sixty. Both names will appear in the book as having set records, but under different conditions." He also emphasized the standard would be applied to all such records. Frick even enjoyed watching on television when Maris hit his sixtieth—during the last eight games—and seeing him with Ruth's widow, holding the home run ball and kissing her on the cheek. Both he and Clare Ruth also expressed joy Ruth's record held, calling it "a marvelous thing."[63] Frick softened but still held his ground.

The drama would not end, however, especially after Maris hit his sixty-first in the final game. During the offseason, Frick and Maris played off each other in comments, coming to a head in early 1962 at a lunch at Toots Shor's Restaurant honoring Maris. In his comments, Frick erred, stating that Maris had broken a record, but then hedged: "Roger did not break an old record, he set a new record." Maris responded, "I have just learned that Mr. Frick and I have something in common—he doesn't know how to make a speech either." He later qualified his comments, saying neither likes to make a speech and adding, "Through most of last season, I said and repeated, 'a season is a season' and I still think so. However, Mr. Frick is the commissioner. He makes the rules." Two days later, the asterisk became the featured satire at the annual Writers' Association event.[64] Maris never accepted the ruling, and it haunted him the rest of his life.[65]

Frick didn't appear troubled by negative reactions and remained consistent in applying his ruling. In the 155th game of the 1961 season, Jim Gentile hit his fifth grand slam, breaking the league record and tying that set by Ernie Banks. Frick stated it would be treated in the same fashion as had Maris's record.[66] The following year, when the National League expanded, Maury Wills broke Ty Cobb's season record for stolen bases—but required more than 154 games. Frick didn't need to elaborate: "It's a record, whether we say it's a record in 162 games or not there's no question it's a record—the most bases ever stolen in a single season." The Wills achievement generated some controversy because Cobb had played 156 games in 1915 when setting the record, with 2 games tied due to darkness being replayed in full. In effect, both reached ninety-six stolen bases in 156 games.[67] Nonetheless, because Frick's later decisions generated little reaction, most writers seemed to accept separate designations.

Sports history since, however, hasn't been supportive. Bill Veeck led the way in 1962 with his entertaining and opinionated book on his baseball life, coming out soon after he sold the White Sox in 1962. He considered Maris's threat "the greatest single promotional opportunity in the history of baseball and they blew it!" *They* referred to Frick, and the fact that Yankee Stadium was only half full for the final game showed lack of enthusiasm.[68] It was one of numerous criticisms, and others piled on as well. Even Frick did by including *asterisks* in his memoir's title. Criticism mounted, especially following Maris's early death from cancer in 1985. In 1991 the Committee for Statistical Accuracy, a baseball panel chaired by Commissioner Fay Vincent, eliminated all separate records. Maris became the single-season home run king until surpassed by both McGuire and Sosa in the Senior Circuit in 1998 and by Aaron Judge in the American League in 2023. Still, criticisms of Frick continue, impacting how his career is assessed.

However, the ruling remains complicated. He was certainly biased toward Ruth. More important, he failed to use the Records Committee fully. That was, perhaps, "a blatant abrogation." However, he had an excuse. When the Records Committee met in 1960, Frick was at work resolving the franchise issues with New York and LA, absorbing much of his attention. He also claimed to be unaware of the committee's oversight when he made his ruling, though he encouraged it to continue its role going forward. He also admitted he never should have used Ruth's name when declaring separate records.[69] In addition, it was understood that baseball would soon revert to 154 games a season. Further, the ruling seemed intuitively fair—if more games were played and were needed to break a record, separate records were reasonable. This is often viewed as Frick's major legacy. By no means is that true, however.

PITCHERS RECEIVE HELP

The Maris ruling didn't prevent Frick from exploring additional ways to preserve Ruth's record. He first attempted to legalize the "clean" spitball, proposing it to the Rules Committee in 1962. The proposal initially came from Ed Short, White Sox general manager, in October 1961. Although the spitball had been banned since 1920, Short mentioned in the proposal that he had the commissioner's support. Indeed, Frick had conveyed such on numerous occasions: "I believe that the spitter would be a fine thing for the game. It would help the pitchers, reduce the home-run epidemic to healthy proportions, cut down on free swinging and give us a lot of new angles to talk about and work out." With Frick and Cronin's support, restoring the spitball appeared likely until Giles spoke strongly against legalization, calling it a "freak pitch that never had its place in baseball." Further, he believed fans preferred higher-scoring games, which the spitter would reduce. The Rules Committee agreed, voting 8–1 to continue its prohibition. Jim Gallagher explained his committee saw no compelling reason to restore the outlawed pitch.[70] The 1962 season would be played under the same guidelines as 1961.

If Frick was disappointed, he didn't indicate such, perhaps because he had already devised another approach. He may have read a letter to *The Sporting News* editor in which a fan from Minnesota recommended an enlarged strike zone. Months transpired before the commissioner offered a statement in the form of a proposal. During a Houston speech, Frick called for restoring the old strike zone—from the top of shoulders to the bottom of the knees. Since 1950, the zone had been shrunk to the bottom of the shoulders and top of the knees. He claimed the enlarged zone would speed up the game by reducing home runs and walks. Although the speech wasn't covered much, Spink recommended adoption of the zone as Frick recommended.[71] That would prove prophetic.

Jim Gallagher had resigned as Rules Committee chair after thirteen years, as he no longer worked in baseball. Frick took advantage, replacing him with Charles Segar, baseball's secretary-treasurer and previously Frick's administrative assistant. As a writer observed, "It marks the first time the commissioner's office has taken over the playing rules group." It was speculated the appointment stemmed from Frick's frustration in losing the spitball vote; some conjectured that he would attempt to have the new committee legalize it.[72] He did not. Instead, Frick had moved on, convinced the larger strike zone would accomplish similar goals. What better way to ensure it than by putting someone from your office in charge? C. C. Johnson Spink supported the appointment, saying Segar was well grounded in the rules, and "most thoughtful people will applaud the promotion." Spink added a cautionary note: "It is conceivable that Segar might some time find himself in a compromising situation."[73] Because Frick had a purpose in mind when Segar was appointed, the statement suggests the compromising situation was already present.

The Rules Committee met in late January 1963 to consider the new zone. Shortly before, Frick cautiously lobbied the group though remained coy on the outcome. Segar was equally elusive, suggesting the agenda wasn't finalized. Frick also emphasized he still supported the spitter, though it was no longer a priority. It was not a surprise, then, when the Rules Committee approved the larger strike zone. Segar announced the unanimous vote, describing it as a return to the zone used until 1950. It was widely felt the new zone would benefit pitchers and speed up games by reducing walks. Many pitchers were supportive, though some remained skeptical of any beneficial impact. There was concern on how it would affect hitters. Yankees great Joe DiMaggio thought the new zone could impact home run hitters, especially those he considered free swingers. He stressed hitters would have to adjust to be successful.[74] It was largely expected the change would have an impact, but nobody was sure how much.

In fact, the change was profound, directly and indirectly. Batting averages dropped precipitously in both leagues in 1963, with the American League falling from .255 to .247 and the Nationals even greater, from .261 to .245. That decline continued through 1968, causing the Rules Committee, long after Frick retired, to return to the 1962 zone. Even with that, neither league returned to 1962 levels. The Junior Circuit took drastic action to address that in 1973, adopting the designated hitter (DH).[75] With the pitcher no longer required to bat, it surpassed the National League in batting average every year from 1973 until 2020, which was the only exception until the Senior Circuit adopted the DH in 2022. Further, if Frick's subliminal goal was protecting Ruth's record, he succeeded. It had taken thirty-four years for Maris to surpass Ruth and another thirty-seven years before Mark McGuire and Sammy Sosa surpassed both in 1998. Frick may not have anticipated the DH or the preservation of Ruth's record for almost four more decades, but both were byproducts of his strike-zone change.

COLLEGE BASEBALL WINS RESPECT

In World War II's aftermath, baseball prospered. Huge crowds attended games, and the Minors expanded exponentially; both occurred at college baseball's expense, which faced many challenges. First, the rapid growth of professional ball produced a huge need for players, thereby depleting college rosters. Not only could players be signed before enrolling, but they also could be drafted at any time. Most college players were signed by lower-level clubs, complicating the problem. Although signing bonuses were small, the opportunity to reach the Majors was tempting, even for players on scholarships. That remained unresolved for much of Frick's tenure. A second challenge stemmed from lack of summer playing opportunities for those who hadn't turned professional. A third problem stemmed from ballplayers signing pro contracts before or during college. Most would never reach the Majors but couldn't afford college while playing ball or after retiring, as many by then were married with families. Frick faced these challenges while dealing with the often-hostile relationship with the NCAA.

The first of the challenges—protection of college ballplayers after they started playing—proved to be difficult. A few months into his tenure, Frick was confronted with demands from the American Association of College Baseball Coaches, addressing the lack of an agreement with professional baseball since 1945. To reestablish one, the association presented three demands: First, no college player would be allowed to sign a pro contract until his college was completed, his class had graduated, or he was declared a hardship case by both the college dean and the commissioner. Coaches acknowledged the demands were new. Frick responded slowly, in January 1953, when he requested that the NCAA appoint a committee of three to meet with baseball representatives to consider the requests, which occurred in February. It was the first positive move from baseball in years, starting a long road to resolution.[76]

A year later, with the NCAA and Association of College Baseball Coaches working toward an agreement, it was apparent baseball executives were stalling. Colleges proposed preventing players from negotiating or signing professional contracts, beginning with a player's sophomore year. Whereas Frick and the two league presidents were supportive, the National League magnates voted it down in December 1953 and the Junior Circuit postponed action until July. In an attempt to gain more serious consideration, coaches collectively prohibited pro scouts from attending games. The Summer Meetings produced an apparent breakthrough, with both leagues agreeing to prohibit signing college players during the period requested. While calling it a "revolutionary" action by magnates, the reporter acknowledged it still put baseball behind both pro football and basketball in protecting college athletes.[77]

That decision didn't end the saga. The Minors, blaming the Majors for their financial problems, declared independence when they could. At their annual meeting in 1954, the Minor Leagues voted down the agreement. Disappointed, Frick requested another vote, stressing that "the cooperation of baseball with the colleges is of extreme importance." By a slim two-vote margin, the Minors ignored him. When Frick spoke to the coaches at their annual meeting in early 1955, he conveyed disappointment and pledged to do all in his power to have Minor League clubs owned by the Majors honor it, excepting hardship cases. With that pledge, the commissioner received a standing ovation.[78] There was still hope for progress.

It was short-lived, however. At their annual meeting in 1956, the Minors lifted all restrictions on drafting college players, with the Majors following suit. Though not pleased, Frick believed he had no choice but to enforce the result, rationalizing, "I would like to see a workable rule adopted. But since the minor leagues have no college rule, it was a joke for the majors to have one since they were merely signing college players through the back door." College coaches, as expected, objected, but for all practical purposes no progress had occurred despite Frick's efforts.[79] Matters were back to square one.

In a speech to the Executive Club of Chicago early in 1957, Frick altered his position, claiming college coaches caused part of the problem. Beyond the Minors' unwillingness to participate, the commissioner claimed many coaches had little interest in their athletes' education: "If college coaches come to me and say they are interested in a boy getting an education, the commissioner will go for it. But too often they're not interested in his education. They're interested in his eligibility." The sports editor of the *Detroit Free Press* suggested the problem was even deeper; he asserted that some coaches demanded money to allow their players to be signed.[80] Given that, it appeared even more difficult to keep players in college and provide their teams' stability.

Efforts to meet and resolve the deadlock were made during the next two years, but none produced a solution. More than a year after an agreement was discarded in 1956, John Kobs, Michigan State coach and a negotiation leader, spoke out strongly against professional baseball: "We feel . . . we've had exceptionally shabby treatment at the top. . . . We do not believe Frick has ever been very sympathetic to our situation or has been much interested in the Majors reaching an agreement with us." He recommended coaches post signs stating pro scouts are unwelcome. Some clubs attempted to work with college coaches, but their efforts were haphazard. At Frick's urging, a meeting was set up in Detroit in July 1958 between four coaches, including Kobs and Eppie Barnes of Colgate, and four younger general managers. John McHale of the Tigers hosted the meeting. Barnes, a dean among college coaches, worked with Frick to arrange the session. Though a positive step, little was expected from it. McHale suggested a report would be produced but didn't anticipate further meetings.[81] For years afterward, there was no apparent progress. Players were signed—scouts in attendance or not—and college team rosters were disrupted.

Although agreement remained unachievable, it is notable that between 1958 and 1963, when a deal was finally reached, colleges were mostly silent on the matter, suggesting discussions were continuing. C. C. Johnson Spink proposed in 1958 that the two sides compromise by the Major League club paying the college education of signed players while they remained in school. During that same period, the Majors' support for summer college baseball leagues was suggested, implied by a *New York Times* article in 1964 in which Eppie Barnes acknowledged, "The N.C.A.A.'s professional baseball committee has been working with the commissioner's office for four or five years."[82] Scholarships and summer leagues were clearly segments of those conversations.

Finally, a resolution was achieved in 1963 addressing all three issues. On drafting players, it was agreed none would be chosen until after sophomore year, giving them two full seasons to decide whether to continue their education or pursue pro ball. Both the Majors and Minors signed off, reaching a previously unobtainable accord. Frick conducted the vote in May, conveying a new era of accommodation. Lee MacPhail, president of the Orioles and a participant at the 1958 Detroit meeting, encapsulated the change: "Recently, pro baseball and the colleges have worked together in the best co-operative spirit to encourage baseball and smooth out any areas of friction." Months later, Spink offered his view: "Now, through common-sense negotiations on both sides, accord is being achieved. This will work to the benefit of both baseball and colleges."[83] It took considerable perseverance and patience, including numerous unpublicized discussions, but peace was finally achieved. Without question, the other two issues—a summer league and a college scholarship fund—assisted in reaching the agreement.

For the summer league, the breakthrough was the announcement of the Central Illinois League in 1963, funded in part by a $50,000 grant from Major League Baseball. The league would play in six towns in central Illinois, with teams managed by college coaches. Even though the Majors provided most of the funding, it would not manage the operation; it provided only financial oversight through the National Collegiate Baseball Foundation, a new entity in Frick's offices. The new league, certified by the NCAA, allowed players to maintain amateur status. Further, it provided players with jobs where they played. It was intended as a model for future expansion.[84]

The *Chicago Tribune* was strongly supportive; it published a two-day in-depth study that tied the league to the new scholarship program. Like the summer league, the scholarships broke new ground. Every player signing a professional contract would be granted up to $8,000—a thousand each semester—at the college of his choice after signing a professional contract.

Frick conveyed excitement about the league, calling it a true joint venture: "The formative years for a professional baseball player are 17 to 20. We must provide opportunity for these boys. They must play during the summertime. At present, the colleges do not offer this opportunity."

Although the first season had the usual struggles of a start-up, its success was evident. Some players signed pro contracts, and numerous scouts attended games. Frick had a major role in assisting the program's initial stage.[85]

By the end of 1964 Frick was ready to announce its expansion. Coming off successful Winter Meetings in which the commissioner was granted additional powers and established the player draft, Frick announced up to $750,000 would be set aside to establish up to four additional college leagues. Two months later, he qualified it as a $75,000 grant to various already-established leagues. The funds would purchase equipment and uniforms and pay for umpires and league expenses. He also announced that the National Collegiate Baseball Foundation would move to Kansas City to work more closely with the NCAA, which was headquartered there.[86] Both the money and the move suggested the summer league program was growing and was worthy of baseball's commitment.

That was also true of the scholarships. At a New York banquet in February 1965, Frick announced that 292 players signing Minor League contracts were eligible or already receiving money. That success countered criticism from some coaches still claiming that professional baseball interfered with college education. Frick asserted, "I'm annoyed at coaches who say pro baseball is wrecking education. . . . We are actually fostering education."[87] Although the program was in its infancy as Frick retired, it opened college opportunities to many young ballplayers. Along with summer leagues and protection of college players through sophomore year, Frick had substantially reduced the tensions with colleges that had endured during most of his tenure.

Frick's lesser legacies had important impacts on baseball, like those discussed in previous chapters. For many, the results were mixed, hence this chapter title. It is useful to separate the changes discussed into good, bad, and ugly categories.

There were many good outcomes. Sending clubs to Japan, accompanied by the commissioner or league president, was highly beneficial following World War II. The State Department certainly thought so and continued to authorize the trips. They also fostered the first Japanese player appearing in the Majors. Frick's strong support of the Rules Committee decision to remove gloves, in spite of opposition, guaranteed its implementation. His dealings with players, especially during his later years, generated good relations. The Cy Young Award for pitchers remains a legacy. While controversial, his removal of two Cincinnati Redlegs from the 1957 All-Star squad produced a more representative team. The establishment of minimum distances for foul poles and straight-away center field reduced cheap home runs. The creation of a larger strike zone, with major long-term impacts, accomplished what Frick wanted—fewer home runs. Finally, his efforts brought peace between the Majors, Minors, and college baseball. All were important achievements.

There were also bad results. The controversy over Masanori Murakami, caused by cultural misunderstandings and baseball's reserve clause, negatively impacted relations between Japan and the United States. The boycott by player reps of their meeting with Frick was a setback in their relations, precipitating the ultimately powerful Players' Association. Frick's insistence on only one Cy Young Award didn't make sense and was changed after he retired. Conducting two All-Star Games for four seasons fostered harmony with players and added to their pension, but it diminished the game's significance. Finally, the enlargement of the strike zone reduced both home runs and batting averages for years, even after it was restored to its pre-1963 range. If hitting and power stimulated fan interest, that change diminished it. Those bad impacts, however, didn't seem to outweigh the good.

The term *ugly* is subjective—what may seem so to one might be attractive to another. Frick's efforts to protect the reserve clause in the Murakami case may have seemed noble to magnates, but it likely hindered opportunities for Japanese players for decades. Similarly, the Players' Association certainly became beneficial to many players but also led to free agency, much to the chagrin of fans who witnessed star players depart their clubs. Frick was likely correct that players and managers were better qualified than fans to select All-Stars, but fan interest diminished when they didn't have a vote. Changing the strike zone benefited pitchers, as Frick intended, but the decline in batting averages ultimately produced the designated hitter, mourned by many fans. Finally, Frick's ruling on Roger Maris's home run record remains arguable, but it is certainly the ruling he is most remembered for—over any other accomplishment during his thirty-one years in baseball. That, by itself, was ugly to Frick's reputation and memory.

12

Creating and Decking the Hall

At the entrance to the Baseball Hall of Fame are portraits of its "founding fathers"—Stephen Clark and Ford Frick. Far back on the right-hand side of the hall is Frick's plaque, proudly claiming the founding as one of his three achievements. Though true, the assertion is misleading. Frick did not suggest Cooperstown as the location—that seed was planted while he was still a boy. Nor was he the first National League executive to show interest in Cooperstown—his predecessor, John Heydler, had been supportive in 1920. Nor was the museum his idea—that came from Stephen Clark's assistant, Alexander Cleland, the museum's driving force. It clearly was Frick's idea for a hall to honor baseball's greats, and he also played a role in establishing the selection procedure. Further, he was crucial in gaining the support of baseball for the concept and the ceremonies for the first inductions in 1939—the alleged centennial of the game's founding. Equally important, Frick provided ongoing support for the hall throughout his thirty-one years as a baseball executive and even in retirement—his commitment endured for the remainder of his life. The hall was both Frick's first major achievement and a personal commitment.

AN IDYLLIC LOCATION

Driving to Cooperstown, one is impressed with two things—the beauty of the area and its remoteness. The village, with a population of roughly two thousand, is a classic early nineteenth-century community. Many buildings date from that era—though not the hall. Main Street, where most businesses are located, is only three blocks long, running from the courthouse at the west end to the hall at the east. Two blocks north is Otsego Lake, a glacier-carved lake busy with nautical activity during the summer. The lake is surrounded by hills, notable for the lack of development on it except for a motel by the docks and a resort and golf course to the west. Otherwise, residences are scarce, which has preserved a natural beauty. The lake is also notable for being the origin of the Susquehanna River which empties into the Chesapeake Bay. A first-time visitor is struck by the overall beauty.

It is a historic town. Founded by William Cooper in 1786, his son—James Fenimore—grew up in the village. He was one of the more prolific early American authors. Many of Cooper's better-known stories reflect his interactions with Native Americans while he lived in Cooperstown. He was captivated by the area's beauty. His best-known novel, *The Last of the Mohicans*, was inspired by local natives, the village's early history, and the lake; the novel gave his hometown a national reputation. The community is vibrant with numerous shops and restaurants along Main Street's three blocks. Hotels, motels, and bed and breakfasts are close by, which reflects the town's status as a tourist attraction. More of that is evident if one approaches from the south on State Highway 28. Hotels and restaurants start four miles from town, most in proximity to a huge baseball facility, Cooperstown Dream Park, which is active during the summer months with a variety of Little League tournaments. Most tournaments provide at least one visit to the hall, ensuring three months with a high volume of visitors. The Hall of Fame is proof of the axiom "If you build it, they will come."

When one spends some time in Cooperstown, one notices something else—many Main Street stores are baseball-souvenir shops, stocked with baseball cards and other memorabilia. Simply put, many shops wouldn't exist without the Hall of Fame, and many stores are closed during the off-season. A visitor realizes that without the museum, the downtown would be far less vibrant.

The vibrancy was likely Stephen Clark's intent when he began his effort to create a museum. He capitalized on the legend that Abner Doubleday invented baseball there in 1839. Clark was the driving force in making the isolated village a place people would visit. The timing of Clark's effort was not a coincidence because the supposed anniversary was approaching. Further, like other small, isolated communities, Cooperstown had been severely impacted by the Depression—it had lost its railroad service, which was a major indicator the community was beginning a downward spiral. Clark had the wherewithal to turn the town's fortunes around, but he needed a good story to supplement his influence and money to create a museum.

THE ORIGIN STORY AND DEBATE

To young baseball fans in the 1950s, it was common knowledge baseball was invented in Cooperstown, New York, in 1839 by Abner Doubleday. Someone had to invent the game somewhere, and because the Hall of Fame was in Cooperstown, further explanation was unnecessary. In reality, that was a myth, stemming from the recollections of someone who departed Cooperstown at fourteen in 1848 but claimed to be present when Doubleday laid down the ground rules for baseball. How the memories of an elderly Colorado mining engineer would shape baseball history is an intriguing story.

Its roots lay in a dispute between two men instrumental in shaping early baseball. One, Henry Chadwick, is often considered the father of baseball. Although he never played, he reported on baseball for various newspapers in New York City before it became professional, and he developed the first statistics and the symbols used to keep track of the game—the box score. Born in England, he emigrated to the United States at twenty-three. Even before ballplayers were paid, he published an annual book, *Beadle's Dime Base-Ball Player*, summarizing the season. In later years, he produced the annual *Spalding Base Ball Guide*, the official compilation of the season and the sport's primary publication. He compiled the book for decades until his death in 1908.

Albert Goodwill Spalding, for whom the *Guide* was named, is the other party in the dispute that determined the hall's location. Born in Byron, Illinois, a small town southwest of Rockford, he became a star pitcher for the Boston Red Stockings in the National Association of Professional Base Ball Players, the initial professional organization. When it folded with the creation of the National League in 1876, he was plucked from Boston by William Hulbert, the league's founder, to join the Chicago White Stockings. Spalding and his brother also capitalized on the growing popularity of sports in the 1870s by establishing the Spalding Sporting Goods Company. Along with his business, he remained involved with Hulbert and the Chicago club after retiring as a player in 1877. He controlled the team after Hulbert's death in 1881 and remained an important force in the league. In fact, he had a part in consolidating the three competitive leagues into the twelve-team National League following the 1890 and 1891 seasons. Soon after, Spalding ended his baseball involvement to focus on his sports company.

The two men worked closely through much of their careers after Spalding hired Chadwick to compile his annual guide. They remained associates until Chadwick's death, but they disagreed sharply on baseball's origin. Chadwick had played rounders in England and was aware settlers brought it to the colonies. He was convinced rounders had evolved, ultimately becoming baseball in New York City through the efforts and competition of various clubs. From there, baseball slowly evolved further into the professional game. Spalding disagreed, as he was convinced baseball was uniquely American. In fact, he rejected any other game affecting its development and became more convinced after he watched a game of rounders played in England. By contrast Chadwick—perhaps given his birthplace—was receptive to an evolutionary process.

As their differences grew at the turn of the century, Spalding resolved to pursue the issue more diligently. In the 1905 edition of the *Base Ball Guide*, he asserted that baseball was uniquely American and followed it up by establishing a formal commission, known as the Mills Commission, of men connected to baseball to determine the game's origin. The chairman was Abraham G. Mills, a former player and National League president from 1882 to 1884. By 1905 he was a business executive. Among the commission members were Nicholas E. Young, who succeeded Mills as league president; Morgan G. Buckeley, the league's first president in 1876 and later a U.S. Senator; Alfred J. Reach, founder and head of a rival sporting goods company; George Wright, an early standout player; and James E. Sullivan, president of the American Amateur Athletic Union and also the commission's secretary.[1]

As distinguished as this commission appeared, little evidence suggests they ever met or even examined input. Although Sullivan received hundreds of suggestions, none was presented to the commission. Instead, Spalding sent Mills three letters he had received in 1907 from Abner Graves, the retired mining engineer, stressing that they should receive special attention. They did, indeed. Graves recalled that Abner Doubleday, either in 1839 or 1840, laid out a baseball diamond with his military-school classmates and other townsfolk and established the game's rules. There were three bases, all safe zones, and a home base that, if reached, produced a run. The game was played on a field, a cow pasture, on the south side of Main Street. With such details, a commission meeting wasn't necessary. Spalding and Mills received what they had wanted.

Doubleday was an ideal candidate. He was a West Point graduate and Civil War hero and was at Fort Sumpter when the first Civil War shots were fired. Later, Doubleday commanded troops at Gettysburg that were instrumental in stopping Pickett's Charge. Baseball's founder was the hero of a significant battle. Mills had known Doubleday, as both were members of a New York City veterans' group, and Mills had served as one of his honor guards at the funeral.[2] The Doubleday connection was also special for Spalding because both were associated with the Theosophical Society, a religious philosophy based on the commonality of human cultures. For Mills, Doubleday was someone he knew and admired. For Spalding, Doubleday was someone who shared his beliefs. For both, he was a Civil War hero.

There was additional importance for Spalding. He was aware of the conviction that baseball had originated in New York City, and both he and Chadwick initially accepted that premise, though Spalding did so with reservations. Having grown up in a small town, it was more fitting to him that baseball's origin would be rural, more in tune with the wholesome image of Americana than cities were in 1907. Cooperstown fit that expectation. In effect, Spalding now had the ideal person and place for baseball's origin—a game created in small-town America.

It was such a good story that little, if anything, was done to fact-check it. Spalding and Mills were aware that baseball's creation was credited to the Knickerbockers club in New York City, which played their games on the Elysian Fields in New Jersey. Alexander Joy Cartwright, one of the Knickerbockers, was allegedly instrumental in establishing the ground rules. There was even an effort by the Spalding commission, albeit half-hearted, to explore a possible connection between the Cooperstown origin and Cartwright. Mills had accepted the Knickerbocker theory prior to Graves's letters but glossed over it in his final report, concluding with certainty that baseball originated in Cooperstown, likely in 1839.[3] A little research would have provided a cautionary note before publicizing Graves's story. First, Abner Doubleday wasn't in Cooperstown in 1839 or 1840. He had matriculated at West Point in the summer of 1838, residing there full-time until graduation in 1842. That alone would have ruled out either year. Further, those close to Doubleday knew he never demonstrated any interest in outdoor sports. In particular, well before his death in 1893, professional baseball had become highly popular in his New York City home, yet he never claimed any association with the game's origin.

A similar investigation on Graves would have also raised skepticism. His background story was true. He was born and raised around Cooperstown, though he departed at fourteen, never to return. He lived an eventful life, had married well, and was successful in the mining business. However, his recollection of playing in the first game with Doubleday was unlikely because Graves would have been five in 1839. If he was a year off, when Doubleday was still in Cooperstown, Graves would have been four, in either case too young to participate or even to remember it.[4]

Any investigation obviously didn't happen, as Spalding published Graves's version in his 1908 baseball guide. Chadwick, still the author of the guide, had no choice but to execute his boss's dictate, though he remained convinced the game evolved from rounders as later evidence would indicate. However, he had little, if any, time to counter Spalding's claim—he died later that year. Spalding's nemesis was no longer around to contest the Cooperstown thesis. But that didn't matter much to Spalding at that point, because he had moved to San Diego to spend his remaining years focused on his Theosophical faith. What had mattered to him was a story that credited baseball with a unique origin in a small, rural, and historical town—a true American saga in every way. All he needed was for others to perpetuate the myth.[5]

A key person to do so was Sam Crane, a Major League ballplayer and subsequently a New York City sportswriter. From that later vantage point, shortly after Spalding published his origin story, Crane became one of Cooperstown's biggest advocates. Although not a prominent sportswriter, he made several visits to the village and generated interest among locals—a necessary ingredient to create something tangible out of Graves's myth.[6] That first step led to construction of a baseball diamond on the land where it supposedly had originated. Local officials purchased the Phinney cow pasture behind the Main Street stores and built a ball diamond. Two of the townspeople who had constructed it also met with new National League president John Heydler, who proved supportive. The men then recruited two teams from the area to play a game on the diamond in September 1920. Heydler came to dedicate the field and umpire the first inning.[7] It was an important start, especially with support coming from a top baseball executive. After that, however, the project languished for years, due to lack of interest and funding.

That changed during the Depression, especially with the election of Franklin Delano Roosevelt in 1932. With the creation of the Work Projects Administration by the National Recovery Act in 1933, money was available for restoration work. One of the recipients was Doubleday Field, and construction of a new diamond and grandstands was started in early 1934. It became the catalyst for the hall.

SEWING IT TOGETHER

Another prominent family associated with the village would provide the impetus to create a tourist attraction. Interestingly, that family never called the village home; instead, the family patriarch built a summer residence there for his wife, a Cooperstown native. That generated an ongoing connection that paid dividends a century later, when a descendant witnessed the construction of Doubleday Field in the spring of 1934.

That descendant was Stephen Clark. His grandfather Edward Clark, whose spouse was from Cooperstown, built the summer home in the 1850s. By that time he was partner in a successful New York City law firm that was retained by Isaac Singer, inventor of a sewing machine superior to any competitors. Singer encountered many patent challenges, and Clark, an expert on patent law, negotiated an arrangement by which he received half the profits. In return, Clark oversaw the company's operations, a skill Singer apparently lacked. The Singer machine became incredibly popular, and Edward Clark accumulated one of the great nineteenth century fortunes.[8] Clark also inculcated a sense of civic responsibility and affection for Cooperstown to his son and grandsons that later proved highly beneficial.

Of the four grandsons, Edward and Stephen were the most generous to their second home. Edward built a mansion on Otsego Lake that Stephen later purchased and converted to an art museum. He also built the Otesaga Hotel, Cooperstown's premier resort today. His brother, Stephen, however, proved to be even more beneficial. With the village deep in the Depression in the mid-1930s, the railroad line discontinued, and the population declining, Stephen believed Cooperstown could attract tourists with museums, three of which he ultimately created. He also established the local hospital and a health and fitness center, and he set up endowments for local development and scholarships. Thanks to the Doubleday myth, a baseball museum became a logical choice, though it wasn't Clark's idea. Instead, it came from his associate, Alexander Cleland.

Cleland had worked for years with Stephen as director of the Clark House, a home and provider of services for male immigrants integrating into New York City. Cleland had emigrated from Scotland and developed a reputation as an immigration expert, which led to being hired by Clark. Like Clark, Cleland was not a baseball fan, but a Cooperstown meeting piqued his interest. While there, Cleland met workmen rebuilding the ball diamond. Their enthusiasm for the project and excitement about a possible celebration of baseball's one hundredth anniversary in five years gave Cleland an idea. Upon returning to New York, he put together a plan to build a baseball museum by Doubleday Field and presented it to Clark.[9] The Singer heir loved it. They quickly sketched plans for the building and devised a method of funding.

Late in the summer of 1934, Clark and Cleland presented their plan to the village trustees. By then an old ball had been found in an abandoned barn inside a trunk that had belonged to Abner Graves. Clark purchased the ball for $5, naming it the "Doubleday ball."[10] The discovery gave proof to the origin story and was a natural item for the museum, adding momentum and encouraging local support. In October the trustees passed a resolution stating that they "hereby designate and appoint Mr. Alexander Cleland of New York City as their representative in New York in the promotion of a movement to erect at Doubleday Field in the Village of Cooperstown a suitable memorial that shall be a national baseball shrine."[11] By then Cleland had elicited support from Walter Littell, editor and publisher of the local papers, who played a major role in keeping the community informed.[12] Support and funding were in place.

What remained critical to the project, however, was support from baseball, and attempts were made early to achieve it. Since Heydler had been supportive earlier, he was the first official contacted. Still supportive, he indicated he was retiring as National League president and referred the matter to his successor, Ford Frick. At the end of January 1935 Cleland wrote to Frick, requesting a meeting along with his support. While he didn't achieve a meeting initially, he did receive support for the museum— Frick assured Cleland he had the league's approval and offered "the fullest cooperation in any project you may evolve."[13] Cleland had the necessary initial commitment. Everything appeared sewed together, but the cooperation was only the start of what would become a much larger concept and event.

The initial support from Frick didn't impact the museum concept. Until May 1935 Cleland's correspondence made no mention of a Hall of Fame. Cleland had hoped to meet with Frick sooner, but it didn't happen until May. Frick was the holdup, as he was busy learning his new job as league president and grappling with its early problems. He had also prioritized visiting all eight clubs during spring training. When they finally met, the session reshaped Cleland and Clark's vision.

Frick proposed the idea for the Hall of Fame at that meeting. The first reference to it occurs in a letter dated May 13 from Cleland to Roy Witmer of the National Broadcasting Company. Cleland asked how to solicit names for selecting fifty baseball immortals to be in "baseball's hall of fame."[14] The concept was new to Cleland, but not to Frick. New York University had a Hall of Fame for Great Americans, started in 1901, which recognized George Washington among others. Frick likely visited the attraction because he had been in New York for almost fourteen years and had been on the campus, having broadcast at least one of the university's football games. In his memoir, Frick claims to have visited a few days before meeting with Cleland.[15] Still, no publicity about the idea came out of their meeting.

It's likely the delay was to allow time to develop the concept. That summer, a Cooperstown newspaper mentioned the idea, referencing "the plan to create a Hall of Fame in the National Baseball Museum in this village, which was recently suggested by Ford Frick, President of the National League, to Alexander Cleland, Secretary of the museum and Doubleday Field movement." The article explained the hall would be "a preliminary to the elaborate program planned in observance of baseball's centennial at Cooperstown in 1939."[16] It's likely this story was published after Frick's August meeting with Cleland, when the process for selecting players was also formalized.

That August meeting in Frick's office included Cleland and Clark, along with three media representatives. They provided the key to a major question: how do you select the greats for the Hall of Fame? The media representatives were from the three major news services—Davis Walsh of the International News Service, Alan Gould of the Associated Press, and Henry Farrell of United Press. Collectively, the six men decided the selections would be made by the Baseball Writers' Association of America

(BBWAA), with the more recent players selected by sportswriters who had covered them. Gould suggested that a 75 percent vote be required for induction.[17] Cleland posited that fans make the selection, which was glossed over, perhaps from concern it would turn the selection into a popularity contest rather than an evaluation of accomplishments. The group stipulated that a player must be retired, and later that became a five-year requirement. Aspects of the process would evolve, with committees established in later years to deal with the nineteenth century and other categories.[18] Still, the basic format for selection was established at this meeting, much of it remaining in place today.

After that meeting, the establishment of the Hall of Fame and the museum became a national story. The *New York Times* announced a hall for baseball stars, determined by sportswriters and editors, with the BBWAA providing oversight. The article mentioned that the meeting occurred in Frick's office with Cleland present and the initial selection would be limited to ten players, five from the last century and five from the current one. The inductees would be honored during the centennial celebration in 1939.[19] A baseball Hall of Fame was now public knowledge, and although the museum remained important, it now was secondary. Further, the museum had become something larger.

Considerable work remained. Cleland had hoped to involve Landis. While Frick provided a supportive role, Landis was the commissioner—supposedly the "czar of baseball." When Cleland met with Frick, he also wrote to Landis, requesting him to chair a national committee. A month later, with no response, Cleland wrote the commissioner's secretary, Leslie O'Connor, asking for assistance. This time he received a response from Landis, though not what he anticipated. Landis had no interest in chairing a committee. Further, the matter wouldn't be brought up until the 1935 joint meeting of the two leagues in early December; because the celebration wasn't until 1939, that should provide plenty of time, according to Landis.[20] He clearly wasn't interested.

Landis also downplayed it at the joint meeting. The day before, at the National League meeting, the owners committed $10,000 for the Cooperstown centennial fund, even though it had just allocated $36,000 to stabilize the financially struggling Boston Braves.[21] At Landis's meeting, the only result was an advisory council to provide baseball input for the centennial, with more discussion spent on the issue of discounting grandstand seats for children.[22] Cleland was left uncertain about baseball's support.

In the meantime, establishment of the hall and museum proceeded. The first vote for induction was held in late 1935 and early 1936. The vote for nineteenth-century players proved complicated, as no one received 75 percent of the votes, but the vote for the modern era succeeded. Five players from that era surpassed the threshold—Ty Cobb, Babe Ruth, Walter Johnson, Christy Mathewson, and Honus Wagner. Changes were later made to the nineteenth-century process. Because fewer than ten were chosen, the BBWAA decided to conduct an annual vote. In January 1937 three more inductees were announced—Cy Young, Tris Speaker, and Napoleon Lajoie. By that time the quota of ten was dropped, and any eligible player receiving the proper number of ballots would be inducted.[23] Although the hall selections progressed nicely, baseball had done little to prepare for the centennial.

When the leagues met in December 1937, the advisory council created two years earlier had done little, causing Frick to strongly express his concerns. He first conveyed doubts about the council, less for its lack of accomplishment, but rather for being limited to the Majors. He proposed a separate committee—including the Minors, colleges, and other baseball organizations—funded by the commissioner's office. He also pushed for a major financial commitment, as the Minors already offered $25,000. He proposed $100,000 to the centennial for a national program, including a paid director who would bring along "a high-class promotional group of men." He added, "It can be a tremendous national thing. It is the biggest thing in baseball. It can make 1939 the biggest thing baseball has ever had." Branch Rickey and Clark Griffith spoke positively, and Tom Yawkey, Red Sox owner, motioned that $50,000 come from each league. It passed. Landis remained silent, though not throwing cold water on the proposal.[24] The centennial finally had the support needed from baseball to make it a first-class affair.

That was assured by hiring Steve Hannagan, whose firm would coordinate the publicity and events. Hannagan, like Frick a native Hoosier, had managed a New York publicity firm for over a decade, representing clients like the Indianapolis 500. He was joined by Al Stoughton, a Bucknell alum, for years the university's publicist, and also a nephew of Hall of Famer Christy Mathewson. Together, they developed a massive national campaign capitalizing on the Doubleday connection—baseball created by a national hero—while also appealing to the general public. They stressed the patriotism of baseball, the national game. Hannagan may have been influenced by how Germans publicized the 1936 Olympics, stressing nationalism, health, and participation. Utilizing local newspapers, along with radio and movie newsreels, Hannagan and Stoughton stimulated a nationwide interest that reached well beyond diehard baseball fans.[25] They achieved the national prominence Frick had imagined.

Not all went smoothly. In 1937 and 1938, Cleland received numerous letters from Bruce Cartwright of Honolulu and the Hawaii Chamber of Commerce. Cartwright was the grandson of Alexander Joy Cartwright, who left New York City for Honolulu and later claimed to have developed the rules of baseball in 1845 and promoted the sport as he crossed the continent. Grandson Bruce and the chamber hounded Cleland, maintaining that Doubleday was being recognized for what Cartwright had accomplished. In a letter to Cleland, Frick suggested a solution: "The Centennial of baseball is a centennial of a game rather than of individuals . . . there is no tendency on the part of organized baseball at least to give all the credit to Abner Doubleday and to overlook Cartwright. . . . Mr. Cartwright certainly will be included among the immortals whose names will be perpetuated in the museum."[26] That soothed Cartwright's discontent.

The centennial, on June 12, 1939, was a huge success, with thousands of spectators cramming the streets of Cooperstown. All living inductees were present, though Ty Cobb arrived late. James Farley, postmaster general, provided an official presence by selling a commemorative stamp at the post office. Charles J. Doyle, president of the BBWAA, was master of ceremonies, and the Cooperstown mayor offered a welcome. John Heydler gave an address about the centennial, and Landis offered a dedicatory address. Frick was not left out—he joined William Harridge and William Bramham, head of the Minor Leagues, to cut the ribbon opening the museum. Doyle returned to the podium to do the roll call. The ceremonies then moved to Doubleday Field, where local high school boys enacted a game of town ball, followed by a game from the 1850s between two New York clubs, enacted by U.S. Army soldiers. The climax was a game played between the National and American Leagues, with two players representing each of the sixteen ball clubs. Each league provided an umpire, and the clubs were managed by two of the inductees—Honus Wagner for the National League and Eddie Collins for the Junior Circuit. All eleven living members of the Hall of Fame became the "Coaches and Board of Strategy."[27] It was, indeed, a great day in Cooperstown.

Kenesaw Mountain Landis played an appropriate role in the celebration, but that didn't suggest his support. As Frick summarized, "He couldn't see it. He said his office couldn't become involved in any local promotion. The judge maintained that aloofness throughout the rest of his life. He did attend the dedication celebration, made a fine dedication speech, and entered fully into the spirit of the day—but so far as I know he never again went near Cooperstown."[28] Because no inductions took place between 1936 and 1946, there was also no occasion for Landis to preside. His spirit was there in 1946, however. Shortly after his death, a special committee, including Stephen Clark, convened; it dispensed with the five-year wait, and the vote of the six members, including three magnates and two sportswriters, for Landis's induction was unanimous.[29] There was already precedent, as each league's first president had been inducted in 1939. Landis may have wanted little to do with the hall, but he became a permanent member.

A LIFETIME COMMITMENT

For Frick, the hall became an important part of his life, even after his induction. During his thirty-one years in baseball, he rarely missed an induction ceremony. The one in 1946 was the first after the inaugural, and the new commissioner, Albert Benjamin "Happy" Chandler presided, though Frick also spoke. The keynote was given by New York Governor Thomas Dewey, who had lost his presidential campaign two years earlier. He threw out the first pitch at the game, which drew over ten thousand fans.[30] During subsequent years, Frick was the primary official at three inductions, and Chandler was not at any, suggesting the hall wasn't a high priority for him. Frick's comments in 1947 were highly patriotic, calling baseball "as democratic as a town meeting, and as American as wheat and corn." In 1950, when the west wing of the museum was dedicated, Frick stressed, "We are dedicating anew our faith in American traditions and American ideas."[31] Frick presided again in 1951 since Chandler had just resigned; this time, he focused on the pending congressional hearings, expressing confidence that "the committee will clear away the mists and open a new highway for baseball through the years ahead."[32] Frick would set the standard for future commissioners to attend.

Throughout his tenure as commissioner, Frick never weighed in on Hall of Fame candidates and let the BBWAA and Veterans Committee do their work. The commissioner's role was a passive one, merely welcoming new members and giving an appropriate speech. He never intervened to tip the scales. That changed in retirement when Frick was named chairman of the Veterans Committee in 1966, replacing the late Branch Rickey. Frick expected a normal meeting with the usual candidates—those passed over by the BBWAA for not reaching 75 percent of the vote and out of baseball for five years. However, he was approached by a sportswriter requesting that the committee bypass the five-year rule for Casey Stengel, who was retiring as the Mets' manager. The committee waved the five-year rule for any manager, executive, or umpire sixty-five or older.[33] An enthusiastic supporter, Frick went even further by formulating plans on how to provide Stengel special early recognition.

The relationship between Frick and Stengel dated back to when Frick began his tenure in 1934. The new manager offered sarcastic comments about league umpires at a banquet honoring Frick. Stengel's barbs initiated a heavy barrage of similar comments from Frick's former sportswriter colleagues, some accusing him of jumping to the enemy.[34] Stengel had set the tone for the ribbings, making it clear Frick had entered a different world. It initiated their relationship.

It wouldn't take long for it to continue. During the 1935 season, Frick fined the then Dodgers' manager, not for misbehavior, such as cursing or kicking an umpire, but instead for arguing over an issue continuously rather than submitting a protest. In effect, Stengel was fined for filibustering a game.[35] Other fines were administered by Frick to Stengel while the latter managed National League clubs through 1943. When he returned with the Yankees in 1949, Frick had little reason to interact, as manager issues were league matters. However, when Stengel became the Mets' manager in 1962, he crossed a line, which prompted Frick's involvement. Baseball had a rule against posing in uniform for a television commercial that promoted alcohol. In this case, in an ad for a local beer, Casey was in uniform demonstrating bunting to the poster girl—Kathy Kersh—who was standing behind him holding a ball. Frick fined the manager $500 and noted, "If Casey is going to teach bunting he should be more careful to keep his eye on the ball. It's behind him in the picture."[36] It proved an expensive return for Stengel.

It was fitting that when both retired they would be brought together again. Frick announced the decision to reduce the waiting time at the New York BBWAA dinner in 1966 but did not mention particulars. The article speculated Stengel might be a beneficiary but added it wouldn't occur until 1967, though the two were together on the dais when Frick made the announcement.[37] Frick had offered no indication otherwise. He had been intentionally coy because he had already planned the surprise. A vote had been taken by mail by the Veterans Committee, and the results were unanimous to induct Stengel that year. The decision remained a secret; even Commissioner William Eckert wasn't informed until a day before its announcement. Those few who knew helped stage the surprise at the Mets' first spring training game in early March. While Eckert was present, Frick presided at the ceremony and presented Stengel with a replica of a Hall of Fame plaque. A surprised and elated Stengel walked up to both the first and third base stands while displaying his honor, with rousing ovations raining down. A New York sports columnist, calling it "a most proper coronation ceremony," said Frick had "pushed through the drive to its happy conclusion."[38] The formal induction would not occur until July, but Stengel had already received well-deserved recognition.

At the formal induction that summer, only one other player—Ted Williams—was honored; one of the greatest players was joined by one of the greatest managers. The notoriety of the two men brought the largest turnout at an induction since the initial one. It also was noteworthy given Williams's speech, expressing a wish that generated controversy for the hall the next five years: "I hope someday Satchel Paige and Josh Gibson can be added here in some way as a symbol of great Negro players. They are not here only because they didn't get a chance."[39] It was the first recognition from an inductee that some of the greatest ballplayers hadn't had the opportunity for recognition.

That precipitated a debate between offering a full induction or a separate wing for Negro League players. Frick's Veterans Committee didn't appear to give the issue attention. Members selected a number of greats, including Branch Rickey, Lloyd Waner, Kiki Cuyler, Goose Goslin, Stan Coveleski, and Waite Hoyt, and at one meeting, in 1968, Frick suggested adding a wing to house the library.[40] At the induction that summer, he presented the library with the first copy of Babe Ruth's book of baseball to roll off the press, which Frick had ghostwritten. The copy was signed by Ruth, Lou Gerhig, former Yankees manager Miller Huggins, and Yankees owner Jacob Ruppert. When Coveleski and Hoyt were selected in 1969, Frick noted, "We wanted to elect them while they were still around to smell the roses."[41] While Williams's wish still percolated, Frick's committee maintained the status quo by remaining silent on Negro League standouts.

In early January 1970 Frick submitted his letter of resignation from the Veterans Committee.[42] There was speculation he offered it because he opposed the hall's direction on the Negro League issue—treating its standouts the same as Major Leaguers. While there is no record of Frick's position, he was a traditionalist and likely believed recognition of Negro League players should be treated separately because most hadn't experienced the Majors. Thus, a separate wing made sense. The counterargument was that those players would receive the same separate-but-equal treatment rendered by a late nineteenth-century Supreme Court decision that was reversed in 1954. Considerable criticism came from the press over the hall even considering separate treatment. If Frick did disagree, however, which was likely, it didn't affect his involvement. When Satchel Paige was inducted in 1971, Frick was present. He was there again the following year for Josh Gibson's induction.[43] The Negro League issue did not prompt his resignation or alter his involvement in any way.

Instead, he had resigned the Veterans Committee because he couldn't serve if it considered him for induction. It didn't accept the resignation until the day before its meeting, though it had been offered a month earlier. The next day, Frick was selected unanimously. Many had worked with him, including Joe Cronin, Warren Giles, Charles Segar, and Will Harridge. Including the sportswriters on the committee, Frick was truly selected by peers. He declared that he was "proud, flattered, and humbled."[44] He continued serving on the Board of Directors of the Hall and Museum, retiring in 1977 only after a stroke rendered him paralyzed and unable to speak.[45] That ended more than forty years of involvement.

The highlight was his induction. By 1970 baseball had fired William Eckert, the man who replaced Frick, and Bowie Kuhn now presided over the induction, following the precedent Frick had established. The new commissioner acknowledged, "More than anyone else, Ford Frick has brought us here today and through the years. He is the father of the Baseball Hall of Fame. It was his foresight and determination that brought it into existence."[46] In the audience were family—wife Eleanor; son Fred and Fred's spouse, Jere; and grandchildren Kelley and Ford. Perhaps thinking of them, Frick's speech addressed youth and the hall. "Children have the right to dream and to have their heroes to idolize. Baseball provides them [the heroes]. . . . Baseball will continue to grow because it exemplifies what is perfect in men. But without memories of the past, there could be no dreams of the future. Without those yesterdays, there could be no bright tomorrows."[47] His plaque in the hall mentions three accomplishments: president of the National League, commissioner of baseball, and founder of the Hall of Fame. All three encapsulated significant achievements during his baseball career.

Frick was not responsible for many facets of the hall. He was not involved with the location, didn't have the idea of a museum, nor did he do the spade work. Stephen Clark and Alexander Cleland were the driving forces behind the concept, as well as the first celebration. That said, someone in baseball had to be supportive. John Heydler had done so earlier, but someone had to take the baton when he retired. Landis certainly didn't want it. Will Harridge didn't either. Perhaps Frick was influenced by Heydler, but it was Frick who had to get behind the concept and carry the water to ensure its success. He did that. He had the idea for the Hall of Fame and continued to promote it to gain support from baseball. It is fair to conclude that without Frick, there would not be the Hall of Fame and Museum in Cooperstown. Like many of the other accomplishments discussed in this book, it was a lasting legacy, one Frick remained committed to for the remainder of his life.

ACKNOWLEDGMENTS

If I hadn't been convinced to teach a winter term baseball history class at DePauw University twenty-five years ago, this book would never have materialized. Jeffrey Hollander was the coordinator, his persuasion reflecting an effort for a more rigorous, yet popular class for January. Through years of teaching the class, I became aware of DePauw alum Ford Frick, his baseball leadership, along with his contributions to both journalism and radio broadcasting. My interest was piqued as I realized how poorly regarded Frick was by scholars, in spite of baseball's many changes during his thirty-one years.

DePauw provided me with an excellent support network. The late John Dittmer, professor emeritus of history, read and commented on all the chapters. Librarian Tiffany Hebb was helpful throughout my research. Recently retired archivist Wes Wilson assisted me with materials during Frick's student years at DePauw. Jinsie Bingham provided a place to stay on my research trips as well as historical tidbits on Greencastle. Coworkers Chris Newton and Marilyn Culler, along with history professor and baseball fan David Gellman, offered support at various times. Although student transcripts are not public, I am indebted to June Wildman, assistant registrar at DePauw in 2015, for the information on grades. Archivist Wes Wilson confirmed Frick was not inducted into Phi Beta Kappa. Others, outside DePauw, also offered help, including Barry Ferris, president of the alumni board of Palmer High School, formerly Colorado Springs High School, where Frick taught. Jessy Randall, curator and archivist at Special Collections at Colorado College, was helpful in locating sources on Frick. William Marshall, librarian at the University of Kentucky, provided me a copy of the MacPhail Report and introduced me to the Chandler papers.

The staff at the Giamatti Research Center at the National Baseball Hall of Fame and Museum in Cooperstown, New York, has been supportive since I first came to do research in 2007. Freddie Berowski helped initially. Jim Gates stepped in when I focused on this book in 2014. Two staff members—Cassidy Lent and Mark Rothenberg—both joined Gates at our first meeting and have been helpful numerous times since. Rothenberg's replacement, Rachel Wells, assisted me on my last trip. Friends made through the Cooperstown Symposium and the Society for American Baseball Research have provided important contributions. Cassidy Lent has been helpful throughout the process. Jim Gates read and critiqued the chapter on Cooperstown. Paul Hensler read both the preface and the chapter on expansion with helpful comments. Ed Edmonds read and offered comments on the antitrust chapter and provided me with all the congressional hearings examined. David Krell has been supportive at various times. In all cases, they bear no responsibility for conclusions reached. Andy McCue offered suggestions on more than one occasion, as has Steven Wisensale. The late Bill Marshall, while still at the University of Kentucky, helped with my research there and provided ongoing encouragement for me to pursue a reassessment of Frick. The resources and contributions of the Society for American Baseball Research (SABR) and its members were useful in providing access to *The Sporting News* and biographies of baseball personalities.

Many friends have helped. Ned and Sue Lee housed me during my research in Fort Wayne. Will Carroll has constantly nagged me to keep writing. So has Jay Hook. Little did he realize he would become a subject. Gary Benjamin, over numerous lunches, had little choice but to listen to whatever I was researching or writing about. Ed Folsom, close to a lifelong friend, has discussed book ideas and content with me for longer than this book was in the making. His advice was useful in many areas.

Frick's descendants were exceptionally helpful, especially at the beginning. Grandson Ford and spouse Ann had me for dinner in Denver and helped later with contacts at Colorado College. Kelly Frick Richards, Frick's granddaughter, entertained me at her home in Vinal Haven Island, Maine, for a day, providing useful family history. She also made sure I made it to the 4:00 p.m. ferry to assure she wouldn't be stuck with me overnight. The late Jere Frick, their mother, was very informative and also put me in touch with a very insightful Emil "Buzzie" Bavasi. Terry Housholder, former editor of the *News Sun* (Kendallville IN), took me around Noble County and helped determine that Frick, in his youth, apparently imagined a Cubs exhibition game there in 1907.

Special mention goes to the staff at the University of Nebraska Press for their support and patience, and to copyeditor Joseph Webb for stylistic and substantive improvements to the manuscript.

Finally, thanks to my wife, Lynn, for her tolerance and technical support at critical times. And thanks to my family, sons Jeff and Brad and daughter Mindy, as well as to their spouses, Christy, Amy, and Kevin. Finally, thanks to all my grandkids—Brenden, Caden, Zoey, Bridget, Colin, and Ailis—for constantly making life special.

Portions of chapter 3 were previously published in "The Season That Almost Wasn't," *Nine* 27, no. 1 (2018): 25–40.

Portions of chapter 4 were previously published in "Ford Frick and Jackie Robinson: The Enabler," in *Jackie: Perspectives on 42*, ed. Bill Nowlin and Glen Sparks (Phoenix AZ: Society for American Baseball Research, 2021), 114–21.

NOTES

PREFACE

1. "Senator Chandler in Talk with Frick," *New York Times*, April 27, 1945.
2. "Chandler Angers Baseball Leaders," *New York Times*, October 8, 1945.
3. Arthur Daley, "The Pension Plan," Sports of the Times, *New York Times*, December 11, 1953.
4. "Baseball Now a Monopoly, Says Chandler," *Chicago Tribune*, April 29, 1958.
5. To Complete the Report, *Chicago Tribune*, July 15, 1959.
6. Insiders Say, *The Sporting News*, February 21, 1970, 4.
7. Veeck and Linn, *Veeck as in Wreck*, 240.
8. Veeck and Linn, *Veeck as in Wreck*, 242.
9. Veeck and Linn, *Veeck as in Wreck*, 243.
10. Veeck and Linn, *Veeck as in Wreck*, 250. When interviewing Veeck's son Mike, I asked why his dad disliked Frick. He responded, "He disliked anyone wearing a tie." Mike Veeck, in discussion with the author, March 23, 2008.
11. Voigt, *American Baseball*, 3:94–95.
12. Marshall, *Baseball's Pivotal Era*, 395. The late Bill Marshall was very helpful, facilitating my examination of Chandler's papers at the University of Kentucky Library and providing a copy of the MacPhail Report. In later correspondence, he encouraged me, saying Frick "badly needs rehabilitation." William Marshall, email message to author, November 5, 2010. He also viewed Chandler as "overly sensitive to criticism and paranoid. You were either for him or against him. His world could be very black and white." Frick was not viewed as "for Chandler." William Marshall, email message to author, February 20, 2016. Not surprisingly, I disagree with Marshall's assessment of Frick in his book.
13. Moffi, *Conscience of the Game*, 142.
14. Buhite, *Continental League*, 48–49.
15. For additional historiography on Frick, see Bohmer, "Reshaping Baseball."

16. Carvahlo, *Frick**, 271. I disagree with Carvahlo numerous times, letting my analysis make the case. I believe facts demonstrate Frick contributed significantly to the changes occurring during his tenure.
17. Holtzman, *Commissioners*, 119–20.
18. Holtzman, *Commissioners*, 286–87. The last comment, on enforcing rules the owners had made, was provided by Buzzie Bavasi. Emil "Buzzie" Bavasi, in discussion with the author, May 31, 2007.
19. Frick, *Games*, 210.
20. Frick, *Games*, 212.
21. Frick, *Games*, 215.
22. Frick, *Games*, 219.
23. Lewis, "Bud Selig's Use of Smart Power," 195, 201–2. Lewis quotes me describing Frick as "a typical CEO of the era, who worked his way up through the ranks, shunned publicity, delegated significantly, and worked behind the scenes to accomplish goals pragmatically." That's all true, despite my opposite conclusion. Dwight D. Eisenhower was also a 1950s-style executive, and most historians regard him as one of the most successful presidents. The same is true for Frick among the commissioners.
24. The personal observations on Frick come from interviews with the four. Emil "Buzzie" Bavasi, discussion; Angela "Jeri" Frick, in discussion with the author, April 12, 2007; Ford Frick, grandson, in discussion with the author, April 16, 2014; and Kelly Frick Richards, in discussion with the author, October 4, 2014.

1. BEFORE REACHING THE MAJORS

1. The conservative takeover of the Zurich Canton and the liberal return to power are discussed in Lerner, *Laboratory of Liberty*, 256–58, and Walton, *Richard Wagner's Zurich*, 26–29. My supposition is based on the family's religion in Noble County. The various connections were found on Ancestry.com, using federal censuses from 1840 through 1870. Immigration records were also found through that site. The land acquisitions are in *Transfer Books of Noble County, 1848–1854*, June 27, 1850, and November 1853, in the Noble County Court House. The value of their farms is from the 1870 census.
2. Noble County History Book Committee, *History of Noble County*, 142.
3. Landon, Gagen, and Knopp, *History of Schools in Noble County*, 19, 33.
4. *Transfer Books of Noble County, 1887–1894*, October 15, 1889, Noble County Court House.
5. *Transfer Books of Noble County, 1895–1903*, April 29, 1895, Noble County Court House.

6. Noble County Historical Society, *Pioneer Echoes*, October 2005, 5.
7. 1910 federal census, Brimfield IN, Orange Township.
8. Frick, *Games*, 3.
9. 1900 federal census, Orange Township, Indiana.
10. Noble County Historical Society, *Pioneer Echoes*, April 1991, 3.
11. Frick, *Games*, 4–5.
12. Every issue of the *Kendallville News-Sun* from March through October 1907 was examined, including the year before and after. No mention of the game was in stories or advertisements. The local paper was a logical way to generate ticket sales. Further, a Major League club in town was news.
13. Frick, *Games*, 3.
14. The information was likely recounted to Frick's granddaughter, Kelly Frick Richards, by elderly family member Mary Jane Leipid. Kelly Frick Richards, email to author, July 10, 2025.
15. Indeed, the farm of sister Sophronia and her husband, Orlando, was likely where young Ford may have farmed.
16. "A Distinctive Mark: Ford Frick's Thirty-One Years as a Baseball Executive," unpublished manuscript in possession of the author, n.d. The author is anonymous. The quote is taken from Robert A. Reed in the *Fort Wayne Journal-Gazette* in 1934.
17. Scrapbook of M. F. Owen, Noble County Library, vol. 20, 5708–9. Millard Fillmore Owen was a hotel and restaurant keeper in Rome City, maintaining a scrapbook for over fifty years. Ford Frick is mentioned a few times. Frick acknowledged a relationship in a letter: "Condolences on Owen's passing. I don't know of any man who rated higher in my affection than did Mr. Owen. He was kind and good to me when kindness meant so much." Vol. 26, 7283. Did Owen provide Frick lodging in return for work at the hotel during cold and stormy days? Given the five-plus mile sojourn each way, that was a way to avoid arduous travel.
18. "Distinctive Mark," 1.
19. "Distinctive Mark," 1. The International School of Business, still in Fort Wayne, was able to confirm Frick was a student but unable to locate records.
20. Terry Housholder, "Noble County's Ford Frick a Pioneer of National Pastime," *Kendallville News-Sun*, April 13, 1978.
21. Two DePauw books were particularly useful: Manhart, *DePauw through the Years*, especially 1:247–70, and Sweet, *Indiana Asbury-DePauw University, 1837–1937*, especially 186–202.
22. "College Folk Shifting Vocations," *DePauw Daily*, October 22, 1912. The semester numbers fluctuated closely around those given.

23. *DePauw University Catalogue, 1914–15*, 27, Roy O. West Library Archives.
24. *DePauw University Catalogue, 1914–15*, 27–28, Roy O. West Library Archives.
25. "Prices and Wages by Decade: 1910–1919," University of Missouri Libraries, last updated August 19, 2025, https://libraryguides.missouri.edu/pricesandwages/1910-1919. The wages are listed as the average daily wage for the New York Central & Hudson River Railroad in 1911–12. Jacob Frick's actual wage is unknown, but given his low-level supervisory position, the figure is close.
26. *DePauw University Catalogue, 1913–14*, 59, Roy O. West Library Archives.
27. "A Fraternity Pan-Hellenic?" *DePauw Daily*, April 20, 1915.
28. Today's Editorial, *DePauw Daily*, December 16–19, 1913. The *Daily* was cautious in taking strong positions in the editorials but made clear its support of prohibition.
29. "Dry Greencastle," *DePauw Daily*, January 6, 1914.
30. "Wabash Defeats DePauw," *DePauw Daily*, October 12, 1912; and "Coach Cunningham Suffers Severe Attack of Indigestion," *DePauw Daily*, October 15, 1912.
31. "Advise New Constitution," *DePauw Daily*, November 19, 1912.
32. "Warning Sounded to Students Who Drink or Gamble," *DePauw Daily*, February 17, 1914.
33. "An Official Announcement," *DePauw Daily*, September 21, 1914.
34. "President Addresses Superintendents," *DePauw Daily*, November 14, 1911.
35. "Notice," *DePauw Daily*, October 28, 1914.
36. Ford Frick, "Address for Centennial Celebration Indiana Alpha Chapter Phi Kappa Psi," Greencastle IN, June 5, 1965, 5, unpublished manuscript in possession of author, also at Phi Kappa Psi records, box DC1723, 1910–1929, folder 1, Roy O. West Library Archives. The excursion was called "The Drive."
37. Frick, "Address for Centennial," 5.
38. "Good-Bye Little Drug Shop," *DePauw Daily*, October 17, 1913.
39. Frick, "Address for Centennial," 4.
40. "Petitions Filed for Positions on *Daily*," *DePauw Daily*, May 1, 1912; and "New Men Chosen for *Daily* Staff," *DePauw Daily*, May 16, 1912. The first source mentions the five men trying out, and the second one announces Frick as the sophomore editor.
41. DePauw University, *Mirage, 1911–12*, 223–24, Roy O. West Library Archives.
42. Phillips and Baughman, *DePauw: Pictorial History*, 89.

43. "False Simplicity," *DePauw Daily*, April 11, 1912. If the room offered indoor plumbing, it was an improvement for young Ford.
44. DePauw University, *Mirage, 1912–13*, 182, Roy O. West Library Archives.
45. "Independents Nominate Ticket," *DePauw Daily*, September 24, 1912; and "Sophomore Ticket Elected," *DePauw Daily*, September 25, 1912. The numbers suggest only sophomores voted for their officers.
46. "Diamond for First Practice," *DePauw Daily*, April 1, 1913.
47. "Baseball Notes," *DePauw Daily*, April 15, 1913.
48. There is other anecdotal evidence. In 1863 Jacob's younger brother was born and named Stephen Douglas after the late Illinois senator, suggesting a Democratic lean.
49. *Postal Salaries: Final Report of the Joint Commission on Postal Studies*, S. Doc. 66-422, 66th Cong., 3rd sess., U.S. Congressional Serial Set no. 7789, at 221–23 (1921).
50. Frick, "Address for Centennial," 5.
51. Phi Kappa Psi records, box DC1723, 1910–1929, folder 1, Roy O. West Library Archives. In order, the quotes are from the minutes of meetings on October 28, 1914; November 18, 1914; December 21, 1914; January 11, 1915; and March 29, 1915.
52. Phi Kappa Psi records, minutes of January 11, 1915, box DC1723, 1910–1929, folder 1, Roy O. West Library Archives.
53. Personals, *DePauw Daily*, April 28, 1915. His fraternity brothers may have had another reason. Around midnight of November 11, 1914, a fire broke out in the house's phone booth. Frick discovered it, alerting his sleeping brothers, who doused the flames. "Fire Causes Damage in Phi Psi House," *DePauw Daily*, November 12, 1914.
54. Frick, "Address for Centennial," 3.
55. Editors for the *DePauw Daily*, *DePauw Daily*, October 28, 1914; and Editors for the *DePauw Daily*, *DePauw Daily*, March 9, 1915. Frick disappears from the list in late October, reappearing in early March.
56. Ford C. Frick, "Prepared for Earlham," *DePauw Daily*, November 22, 1912.
57. Ford C. Frick, "Hebe for Short," *DePauw Daily*, October 8, 1914.
58. "Faculty Supervision of *DePauw Daily* Not Favored by F. C. Tilden," *DePauw Daily*, December 11, 1914.
59. "Council Recommends Tuition Plan Voted through Yesterday," *DePauw Daily*, May 19, 1915.
60. "Guthrie on Trail of $1000 to Ensure Publication of *Mirage*," *DePauw Daily*, November 18, 1913.
61. "Frick at Head of Liberal Ticket in Heavy Sweep of *Mirage* Offices," *DePauw Daily*, October 21, 1915.

62. "Two New Departments to 1914 *Mirage*, Says Editor-in-Chief Frick," *DePauw Daily*, February 27, 1914.
63. "Purple Covers of 1915 Yearbook Will Open Tomorrow Afternoon," *DePauw Daily*, May 27, 1914.
64. DePauw University, *Mirage, 1913–14*, 188, Roy O. West Library Archives.
65. DePauw University, *Mirage, 1913–14*, 269, Roy O. West Library Archives.
66. "Secondary Champions Take Quakers Today in Frolicsome Tune," *DePauw Daily*, May 22, 1914.
67. "Zip Abounds Today as Baseball & Football Aspirants Work Out," *DePauw Daily*, March 19, 1915.
68. "Grim's Guillotine Leaves Twenty-Five on DePauw Diamond," *DePauw Daily*, March 29, 1915; "Varsity, Yannigans Play First Real Ball on M'Keen Lot Today," *DePauw Daily*, March 30, 1915; and "End of Today's Fray Relegates Scrubs to Cellar by 9–3 Score," *DePauw Daily*, March 31, 1915.
69. "Graduate Manager Ellis and Student Manager Frick Will Accompany the Team," *Indianapolis Star*, May 19, 1915. The late Pete Cava, fellow SABR member in the Oscar Charleston chapter, provided the clipping, in author's possession.
70. "Team Is Now Assured, Fourteen Men Report," *DePauw Daily*, December 2, 1914.
71. "Plans for Freshmen Basketball Fall Through When Armory Is Found Unsafe," *DePauw Daily*, December 17, 1914.
72. "Vigilance Committee Is Reorganized and Officers Are Elected for Semester," *DePauw Daily*, February 4, 1915.
73. DePauw University, *Mirage, 1914–15*, 80, Roy O. West Library Archives.
74. "Bishop Quayle Will Give Commencement Address to Seniors," *DePauw Daily*, February 25, 1915.
75. "Present Senior Class to Hold Commencement Outdoors," *DePauw Daily*, March 9, 1915.
76. "Seniors Announce the Program for Annual Class Day Exercise," *DePauw Daily*, May 18, 1915.
77. "'One of the Faculty' Given at Opera House by Sigma Delta Chi," *DePauw Daily*, April 23, 1914.
78. Phi Kappa Psi records, box DC1723, 1910–1929, folder 1, Roy O. West Library Archives.
79. In an anonymous column in the November 19, 1914, issue of the *Daily* on page 3, titled "Reveries of a Would-Be-Cynic," the heading is followed by a famous Kipling quote: "A woman is a woman, but a good cigar is a smoke." The column explains why its author doesn't date DePauw coeds, concluding they "touch very lightly upon such weighty subjects as I had expected sincere college co-eds would have uppermost in their minds."

That could have been written by numerous students, except that in the *Mirage* of Frick's senior year, at the end of the caption under his picture, was the identical quote. Was that coincidence or an explanation for his graduating unattached? A year and a half later, he married.

80. Frick, "Address for Centennial," 4, 5.
81. "Professor Barnes New Book Now in Use Here," *DePauw Daily*, September 19, 1913.
82. "Few Professions Call Bulk of this Years' Grads in Life Work," *DePauw Daily*, April 29, 1915.
83. *Greencastle Banner*, June 10, 1915. Quotation from article snippet is in author's possession.
84. Frick, "Address for Centennial," 6.
85. Angela Frick, discussion. Frick's daughter-in-law felt Fred had a good experience at DePauw, but it wasn't his preference.
86. Bavasi, discussion. Ford convinced Bavasi's mother DePauw was a Catholic college. Buzzie knew differently but was pleased to join his friend.
87. Ree, *Walsenburg*, 229.
88. Daniel M. Daniel, "Frick, New National League Head, Born Poor Farm Boy, Received First Break When NY Called Him," *The Sporting News*, November 15, 1934.
89. Carvalho, *Frick**, 30.
90. "Ford C. Frick of This City and Miss Eleanor Cowling of Walsenburg Were Married at the Home of the Bride Yesterday. Mr. Frick is a teacher in the commercial department of the Colorado Springs High School and formerly resided in Walsenburg. Mrs. Frick was a student at Colorado College for some time." *Colorado Springs Gazette*, wedding announcement, September 19, 1916. Carvalho suggested Cowling was Frick's student. Given age closeness and her college attendance, that's unlikely.
91. Kelly Frick Richards, discussion.
92. Ree, *Walsenburg*, 114.
93. Ree, *Walsenburg*, 54.
94. Ree, *Walsenburg*, 57.
95. Draft registration card for Ford C. Frick, June 5, 1917, National Archives and Records Administration, Ancestry.com, accessed July 20, 2025.
96. *Colorado Springs Gazette*, announcements, November 6, 1917. There are numerous later accounts of his work for the *Gazette*, including in 1951, when he was named commissioner. See, for example, "Frick Started Climb to New Post as Local Sports Scribe," *Colorado Springs Gazette-Telegraph*, September 21, 1951. That article suggests he was a professor at Colorado College before accepting the *Gazette* job, leaving teaching to work at the paper full-time. The limited historical record suggests the

opposite—newspaper first, then part-time work at the college. In either case, both were disrupted by World War I and the pandemic.

97. "Thirteen New Faculty Members at Colo. College," *Colorado College Tiger*, October 1, 1918.
98. Colorado College, *Pikes Peak Nugget*, 1918–19, 19, Colorado College Library.
99. Colorado College, *45th Annual Catalogue, 1918–19*, Colorado College publication bulletin series no. 52, general series no. 2 (Colorado Springs CO: 1919), 83.
100. "Epidemic of Influenza Is Practically Arrested," *Colorado College Tiger*, October 11, 1918.
101. "Frick Started Climb," *Colorado Springs Gazette-Telegraph*.
102. 1920 federal census, Denver City, January 12, 1920.
103. "Frick Started Climb," *Colorado Springs Gazette-Telegraph*.
104. Morris Fraser, "Ex-Baseball Commissioner Got Start on *Gazette Telegraph*," *Colorado Springs Gazette-Telegraph*, March 3, 1972.
105. *Colorado Springs Telegraph*, ca. 1920, in author's possession.
106. "Frick Slugged Grand Slam for *Gazette*," *Colorado Springs Gazette-Telegraph*, March 23, 1997.
107. "Former Gazette Sportswriter Founded Baseball Hall of Fame," *Colorado Springs Gazette-Telegraph*, May 22, 1993; and Carvalho, *Frick**, 34–36.
108. Holtzman, *No Cheering*, 207–8.
109. Holtzman, *No Cheering*, 206.
110. Frick, *Games*, 27–28.
111. Holtzman, *No Cheering*, 210; and Carvalho, *Frick**, 42. Carvalho, a journalism professor, felt Frick's work as a ghostwriter was a conflict of interest. It wasn't considered such at the time.
112. Angela Frick, discussion.
113. Frick, *Games*, 85.
114. Frick, *Games*, 85–86.
115. "Baseball Diners Sheer for Walker," *New York Times*, March 22, 1926; and John Drebinger, "Baseball Writers Frolic Before 700," *New York Times*, February 5, 1934. The 1934 dinner was the eleventh annual minstrel display, suggesting Frick's involvement from the start. The 1934 performance was his last, coming immediately before his hire as public relations director.
116. Dan Daniel, "Frick, New National League Head, Born Poor Farm Boy, Received First Break When New York Called Him," *The Sporting News*, November 15, 1934, 5.
117. Daniel, "Frick," 5.
118. John Drebinger, "Club Owners of the N.L. Elect Frick as Successor to Heydler," *New York Times*, November 9, 1934.

119. Daniel, "Frick," 5.
120. "Nation-Wide Hook-Up for the Series Ready; Broadcasting Will Start at 1 P.M. Tomorrow," *New York Times*, September 30, 1930.
121. "Game to Be Widely Heard," *New York Times*, November 25, 1930.

2. A DEPRESSING, CHALLENGING START

1. Scheduling Meeting of the National League of Professional Baseball Clubs, February 6, 1934, box 7, folder 10, 6–7, Meetings of the National League of Professional Baseball Clubs, Giamatti Research Center. Carvalho suggests Frick was replacing Cullen Cain, who left two years before. Carvalho also suggested, perhaps reflecting Frick's own speculation, that John McGraw recommended Frick. Heydler made no such indication. Carvalho, *Frick**, 54–55.
2. National League Scheduling Meeting, February 6, 1934, box 7, folder 10, 9, 10, 18, 20–21, 22, Giamatti Research Center.
3. Joe Vila, "Terry 'Rides' Carey at Writers' Feast," *The Sporting News*, February 15, 1934, 5.
4. "Sunday Home Games Evenly Divided among N.L. Clubs This Year," *New York Times*, February 7, 1934.
5. Dick Farrington, Fanning with Farrington, *The Sporting News*, May 5, 1934, 4.
6. Winter Meetings of the National League of Professional Baseball Clubs, December 11, 1934, box 7, folder 13, 12, 16, Giamatti Research Center.
7. National League Board of Directors Meeting, November 2, 1934, box 7, folder 12, 1, Giamatti Research Center.
8. Special Meeting of the National League President, November 8, 1934, box 7, folder 12, 2, Giamatti Research Center.
9. Daniel M. Daniel, "Rambling Round the Circuit with Pitcher Snorter Casey," *The Sporting News*, November 15, 1934, 4.
10. "National League Meets to Name President," *Chicago Tribune*, November 8, 1934.
11. John Drebinger, "Frick Is Favored for Baseball Post," *New York Times*, November 8, 1934.
12. John Drebinger, "Club Owners of the National League Elect Frick as Successor to Heydler," *New York Times*, November 9, 1934.
13. J. Taylor Spink, "Frick and Traband," editorial, *The Sporting News*, November 15, 1934, 4.
14. Daniel, "Frick," 5.
15. Dan Daniel, "Yanks Make Offer for Manush, Myer," *The Sporting News*, November 15, 1934, 2.

16. "Baseball Writers Honor Frick at Dinner; Landis Is Among the 140 Guests Present," *New York Times*, December 6, 1934.
17. John Drebinger, "Leaders in Many Branches of Sports Attend Dinner of Baseball Writers," *New York Times*, February 6, 1935.
18. Daniel, "Frick," 5. As a sportswriter and ghostwriter, Frick told a good story. He apparently could also do so about himself.
19. "Nation-Wide Hookup for the Series Ready," *New York Times*, September 30, 1930.
20. National League Winter Meetings, December 11, 1934, box 7, folder 14, 76–87, Giamatti Research Center.
21. National League Winter Meetings, December 11, 1934, box 7, folder 14, 179–211, Giamatti Research Center.
22. Warfield, *Roaring Redhead*, 30–31.
23. National League Winter Meetings, December 11, 1934, box 7, folder 14, 186, Giamatti Research Center.
24. National League Winter Meetings, December 11, 1934, box 7, folder 16, 211, Giamatti Research Center.
25. J. Taylor Spink, Three and One: Looking Them Over with J. Taylor Spink, *The Sporting News*, January 3, 1935, 4.
26. Pietrusza, *Judge and Jury*, 388.
27. Edgar G. Brands, "Initial Test of Nocturnal Game at Cincinnati Proves Its Practicality as Added Feature of Major Leagues," *The Sporting News*, May 30, 1935, 3.
28. Tom Swope, "Reds Draw 152,270 at 18 Home Games," *The Sporting News*, May 30, 1935, 2.
29. Brands, "Initial Test," 3. The first night game was supposed to be played May 24. Rain forced postponement, providing Frick an opportunity to visit his son, Fred, at DePauw.
30. Warfield, *Roaring Redhead*, 64–66.
31. Three SABR biography projects provided the background on this: Rory Costello, "James Gaffney," Society for American Baseball Research, n.d., https://sabr.org/bioproj/person/james-gaffney/; Bob LeMoine, "Judge Emil Fuchs," Society for American Baseball Research, n.d., https://sabr.org/bioproj/person/judge-emil-fuchs/; and Bob LeMoine, "Boston Braves Team Ownership History," Society for American Baseball Research, ca. 2017, https://sabr.org/bioproj/topic/boston-braves-team-ownership-history/. For the last source, see especially the section on Fuchs.
32. National League Board of Directors Meeting, December 11, 1934, box 7, folder 13, 22–30, Giamatti Research Center.

33. National League Winter Meetings, December 12, 1934, box 7, folder 14, 167–69, Giamatti Research Center; "Dog-Race License Sought by Braves," *New York Times*, December 8, 1934; and "Dogs Shall Not Run for Braves Say Boss Frick," *Chicago Tribune*, December 8, 1934.
34. Three *New York Times* stories best demonstrated Frick's problem: "Dog Racing Asked for Braves Field," *New York Times*, January 13, 1935; John Drebinger, "National League Meeting Called to Decide on Future of Homeless Braves," *New York Times*, January 15, 1935; and "Charles F. Adams, VP and Major Owner of Braves, Will Not Take Over Club from President Fuchs," *New York Times*, January 17, 1935.
35. Special Meeting of the National League of Professional Baseball Clubs, January 18, 1935, box 7, folder 18, 62, Giamatti Research Center.
36. Special Meeting of the National League of Professional Baseball Clubs, January 18, 1935, box 7, folder 18, 77, Giamatti Research Center.
37. John Drebinger, "National League Reaffirms Ban on Dog Racing; Braves to Stay in Own Park," *New York Times*, January 19, 1935.
38. "Rule Permitting Night Baseball with Restriction Passed by National League," *New York Times*, February 6, 1935.
39. J. Taylor Spink, "Frick Wins His Spurs on the Dog Racing Situation," *The Sporting News*, January 24, 1935, 4.
40. "Sees Ruth Aiding League," *New York Times*, March 6, 1935; and "Frick Predicts Ruth in National League Will Draw 500,000 More Fans," *Chicago Tribune*, March 17, 1935.
41. The Braves benefitted for the first month and a half. Surdam, *Wins, Losses, and Empty Seats*, 290.
42. Summer Meetings of the National League of Professional Baseball Clubs, July 7, 1935, box 7, folder 17, 58–59, 59–64, 81–83, 91–92, Giamatti Research Center.
43. LeMoine, "Boston Braves Team Ownership"; and LeMoine, "Judge Emil Fuchs."
44. "Fuchs, in Post Since 1925, Quits as Head of Braves," *New York Times*, August 1, 1935.
45. Tommy Holmes, "Bordabaray's 'Spinach' Sprouts New Ambition," *The Sporting News*, November 14, 1935, 2.
46. "National League Takes Over Braves Franchise," *Chicago Tribune*, November 27, 1935.
47. National League Winter Meetings, December 10, 1935, box 7, folder 19, 13–25, Giamatti Research Center.
48. National League Winter Meetings, December 10, 1935, box 7, folder 19, 12, Giamatti Research Center.

49. Rory Costello, "Bob Quinn," Society for American Baseball Research, n.d., https://sabr.org/bioproj/person/bob-quinn/.
50. "New England Syndicate Buys Control of Bees," *Chicago Tribune*, April 21, 1941.
51. "Three Boston Contractors, Including Perini, Purchase Braves," *New York Times*, January 22, 1944.
52. Andy McCue, "Los Angeles/Brooklyn Dodgers Team Ownership History," Society for American Baseball Research, last modified November 28, 2017, https://sabr.org/bioproj/topic/los-angeles-brooklyn-dodgers-team-ownership-history/.
53. McCue, "Los Angeles/Brooklyn Dodgers."
54. "Dodgers Vice President Joseph Gilleaudeau Announces Dodgers for Sale for 2 Million," *New York Times*, March 26, 1936, 28. The announcement may have been a reaction to the Braves hiring Bob Quinn months earlier because he had been their general manager.
55. "Sale Rumor Puts Ruth in Dodger Job," *New York Times*, October 7, 1936; and "MacPhail Rumored to Be Hired as Dodger G.M.," *Chicago Tribune*, October 17, 1936.
56. Barber, *1947*, 15; and Mann, *Baseball Confidential*, 154. McCue, "Los Angeles/Brooklyn Dodgers" also supports their thesis.
57. MacPhail's biographer believes Frick was the driving force. Warfield, *Roaring Redhead*, 72. When the hiring was announced, one paper acknowledged Frick's role: "Dodgers Set to Name MacPhail GM," *Chicago Tribune*, January 8, 1938.
58. Roscoe McGowen, "Tamulis Behind 15-Hit Barrage, Checks Phils for Dodgers, 13–2," *New York Times*, July 9, 1938.
59. Roscoe McGowen, "MacPhail Hires Ruth as Coach for $15,000," *New York Times*, June 19, 1938.
60. "Dodger Baseball to Be Broadcast," *New York Times*, December 7, 1938; McCue, "Los Angeles/Brooklyn Dodgers"; and Warfield, *Roaring Redhead*, 73.
61. McCue, "Los Angeles/Brooklyn Dodgers."
62. Rich Westcott, "Philadelphia Phillies Team Ownership History," Society for American Baseball Research, last modified October 1, 2018, https://sabr.org/bioproj/topic/philadelphia-phillies-team-ownership-history/.
63. Rossi, "Nugent Era," 15–16.
64. Westcott, "Phillies Ownership." For a discussion of the ballpark, see Goldberger, *Ballpark*, 56–57.
65. Special Meeting of the National League of Professional Baseball Clubs, November 26, 1935, box 7, folder 18, 12, 64, Giamatti Research Center; National League Scheduling Meeting, February 4, 1936, box 7, folder

20, 53–56, Giamatti Research Center; and National League Scheduling Meeting, February 6, 1940, box 8, folder 9, 29, 41, Giamatti Research Center.

66. National League Winter Meetings, December 10, 1940, box 8, folder 13, 84–86, Giamatti Research Center.
67. National League Summer Meetings, July 7, 1941, box 8, folder 15, 16–17, 20–23, Giamatti Research Center; and "Drops Plans to Buy Phils," *New York Times*, September 24, 1941.
68. National League Winter Meetings, December 10, 1941, box 8, folder 16, 159–60, Giamatti Research Center.
69. Special Meeting of the National League of Professional Baseball Clubs, January 17, 1942, box 8, folder 17, 2–33, Giamatti Research Center.
70. National League Scheduling Meeting, February 2, 1942, box 8, folder 18, 184–203, Giamatti Research Center; and "National League Plans More Night Games," *Chicago Tribune*, January 18, 1942.
71. National League Board of Directors Meeting, November 4, 1942, box 9, folder 1, 2–7, 69–71, Giamatti Research Center.
72. National League Board of Directors Meeting, November 4, 1942, box 9, folder 1, 90–91, 137, 170, 174–75, Giamatti Research Center. Veeck and the Phillies are discussed in chapter 5. Neither Nugent nor Frick regarded Veeck's interest as serious.
73. "League Ready to Step In and Order Phils Sold," *Chicago Tribune*, November 12, 1942.
74. National League Board of Directors Meeting, November 30, 1942, box 9, folder 2, 17, 36–37, 63, Giamatti Research Center. The lead purchaser was likely John B. Kelly, a local builder, a former Olympic rowing star, and Grace Kelly's father.
75. National League Winter Meetings, December 1–2, 1942, box 9, folder 3, 84, 105, Giamatti Research Center; and John Drebinger, "Plight of the Phillies?" *New York Times*, December 1, 1942.
76. National League Scheduling Meeting, February 9, 1943, box 9, folder 4, 38, Giamatti Research Center. Most of the 166 pages of minutes focused on the deal.
77. "Phils Sold to Cox, with Group to Get Title on March 3," *New York Times*, February 21, 1943; and J. Taylor Spink, "Men of Courage and Vision Take Hold of Phils," *The Sporting News*, March 4, 1943, 4.
78. Westcott, "Phillies Ownership."
79. "Frick Rulings Hit by Phillies' Owner," *New York Times*, July 4, 1943; National League Summer Meetings, July 12, 1943, box 9, folder 6, 32–36, Giamatti Research Center; and "Apology Issued by Phils' Owner," *New York Times*, July 10, 1943.

80. Westcott, "Phillies Ownership"; and Stan Baumgartner, "Cox Is Banned by Landis after Betting Probe," *The Sporting News*, November 25, 1943, 6.
81. Stan Baumgartner, "Bob Carpenter, 'My Boy' to Dad, Kid of Prexies," *The Sporting News*, December 2, 1944, 4.
82. National League Summer Meetings, July 7, 1941, box 8, folder 15, 17–19, Giamatti Research Center.

3. STAYING ALIVE

1. J. G. Taylor Spink, "Draft Again Given Little Attention by Majors," *The Sporting News*, October 10, 1940, 4.
2. National League Summer Meetings, July 6, 1942, box 8, folder 19, 7, Giamatti Research Center.
3. National League Summer Meetings, July 6, 1942, box 8, folder 19, 56–57, Giamatti Research Center.
4. National League Scheduling Meeting, February 8, 1944, box 9, folder 8, 27–29, Giamatti Research Center.
5. Ford C. Frick, "Frick Foresees Interesting Race for National League This Year," *New York Times*, January 7, 1941.
6. Major League Notes, *The Sporting News*, April 16, 1942, 9.
7. Shortly after graduating in 1938, Fred Frick joined his father in Chicago, where he was meeting with Landis. After introductions and some conversation, the commissioner pointed his finger in Fred's chest, exclaiming, "Young man, you sound just like a New Dealer." Angela Frick, discussion.
8. Pietrusza, *Judge and Jury*, 432.
9. Pietrusza, *Judge and Jury*, 433.
10. Joint Meeting of the National and American League Baseball Clubs, December 11, 1940, box 4, folder 6, 7–11. Giamatti Research Center.
11. Joint Meeting of the National and American League Baseball Clubs, December 11, 1940, box 4, folder 6, 45–49, Giamatti Research Center.
12. Joint Meeting of the National and American League Baseball Clubs, December 11, 1941, box 4, folder 6, 3–16, Giamatti Research Center.
13. Joint Meeting of the National and American League Baseball Clubs, December 11, 1941, box 4, folder 6, 21–23, Giamatti Research Center.
14. National League Scheduling Meeting, February 2, 1942, box 8, folder 18, 4, Giamatti Research Center. Frick actually convened a secretive league meeting on January 17, 1942, following FDR's letter. He initially denied the meeting, then acknowledged the magnates had discussed increasing night games and how to raise defense bonds. When asked if the Phillies were discussed, Frick was evasive, stating the meeting

wasn't called for that purpose. "National League Plans More Night Games at Secret Meeting," *Chicago Tribune*, January 18, 1942. In fact, it did address the Phillies' crisis. Special Meeting of the National League of Professional Baseball Clubs, January 17, 1942, box 8, folder 18, 1–23, Giamatti Research Center. On page 24, there was only passing reference to FDR's letter.

15. National League Scheduling Meeting, February 2, 1942, box 8, folder 18, 16, 30, Giamatti Research Center.
16. National League Scheduling Meeting, February 2, 1942, box 8, folder 18, 162–69, Giamatti Research Center.
17. Joint Meeting of the National and American League Baseball Clubs, July 6, 1942, box 4, folder 9, 5–6, Giamatti Research Center.
18. Joint Meeting of the National and American League Baseball Clubs, July 6, 1942, box 4, folder 9, 11–21, Giamatti Research Center.
19. Joint Meeting of the National and American League Baseball Clubs, July 6, 1942, box 4, folder 9, 25, Giamatti Research Center.
20. Midsummer Meeting of the National League Baseball Clubs, July 10, 1944, box 9, folder 9, 2–7, 21, 32, Giamatti Research Center.
21. The saga of the dim outs can be found in the *New York Times*: "Night Games Under Review by Army," *New York Times*, April 30, 1942, 10; John Drebinger, "Dodgers Defeat Giants in Twilight Game Raising $59,859 for Navy Relief," *New York Times*, May 9, 1942, 16; "6:30 Start for All-Stars," *New York Times*, June 17, 1942, 28; and James D. Dawson, "LaGuardia Permits Giants and Dodgers to Resume Night Baseball This Year," *New York Times*, January 25, 1944, 22. New York was the only city where night games were prohibited, although neither Boston ballpark had lights.
22. Midsummer Meeting of the National League Baseball Clubs, July 6, 1942, box 6, 8, Giamatti Research Center.
23. Joint Meeting of the National and American League Baseball Clubs, July 6, 1942, box 4, folder 9, 9–10, Giamatti Research Center.
24. "Cross-Country World Series Is Given a Hearing," *Chicago Tribune*, June 30, 1942. This is the only instance the author could find of the proposal mentioned in news coverage.
25. Joint Meeting of the National and American League Baseball Clubs, July 6, 1942, box 4, folder 9, 44–45, 52, 61, 66, Giamatti Research Center.
26. Joint Meeting of the National and American League Baseball Clubs, July 6, 1942, box 4, folder 9, 43–44, 52–62, 74, Giamatti Research Center.
27. Joint Meeting of the National and American League Baseball Clubs, July 6, 1942, box 4, folder 9, 48, 63–68, 80–81, 87–90, 119, Giamatti Research Center.

28. Pietrusza, *Judge and Jury*, 14–18, 36–40. Landis secured appointments from presidents of both parties.
29. "Frick Refuses to Air Result of Draft Talk," *Chicago Tribune*, January 24, 1945.
30. Arthur Daley, "Baseball Learns the Score," Sports of Our Times, *New York Times*, January 25, 1945; and Arthur Daley, "Short Shots in Sundry Directions," Sports of Our Times, *New York Times*, January 29, 1945.
31. National League Scheduling Meeting, February 4, 1941, box 8, folder 18, 11–16, 17, 46–47, Giamatti Research Center.
32. Dan Daniel, "N.L. Setting Aside 7-Game Light Rule, Seeks Limit of 14," *The Sporting News*, January 22, 1942, 1. At the end, Daniel mentions Frick had a meeting in DC on January 19.
33. National League Scheduling Meeting, February 2, 1942, box 8, folder 18, 77–78, Giamatti Research Center.
34. J. G. Taylor Spink, "Ford Frick Sets an Example," *The Sporting News*, March 12, 1942, 4.
35. National League Summer Meetings, July 7, 1943, box 9, folder 6, 8, Giamatti Research Center.
36. National League Scheduling Meeting, February 8, 1944, box 9, folder 8, 8–11, 27–28, 134–39, Giamatti Research Center.
37. National League Winter Meetings, December 10, 1940, box 8, folder 13, 64, Giamatti Research Center.
38. Shirley Povich, "$42,000 in Equipment Begins Moving to U.S. Camps," *The Sporting News*, January 8, 1942, 2.
39. National League Winter Meetings, December 9–10, 1941, box 8, folder 16, 65–75, Giamatti Research Center.
40. National League Scheduling Meeting, February 2, 1942, box 8, folder 18, 109–11, 132–36, 146–49, Giamatti Research Center. Even after discussion, Crosley questioned the fund. National League Scheduling Meeting, February 2, 1942, box 8, folder 18, 144, Giamatti Research Center.
41. Scribble by Scribes, *The Sporting News*, April 16, 1942, 4.
42. "Majors to Send 36,000 balls, 9,000 Bats and Catching Equipment to Men in Service," *New York Times*, December 27, 1942.
43. Goldstein, *Spartan Seasons*, 64–65.
44. Goldstein, *Spartan Seasons*, 67, 68–69.
45. "Baseball Contributes to War Fund and Red Cross," *New York Times*, September 11. 1943.
46. "Baseball's Value Cited," *New York Times*, April 27, 1944.
47. National League Scheduling Meeting, February 2, 1942, box 8, folder 18, 106–7, 150–52, Giamatti Research Center.

48. Harry Cross, "Dodger, Yank, Giant Starts 'Sell' for $123,850,000 in War Bonds," *The Sporting News*, June 17, 1943, 5.
49. U.S. Congress, *House of Representatives Hearings Before the Subcommittee on Monopoly and Antitrust of the Committee of the Judiciary*, 41 (1951) (statement of Ford C. Frick).
50. Obemeyer, "War Games," 23–24.
51. "Baseball Men Scoff at Idea of '43 Changes," *Chicago Tribune*, October 28, 1942.
52. Edgar G. Brands, "Majors and Minors Plan Chicago Meets," *The Sporting News*, October 15, 1942, 16.
53. "Baseball Heads Ridicule Proposal to Regroup Big Leagues Next Year," *New York Times*, October 28, 1942.
54. "ODT Asks Majors to Curtail Travel," *New York Times*, December 1, 1942.
55. National League Winter Meetings, December 1, 1942, box 9, folder 3, 159, Giamatti Research Center.
56. Goldstein. *Spartan Seasons*, 99.
57. Special Joint Meeting of the National and American League Baseball Clubs, January 5, 1943, box 5, folder 2, 44–46, 47–48, Giamatti Research Center.
58. Goldstein, *Spartan Seasons*, 101.
59. "World Series to be One-Trip Affair; Starts Here Oct. 5," *New York Times*, September 12, 1943. This wasn't an issue in the 1944 because the Series involved the two St. Louis clubs.
60. "Government Urges Change in Majors to Curtail Travel," *New York Times*, February 11, 1945.
61. "ODT Asks 25% Cut in Baseball Travel," *New York Times*, February 22, 1945.
62. Roscoe McGowen, "Majors to Retain 3 East-West Trips," *New York Times*, February 23, 1945.
63. An earlier version of this section is Bohmer, "Season That Almost Wasn't," 25–40.
64. "Roosevelt Stand Seen as Blackout for Pro Athletes," *New York Times*, January 7, 1945.
65. "Swope Promises Full Compliance," *New York Times*, December 24, 1944.
66. "Big Leagues Plan to Continue Play," *New York Times*, December 27, 1944.
67. "Harridge, AL Head, Pleased by Roosevelt Statement," *New York Times*, January 17, 1945.
68. John Drebinger, "Frick Says Majors Have Free Choice," *New York Times*, January 24, 1945.
69. "Frick Refuses to Air Result of Draft Talk," *Chicago Tribune*, January 24, 1945.

70. Arthur Daley, "Baseball Learns the Score," Sports of the Times, *New York Times*, January 25, 1945.
71. National League Scheduling Meeting, February 3, 1945, box 10, folder 1, 14–16, 18, 22–24, Giamatti Research Center.
72. National League Scheduling Meeting, February 3, 1945, box 10, folder 1, 27–30, Giamatti Research Center.
73. National League Scheduling Meeting, February 3, 1945, box 10, folder 1, 24–25, 33, 42, 108, Giamatti Research Center.
74. National League Scheduling Meeting, February 3, 1945, box 10, folder 1, 34–35, Giamatti Research Center.
75. John Drebinger, "New Joint Agreement Reached," *New York Times*, February 4, 1945.
76. Edward Prell, "Harridge, Frick to Ask Yes or No on '45 Baseball," *Chicago Tribune*, February 20, 1945.
77. "Frick Optimistic after Byrnes Talk," *New York Times*, February 21, 1945.
78. "ODT Asks 25% Cut in Baseball Travel," *New York Times*, February 22, 1945.
79. "Ball Players in War Work Free to Play," *Chicago Tribune*, March 22, 1945.
80. "Baseball Leaders Generally Elated," *New York Times*, March 22, 1945.
81. J. G. Taylor Spink, "Another Go-Ahead Signal for Baseball," *The Sporting News*, March 1, 1945, 10.
82. Ford Frick, "Season Outlook?" *New York Times*, April 15, 1945.
83. "Lifting of Sports Curbs Opens Way for All Big Fall and Winter Events," *New York Times*, August 18, 1945.
84. Obemeyer, "War Games," 23–24. Obemeyer seems overly critical because he acknowledges baseball never asked for special favors. Given the risk of suspension, its contributions seem generous, albeit self-serving.

4. CHANGE IS GOING TO COME

1. Joint Meeting of the National and American League Baseball Clubs, July 8, 1946, box 6, folder 8, 15, Giamatti Research Center. Unlike most meetings, there are no minutes from July 7. At the joint meeting the next morning, the minutes are short.
2. Marshall, *Baseball's Pivotal Era*, 56. Marshall devotes a chapter on the Mexican League. See pages 45–63.
3. A detailed account of Murphy's efforts is in Burk, *Much More Than a Game*, 87–95. See also Lowenfish and Lupien, *Imperfect Diamond*, 139–53.
4. *Report of Major League Steering Committee for Submission to The National and American League at Their Meeting in Chicago*, August

27, 1946, 1, Albert Benjamin "Happy" Chandler Papers, University of Kentucky Library.

5. *Report of Major League Steering Committee*, 10–17.
6. *Report of Major League Steering Committee*, 19–20.
7. *Report of Major League Steering Committee*, 20.
8. Lowenfish, *Branch Rickey*, 449–51. Bill Veeck, the first to integrate the American League, was present, having recently purchased the Indians.
9. Joint Meeting of the National and American League Baseball Clubs, August 28, 1946, box 6, folder 8, 7–21, Giamatti Research Center. The session also approved a 168-game season, which received more press, albeit negative. It was soon rescinded. On page 31 was a parting note from Chandler: nothing should be said to the press. He was likely referring to the day before.
10. Lowenfish, *Branch Rickey*, 377–79; and Tygiel, *Baseball's Great Experiment*, 69–70.
11. Lowenfish, *Branch Rickey*, 359.
12. Wes Wilson, email message to author, February 18, 2020. Until 2019 Wilson was DePauw's archivist.
13. "Baseball Diners Cheer for Walker," *New York Times*, March 22, 1926; "Notables of Sport See Writers Frolic," *New York Times*, February 2, 1931; and John Drebinger, "Baseball Writers Frolic Before 700," *New York Times*, February 5, 1934. The quote is from 1931. The 1926 performance was in St. Petersburg, Florida, during spring training, but others were in New York City in February. Frick was the interlocutor, perhaps since 1926.
14. The frequency of these games is discussed in Epplin, *Our Team*, 27–28, 85–87, 132–40, 192–96.
15. Lamb, "Baseball's Whitewash," 1–2. Lamb expands on the topic in *Conspiracy of Silence*, 133–35.
16. Lamb, "Baseball's Whitewash," 12, 16.
17. Lamb, "Baseball's Whitewash," 9, 15.
18. Ted Benson, "League Open to Negroes Says Frick, League Prexy," *Chicago Defender*, August 29, 1936.
19. Veeck and Linn, *Veeck as in Wreck*, 171–72. The team was sold in early 1943, a year earlier. Veeck's contact with Frick was actually in October 1942.
20. Tygiel, *Baseball's Great Experiment*, 40–41.
21. Jordan, Gerlach, and Rossi, "Baseball Myth Exploded."
22. Tygiel, "Revisiting Bill Veeck," 109–14. See especially pages 110, 112, and 114.
23. Dickson, *Bill Veeck*, 79–80, 357–66.

24. Macht and Warrington, "The Veracity of Veeck."
25. "Veeck Bids for Phils," *The Sporting News*, October 22, 1942, 10.
26. National League Board of Directors Meeting, November 4, 1942, box 9, folder 1, 90–91, 137, Giamatti Research Center.
27. Stan Baumgartner, "Sale or No, Phils Don't Want Vaughan," *The Sporting News*, November 19, 1942, 7. The article quoted Nugent: "Veeck stopped by to see me on his way to the World Series and did not mention even being interested in the club." As owner of the Milwaukee Brewers, Veeck developed a reputation as a maverick, creative owner. *The Sporting News* referred to him as "Sport Shirt" for his refusal to wear coat and tie. He was a magnet for media attention. Given the logistics, especially the number of people necessary, the lack of coverage brings Benjamin Franklin to mind: "Three can keep a secret, if two of them are dead." If Veeck harbored ideas, they didn't proceed much further.
28. Lowenfish, *Branch Rickey*, 419. For a less sanitized version, see Tygiel, *Baseball's Great Experiment*, 170.
29. The story has numerous renditions; the best, perhaps, is in Dickson, *Leo Durocher*, 159–60.
30. Dickson, *Leo Durocher*, 156–58.
31. Dickson, *Leo Durocher*, 167.
32. "Chandler Refuses to Delay Hearing," *New York Times*, March 23, 1947.
33. Dickson, *Leo Durocher*, 165–66.
34. Dickson, *Leo Durocher*, 166–67.
35. Tygiel, *Baseball's Great Experiment*, 177.
36. Lowenfish, *Branch Rickey*, 425.
37. Chandler and Trimble, *Heroes*, 226–29.
38. "Dodgers Pick Durocher Successor Today," *Chicago Tribune*, April 10, 1947.
39. Dickson, *Leo Durocher*, 173.
40. James Dawson, "Chandler Summons MacPhail of Yanks to Hearing in Cincinnati Next Week," *New York Times*, April 26, 1947.
41. Tygiel, *Baseball's Great Experiment*, 184.
42. Roscoe McGowen, "Brooklyn Defeats Leonard in 8th, 1–0," *New York Times*, April 23, 1947; Joesph M. Sheehan, "Hatten Triumphs for Brooklyn, 5–2," *New York Times*, April 24, 1947; and Roscoe McGowen, "Walker's 2-Run Single in First Downs Phillies for Branca, 2–0," *New York Times*, April 25, 1947. McGowen noted Chapman was missing.
43. "'Jackie Just Another Player to Us—With No Favors,' Says Chapman," *The Sporting News*, May 14, 1947, 6.
44. Stanley Woodward, Views of Sport, *The Sporting News*, May 21, 1947, 4. The column is verbatim from the *New York Herald Tribune* on May 9.

45. Tygiel, *Baseball's Great Experiment*, 182–83; and Marshall, *Baseball's Pivotal Era*, 140.
46. Woodward, Views of Sport, 4.
47. "Says Cards Strike Plan against Negro Dropped," *New York Times*, May 9, 1947.
48. "Robinson Reveals Written Threats," *New York Times*, May 10, 1947.
49. Arthur Daley, "The Passing Baseball Scene," Sports of Our Times, *New York Times*, May 13, 1947.
50. Stan Woodward, "Essentially Right and Factual," Views of Sport, *The Sporting News*, May 21, 1947, 4.
51. Corbett, "Strike against Jackie Robinson."
52. Frick, *Games*, 97–98. Close to retirement, Frick claimed the Cardinals' strike was "quickly brought to a halt by me as President of the National League." Robinson, *Baseball Has Done It*, 113.
53. Buzzie Bavasi, email message to author, January 22, 2008. Bavasi was insistent about the meeting and about Frick presenting the ultimatum directly. Bavasi was known for stories, and his comments were based on decades-old memories, but it was the only revision he adamantly suggested to me. An intriguing account on the story's development is in Kahn, *The Era*, 57–62.
54. Major Flashes, *The Sporting News*, February 25, 1948, 23; "Honor Robinson, Rickey: Frick Also Cited for Breaking Color Barrier in Baseball," *New York Times*, February 16, 1948; and "Intolerance Group Presents Awards," *New York Times*, April 12, 1948.
55. This is not to say Chandler had no role. A good case is made that he helped by not using his powers negatively. Hill, "Commissioner A. B. 'Happy' Chandler." Hill stresses Chandler's role wasn't formal.
56. "Umpires Irk Robinson," *New York Times*, April 21, 1951.
57. "Dodger Office Backs Jackie; Ford Frick Explains Blast," *The Sporting News*, May 9, 1951, 2.
58. "Dodger Trio Fined for Boston 'Scene,'" *New York Times*, September 29, 1951.
59. Tygiel, *Baseball's Great Experiment*, 295.
60. "Bavasi Berates Bombers," *New York Times*, December 3, 1952.
61. Robinson, *I Never Had It Made*, 102. Robinson added, "Without that kind of support from some of the people in baseball who had power, I could not have made it, no matter how well I performed, no matter how loyal black people were."
62. Robinson, *Baseball Has Done It*, 212.
63. Robinson. *Baseball Has Done It*, 109. Frick's assessment seems cowardly, being passive while waiting for people to "come around." As he

approached retirement, he didn't seem to evolve. In that same period, however, Frick prevented a Minor League franchise in Little Rock from operating unless it integrated the ballpark.

5. SECOND TIME'S A CHARM

1. Pietrusza, *Judge and Jury*, 444–51. Leslie O'Connor stated publicly, "A few weeks will fix him up fine. When he comes out, he'll be better than ever" (449).
2. Pietrusza, *Judge and Jury*, 450–51.
3. Irving Vaughn, "Majors Meet Today; Hint Landis Will Quit," *Chicago Tribune*, November 17, 1944.
4. Irving Vaughn, "Major Chiefs OK Landis for 7 More Years," *Chicago Tribune*, November 18, 1944; and "Baseball Heads Will Recommend New Seven-Year Term for Landis," *New York Times*, November 18, 1944.
5. "Landis Is Praised by His Colleagues," *New York Times*, November 26, 1944.
6. John Drebinger, "Majors Not to Act on Successor until Chicago Meetings," *New York Times*, November 18, 1944.
7. Arch Ward, In the Wake of the News, *Chicago Tribune*, November 30, 1944.
8. National League Winter Meetings, December 11–12, 1944, box 8, folder 11, 34–35, Giamatti Research Center.
9. John Drebinger, "Majors Set Plans to Pick New Head," *New York Times*, December 13, 1944.
10. National League Scheduling Meeting, February 3, 1945, box 10, folder 1, 79–80, 109, 111–12, Giamatti Research Center.
11. John Drebinger, "Majors Sign Pact, but Delay Action on Commissioner," *New York Times*, February 4, 1945. The article provides details of the new national agreement.
12. "O'Connor Declines to Take Landis Job," *New York Times*, November 28, 1944; and John Drebinger, "Election of Frick Looms Next Month," *New York Times*, January 14, 1945.
13. Joe Williams, "The Scooper Reports on the B.B. Meeting," *The Sporting News*, December 21, 1944, 4.
14. "Griffith Leaning to Choice of Frick," *New York Times*, January 30, 1945.
15. Ward Morehouse, "Ford Frick: . . . He Isn't Trying on Landis' Toga for Size—Yet," *The Sporting News*, January 25, 1945, 3.
16. John Drebinger, "Majors Set to Pick Commissioner Here," *New York Times*, February 2, 1945.
17. "Delay in Naming Baseball Commissioner Expected by Big League Officials in West," *New York Times*, January 21, 1945.

18. John Drebinger, "Majors Ready to Pick Czar Soon, Probably before Season Is Opened," *New York Times*, February 5, 1945.
19. John Drebinger, "Drive to Fill Position of Landis Hits Snag," *New York Times*, February 3, 1945. The previous day Drebinger believed Frick would be selected.
20. John Drebinger, "Four Baseball Men Sift Field for Czar," *New York Times*, February 9, 1945.
21. John Drebinger, "Baseball Outlook in Capital Better," *New York Times*, February 9, 1945.
22. Carl T. Felker, "Writers Veer to Outsider as Leader," *The Sporting News*, February 15, 1945, 3.
23. J. G. Taylor Spink, "The Inside Story—Vote-By-Vote," Looping the Loops, *The Sporting News*, May 3, 1945, 4.
24. Marshall, *Baseball's Pivotal Era*, 18. Branch Rickey took notes, allowing reconstruction of the process.
25. Spink, "Inside Story," 4.
26. Marshall, *Baseball's Pivotal Era*, 21.
27. Spink, "Inside Story," 5.
28. Marshall, *Baseball's Pivotal Era*, 25–27.
29. Marshall, *Baseball's Pivotal Era*, 20–21.
30. "Senator Chandler in Talk with Frick," *New York Times*, April 27, 1945.
31. Vincent X. Flaherty, "Chandler Takes Firm Grasp on Reins of Game," *The Sporting News*, July 19, 1945, 5.
32. Joint Meeting of the National and American League Baseball Clubs, July 12, 1945, box 6, folder 4, 10, 12, Giamatti Research Center.
33. "Chandler Angers Baseball Leaders," *New York Times*, October 8, 1945.
34. Irving Vaughn, "Big Leagues Rally Behind Chandler; Kill Ouster Rumor," *Chicago Tribune*, October 9, 1945.
35. "Chandler Resigns Seat in U.S. Senate," *New York Times*, October 10, 1945.
36. "Gardella Asks Damages," *New York Times*, October 3, 1945.
37. "Suspension Stirs American League," *New York Times*, October 31, 1945.
38. Marshall, *Baseball's Pivotal Era*, 378; and John P. Carmichael, "Magnates Resented Chandler's Desire to Know Where He Stood," *The Sporting News*, December 20, 1950, 2.
39. "Cards Defy Chandler, Frick," *Chicago Tribune*, June 10, 1950; and Arch Ward, In the Wake of the News, *Chicago Tribune*, June 12, 1950.
40. "Cards Drop Sunday Night Game Plan," *Chicago Tribune*, June 13, 1950.
41. Marshall, *Baseball's Pivotal Era*, 380.
42. "Chandler Assured of Retaining Post," *New York Times*, November 18, 1950.

43. Edgar G. Brands, "Chandler Stands Pat Despite Ouster Coup," *The Sporting News*, December 20, 1950, 3. Some conjectured Wrigley or Yawkey opposed Chandler.
44. Edward Prell, "Majors Reported Impatient to See Chandler Leave," *The Sporting News*, April 11, 1951, 4.
45. Roscoe McGowen, "Chandler Matter May Rest Till '52, Says Owner Perini," *New York Times*, February 4, 1951; and "Major League Meeting to Select Baseball Commissioner Called for March 12," *New York Times*, February 8, 1951.
46. "Pro and Con Views of Sport Scribes on Chandler's Ouster," *The Sporting News*, December 20, 1950, 2.
47. "Chandler Loses His Baseball Post; Eyes Vacant Seat in U.S. Senate," *New York Times*, March 13, 1951.
48. Edward Prell, "Impatient," *The Sporting News*, April 11, 1951, 4.
49. "Players Commissioner Idea Stirs Baseball Heads," *New York Times*, March 21, 1951.
50. "See Chandler Plan Approved by Club Owners," *Chicago Tribune*, June 8, 1951.
51. Joe King, "Choose Commissioner Now—O'Malley," *The Sporting News*, July 4, 1951, 3.
52. Dan Daniel, "Griff for 'Strong National Figure,'" *The Sporting News*, July 4, 1951, 2, 10. In that issue, Spink supported Frick. "Ford Frick, literally right under the club owners' noses, it would seem to *The Sporting News*, is the man to lead them out of the existing wilderness." J. G. Taylor Spink, "Frick's Stock on the Rise," *The Sporting News*, July 4, 1951, 12.
53. "Ryan Requests Commissioner before Series," *Chicago Tribune*, August 26, 1951.
54. Walter Trohan, "MacArthur Rejects Job of Baseball Boss," *Chicago Tribune*, August 28, 1951; and J. G. Taylor Spink, "Game Sought Gen. O'Donnell as Boss," *The Sporting News*, August 29, 1951, 1.
55. Dan Daniel, "Yankees Reported Ready to Renew Farley Backing," *The Sporting News*, September 5, 1951, 6.
56. "Lausche Withdraws as Candidate for Baseball Commissioner Position," *New York Times*, September 16, 1951.
57. Irving Vaughn, "Major Leagues May Elect New Chief Today," *Chicago Tribune*, September 20, 1951.
58. "200 at Klem Funeral," *New York Times*, September 20, 1951.
59. "Giles and Frick Head Candidates in Baseball Vote Listed for Today," *New York Times*, September 20, 1951.
60. The vote summary and Giles's withdrawal is in Joseph M. Sheehan, "Frick Elected Commissioner of Baseball for Seven Years," *New York*

Times, September 21, 1951. That Cincinnati cost Giles the position is mentioned by Oscar Ruhl, The Ruhl Book, *The Sporting News*, October 3, 1951, 39. Ruhl thought eastern club owners were responsible for blocking Giles, but most were American League owners. In the Ruhl column, one owner noted, "When an N.L. player had a grievance, he'd wait until his club played Cincinnati, and he could go up to visit the commissioner. A.L. players never get to Cincy, so they had to make trips at their own expense to see Chandler."

61. "Police Break the News to Frick as He Prepares for Bed," *The Sporting News*, September 26, 1951, 4.
62. Irving Vaughn, "Frick Heads Baseball after 12 Hour Vote," *Chicago Tribune*, September 21, 1951.
63. "Frick Is in No Hurry to Take Over; He'll Await Successor," *Chicago Tribune*, September 22, 1951.
64. Frederick G. Lieb, "'Horse Sense' Policy Pledged by Frick," *The Sporting News*, October 3, 1951, 3.
65. Arch Ward, In the Wake of the News, *Chicago Tribune*, September 24, 1951.
66. J. G. Taylor Spink, "Game Chooses Sound, Experienced Leader," *The Sporting News*, September 26, 1951, 12.
67. Carvalho, *Frick**, 149. Chandler was ousted in 1950, not 1951.
68. "Baseball Finds Its Man," editorial, *New York Times*, September 22, 1951.

6. NATIONALIZING THE GAME

1. An excellent study is G. Edward White, *Creating the National Pastime*, especially 275–306.
2. "Mize-to-Giants Deal Surprises Breadon," *The Sporting News*, December 18, 1941, 2. Barnes added that if the Browns moved, LA was their top choice. See also Edgar C. Brands, "Majors Gird to Carry On during U.S. Emergency; Vote Funds to Give Equipment to Men in Service," *The Sporting News*, December 18, 1941, 7. In the same issue, J. G. Taylor Spink predicted Major League baseball in LA in less than a decade. See page 4. It took sixteen years.
3. "Coast Circuit Asks Big League Status," *New York Times*, December 5, 1945.
4. John Drebinger, "Big League Status Is Denied to Coast," *New York Times*, December 12, 1945.
5. Frederick G. Lieb, "Inside Browns' Near Shift to L.A. Revealed," *The Sporting News*, January 17, 1946, 2.
6. "Chandler in Los Angeles," *New York Times*, August 29, 1947; Cory Virgil, "Coast Bolts Door against Major Invasion," *The Sporting News*,

September 10, 1947, 1, 4; and "Nice Ride to California for Committee of Majors," *The Sporting News*, September 10, 1947, 4.

7. Dan Daniel, "Majors Reject Coast Bid for Big Time Rating," *The Sporting News*, December 17, 1947, 5. The National League voted to add two teams, but the American League rejected that, 5–2. Rowland was concerned the National League intended to invade his larger cities.
8. "Frick Sees Major Clubs for Coast, but Not Soon," *The Sporting News*, December 1, 1948, 4; and Dan Daniel, "Frick Foresees Changes in Major Map," *The Sporting News*, May 17, 1950, 1–2.
9. Jack MacDonald, "'Draft Relief or O.B. Bolt,' Coast's Ultimatum," *The Sporting News*, September 5, 1951, 9.
10. Dan Daniel, "Revolutionary Plan for More Major Leagues," *The Sporting News*, November 7, 1951, 2, 4. The news was announced by Frank Shaughnessy, president of the International League, who sat in on the discussions.
11. Dan Daniel, "Frick Outlines Plan to Build Up New Majors," *The Sporting News*, November 21, 1951, 13.
12. Joseph Sheehan, "Plan Arranged for Minor Leagues to Reach Major Status," *New York Times*, November 15, 1951.
13. Daniel, "Frick Outlines Plan," 13.
14. Charles Weatherby, "Danny Gardella," Society for American Baseball Research, n.d., https://sabr.org/bioproj/person/danny-gardella/.
15. U.S. Congress, *House of Representatives Hearings Before the Subcommittee on Monopoly and Antitrust of the Committee of the Judiciary*, 2 (1951).
16. U.S. Congress, *House of Representatives Hearings Before the Subcommittee on Monopoly and Antitrust of the Committee of the Judiciary*, 20–21, 26, 29 (July 30, 1951).
17. U.S. Congress, *House of Representatives Hearings Before the Subcommittee on Monopoly and Antitrust of the Committee of the Judiciary*, 79–102 (July 31, 1951). The quote is from page 87.
18. U.S. Congress, *House of Representatives Hearings Before the Subcommittee on Monopoly and Antitrust of the Committee of the Judiciary*, 111, 123 (July 31, 1951).
19. U.S. Congress, *House of Representatives Hearings Before the Subcommittee on Monopoly and Antitrust of the Committee of the Judiciary*, 1056, 1057 (October 23, 1951).
20. J. G. Taylor Spink, "New Rule Sets Up Major 'Moving Van,'" *The Sporting News*, November 19, 1952, 1, 6; and Edgar Munzel, "'Most Two-Club Cities Doomed'—Lane," *The Sporting News*, November 26, 1952, 1.

21. National League Winter Meetings, December 5–6, 1952, box 29, folder 3, 81, 103, Giamatti Research Center.
22. Irving Vaughn, "Report Braves Ready to Shift to Milwaukee," *Chicago Tribune*, December 12, 1952; and Joe King, "Path Opened for Browns Shift to Milwaukee," *The Sporting News*, December 17, 1952, 2.
23. A good summary of relocations during Frick's tenure is Tygiel, *Past Time*, 165–97.
24. Veeck and Linn, *Veeck as in Wreck*, 221–29; and Dickson, *Veeck: Maverick*, 188.
25. "Saigh Gets Jail Term; Cardinals Fate Moot," *New York Times*, January 29, 1953.
26. "Busch, Brewer, Buys the Cardinals; Pays $3,750,000 for St. Louis Club," *New York Times*, February 21, 1953.
27. "Baltimore Elated," *New York Times*, March 15, 1953; and "Talk of Browns Move Too Late, Says Ford Frick," *Chicago Tribune*, March 7, 1953.
28. "Governor and Senate Add Weight to Milwaukee Franchise Request," *New York Times*, March 6, 1953.
29. "Braves Seek Curb on Shifting Clubs," *New York Times*, March 12, 1953.
30. "Tug of War Pulls Browns Two Ways," *New York Times*, March 13, 1953. The Baltimore mayor was Nancy Pelosi's father.
31. "Way Seen Clear for Browns and Braves Shifts Following Baseball Conference," *New York Times*, March 16, 1953.
32. "League Forbids Browns Shift in 1953," *Chicago Tribune*, March 17, 1953.
33. Arthur Daley, "After the Knockout," Sports of the Times, *New York Times*, March 18, 1953. Other reasons included Veeck's conflicts on issues like sharing television revenue. Dickinson, *Veeck: Maverick*, 217. Clearly, Veeck's innovations concerned magnates. Still, many who allowed his purchase of the Browns were around when he bought the White Sox.
34. Joseph C. Nichols, "Braves Send 36,000 Home Happy by Halting Cards in Tenth, 3–2," *New York Times*, April 15, 1953.
35. "Frick Cried over Beer So Cards Name Park for Busch and Budweiser Goes Down the Drain," *New York Times*, April 11, 1953; "Busch Buys Sportsman Park from Browns, $400,000 Improvement Program Started," *The Sporting News*, April 15, 1953, 8; and "6,000 Shares Browns' Stock in Baltimore," *The Sporting News*, April 22, 1953, 21.
36. J. G. Taylor Spink, "Webb Seeks K.C. as Major League Entry," *The Sporting News*, July 22, 1953, 1–2.
37. "Big Leagues Vying for Coast Entries," *New York Times*, July 19, 1953.

38. Ray Gillespie, “Prospector Veeck Maps His Report on New Homesites,” *The Sporting News*, September 2, 1953, 6; and J. G. Taylor Spink, “Los Angeles Slated for Big Time Berth—but in National League,” *The Sporting News*, September 9, 1953, 1–2.
39. Robert L. Burnes, “Receivership Threat Sped Browns’ Shift,” *The Sporting News*, October 7, 1953, 3, 4.
40. Doug Skipper, “Connie Mack,” Society for American Baseball Research, n.d., https://sabr.org/bioproj/person/connie-mack/.
41. “Curb Gossip on Franchise Shifts: Frick,” *Chicago Tribune*, May 8, 1954.
42. “Johnson Tells $4,000,000 Bid for Athlctics,” *Chicago Tribune*, August 4, 1954.
43. Lee E. Cooper, “Yankees Sell Stadium, Rent it Back in a Three-Way $6,500,000 Deal,” *New York Times*, December 18, 1953; and “League Votes Today on A’s Shift,” *Chicago Tribune*, November 8, 1954.
44. “‘No Park, No Franchise,’ Frick Tells L.A.,” *The Sporting News*, August 18, 1954, 11; Warrington, “Departure without Dignity,” 103; and Katz, *Kansas City A’s*. Katz provides an excellent discussion of the complicated sale to Johnson and the problems created later by trades. Pages 1–112 detail the sale, timelines, and involved parties.
45. The Dodgers and Giants are the most researched relocations. Three extensive examinations are Treder, *Forty Years*, 181–92; D’Antonio, *Forever Blue*, especially 227–55; and Murphy, *After Many a Summer*. McCue, *Mover and Shaker*, 128–60, is an excellent synopsis of O’Malley’s efforts to stay in Brooklyn.
46. McCue, *Mover and Shaker*, 137–39.
47. McCue. *Mover and Shaker*, 140–41.
48. “‘No Park, No Franchise,’ Frick Tells Los Angeles,” *The Sporting News*, August 18, 1954, 11; “’Frisco Acts to Coordinate Big League Plans with L.A.,” *The Sporting News*, September 19, 1954, 10; “Frick Tells ’Frisco It Needs Big Park to Get Major Ball,” *The Sporting News*, October 13, 1954, 6; Jack McDonald, “’Frisco Approves New Stadium in Bid for Big Time,” *The Sporting News*, November 10, 1954, 2; “Leo Eyeing ’Frisco, Tabs Dark as Giants Pilots Timber,” *The Sporting News*, November 10, 1954, 2; “Frick Enthused over ’Frisco Approval of Major Stadium,” *The Sporting News*, November 17, 1954, 8; and “Starr, Mulligan, Torrence Top Field to Succeed Rowland and Coast Prexy,” *The Sporting News*, November 24, 1954, 11.
49. These events occurred within three weeks of each other. Joe King, “Stoneham 100% N.Y., ‘Giants New York Team,’” *The Sporting News*, November 24, 1954, 8, in the same issue that Rowland announced his retirement; “Big League Ball Coming to West Coast Fast, Says P.K.,” *The*

Sporting News, December 1, 1954, 6; and "Third Major Loop Favored by Frick," *The Sporting News*, December 15, 1954, 10.

50. "Cal Griffith Again Denies Nats Will Move Next Year," *The Sporting News*, September 26, 1956, 10.
51. McCue, *Mover and Shaker*, 145–46. The March 13, 1957, issue of *The Sporting News* had numerous stories about the Dodgers pursuing LA, including a picture of O'Malley and Duke Snider with LA mayor Norris Poulson and Los Angeles County board member Kenneth Hahn: Jack McDonald, "Coast Okays Brooklyn as Angel Owner," 25; John B. Old, "Envoys from L.A. Dangle Lure of 60,000-Seat Park for Bums," 25; *Californians Make Pitch at Vero Beach*, photograph, 25; the following page, 26, includes Rube Samuelson, "L.A. Awaits Park Moves as Tip-off"; "$50,000 Sought in 'Frisco in Stadium Study," 26; "If Dodgers Move, S.F. Should Act Quickly for Giants," 26; and "Dodgers to Go West in '58, Three L.A. Scribes Predict," 26.
52. "Frick Blacks Out Talk of Club Shifts," *Chicago Tribune*, May 11, 1957.
53. "Major League Shift May Be Set in July," *Chicago Tribune*, May 12, 1957.
54. Robert Cromie, "Dodgers, Giants Get O.K. to Move West," *Chicago Tribune*, May 29, 1957.
55. "Highlights of Frick's Statement at Hearings," *The Sporting News*, June 26, 1957, 13–14.
56. C. P. Trussell, "O'Malley Says City Balks Dodgers Plan," *New York Times*, June 27, 1957.
57. U.S. Congress, *Bills to Amend the Antitrust Laws to Protect Trade and Commerce Against Unlawful Restraints and Monopolies*, 1939–51 (June–August 1957).
58. Frick already met with affected Minor Leagues' executives, including Leslie O'Connor, now Pacific Coast League president, the focus being relocation possibilities. Frick claimed the meeting was exploratory, but it was also an effort to preempt any lawsuit. John Drebinger, "Frick Meets with Minor Leagues on Possible Franchise Changes," *New York Times*, July 11, 1957.
59. Bill Becker, "Giants Will Shift to San Francisco for 1958 Season," *New York Times*, August 20, 1957; and "Giants Trade Minneapolis Franchise to Red Sox for San Francisco Club," *New York Times*, October 16, 1957.
60. Emanuel Perlmutter, "Dodgers Accept Los Angeles Bid to Move to Coast," *New York Times*, October 9, 1957; Charles Bennett, "Nelson Rockefeller Offers Aid to Keep Dodgers in the City," *New York Times*, September 11, 1957; and Arthur Daley, "The Answer Is No," Sports of Our Times, *New York Times*, October 17, 1957.

61. Lawrence E. Davies, "Giants Are Cheered by 125,000 in Parade through San Francisco," *New York Times*, April 15, 1958.
62. The quote is from the late Russ Kemmerer, a Senators pitcher in the late 1950s. He repeated it annually in my baseball history class.
63. Louis Effrat, "Senators Silent as League Meets," *New York Times*, July 10, 1958.
64. "Frick Says Unlimited Telecasts Will Kill Baseball in Ten Years," *New York Times*, July 17, 1958; and "Senate Is Urged to Limit Number of Players Controlled by Majors," *New York Times*, July 18, 1958.
65. "Senator Shift Faces Battle," *Chicago Tribune*, August 24, 1958; "Frick Denies Major Expansion Will Be Asked by A.M. Tuesday," *New York Times*, September 4, 1958; and Arthur Daley, "A Capital Offense," Sports of the Times, *New York Times*, September 5, 1958.
66. "Veto American League Franchise Shift," *Chicago Tribune*, September 9, 1958.
67. Shirley Povich, "Cal Says Nats' Stay in Capital Depends on Stadium Solution," *The Sporting News*, September 19, 1958, 8.
68. Shirley Povich, "Cal and Frick Tangle over Move," *The Sporting News*, October 14, 1959, 4.
69. Shirley Povich, "Nats' Pat Stand Calms Crisis in Capital," *The Sporting News*, October 28, 1959, 5–6.
70. Ironically, attendance increased their last two years to almost 750,000 in 1960.
71. William Bartholomay, in discussion with the author, November 22 and December 20, 2017.
72. Edward Prell, "11 Man Group Purchases Chuck Comiskey's 46% of White Sox," *Chicago Tribune*, December 16, 1961.
73. "Wisconsin Men Buy Braves for $5,500,000; Club Will Stay in Milwaukee," *New York Times*, November 17, 1962. Bartholomay stressed relocation wasn't considered at purchase. Bartholomay, discussion, November 22, 2017.
74. Bartholomay, discussion, November 22, 2017.
75. John Drebinger, "Finley Will Open in Kansas City but Promised Court Action Soon," *New York Times*, January 18, 1964; and "A's Can't Move, Says Frick," *Chicago Tribune*, January 31, 1964.
76. Joseph Durso, "Braves Ready to Transfer Franchise from Milwaukee to Atlanta Next Year," *New York Times*, July 3, 1964; and "Giles Discourages Pool of TV Money," *New York Times*, July 19, 1964.
77. "Frick Warned Milwaukee Is Ready to Sue," *Chicago Tribune*, October 10, 1964.

78. Joseph Durso, "Braves Put Off Request to Move to Atlanta Because of a Restraining Order," *New York Times*, October 23, 1964.
79. "League Refuses to Allow Braves to Move till '66," *New York Times*, November 8, 1964; and "Atlanta Club Is Purchased by Braves for $285,000," *New York Times*, November 30, 1964.
80. Bob Wolf, "Celler Supports Milwaukee Plan to Sue Braves," *The Sporting News*, February 20, 1965, 15–16.
81. Furman Bisher, "Another Injunction—This Time Atlanta Fires One at Milwaukee," *The Sporting News*, January 1, 1966, 10.
82. Bob Wolf, "Milwaukee County Decides to Drop Braves Litigation," *The Sporting News*, February 11, 1967, 26.
83. Bob Wolf, "Milwaukee Rates a Place in Expansion Plan," *The Sporting News*, November 27, 1965, 11.

7. NOT A MINOR PROBLEM

1. Lowenfish, *Branch Rickey*, 121–24.
2. Pietrusza, *Judge and Jury*, 361–69.
3. An excellent analysis of the Minor League's relationship with the Majors is Gietschier, *Baseball*, 107–21. He noted the need for more research.
4. Edgar G. Brands, "Swift Farm Expansion Overpowers Minors," *The Sporting News*, March 26, 1947, 1.
5. Jerome Holtzman et al., "Baseball—Minor Leagues, Teams, Players," *Britannica*, last updated July 25, 2025, https://www.britannica.com/sports/baseball/The-minor-leagues.
6. Stan Baumgartner, "Game to Set Dials Right on Television," *The Sporting News*, November 10, 1948, 1.
7. Edgar G.Brands, "21 Cities Erased from O.B. Map by Farm Slashes," *The Sporting News*, January 18, 1950, 14.
8. "Minor Leagues Hit by Big League Broadcasts," *New York Times*, July 11, 1950.
9. Edgar G. Brands, "Major Aircasts Imperil Minors—Trautman," *The Sporting News*, December 6, 1950, 4; and Edgar G. Brands, "Basis for Radio, TV Solution Drawn Up," *The Sporting News*, December 13, 1950, 14.
10. "N.L. Owners to Form New Radio Policy," *New York Times*, January 5, 1951.
11. "Clubs Televising All Games Had Increases, TV Declares," *The Sporting News*, December 12, 1951, 18.
12. Dan Daniel, "O.B. Spikes Celler Probers' Complaints," *The Sporting News*, December 17, 1952, 1, 4.

13. "Frick Appoints Six to Study Radio-TV," *New York Times*, December 31, 1952.
14. Arthur Daley, "Cassandra Speaks," Sports of the Times, *New York Times*, February 3, 1953.
15. U.S. Congress, *Bill to Authorize the Adoption of Certain Rules with Respect to the Broadcasting or Telecasting of Professional Exhibitions*, 2–5 (May 6, 1953).
16. U.S. Congress, *Bill to Authorize the Adoption of Certain Rules with Respect to the Broadcasting or Telecasting of Professional Exhibitions*, 8–12, 19, 23 (May 6, 1953) and 104–10 (May 11, 1953).
17. U.S. Congress, *Bill to Authorize the Adoption of Certain Rules with Respect to the Broadcasting or Telecasting of Professional Exhibitions*, 8 (May 6, 1953) and 69–70 (May 8, 1953); and Jack Walsh, "Congress Told Dept. of Justice Ties Majors' Hands on Air Curb," *The Sporting News*, May 13, 1953, 16.
18. Jack Walsh, "Sen. Johnson 'Optimistic' Over Aircast Relief," *The Sporting News*, May 20, 1953; and "Need for TV Action Becomes Plainer," *The Sporting News*, May 27, 1953, 12.
19. "Frick Predicts Doom of Minors Unless Telecasts Are Controlled," *New York Times*, June 28, 1953.
20. "Make Majors Pay to Air Games in Minors—Shag," *The Sporting News*, February 10, 1954, 8; and Dan Daniel, "Frick Spikes Aid-to-Minors Proposal," *The Sporting News*, February 17, 1954, 1, 2.
21. Cy Kritzer, "'Combine Major and Minor Rule'—Frick," *The Sporting News*, June 2, 1954, 1, 2.
22. J. G. Taylor Spink, "Limit Radio, Drop Farms, Griffith Urges," *The Sporting News*, August 4, 1954, 1, 2.
23. "Lawrence Organizes Minor Group to Sue Majors for 50 Million," *The Sporting News*, September 29, 1954, 27; and Dan Daniel, "Commissioner Undisturbed by News of Proposed Suit," *The Sporting News*, September 29, 1954, 27. All except Portsmouth, Virginia, dropped out, reducing the amount to $250,000. Frick testified, asserting Major League Baseball lacked control due to the Justice Department. The court decided for the Major Leagues.
24. Brad Willson, "Major Farm Directors Huddle over Ways to Help Low Minors," *The Sporting News*, September 15, 1954, 13.
25. John Drebinger, "Big Leagues Revamp Working Agreement with Minors," *New York Times*, December 8, 1954; and Harold Rosenthal, "Majors Refuse Minors' Plea to Cut Radio-TV," *The Sporting News*, December 15, 1954, 7.

26. John Drebinger, "Majors Continue Bonus Rule and Reject Player Demands," *New York Times*, December 6, 1955.
27. Walt Hickey, "Minors Cut to 27 Loops as Class C Provincial Folds," *The Sporting News*, April 25, 1956, 6.
28. John Drebinger, "Minors Call on Congress to Reopen Inquiry on Baseball," *New York Times*, December 6, 1957; "Baseball TV Faces Trust Threat," *Chicago Tribune*, December 12, 1957; John Fisher, "Solons Promise Help 'Within the Law' on TV Problems," *Chicago Tribune*, January 15, 1958; and "Majors Name Committees to Aid Minors," *Chicago Tribune*, May 6, 1959.
29. "Frick Says Broadcasters Fight Measures to Curb Baseball TV," *New York Times*, September 3, 1959.
30. Dave Brady, "TV Officials Blast Game's Pleas for Minor Blackouts," *The Sporting News*, September 9, 1959, 25.
31. "Major League Miscellaneous Year-by-Year Averages and Totals," Baseball Reference, accessed July 10, 2025, https://www.baseball-reference.com/leagues/majors/misc.shtml.
32. Cy Kritzer, "Buffalo Boss in 'Monopoly' Probe Threat," *The Sporting News*, June 6, 1956, 16.
33. Carl Lundquist, "Opening-Day Cut to 28 Players by Majors Planned," *The Sporting News*, September 26, 1956, 4.
34. Joe Reichler, "Minors, Like Mighty Casey, Whiffed on Golden Chance," *The Sporting News*, November 12, 1958, 10.
35. Edward Prell, "Help Minor Leagues, Frick Urges Majors," *Chicago Tribune*, April 25, 1956.
36. "O'Malley Proposal Would Enable Minors to Share in TV Receipts," *New York Times*, November 29, 1955.
37. John Drebinger, "Miami Franchise Is Center of Interest at Minor League Meeting in Columbus," *New York Times*, November 30, 1955.
38. John Drebinger, "Court Puts Off Assault Hearing," *New York Times*, October 12, 1956; "Frick Selects Six to Direct Funds in Majors," *Chicago Tribune*, October 31, 1956; and "DeWitt in New Post," *New York Times*, December 4, 1956. DeWitt, a native of St. Louis, was part owner of the Browns since 1936 until Veeck sold.
39. Clifford Kachline, "Aid Plan Makes Game One Happy Family," *The Sporting News*, December 12, 1956, 15.
40. J. G. Taylor Spink, "New Major-Minor Teamwork for '57," editorial, *The Sporting News*, December 19, 1956, 12.
41. Jack MacDonald, "PCL Asks 25 Cents on Each Admission for Major Invasion," *The Sporting News*, November 13, 1957, 8; Dan Daniel, "Well-

Kept Secret, Hush-Hush Meet on Minors Map," *The Sporting News*, November 13, 1957, 9; and John Drebinger, "Phoenix, Spokane and Salt Lake City Are Admitted to Coast League," *New York Times*, December 3, 1957.

42. Edgar Munzel, "Shag Hurls Sunday TV Fight in Majors' Teeth," *The Sporting News*, December 11, 1957, 5.
43. "Minor Aid Fund Replenished, Now Back at $500,000 Level," *The Sporting News*, November 5, 1958, 6. The title suggests the fund was cut previously. If so, it wasn't mentioned.
44. Oscar Kahan and Clifford Kachline, "Frick Helps Save Minor Realignment," *The Sporting News*, December 10, 1958, 7.
45. J. G. Taylor Spink, "Independents' Big Cut in Million Fund," *The Sporting News*, June 24, 1959, 1, 4; and Ray Gillespie, "Minors Moan over Strings on Handouts," *The Sporting News*, September 9, 1959, 1, 8.
46. Clifford Kachline, "Majors Stash 847 Gs for Minors Safety," *The Sporting News*, December 16, 1959. A new league debuted in 1960, the Western Carolina, affiliated with the Continental League. Originally intended as a pooling operation, Frick altered it so each club identified with a specific franchise. Since the Continental League never materialized, the league reaffiliated. Buhite, *Continental League*, 106–44, especially 115–16.
47. Clifford Kachline, "$800,000 in Aid Money Sent to 200 Minor Clubs," *The Sporting News*, October 26, 1960, 17. The amount was less than publicized but larger than prior.
48. Lloyd McGowan, "Shag for Development Bureau to Organize Industrial Teams," *The Sporting News*, September 8, 1954, 6. The entire page was devoted to pros and cons.
49. J. G. Taylor Spink, "Organized Ball to Add Industrial Loops," *The Sporting News*, September 1, 1954, 12.
50. John Drebinger, "Frick Meets with Minor Leagues on Possible Franchise Changes," *New York Times*, July 11, 1957; and John Drebinger, "Minors Call on Congress to Reopen Inquiry on Baseball," *New York Times*, December 6, 1957.
51. Lowell Reidenbaugh, "What's Wrong with Minors? No Action," *The Sporting News*, November 12, 1958, 1, 8, 10; and Kahan and Kachline, "Frick Helps," 7.
52. Ray Gillespie, "Realignments Seen by DeWitt as 'Trial Runs' This Season," *The Sporting News*, March 4, 1959, 6.
53. Clifford Kachline, "Pitch to Shake Up Minor's Structure Hits Roadblock," *The Sporting News*, December 6, 1961, 7. Another article on the same page by Oscar Kahan demonstrated many lower-level clubs still

struggled. Oscar Kahan, "Only 6 Clubs to Operate in '62 Southern," *The Sporting News*, December 6, 1961, 7.

54. Joe King, "Frick Tackles Minors' New Setup," *The Sporting News*, April 25, 1962, 3, 6. The quote is from another article: "Frick Confident of Minors' Overhaul for '63 Campaign," *The Sporting News*, April 25, 1962, 3.
55. Dan Daniel, "Frick Group Blueprints O.B. Shakeup," *The Sporting News*, May 16, 1962, 1, 2; and Editorial, "Is Drastic Step Really Necessary?" *The Sporting News*, May 16, 1962, 12.
56. Edgar Munzel, "Majors Guarantee to Back 100 Minor Clubs," *The Sporting News*, June 2, 1962, 13; and "Putting Minors on Solid Footing," *The Sporting News*, June 2, 1962, 12. There was little coverage other than that in *The Sporting News*. Big-city sports news outlets appeared to have little interest in the Minors.
57. Clifford Kachline, "Overhaul of Minors Flops; Farm Chiefs Try to Mend Flaws," *The Sporting News*, October 6, 1962, 24.
58. Oscar Kahan, "Frick Ties Up Loose Ends in Minor Leagues," *The Sporting News*, December 15, 1962, 8.
59. Clifford Kachline, "Majors Pick Up $10 Million Tab in Minors," *The Sporting News*, December 15, 1962, 5.
60. The need for eight teams was brought up frequently in discussions to constitute Minor Leagues. Sullivan, *Late Innings*, 175–77.
61. "Frick Working on Realignment of Two Triple-A Minor Leagues," *New York Times*, November 19, 1963.
62. "Circuit's Range Now 4,500 Miles," *New York Times*, December 3, 1963.
63. "George H. Trautman, 73, Dead; Headed Minor-League Baseball," *New York Times*, June 25, 1963.
64. John Drebinger, "Majors and Minors Plan a Closer Tie," *New York Times*, November 15, 1963.
65. Clifford Kachline, "'Minors Must Expand' Says New Boss Piton," *The Sporting News*, December 14, 1963, 11.
66. C. C. Johnson Spink, "Minors on Stronger Footing," *The Sporting News*, April 24, 1965, 14.
67. See, for example, Snyder, *A Well-Paid Slave*, 42–51; and White and Dillow, *Uppity*, 30–43, for African American player experiences.
68. John Drebinger, "The Little Rock Story," Sports of Our Times, *New York Times*, August 23, 1963.

8. THE HARDBALL POLITICS OF EXPANSION

1. Irving Vaughn, "Majors Weigh Coast Bid," *Chicago Tribune*, December 11, 1945; Irving Vaughn, "Majors Deny Membership to Coast League,"

Chicago Tribune, December 19, 1945; and John Drebinger, "Big League Status Is Denied to Coast," *New York Times*, December 12, 1945.

2. Virgil Cory, "Coast Bolts Door against Major Invasion," *The Sporting News*, September 10, 1947, 1; and "Nice Ride to California for Committee of Majors," *The Sporting News*, September 10, 1947, 4.
3. Dan Daniel, "Majors Reject Coast Bid for Big Time Rating," *The Sporting News*, December 17, 1947, 5.
4. "Frick Sees Major Clubs for Coast, but Not Soon," *The Sporting News*, December 1, 1948, 4.
5. Cy Kritzer, "3rd Major Talk Fails to Stir Happy," *The Sporting News*, May 10, 1950, 30.
6. Dan Daniel, "Frick Foresees Changes in Major Map," *The Sporting News*, May 17, 1950, 1.
7. Jack McDonald, "'Draft Relief or Organized Baseball Bolt,' Coast's Ultimatum," *The Sporting News*, September 5, 1951, 5.
8. "Big Time Expansion Blueprint," *The Sporting News*, November 21, 1951, 13.
9. John B. Old, "Coasters Can Get Ready in 5 Years, Rowland Asserts," *The Sporting News*, November 21, 1951, 13.
10. Dan Daniel, "Frick Outlines Plan to Build Up New Majors," *The Sporting News*, November 21, 1951, 13.
11. "Council Sets Up 11 Requirements for Loops to Gain Major Status," *New York Times*, November 29, 1951.
12. Arch Ward, In the Wake of the News, *Chicago Tribune*, April 9, 1952.
13. Irving Vaughn, "Coast Hesitant in Its Bid for Major Status," *Chicago Tribune*, April 20, 1952.
14. John B. Old, "Game's Head Sees Coast's Rise as Unit," *The Sporting News*, April 2, 1952, 13.
15. "Harridge and Giles Deny Reported Franchise Move," *The Sporting News*, May 7, 1952, 24.
16. "Major Expansion Is Certain, Frick Tells 'Em in Honolulu," *The Sporting News*, October 21, 1953.
17. John Drebinger, "Frick Emphasizes 'Urgent' Need for Expansion of Major Leagues," *New York Times*, November 8, 1953.
18. "Greenberg to Urge 10 Club A.L. Circuit," *Chicago Tribune*, November 15, 1954.
19. "A.L. Votes to Push Expansion Moves; N.L. Acted Nov. 22," *The Sporting News*, December 15, 1954, 7.
20. Dan Daniel, "Plans for Expansion Placed on Shelf at New York Sessions," *The Sporting News*, February 9, 1955, 21.

21. Roscoe McGowen, "Maglie and Giants Are Reported $2000 Apart on Hurler's Salary," *New York Times*, February 10, 1955.
22. "Three Major Leagues in Frick's Crystal Ball," *New York Times*, May 8, 1957.
23. J. G. Taylor Spink, "Time for Orderly Planning," editorial, *The Sporting News*, June 5, 1957, 12.
24. "Frick Calls St. Louis Meeting with Minors' Reps on July 10," *The Sporting News*, June 26, 1957, 16.
25. McCue, *Mover and Shaker*, 156–57. In a discussion between the author and McCue on March 9, 2023, he doubted O'Malley intended to relocate but believed circumstances ultimately pushed him.
26. Arthur Daley, "The Answer Is No," Sports of the Times, *New York Times*, October 17, 1957.
27. "Mayor Appoints 4 Men to Seek Second Baseball Club for City," *New York Times*, November 30, 1957; and Shapiro, *Bottom of the Ninth*, 27.
28. John Drebinger, "Redlegs' Owner Hints of Settling Club in New York," *New York Times*, December 30, 1957.
29. Edward Prell, "Majors Gird for New York Territorial Fight," *Chicago Tribune*, September 27, 1957.
30. "International League Claims Jersey City as a Step toward Third Major Loop," *New York Times*, October 18, 1957.
31. John Drebinger, "Fight on Issue of New York Territorial Rights Marks Majors' Joint Meeting," *New York Times*, December 7, 1957.
32. John Drebinger, "Baseball Committee Clears Way for Second Major League Team in New York," *New York Times*, January 4, 1958.
33. John Drebinger, "Frick Offers Baseball Advice," *New York Times*, January 3, 1958. That was an interesting comment because O'Malley was financing his ballpark.
34. Harold Rosenthal, "Door Left Ajar for N.L. Return to New York," *The Sporting News*, February 5, 1958, 13.
35. Hal Middlesworth, "Tigers Opposed Open Territorial Rule to Protect Big Investment," *The Sporting News*, February 5, 1958, 22.
36. Bob Broeg, "Compromise Likely on Territorial Rights," *The Sporting News*, February 5, 1958, 13, 22.
37. "Baseball Leaders Act to Speed Return of National League Team to This City," *New York Times*, April 29, 1958.
38. Frederick G. Lieb, "N.L. Weighing Expansion to 10 Clubs," *The Sporting News*, July 16, 1958, 1, 2; and Roscoe McGowen, "Mayor Tells National League of Flushing Meadow Proposal," *New York Times*, July 8, 1958.
39. "Frick Denies Major Expansion Will Be Asked by Him Tuesday," *New York Times*, September 4, 1958; and Edgar Munzel, "Leagues to Hold at

Eight Clubs, Will Try to Build from Within," *The Sporting News*, September 17, 1958, 7.

40. Arthur Daley, "Was This Trip Necessary?" Sports of the Times, *New York Times*, September 12, 1958.
41. "12 Team Leagues Near, Frick Says," *New York Times*, April 13, 1958.
42. Louis Effrat, "Frick Attacks 'Sledge-Hammer' Tactics of City's Bid for New Major Club," *New York Times*, November 14, 1958. Russell D. Buhite asserted the lack of movement, especially by the National League, was the impetus for Shea. Buhite, *Continental League*, 42–43.
43. Effrat, "Frick Attacks," 32.
44. "'Third League' Proposal Stirs Mixed Reaction," *The Sporting News*, November 26, 1958, 5; John Drebinger, "City Preparing 'Concrete' Offer to Frick on Third Big League," *New York Times*, November 15, 1958; and Lowenfish, *Branch Rickey*, 546.
45. Drebinger, "City Preparing 'Concrete' Offer."
46. "Dead Set Against Third League: Giles," *Chicago Tribune*, November 18, 1958.
47. "Frick Favors Expansion, 2nd New York Team," *Chicago Tribune*, November 19, 1958.
48. Dan Daniel, "N.L. Arousing Real Hope for Team in New York," *The Sporting News*, December 17, 1958, 2.
49. "Third Big League Reported Nearer," *New York Times*, April 14, 1959.
50. "Majors Invite a Third League, City Preparing Baseball Plan," *New York Times*, May 22, 1959.
51. Earl Flora, "Conditions for New Circuit Listed at Top-Level Huddle," *The Sporting News*, May 27, 1959, 13.
52. David Conlin, In the Wake of the News, *Chicago Tribune*, May 28, 1959.
53. Arthur Daley, "Trojan Horse," Sports of the Times, *New York Times*, May 26, 1959.
54. Burton Hawkins, "Talk of Third Major League Called Politics," *The Sporting News*, July 1, 1959, 12.
55. Roscoe McGowen, "Shea Declines Kefauver Offer of Bill to Aid 3rd Major League," *New York Times*, July 2, 1959.
56. Dick Young, "Third Major League Formed," *Chicago Tribune*, July 28, 1959.
57. William Conklin, "Shea Criticizes Circuit Heads for Comments on Third League," *New York Times*, July 29, 1959.
58. "Frick Talks of Baseball Harmony," *New York Times*, July 30, 1959.
59. "Kefauver Advises Majors to Aid Third League," *New York Times*, August 1, 1959.

60. John Drebinger, "That Third-League Theme," Sports of the Times, *New York Times*, August 16, 1959; and "Shea May Seek 10-Club Set Up in Meeting with Majors Today," *New York Times*, August 18, 1959.
61. Howard M. Tuckner, "Rickey Will Head Continental League," *New York Times*, August 19, 1959.
62. *To Limit the Applicability of the Antitrust Laws: Hearings Before the H.R. Subcomm. on Antitrust and Monopoly of the Comm. on the Judiciary*, 86th Cong., in U.S. Congress, *Hearings on Antitrust Dichotomy in Sports*, 214–51 (September 4, 1959). Frick's comments about the Continental League are on 221–23. The general discussion on controlling players is on 214–51.
63. "Shea Indicates Increasing Lack of Harmony Between Majors, New League," *New York Times*, October 5, 1959.
64. The back and forth occurred over a week, creating a more adversarial relationship. Howard M. Tucker, "Expansion Move Attacked as Plot," *New York Times*, October 23, 1959; John Drebinger, "Cronin Says No New Teams Will Be in American League Lineup in 1960," *New York Times*, October 28, 1959; and "Rickey Asks Frick to Honor Pledge," *New York Times*, October 29, 1959.
65. "Third League Again Threatens to Be Outlaw Circuit If Needed," *New York Times*, November 17, 1959.
66. John Drebinger, "Frick Defends Majors," *New York Times*, November 18, 1959.
67. John Drebinger, "National League Blocks Expansion of Majors, Affirms Pledge to New Circuit," *New York Times*, December 8, 1959.
68. "Frick Predicts Rosy Future for New League," *New York Times*, January 12, 1960.
69. "Northern Teams to Open in South," *New York Times*, February 19, 1960.
70. Buhite, *Continental League*, 111–16. Buhite notes Frick was correct but suggested it was harassment (116). Frick preferred existing league expansion and was a stickler for rules. Those were likely his motivations.
71. "3rd League Demands Help from Majors," *New York Times*, April 16, 1960.
72. "Help Due to Continental, Celler Says," *Chicago Tribune*, April 17, 1960.
73. "Frick Says It's All Talk, No Action, in New Circuit," *New York Times*, April 18, 1960.
74. "Baseball Men Attack Kefauver Bill," *Chicago Tribune*, May 6, 1960.
75. "Frick Vows to Fight Kefauver Proposal," *New York Times*, May 7, 1960.
76. Dan Daniel, "'Kefauver Bill Most Dangerous Yet Introduced,' Frick Warns," *The Sporting News*, May 18, 1960, 7.

77. Howard M. Tuckner, "Shea Hints War against Majors If Kefauver Bill Fails to Pass," *New York Times*, May 13, 1960.
78. Arthur Daley, "Another Summit Meeting," Sports of the Times, *New York Times*, May 17, 1960.
79. *Pursuant to Senate Resolution 238: Hearings Before the S. Subcomm. on Antitrust and Monopoly of the Comm. on the Judiciary*, in U.S. Congress, *To Make the Antitrust Laws Applicable to the Organized Professional Team Sport of Baseball*, 86th Cong., 2nd sess. (May 19–20, 1960). Comments, in order, are on pages 14, 52, 79, 97, and 138. All but the last were offered on the first day. Shea indicated his primary interest was a second team. Johnson remains accurate. Frick and Trautman scored by noting earlier congressional findings and threats to the Minors. Much of the hearing was chaired by Philip Hart, who was more partial to baseball, as he was related by marriage to, and had worked for, an owner. His questioning favored status quo.
80. Dave Brady, "Long, Rocky Route Ahead for Kefauver Bill; Action Unlikely," *The Sporting News*, June 22, 1960, 15.
81. Gordon S. White Jr., "Rickey Says Setback in Senate Won't Hurt Continental League," *New York Times*, June 30, 1960; Dave Brady, "C.L. Hopes Fade after Sport Bill's Failure in Senate," *The Sporting News*, July 6, 1960, 8; and Dan Daniel, "Frick Warns C.L. It Must Act in Hurry," *The Sporting News*, July 6, 1960, 8. For a more in-depth discussion of the vote, see Lowenfish, *Branch Rickey*, 571–72.
82. Robert M. Lipsyte, "N.L. Decision Virtually Assures City of 2nd Baseball Team," *New York Times*, July 19, 1960.
83. Thomas Wicker, "Drive Is Foreseen by 4 Pro Groups," *New York Times*, August 4, 1960.
84. John Drebinger, "Baseball Expands," Sports of Our Times, *New York Times*, August 4, 1960.
85. Buhite, *Continental League*, 2, 3. Beyond having to start from scratch, the Continental League also had to address the pension. Raiding wasn't an option, as Rickey, given his career, had significant reservations about violating the reserve clause.
86. "Frick Considers Los Angeles an 'Open City' for 2nd Club," *New York Times*, August 14, 1960.
87. John Drebinger, "On Sub-Normal Averages," Sports of the Times, *New York Times*, August 18, 1960.
88. Dan Daniel, "Webb and Frick See Peaceful Expansion before '62 Season," *The Sporting News*, September 14, 1960, 9.
89. "National League Gets New York Bid," *New York Times*, October 12, 1960.

90. "American League Ready to Expand," *New York Times*, October 13, 1960.
91. Louis Effrat, "N.L. Admits New York, Houston for 1962," *New York Times*, October 18, 1960.
92. "American League Gets into the Act," *New York Times*, October 18, 1960.
93. John Drebinger, "A.L. in '61 to Add Minneapolis and L.A.," *New York Times*, October 27, 1960.
94. "League Actions Scorned by Shea," *New York Times*, October 27, 1960.
95. John Drebinger, "Frick Approves A.L. Set Up, Concerned about Date Difficulties," *New York Times*, October 28, 1960.
96. Shirley Povich, "Lane, Carroll, MacPhail Barred from Confab," *The Sporting News*, November 2, 1960, 8.
97. Joseph M. Sheehan, "Big League Chiefs Agree to Let Each Other In on Expansion Moves," *New York Times*, November 2, 1960.
98. Jerry Holtzman, "Greenberg 'Pleased and Proud' to Lead A.L.'s Coast Expansion," *The Sporting News*, November 2, 1960, 3, 8.
99. Edward Prell, "Vote for L.A. Carried East by Sox Boss," *Chicago Tribune*, October 18, 1960. Veeck definitely was interested in LA, though he owned a team. Although biographer Paul Dickson made no mention of that interest, Veeck devoted a chapter to it in his first book. When he acknowledged deteriorating health as the cause of his sale of the White Sox, he claimed he could return as a full partner in LA. In that chapter, he also lambasted Frick for failing on his open-city declaration. Veeck and Linn, *Veeck as in Wreck*, 353–72, especially 356, 360, and 367.
100. Bob Hunter, "O'Malley's Old Spar-Mate Returns as A.L. Club Angel," *The Sporting News*, November 2, 1960, 7.
101. Dan Daniel, "Frick Sets Up Barrier to A.L. Expansion Plan," *The Sporting News*, November 23, 1960, 11, 32.
102. Louis Effrat, "Expansion Move Faces Misgivings," *New York Times*, November 16, 1960.
103. John Drebinger, "A.L. Seeks to End L.A. Stalemate Today," *New York Times*, November 17, 1960.
104. Edward Prell, "Quesada Gets Washington Franchise," *Chicago Tribune*, November 18, 1960. In his biography of Greenberg, John Rosengren devotes less than a page to his LA efforts, claiming Frick lacked "the cojones" to oppose O'Malley. The situation was more complicated, but Rosengren perpetuated the myth that O'Malley dominated baseball and stepped over Frick. Rosengren, *Hank Greenberg*, 339.
105. John Drebinger, "A.L. Proposes 1961 Interleague Play as Expansion Compromise," *New York Times*, November 23, 1960; and "A.L. Asks 9 Team Plan with N.L. in '61," *Chicago Tribune*, November 23, 1960.

106. Dan Daniel, "Fans Want Something New, Get It in 9-Club Majors, Inter-Loop Play," *The Sporting News*, November 30, 1960, 1, 2.
107. John Drebinger, "Frick Will Seek Interleague Accord on Expansion at Meeting Here Today," *New York Times*, November 30, 1960.
108. Joseph M. Sheehan, "Expansion Talks to Resume Today," *New York Times*, December 1, 1960.
109. McCue, *Mover and Shaker*, 292. McCue's book provides perspective on O'Malley's goals, most of which he obtained. He conceded 1961 but received $350,000, about half his expenses, for relocating two Minor League clubs. Having the Angels in Chavez Ravine for four years provided rent, half of concessions, and all parking, each contributing to the new ballpark. See also Andy McCue, *Stumbling around the Bases*, 38. Gene Autry, the Angels' owner, estimated the four years cost him an extra $700,000 annually.
110. Arthur Daley, "Trapped in a Corner," Sports of the Times, *New York Times*, November 20, 1960.
111. John Drebinger, "A.L. Gets Plan to Add L.A. Club," *New York Times*, December 4, 1960.
112. Edward Prell, "Baseball Near Expansion Showdown," *Chicago Tribune*, December 6, 1960.
113. Warren Corbett, "Gene Autry," Society for American Baseball Research, n.d., https://sabr.org/bioproj/person/gene-autry/.
114. John Drebinger, "Compromise Reported as A.L. Grants L.A. Franchise," *New York Times*, December 7, 1960.
115. John Drebinger, "L.A. in A.L. in 1961 and N.Y. in N.L. in 1962," *New York Times*, December 8, 1960.
116. John Drebinger, "Frick Is Sure Major Leagues Will Expand to Twelve Teams in a Few Years," *New York Times*, December 9, 1960.
117. Arthur Daley, "How to Lose Gracefully," Sports of the Times, *New York Times*, December 9, 1960. The December 14, 1960, issue of *The Sporting News* even featured, on its page 1, a cartoon of Frick wiping his brow.
118. Bob Burnes, "Expansion Accord Hailed as Guidepost," *The Sporting News*, December 14, 1960, 1, 2, 8. The quotes are from page 8. In the following issue of *The Sporting News*, Frick gave Galbreath credit: "The one man who, more than anybody else, was responsible for that settlement was Galbreath. . . . The controversy was developing into an acrimonious fight. We had an expansion job to do, not to stop a struggle of personalities. . . . Galbreath was the first club owner to sense the dangerous direction in which the dispute had taken." Dan Daniel, "Expansion Peace Bears Galbreath Stamp," *The Sporting News*, December 21, 1960, 6.
119. Corbett, "Rickey's Folly."

9. A POPULAR '60S DRAFT

1. The league meetings reached most major decisions unless leagues differed. Then the commissioner could decide.
2. National League Winter Meetings, December 10, 1945, box 10, folder 4, 140–58, Giamatti Research Center.
3. National League Winter Meetings, December 11, 1945, box 10, folder 4, 401–9, Giamatti Research Center.
4. National League Scheduling Meeting, February 1, 1946, box 10, folder 5, 77–96, Giamatti Research Center.
5. John Drebinger, "Baseball Leagues Virtually Outlaw Bonus Payments," *New York Times*, February 3, 1946.
6. The $6,000 bonus in 1946 is the equivalent of about $99,000 in 2025. CPI Inflation Calculator, accessed July 24, 2025, https://www.officialdata.org/us/inflation/1946?amount=6000.
7. National League Winter Meetings, December 5, 1946, box 10, folder 6, 97–118, Giamatti Research Center. It is unclear whether the amendment passed.
8. National League Winter Meetings, December 13, 1948, box 10, folder 10, 14–15, Giamatti Research Center.
9. "Owners Grant Ball Players 4 Concessions," *Chicago Tribune*, July 12, 1949.
10. "Urge Baseball to Abandon Bonus Rule," *Chicago Tribune*, November 2, 1949.
11. National League Winter Meetings, December 12–13, 1949, box 10, folder 11, 9–10, Giamatti Research Center; John Drebinger, "Chandler Plans to Pave Way Today for Quick Repeal of Baseball Bonus Rule," *New York Times*, December 14, 1949; and John Drebinger, "Giants Get Dark and Stankey of Braves for Gordon, Marshall, Kerr and Webb," *New York Times*, December 15, 1949.
12. Dan Daniel, "March 1 Camp Rule on Way Out—Frick," *The Sporting News*, March 15, 1950, 1, 2.
13. Arthur Daley, "Another Ouster," Sports of the Times, *New York Times*, December 15, 1950.
14. Carl T. Felkner, "Veeck Leads Fight to Restore Bonus Rule," *The Sporting News*, June 18, 1952, 1, 4; and "Frick Sees an Early End to Outlay of Big Bonuses," *The Sporting News*, July 2, 1952, 6.
15. Les Biederman, "Rickey Heads Probers into Bonus Curb," *The Sporting News*, August 20, 1952, 1, 4.
16. David Fleitz, "Eddie Mathews," Society for American Baseball Research, n.d., https://sabr.org/bioproj/person/eddie-mathews/.
17. Arthur Daley, "Youth Must Be Served," Sports of the Times, *New York Times*, March 13, 1952.

18. George Strickler, "Football Draft," *Chicago Tribune*, January 31, 1957.
19. Edgar Munzel, "Year's Ban for Officials, Penalty in New Bonus Rule," *The Sporting News*, October 8, 1952, 6.
20. A $6,000 bonus limit in 1946 equates to roughly $99,000 in 2025, as mentioned in an earlier note. A $4,000 bonus limit in 1953 equals $48,000 in 2025. In effect, the restriction was cut more than half. CPI Inflation Calculator, accessed July 24, 2025, https://www.officialdata.org/us/inflation/1953?amount=4000.
21. Joseph M. Sheehan, "Frick Announced Bonus Outline Going into Winter Meetings," *New York Times*, November 6, 1952.
22. Edgar G. Brands, "Bonus Rule Has Loopholes," *The Sporting News*, December 24, 1952, 10. Although receiving little coverage, the most important rule change was the one facilitating franchise relocation.
23. Dan Daniel, "Leja Hailed as Second Lou, Inks Yank Pact for 100 G's," *The Sporting News*, October 7, 1953, 22; and Evan Katz, "Frank Leja," Society for American Baseball Research, last modified January 2020, https://sabr.org/bioproj/person/frank-leja/. Two bonus-baby players from 1953 to 1957 received over $100,000, one playing over ten years as a journeyman, the other never again reaching the Majors.
24. "MLB Bonus Babies," Baseball Almanac, n.d., https://www.baseball-almanac.com/legendary/Bonus_Babies.shtml.
25. Kaline's statistics and summaries for Koufax and Killebrew are drawn from "Al Kaline," Baseball Reference, n.d., https://www.baseball-reference.com/players/k/kalinal01.shtml; "Sandy Koufax," Baseball Reference, n.d., https://www.baseball-reference.com/players/k/koufasa01.shtml; and "Harmon Killebrew," Baseball Reference, n.d., https://www.baseball-reference.com/players/k/killeha01.shtml.
26. "Roberto Clemente," Baseball Reference, n.d., https://www.baseball-reference.com/players/c/clemero01.shtml; and Hy Turkin, "'Good Prospects Fewer'—Only 15 in Majors Draft," *The Sporting News*, December 1, 1954, 4.
27. Hy Turkin, "Capital Confab to Map O.B. Radio-TV Policy," *The Sporting News*, January 13, 1954, 1, 2.
28. "Bonus Rule to Be Strictly Construed Frick Promises," *The Sporting News*, July 24, 1954, 55; and "Interpretation of Bonus Rule Announced by Frick," *The Sporting News*, February 23, 1955, 17.
29. Dan Daniel, "Paul Sees Vote in December for Unlimited Draft," *The Sporting News*, June 15, 1955, 26; and Edgar Munzel, "Junk Bonus Rule, Briggs Urges," *The Sporting News*, July 27, 1955, 6.
30. Jesse A. Linthicum, "Baltimore's Youth Movement Runs into Some Rough Spots," *The Sporting News*, August 10, 1955, 8.

31. "Orioles Fined $2000, Richards $2500 by Frick," *Chicago Tribune*, September 24, 1955; William J. Briordy, "Richards Draws Bonus Rule Fine," *New York Times*, September 24, 1955; and Jesse A. Linthicum, "$2500 Fine for Richards in Bonus Case," *The Sporting News*, September 28, 1955, 18.
32. "Thomas Borland," Baseball Reference, n.d., https://www.baseball-reference.com/players/b/borlato01.shtml; and Bill Nowlin, "Tom Borland," Society for American Baseball Research, n.d., https://sabr.org/bioproj/person/tom-borland/.
33. Allen Drury, "Frick Sees Peril in Baseball Bill," *New York Times*, June 20, 1957.
34. Brad Wilson, "Frick, Trautman Huddle on Bonus Rule Substitute," *The Sporting News*, September 11, 1957, 4, 6.
35. Ray Gillespie, "Busch to Lead Fight to Put End to Bonus Rule," *The Sporting News*, October 16, 1957, 1, 6; and J. G. Taylor Spink, "Unrestricted Draft Seen Almost Certain," *The Sporting News*, October 30, 1957, 7.
36. Edward Prell, "Kill Both Bonus Rules, Adopt Unrestricted Draft?" *Chicago Tribune*, December 7, 1957; Edgar Munzel, "Bankrolls Now Only Limit on Bonus Bids," *The Sporting News*, December 18, 1957, 11, 12; and Edward Prell, "Vote to Option Present Bonus Kids Expected," *The Sporting News*, December 18, 1957, 12.
37. Jay Hook, in discussion with the author, October 10, 2023.
38. "Jay Hook," Baseball Reference, n.d., https://www.baseball-reference.com/players/h/hookja01.shtml.
39. Clifford Kachline, "Prize Picks Parade in Draft; High Tab May Limit Choices," *The Sporting News*, November 19, 1958, 21; and Oscar Kahan, "Majors Draft 12 Players at Cost of $300,000," *The Sporting News*, December 10, 1958, 11.
40. Jack Walsh, "Frick Certain Majors Will Brake Bonus," *The Sporting News*, July 30, 1958, 1.
41. "Major Leaguers Favor Return to Bonus Rule as Spending Curb," *New York Times*, September 10, 1958.
42. Arthur Daley, "Was This Trip Necessary?" Sports of the Times, *New York Times*, September 12, 1958.
43. Dan Daniel, "Bonus Limit, Draft Pool Proposal Given Frick by Committee," *The Sporting News*, October 29, 1958, 7; Hal Lebovitz, "New Draft Plan Requires More Scouting—Lane," *The Sporting News*, November 19, 1958, 21.
44. "Yankees Fight Unrestricted Draft," *Chicago Tribune*, December 1, 1958.
45. Clifford Kachline, "Minors Vote Unrestricted Draft Trial," *The Sporting News*, December 10, 1958, 9.

46. John Drebinger, "Minors Extend One-Year Draft Rule," *New York Times*, December 4, 1959. The Indians didn't gain much. Lee spent part of a year on the club and was sold to the Angels. He lasted one season. "Mike Lee," Baseball Reference, n.d., https://www.baseball-reference.com/players/l/leemi01.shtml.
47. Oscar Kahan, "Majors Draft 23 Players, Pay 497 Gees," *The Sporting News*, December 7, 1960, 13.
48. Clifford Kachline, "First-Year Rule Triggers Hike in Minors' Selection," *The Sporting News*, December 7, 1960, 14; and Clifford Kachline, "Minors Veto Proposals for Bigger Handouts," *The Sporting News*, December 7, 1960, 11, 16.
49. Ernest Mehl, "Carroll Suggests Free Agent Draft," *The Sporting News*, February 18, 1959, 1.
50. Clifford Kachline, "28 Proposals for Study on Minor Docket," *The Sporting News*, December 2, 1959, 8, 10; and "Frick Has Doubt on Third League," *New York Times*, September 5, 1959, 8.
51. Dan Daniel, "Gallagher Criticizes Defeat of Free-Agent Draft," Over the Fence, *The Sporting News*, December 16, 1959, 10.
52. Dan Daniel, "Majors Hint Move Toward Free-Agent Draft," *The Sporting News*, July 5, 1961, 5, 6.
53. Dave Brady, "Senate-Bill Backers to Huddle with Frick," *The Sporting News*, July 5, 1961, 5; and J. G. Taylor Spink, "Commissioner's Valuable Contribution," editorial, *The Sporting News*, July 26, 1961, 10.
54. J. G. Taylor Spink, "Uneasy Majors Eye Free-Agent Draft," *The Sporting News*, June 28, 1961, 1, 2.
55. Joe King, "Hamey Cites Twin Target in New Bonus Rule," *The Sporting News*, July 12, 1961, 17, 20.
56. John Drebinger, "Frick Hails Move to Halt Wild Bonus Spending," *New York Times*, November 8, 1961.
57. "Plans to Cut Baseball Bonuses Aim to Tighten First-Year Rules," *New York Times*, November 10, 1961.
58. Clifford Kachline, "Bonus-Curb Plan Wins Quick Okay at Minors' Confab," *The Sporting News*, December 6, 1961, 21. The spat is interesting if true. Frick remained close to Bavasi throughout his tenure in baseball.
59. Oscar Kahan, "Total of 35 Choices, Biggest Grab-Bag in 47 Years," *The Sporting News*, December 6, 1961, 9.
60. Clifford Kachline, "'Most Progress in 15 Years,' Frick Declares after Meetings," *The Sporting News*, December 13, 1961, 5.
61. Oscar Kahan, "Big Timers See 40 Per Cent Cut in Bonus Spree," *The Sporting News*, December 13, 1961, 5, 6. Kahan estimated that 1961

bonus expenditures were $8 million to $10 million, reducing costs by 40 percent.

62. Dan Daniel, "'Bonus Rule Proving Effective,' Frick Declares," Over the Fence, *The Sporting News*, May 16, 1962, 12.
63. J. G. Taylor Spink, "Bonus Rule Achieving Results," *The Sporting News*, June 30, 1962, 12; and J. G. Taylor Spink, "More Work Ahead for Bonus Committee," *The Sporting News*, July 21, 1962, 12.
64. Jim Henneman, "Colts Corraling Kid Talent Helped by Bonus Loophole," *The Sporting News*, July 21, 1962, 17.
65. Oscar Kahan, "45 First-Year Kids Grabbed in Draft Raids," *The Sporting News*, December 8, 1962, 13.
66. Clifford Kachline, "Minors Doomed Unless Majors Act," *The Sporting News*, December 8, 1962, 1, 2, 4.
67. Oscar Kahan, "Big Timers Heed Expansion Clubs' Plea, Grant Help," *The Sporting News*, December 14, 1962, 1, 2.
68. As will be discussed in chapter 10, Congress never succeeded, as Frick assembled a powerful grassroots organization. Coupled with Paul Porter's advice, the commissioner considered the exemption secure. Porter is discussed in the next chapter as well.
69. Clifford Kachline, "Free-Agent Draft in Works; Brass Gives 'Go-Ahead,'" *The Sporting News*, January 25, 1964, 4.
70. Barney Kremenko, "Free-Agent Draft by Spring of '65—That's Frick's Goal," *The Sporting News*, April 4, 1964, 10.
71. Joe King, "Will Youngsters Accept Free-Agent Draft?" Clouting 'Em with Joe King, *The Sporting News*, April 18, 1964, 16.
72. Edgar Munzel, "O'Connor No. 1 Foe of Free-Agent Draft," *The Sporting News*, April 11, 1964, 24.
73. Oscar Kahan, "NCAA Seeking Ban on Pro-Sport Draft of College Students," *The Sporting News*, July 18, 1964, 12.
74. Jerome Holtzman, "Majors Split on Free-Agent Draft, Table Plan," *The Sporting News*, August 22, 1964, 2.
75. C. C. Johnson Spink, "Free-Agent Draft Deserves Another Chance," editorial, *The Sporting News*, August 29, 1964, 14.
76. "Major League Owners Urge More Authority for Commissioner of Baseball," *New York Times*, November 7, 1964.
77. Edward Prell, "Baseball Goes Back to 'Landis Code,'" *Chicago Tribune*, December 3, 1964.
78. Joseph Durso, "Baseball's Minors Follow Pro-Football Pattern in Backing Free-Agent Draft," *New York Times*, December 3, 1964.
79. Clifford Kachline, "Frick Lauds 'Great Progress Program,'" *The Sporting News*, December 19, 1964, 1, 2.

80. "Frick Holds Confab to Air New Free-Agent Draft Rules," *The Sporting News*, April 3, 1965, 2.
81. "Free Agent Draft Slated for New York on June 8," *The Sporting News*, May 1, 1965, 12.
82. Leonard Koppert, "Baseball's New Draft: Two Views," *New York Times*, June 6, 1965.
83. C. C. Johnson Spink, "A Progressive Step for Baseball," editorial, *The Sporting News*, June 12, 1965, 14.
84. Clifford Kachline, "Free-Agent Draft Launched without a Hitch," *The Sporting News*, June 19, 1965, 7. Monday's career was solid. Signed a week after drafted for $104,000, he played nineteen seasons with three clubs. "Rick Monday," Baseball Reference, n.d., https://www.baseball-reference.com/players/m/mondari01.shtml.
85. "Reaction By Kids, Parents Very Good, Frick Asserts," *The Sporting News*, June 19, 1965, 44; and David Condon, In the Wake of the News, *Chicago Tribune*, June 23, 1965.
86. Clifford Kachline, "Club Owners Vote Absolute Power to Baseball's Boss," *The Sporting News*, December 19, 1964, 6.

10. PRESERVING THE "EXEMPTION"

1. Banner, *Baseball Trust*, 53–60. Landis agreed baseball violated the Sherman Act but postponed his decision, fearing the liability would be destructive. Banner, *Baseball Trust*, 60.
2. Banner, *Baseball Trust*, 60.
3. Banner, *Baseball Trust*, 69, 72.
4. Banner, *Baseball Trust*, 75–78.
5. Banner, *Baseball Trust*, 81–82.
6. Edmonds, "Over a Century, Part 1," 24–25.
7. Edmonds, "Over a Century, Part 1," 26.
8. Banner, *Baseball Trust*, 88.
9. Vince Guerrieri, "Jorge Pasquel," Society for American Baseball Research, n.d., https://sabr.org/bioproj/person/jorge-pasquel/.
10. "Stephens Quits Mexico; Rejoins Browns," *Chicago Tribune*, April 6, 1946.
11. Weatherby, "Danny Gardella." Gardella was a character, singing opera when inspired and walking down streets on his hands. He was not successful at judging fly balls.
12. Chandler had already reviewed Mickey Owen, who petitioned in August. Chandler rejected him with Frick's support: "Mr. Chandler did the proper thing. It is a good ruling." "Chandler Rules Owen's Ban Stands for Five Years," *Chicago Tribune*, August 15, 1946.

13. Banner, *Baseball Trust*, 98.
14. "Gardella Asks Damages," *New York Times*, October 3, 1947.
15. Banner, *Baseball Trust*, 98.
16. "Decision Reversed in Gardella Suit," *New York Times*, January 28, 1948.
17. J. G. Taylor Spink, "Pasquel Blast Perils Mexican Peace Plan," *The Sporting News*, February 4, 1948, 1, 2; and Dan Daniel, "N.L. Opposes Amesty for Jumpers," *The Sporting News*, February 11, 1948, 1, 2.
18. "Gardella Loses Suit Against the Giants," *New York Times*, July 15, 1948; and Banner, *Baseball Trust*, 98.
19. Thomas Rowan, "U.S. Appeals Court Orders Trial of Gardella Suit against Baseball," *New York Times*, February 10, 1949.
20. "Players Planning to Sue Chandler," *New York Times*, March 7, 1949.
21. Thomas Rowan, "Monopoly Denied in Baseball Case," *New York Times*, April 26, 1949.
22. "Player Limit Suspended, Easing Way for Reinstatement of Exiles," *New York Times*, June 7, 1949; and "Majors Active Player Limit 25 Even for Club with Returnees," *New York Times*, June 9, 1949.
23. "Bill in Congress Proposes to Bar Anti-Trust Prosecution of Sports," *New York Times*, April 6, 1949; and Banner, *Baseball Trust*, 104–6.
24. Banner, *Baseball Trust*, 103.
25. Robin Washington, "The Most Important Congressman You've Probably Never Heard Of," *Forward*, July 2, 2021, https://forward.com/news/472165/voting-rights-act-emanuel-celler-brooklyn-congressman/.
26. "Ty Cobb to Testify," *New York Times*, July 20, 1951.
27. "Frick Defends Baseball," *New York Times*, July 24, 1951.
28. U.S. Congress, *House of Representatives Hearings Before the Subcommittee on Monopoly and Antitrust of the Committee of the Judiciary* (July 30, 31, August 1, 3, 6–8, 10, and October 15–19, 22–24, 1951).
29. U.S. Congress, *House of Representatives Hearings Before the Subcommittee on Monopoly and Antitrust of the Committee of the Judiciary*, 875 (October 19, 1951).
30. U.S. Congress, *House of Representatives Hearings Before the Subcommittee on Monopoly and Antitrust of the Committee of the Judiciary*, 1–3 (July 30, 1951).
31. U.S. Congress, *House of Representatives Hearings Before the Subcommittee on Monopoly and Antitrust of the Committee of the Judiciary*, 46 (July 31, 1951); and John A. McQuiston, "Paul A. Porter, Capital Lawyer Who Held New Deal Posts. Dies," *New York Times*, November 27, 1975. There are varying views on Porter and Chandler. Banner thought Chandler hired Porter, given relationships developed while in Congress. Banner, *Baseball Trust*, 107–9. That's unlikely. While both Democrats,

Celler was a strong supporter of civil rights. Chandler wasn't. While not intervening against Robinson, he supported segregationists politically. A recent book credits Porter, with his political skills, having the most impact in protecting baseball's exemption. Evidence presented here suggests otherwise. Thomas, *Brand New Ballgame*, 98–101.

32. U.S. Congress, *House of Representatives Hearings Before the Subcommittee on Monopoly and Antitrust of the Committee of the Judiciary*, 24 (July 30, 1951). Chapter 1 in this book made clear Frick never lived on a farm and only made the scrub team at DePauw.
33. U.S. Congress, *House of Representatives Hearings Before the Subcommittee on Monopoly and Antitrust of the Committee of the Judiciary*, 26–31 (July 30, 1951) and 33–41 (July 31, 1951).
34. U.S. Congress, *House of Representatives Hearings Before the Subcommittee on Monopoly and Antitrust of the Committee of the Judiciary*, 52–115, 123 (July 31, 1951). The quotes are from pages 70 and 85.
35. U.S. Congress, *House of Representatives Hearings Before the Subcommittee on Monopoly and Antitrust of the Committee of the Judiciary*, 1050–52 (October 23, 1951).
36. U.S. Congress, *House of Representatives Hearings Before the Subcommittee on Monopoly and Antitrust of the Committee of the Judiciary*, 1054–55 (October 23, 1951).
37. U.S. Congress, *House of Representatives Hearings Before the Subcommittee on Monopoly and Antitrust of the Committee of the Judiciary*, 1056–57 (October 23, 1951).
38. U.S. Congress, *Organized Baseball Report of the Subcommittee of Monopoly Power and Antitrust of the Committee on the Judiciary*, 139 (May 27, 1952).
39. U.S. Congress, *Organized Baseball Report of the Subcommittee of Monopoly Power and Antitrust of the Committee on the Judiciary*, 195, 204 (May 27, 1952).
40. U.S. Congress, *Organized Baseball Report of the Subcommittee of Monopoly Power and Antitrust of the Committee on the Judiciary*, 229–32 (May 27, 1952).
41. "Backing of Clause Is Hailed by Frick," *New York Times*, May 24, 1952; and J. G. Taylor Spink, "Up to Game to Solve Own Problems," editorial, *The Sporting News*, June 4, 1952, 10.
42. "Court Dismisses 2 Baseball Suits," *New York Times*, December 6, 1951. Baseball had other antitrust challenges. Gordon McLendon, president of Liberty Broadcasting, sued, accusing it of a "continuing conspiracy to monopolize and restrain competition" in broadcasts. "Liberty Network

Sues Thirteen Baseball Clubs for $12,000,000 over Broadcasting Curbs," *New York Times*, February 22, 1952.

43. Banner, *Baseball Trust*, 113–14, 116–17.
44. Edmonds, "Over a Century, Part 2," 24–25.
45. Edmonds, "Over a Century, Part 2," 26.
46. Edmonds, "Over a Century, Part 2," 26.
47. "Frick Cites Responsibility of Baseball as Game's Executives Hail Decision," *The Sporting News*, November 18, 1953, 8; and J. G. Taylor Spink, "An Early Thanksgiving for Game," editorial, *The Sporting News*, November 18, 1953, 10.
48. J. G. Taylor Spink, "Meetings Face Important Decisions," editorial, *The Sporting News*, December 2, 1953, 12.
49. The details are in the Celler Antitrust Hearings, May 24, 1956, Political Contacts, Correspondence, box 1, folder 12, subfolder March–June 1958, Giamatti Research Center.
50. "Three-I League," Baseball Reference, last modified September 27, 2023, https://www.baseball-reference.com/bullpen/Three-I_League.
51. *Hearings Before the S. Subcomm. on Antitrust and Monopoly of the Comm. on the Judiciary*, in U.S. Congress, *To Limit the Applicability of the Antitrust Laws so as to Exempt Certain Aspects of Designated Professional Team Sports and for Other Purposes*, 85th Cong., 378–79 (1958).
52. Banner, *Baseball Trust*, 134–39.
53. Oscar K. Ruhl, "O.B. First Started Running Anti-Trust Gauntlet in '02," *The Sporting News*, March 20, 1957, 16.
54. "Frick Defended by Keating, Following Blast by Celler," *The Sporting News*, March 20, 1957, 16. Patrick Hillings, from LA, suggested baseball was big business because the Red Sox offered $1 million for Herb Score. "Frick Gets Invitation," *New York Times*, March 20, 1957.
55. Frederick G. Lieb, "Game Tightens Belt in Preparation for Legislative Attack," *The Sporting News*, April 3, 1957, 11.
56. *Organized Professional Team Sports: Hearings Before S. Subcomm. on Antitrust and Monopoly of the Comm. on the Judiciary*, in U.S. Congress, *Bills to Amend the Antitrust Laws to Protect Trade and Commerce Against Unlawful Restraints and Monopolies*, 2–7 (June 17, 1957).
57. *Organized Professional Team Sports*, in U.S. Congress, *Bills to Amend the Antitrust Laws to Protect Trade and Commerce Against Unlawful Restraints and Monopolies*, 91–92 (June 19, 1957).
58. *Organized Professional Team Sports*, in U.S. Congress, *Bills to Amend the Antitrust Laws to Protect Trade and Commerce Against Unlawful Restraints and Monopolies*, 98–100 (June 19, 1957).

59. *Organized Professional Team Sports*, in U.S. Congress, *Bills to Amend the Antitrust Laws to Protect Trade and Commerce Against Unlawful Restraints and Monopolies*, 131 (June 20, 1957).
60. *Organized Professional Team Sports*, in U.S. Congress, *Bills to Amend the Antitrust Laws to Protect Trade and Commerce Against Unlawful Restraints and Monopolies*, 180–81 (June 20, 1957).
61. *Organized Professional Team Sports*, in U.S. Congress, *Bills to Amend the Antitrust Laws to Protect Trade and Commerce Against Unlawful Restraints and Monopolies*, 1250, 1254 (June 24, 1957).
62. *Organized Professional Team Sports*, in U.S. Congress, *Bills to Amend the Antitrust Laws to Protect Trade and Commerce Against Unlawful Restraints and Monopolies*, 1310–13 (June 25, 1957).
63. *Organized Professional Team Sports*, in U.S. Congress, *Bills to Amend the Antitrust Laws to Protect Trade and Commerce Against Unlawful Restraints and Monopolies*, 1796, 1802 (June 26, 1957).
64. *Organized Professional Team Sports*, in U.S. Congress, *Bills to Amend the Antitrust Laws to Protect Trade and Commerce Against Unlawful Restraints and Monopolies*, 1850, 1867, 1872, 1884 (June 26, 1957).
65. Jack Walsh, "Celler, Keating Give 'Sympathy,' Promise Help to Minors on TV," *The Sporting News*, January 22, 1958, 11; and Jack Walsh, "Celler and Keating Planning to Introduce All-Sports Bill," *The Sporting News*, January 22, 1958, 11.
66. J. G. Taylor Spink, "Just an Invitation to Litigation," editorial, *The Sporting News*, February 26, 1958, 12; and "Frick, Owners Say Bill May Kill Baseball," *Chicago Tribune*, March 7, 1958.
67. "Representative Celler Defends His Regulatory Bill," *The Sporting News*, March 12, 1958, 7.
68. Gordon S. White Jr., "Players Swinging at Proposed Bill," *New York Times*, March 20, 1958; and "Players Support Owners on Bill," *New York Times*, March 21, 1958.
69. "Celler Thinks Owners Forced Players Move," *Chicago Tribune*, March 22, 1958.
70. Roberts explained during the first Kefauver session why player reps changed since Lewis claimed owners were supporting the bill. A year later, Frick was asked the same in a Celler hearing. He indicated Roberts requested the meeting for clarification. Lewis was nebulous about the reserve clause in the Celler hearing and waited two months before notifying Celler of the players' position change. Interestingly, the explanation for termination was his testimony before Kefauver in 1958. He didn't testify then but did in the 1957 hearings with his nebulous

answer. Roberts was the ringleader for his dismissal. "Lewis Dismissed as Baseball Players' Lawyer," *New York Times*, March 25, 1959.

71. "Celler Assails Critics," *New York Times*, May 15, 1958.
72. Jack Walsh, "Celler Bill Sent to House Floor, But Dissenters Offer Substitute," *The Sporting News*, June 25, 1958, 14.
73. Jack Walsh, "Sports Bill Wins in House, but Faces Senate Hurdle," *The Sporting News*, July 2, 1958, 20. The victory for Keating may have helped his Senate election.
74. *Legislation to Limit the Applicability of the Antitrust Laws so as to Exempt Certain Aspects of Designated Professional Team Sports: Hearings Before the H.R. Subcomm. of the Comm. of the Judiciary*, 86th Cong., in U.S. Congress, *Hearings on Antitrust Dichotomy in Sports*, 2 (September 2 and 4, 1959).
75. *Legislation to Limit the Applicability of the Antitrust Laws so as to Exempt Certain Aspects of Designated Professional Team Sports*, in U.S. Congress, *Hearings on Antitrust Dichotomy in Sports*, 61, 65–66, 93–94 (September 2, 1959).
76. *Legislation to Limit the Applicability of the Antitrust Laws so as to Exempt Certain Aspects of Designated Professional Team Sports*, in U.S. Congress, *Hearings on Antitrust Dichotomy in Sports*, 214–16 (September 4, 1959).
77. *Legislation to Limit the Applicability of the Antitrust Laws so as to Exempt Certain Aspects of Designated Professional Team Sports*, in U.S. Congress, *Hearings on Antitrust Dichotomy in Sports*, 222–23, 242 (September 4, 1959).
78. "Frick Tabbed to Testify on Package Video Pacts," *The Sporting News*, August 30, 1961, 31; and U.S. Congress, *Telecasting of Professional Sports Contests*, 65–66 (August 28, 1961).
79. *Hearings Before the S. Subcomm. on Antitrust and Monopoly of the Comm. on the Judiciary*, in U.S. Congress, *To Limit the Applicability of the Antitrust Laws so as to Exempt Certain Aspects of Designated Professional Team Sports and for Other Purposes*, 85th Cong., 7 (July 9, 15–18, 22–24, 28–31, 1958).
80. U.S. Congress, *To Limit the Applicability of the Antitrust Laws so as to Exempt Certain Aspects of Designated Professional Team Sports and for Other Purposes*, 85th Cong., 11–21 (July 9, 1958).
81. U.S. Congress, *To Limit the Applicability of the Antitrust Laws so as to Exempt Certain Aspects of Designated Professional Team Sports and for Other Purposes*, 85th Cong., 24 (July 9, 1958).

82. U.S. Congress, *To Limit the Applicability of the Antitrust Laws so as to Exempt Certain Aspects of Designated Professional Team Sports and for Other Purposes*, 85th Cong., 28, 54, 67 (July 9, 1958).
83. U.S. Congress, *To Limit the Applicability of the Antitrust Laws so as to Exempt Certain Aspects of Designated Professional Team Sports and for Other Purposes*, 85th Cong., 297–98, 306–8 (July 18, 1958).
84. U.S. Congress, *To Limit the Applicability of the Antitrust Laws so as to Exempt Certain Aspects of Designated Professional Team Sports and for Other Purposes*, 85th Cong., 84–91, 107–8 (July 15, 1958).
85. U.S. Congress, *To Limit the Applicability of the Antitrust Laws so as to Exempt Certain Aspects of Designated Professional Team Sports and for Other Purposes*, 85th Cong., 157, 159, 161–62, 169–70, 171, 189 (July 16, 1958).
86. U.S. Congress, *To Limit the Applicability of the Antitrust Laws so as to Exempt Certain Aspects of Designated Professional Team Sports and for Other Purposes*, 85th Cong., 113–14, 415, 490 (July 15, 24, and 29, 1958).
87. U.S. Congress, *To Limit the Applicability of the Antitrust Laws so as to Exempt Certain Aspects of Designated Professional Team Sports and for Other Purposes*, 85th Cong., 381–88 (July 24, 1958); and Jack Walsh, "Capital Crammed with Game's History," *The Sporting News*, December 3, 1958, 8.
88. *Hearings Before the S. Subcomm. on Antitrust and Monopoly of the Comm. on the Judiciary*, in U.S. Congress, *To Make the Antitrust Laws Applicable to the Organized Professional Team Sport of Baseball*, 86th Cong., 1st sess., 2–3 (July 28–31, 1959).
89. U.S. Congress, *To Make the Antitrust Laws Applicable to the Organized Professional Team Sport of Baseball*, 86th Cong., 1st sess., 11 (July 28–31, 1959).
90. U.S. Congress, *To Make the Antitrust Laws Applicable to the Organized Professional Team Sport of Baseball*, 86th Cong., 1st sess., 25 (July 29, 1959).
91. U.S. Congress, *To Make the Antitrust Laws Applicable to the Organized Professional Team Sport of Baseball*, 86th Cong., 1st sess., 53–54, 58 (July 29, 1959).
92. *Pursuant to Senate Resolution 238: Hearings Before the S. Subcomm. on Antitrust and Monopoly of the Comm. on the Judiciary*, in U.S. Congress, *To Make the Antitrust Laws Applicable to the Organized Professional Team Sport of Baseball*, 86th Cong., 2nd sess., 4–6 (May 19–20, 1960).
93. *Pursuant to Senate Resolution 238*, in U.S. Congress, *To Make the Antitrust Laws Applicable to the Organized Professional Team Sport of Baseball*, 86th Cong., 2nd sess., 16, 73 (May 19, 1960).

94. *Pursuant to Senate Resolution 238*, in U.S. Congress, *To Make the Antitrust Laws Applicable to the Organized Professional Team Sport of Baseball*, 86th Cong., 2nd sess., 92, 96, 104, 133 (May 19, 1960).
95. U.S. Congress, *To Limit the Applicability of the Antitrust Laws so as to Exempt Certain Aspects of Designated Professional Team Sports and for Other Purposes*, 88th Cong., 26–27, 36, 40 (January 30–31, February 17–18, 1964). Bob Friend's comments are interesting, as he was one of four reps who interviewed, and offered the director's job to, Marvin Miller. Another interesting side note was Hart's questioning the commissioners of the new American and National Football Leagues. Hart suggested a championship game. He mentioned that "it will not be an unattended game." Pete Rozelle countered there would be too much litigation cost. Hart responded, "I imagine court costs would be recovered in the first 10 minutes." Rozelle then said it would dilute the NFL championship game (at 96 and 122).
96. William N. Wallace, "C.B.S. Buys 80% of Stock in Yankee Baseball Team," *New York Times*, August 14, 1964; and Joseph Durso, "Yanks Sale to C.B.S. Stirs Senate Moves for Inquiry," *New York Times*, August 15, 1964.
97. "Bill on Baseball Goes to Congress," *New York Times*, January 5, 1965.
98. Leonard Koppert, "Senate Group Starts Hearings on Baseball Today," *New York Times*, February 18, 1965; Leonard Koppert, "Frick Testifies on Stock Policy at Senate Study of Yanks Sale," *New York Times*, February 20, 1965; and Leonard Koppert, "The Baseball Hearings," Sports of the Times, *New York Times*, February 22, 1965.
99. Dave Brady, "Senate Hearing Aids Support for CBS," *The Sporting News*, March 6, 1965, 2; "Frick Will Testify Today in Milwaukee Antitrust Suit," *New York Times*, November 12, 1965; Leonard Koppert, "National League Faces Antitrust Action after Rejecting New Franchise Bids," *New York Times*, December 3, 1965; and Banner, *Baseball Trust*, 176–81.

11. CHANGES GOOD, BAD, AND UGLY

1. Wisensale, "Cold War," 221.
2. Wisensale, "Cold War," 220–21.
3. Wisensale, "Cold War," 222.
4. N. Sakata, "Capacity Crowds Watch Giants in First Four Japanese Games," *The Sporting News*, October 28, 1953, 17.
5. Shirley Povich, "Eisenhower Receives Japanese Fans' Gift," *The Sporting News*, February 17, 1954, 2.
6. Red McQueen, "Yankee Crowds Total 135,000 for First Four Games in Japan," *The Sporting News*, November 2, 1955, 7; and "Yanks Beat Nankai, 7–0, as Byrne Stars," *New York Times*, October 29, 1955.

7. Roger McGowen, "Baseball Stars Fly to Venezuela," *New York Times*, November 7, 1958; M. J. Gorman, "Major Leagues Make Big Hit in Venezuela Visit," *The Sporting News*, November 19, 1958, 19; and Dan Daniel, "Clinics Venezuela Success May Bring Future Latin Trips," *The Sporting News*, November 26, 1958, 35.
8. "Order Japanese Team to Pay Sox for Stanka," *Chicago Tribune*, February 2, 1961; and C. Paul Rogers III, "Joe Stanka," Society for American Baseball Research, n.d., https://sabr.org/bioproj/person/joe-stanka/.
9. "Frick, Japan to Confer on Player Issue," *Chicago Tribune*, October 23, 1962; "U.S., Japan OK Trading Pact—in Baseball," *Chicago Tribune*, October 29, 1962; and Masaru Fujimoto, "Tiger Tour Hailed as Game's Finest Hour," *The Sporting News*, December 1, 1962, 29.
10. Robert Trumbull, "Murakami Controversy Imperils U.S.-Japan Dealings," *New York Times*, February 5, 1965.
11. "U.S., Japan End War on Giant Hurler," *Chicago Tribune*, April 29, 1965; and Fitts, *Mashi*, 124–35.
12. Hi Turkin, "Batters Get Break in Rules Changes," *The Sporting News*, November 11, 1953, 1, 6.
13. "Old Rule or New, Rosen Still No. 2," *The Sporting News*, November 18, 1953, 14; Hi Turkin, "Path Now Clear for Progress—Frick," *The Sporting News*, November 18, 1953, 1, 2; and J. G. Taylor Spink, "Sacrifice Fly Rule Welcomed Back," editorial, *The Sporting News*, November 11, 1953, 10.
14. Paul Richards to Will Harridge, telegram, March 9, 1954, box 2, folder 8, Rules Committee Files, Giamatti Research Center; Madden, *1954*, 28–29; and Al López to Will Harridge, telegram, March 10, 1954, box 2, folder 8, Rules Committee Files, Giamatti Research Center.
15. Ford Frick to James Gallagher, March 26, 1954, box 2, folder 8, Rules Committee Files, Giamatti Research Center.
16. Ford Frick to All Major League Clubs and to All Minor League Presidents, April 12, 1954, box 2, folder 8, notice no. 9, Rules Committee Files, Giamatti Research Center.
17. "Hear Major Players Get Legal Help," *Chicago Tribune*, August 22, 1953.
18. "Hear Major Players," *Chicago Tribune*; and Lowenfish and Lupien, *Imperfect Diamond*, 184.
19. "Players' Aide, Frick to Meet Tomorrow," *New York Times*, August 23, 1953.
20. Carl T. Felker, "Many Players Rap Hiring of Mouthpiece," *The Sporting News*, September 2, 1953, 1, 2.
21. Louis Effrat, "Council Approves Five Proposals Submitted by Baseball Players," *New York Times*, September 29, 1953.

22. "Players' Lawyer to Press Fight for Revision of Pension Fund," *New York Times*, November 13, 1953.
23. Irving Vaughn, "Baseball Threatens to Kill Pensions," *Chicago Tribune*, December 3, 1953; Irving Vaughn, "Major Leagues Press Fight on Players' Pension Plan," *Chicago Tribune*, December 10, 1953; and "Radio-TV Fund for Pension Chandler Says," *Chicago Tribune*, December 10, 1953.
24. Irving Vaughn, "Baseball Threatens to Kill Pensions," *Chicago Tribune*, December 3, 1953; John Drebinger, "Baseball Players and Frick at Odds," *New York Times*, December 3, 1953.
25. John Drebinger, "Big Leagues Take Steps toward Ending Player Pension Plan in 1955," *New York Times*, December 10, 1953.
26. "Chandler Blasts Baseball Owners," *New York Times*, January 20, 1954.
27. Roscoe McGowen, "Frick Outlines Pension Operations in Action on Heels of 'Sniping,'" *New York Times*, January 22, 1954.
28. "Majors Deny Serious Rift Over Pension," *Chicago Tribune*, January 31, 1954.
29. Roscoe McGowen, "Players' Representatives and Baseball Officials Agree on Pension Plan," *New York Times*, February 17, 1954.
30. J. G. Taylor Spink, "Game Moves to End Talent 'Hoarding,'" *The Sporting News*, July 21, 1954, 1, 2.
31. "Players Group Selects Feller," *New York Times*, October 2, 1956.
32. John Drebinger, "Majors Continue Bonus Rule and Reject Players' Demands," *New York Times*, December 7, 1955; Joseph M. Sheehan, "Baseball Players Protest Owners' Rejection of Demands," *New York Times*, December 15, 1955; John Drebinger, "Frick Assures Baseball Players Demands Will Be Considered Again," *New York Times*, December 16, 1955; and John Drebinger, "Majors Reject Player Pay Raise," *New York Times*, February 5, 1956.
33. "Pay $16,250,000 for All-Star and Series TV," *Chicago Tribune*, July 3, 1956; Arthur Daley, "It's Now a Dream Job," Sports of Our Times, *New York Times*, July 6, 1956; and "Boy, 15, Sends All-Stars into Battle," *Chicago Tribune*, July 11, 1956.
34. Dan Daniel, "Demand for 20 Per Cent Divvy Stuns Owners," *The Sporting News*, December 10, 1959, 5, 6.
35. "Players Endorse Frick on TV Pact," *New York Times*, December 6, 1959.
36. Frick's biographer suggests he lacked firm leadership. Carvalho, *Frick**, 171–75. In fact, while the Atlanta meeting proved a mistake, Frick remained involved, walking a tightrope between owner intransigence and player unrest. That ensured the pension plan's stability.
37. John Lardner, "Perilous Plight of the Pitcher," *New York Times Sunday Magazine*, September 18, 1955.

38. "Young Award Proposed to Honor Ace Pitcher," *New York Times*, December 16, 1955.
39. J. G. Taylor Spink, "Five Points Now Instead of Six," editorial, *The Sporting News*, February 15, 1956, 12.
40. "Frick Seeks Help for Poll on All-Stars," *Chicago Tribune*, May 15, 1956.
41. "Frick's Office Will Conduct All-Star Poll," *Chicago Tribune*, May 22, 1956; and Carl Lundquist, "Five Reds Dominate N.L. All-Star Starters," *The Sporting News*, July 4, 1956, 7.
42. J. G. Taylor Spink, "Time to Abandon Fan All-Star Poll," editorial, *The Sporting News*, July 4, 1956, 12; and Dan Daniel, "Opinion Divided on Fan Poll for All-Star Teams," *The Sporting News*, July 25, 1956, 16.
43. Michael Strauss, "Frick Sidetracks Three Redlegs after Avalanche of Ohio Votes," *New York Times*, June 29, 1957. Because Musial won a very close vote in the end, only two Redlegs were sidetracked.
44. "Redleg Fans Rail against Frick for Vetoing 3 of their All-Stars," *New York Times*, June 30, 1957.
45. J. G. Taylor Spink, "Frick Favors Player Vote for All-Stars," *The Sporting News*, August 7, 1957, 1, 4; Roscoe McGowen, "Managers, Coaches and Players to Pick All-Star Teams," *New York Times*, January 31, 1958; and J. G. Taylor Spink, "Good Picks, but It's Still Fans' Game," editorial, *The Sporting News*, July 9, 1958, 20.
46. Roscoe McGowen, "Majors Weighing Second All-Star Game," *New York Times*, May 2, 1959; "Majors Invite a Third League; City Preparing Baseball Plan," *New York Times*, May 22, 1959; and Arthur Daley, "Too Many Stars," Sports of Our Times, *New York Times*, June 5, 1959.
47. "Players Back 2 All-Star Games if Played within a 4-Day Period," *New York Times*, October 21, 1959; and "Players Endorse Frick on TV Pact," *New York Times*, December 6, 1959.
48. John Drebinger, "Kuenn Will Ask Players to Vote to Restore Old All-Star Set-Up," *New York Times*, July 15, 1960; . . . And to Complete the Report, *Chicago Tribune*, August 2, 1960; and Joe King, "Big Hassle Brewing on All-Star 'Cutback,'" *The Sporting News*, August 10, 1960, 9.
49. "Players Vote for the Continuation of Two All-Star Games a Season," *New York Times*, August 2, 1961; and John Drebinger, "New Bonus Rule Voted by Majors," *New York Times*, December 2, 1961.
50. "Players Ask Majors Reduce '62 Schedule," *Chicago Tribune*, July 9, 1962; Dan Daniel, "Exec Council Nixes Second All-Star Game," *The Sporting News*, October 20, 1962, 6; and Dan Daniel, "Owners and Player Reps Agree to Kayo Second Star Game," *The Sporting News*, December 8, 1962, 20.

51. "Frick Thinks National League Regrets Move Out of New York," *Chicago Tribune*, January 12, 1958; and "Frick Calm but Pitchers Wail at Dodgers' Wall," *Chicago Tribune*, January 21, 1958.
52. "Coliseum Homers Viewed as 'Farce,'" *New York Times*, April 30, 1958; John Rendel, "Frick Asks 325-Feet Minimum at Foul Lines in New Ballparks," *New York Times*, May 6, 1958; and "A Curb on Cheap Homers!" *Chicago Tribune*, July 20, 1958. Frick's comments show concern about Ruth's record three years before the threat.
53. "Order Finley to Knock Down Porch," *Chicago Tribune*, April 12, 1964; and "Finley Yields in Fence Dispute," *Chicago Tribune*, April 14, 1964.
54. "Ruth's Record Can Be Broken Only in 154 Games, Frick Rules," *New York Times*, July 18, 1961. Frick's "distinctive mark" certainly suggested an asterisk.
55. Carvalho and Ankney, "Haunted by Babe," 66.
56. Angela Frick, discussion; "Truman, Spellman Ask about Babe," *New York Times*, August 14, 1948; and "Nation's Leaders Mourn Babe Ruth," *New York Times*, August 17, 1948.
57. Louis Effrat, "Mantle Concedes He Can't Beat Ruth Homer Mark in 162 Games," *New York Times*, September 15, 1961.
58. John Drebinger, "The Home-Run Whirligig," Sports of the Times, *New York Times*, July 30, 1961. Frick approved the committee, perhaps ignoring it given the urgency he felt or concern they'd disagree. However, Frick rarely acted without consultation or a committee to gain support. Evidence suggests Frick did so. A *Sporting News* article in early July, before Frick's ruling, indicates he wanted a conference with the committee regarding the eight extra games. Dan Daniel, "Majors Hint Move Toward Free-Agent Draft," *The Sporting News*, July 5, 1961, 5, 6. The BBWAA committee discussion is on page 6.
59. Arthur Daley, "Protecting the Records," Sports of the Times, *New York Times*, October 23, 1960; and Joe Williams, "Longer Sked No Threat to Babe's Magic 60," *The Sporting News*, December 28, 1960, 9.
60. "Expansion to 24 Major Clubs '62 Possibility, Frick Says," *The Sporting News*, December 28, 1960, 12; and Arthur Daley, "Banditry without Asterisks," Sports of Our Times, *New York Times*, October 1, 1962.
61. C. C. Johnson Spink, "Writers Back Frick's Homer Decision," *The Sporting News*, August 9, 1961, 4.
62. C. C. Johnson Spink, "Homer Decision," *The Sporting News*, August 9, 1961, 4.
63. Dan Daniel, "Cronin Stirs Up Rhubarb, Raps Frick Homer Ruling," *The Sporting News*, September 20, 1961, 9; "No * Will Mar Homer Records,"

New York Times, September 22, 1961; and "Roger Glad Ruth's Mark Safe," *Chicago Tribune*, September 27, 1961.

64. Louis Effrat, "Maris, Frick Make Hit Speeches, Then Strike Words from Record," *New York Times*, January 27, 1962; and Joseph M. Sheehan, "Prizes and Parodies Mark Baseball Dinner," *New York Times*, January 29, 1962.
65. Maris was affected by Frick's bias, but Yankees fans and writers also maligned him, preferring Mantle, if anyone, to surpass Ruth. Maris was harassed even at Yankee Stadium. Clavin and Peary, *Roger Maris*, 166–92.
66. "162-Game Record," *Chicago Tribune*, September 26, 1961.
67. "Steals Two, but Dodgers Lose, 12–2," *Chicago Tribune*, September 24, 1962; and Lee Allen, "Maury's Theft Feats Stir Record Ruckus," *The Sporting News*, October 6, 1962, 10.
68. Veeck and Linn, *Veeck as in Wreck*, 242.
69. Dan Daniel, "Frick Proposes Record Book for 162-Game Chart," *The Sporting News*, January 3, 1962, 14.
70. Edward Prell, "Make Spitball Legal, Suggestion of White Sox," *Chicago Tribune*, October 18, 1961; Dan Daniel, "Frick Sees Splitter as Slab Aid," *The Sporting News*, November 15, 1961, 9; "Giles Opposes Plan to Revive Ball," *New York Times*, November 25, 1961; and John Drebinger, "Baseball Rules Committee Votes, 8 to 1, to Retain Ban on Spitball Pitchers," *New York Times*, November 27, 1961.
71. Jim Wallace, "Enlarge the Strike Zone," letter to the editor, *The Sporting News*, November 29, 1961, 14; "Restore Old Strike Zone, Frick Urges," *The Sporting News*, August 25, 1962, 10; and C. C. Johnson Spink, "Danger in Too Rapid Expansion," editorial, *The Sporting News*, September 1, 1962, 12.
72. "Segar Succeeds Gallagher as Head of Rules Committee," *The Sporting News*, October 27, 1962, 4.
73. C. C. Johnson Spink, "Segar Well Grounded on Rules," editorial, *The Sporting News*, November 10, 1962, 12.
74. Dan Daniel, "Rules Group Urged to Aid Battered Hurlers," *The Sporting News*, January 26, 1963, 36; Bob Joyce, "Hurlers Hail New Strike Zone, Expanded by '10 to 12' Inches," *The Sporting News*, February 9, 1963, 4; and John Drebinger, "New Strike Zone Seen as Problem," *New York Times*, February 13, 1963.
75. "League by League Totals for Batting Average," Baseball Almanac, n.d., https://www.baseball-almanac.com/hitting/hibavg4.shtml.
76. Tom Swope, "College Coaches Renew Plea for Anti-Raiding Pact," *The Sporting News*, January 16, 1952, 16; and Allison Danzig, "Football

Coaches Call for Penalty on False Start by the Offensive Linemen," *New York Times*, January 7, 1953.

77. "Colleges Still Seek Baseball Agreement," *New York Times*, February 16, 1954; and Hy Turkin, "Curb on Campus Recruiting Voted by Majors," *The Sporting News*, August 4, 1954, 7.
78. "Frick Asks Minors to Okay College Rule in Mail Vote," *The Sporting News*, December 22, 1954, 28; and Barney Kremenko, "Frick Promises Major Support of College Pact," *The Sporting News*, January 12, 1955, 20.
79. John Drebinger, "Major League Owners Lift All Restrictions on Signing of College Players," *New York Times*, December 12, 1956.
80. Robert Cromie, "College Baseball Feud Aired by Frick," *Chicago Tribune*, January 26, 1957; and Lyall Smith, "College Coaches Dig Own Grave," Quotes, *The Sporting News*, January 2, 1957, 15.
81. Tommy Devine, "Rah-Rah Mentors Bar Scouts, Except as Cash Customers," *The Sporting News*, May 14, 1958, 20; and Watson Spoelstra, "Majors, College Coaches Huddle," *The Sporting News*, August 30, 1958, 1.
82. C. C. Johnson Spink, "O.B.-College Compromise Needed," *The Sporting News*, March 19, 1958, 12; and William N. Wallace, "Majors Subsidize College Nines with N.C.A.A.'s Cooperation," *New York Times*, December 8, 1964.
83. Oscar Kahan, "Amended Rule on Inking Collegians Gets O.B.'s Okay," *The Sporting News*, August 10, 1963, 22; and C. C. Johnson Spink, "Profitable Peace Between Colleges, O.B.," editorial, *The Sporting News*, January 25, 1964, 12.
84. Oscar Kahan, "Frick's Efforts Open Up Road for Summer Circuit," *The Sporting News*, June 22, 1963, 2.
85. Edward Prell, "Majors Strike Back at Those Who Claim Baseball Is Fading," *Chicago Tribune*, July 7, 1963; and C. C. Johnson Spink, "We Believe," editorial, *The Sporting News*, August 1, 1964, 14.
86. "Majors' Official Vote Restores Commissioner's Broad Powers," *New York Times*, December 5, 1964; and Oscar Kahan, "Expanded College Summer Program to Get $75,000," *The Sporting News*, February 13, 1965, 11.
87. "Frick Questions Tough Eligibility Rules," *The Sporting News*, May 22, 1965, 8.

12. CREATING AND DECKING THE HALL

1. Vlasich, *Legend for Legendary*, 10–11. Pages 1–40 outline how the commission came about.
2. Vlasich, *Legend for Legendary*, 11.

3. Vlasich, *Legend for Legendary*, 18.
4. Vlasich, *Legend for Legendary*, 19–20.
5. Another good source is Block, *Baseball before We Knew It*, especially pages 22–46.
6. Frick, *Games*, 78–79.
7. Vlasich, *Legend for Legendary*, 24–25.
8. Vlasich, *Legend for Legendary*, 26–27.
9. Vlasich, *Legend for Legendary*, 30–31.
10. Vlasich, *Legend for Legendary*, 34–35.
11. Resolution by Cooperstown Village Trustees, October 18, 1934, Alexander Cleland Papers, Giamatti Research Center.
12. Vlasich, *Legend for Legendary*, 34.
13. Alexander Cleland to Ford Frick, January 30, 1935, Alexander Cleland Papers, Giamatti Research Center; and Ford Frick to Alexander Cleland, February 7, 1935, Alexander Cleland Papers, Giamatti Research Center.
14. Alexander Cleland to Roy Witmer, May 13, 1935, Alexander Cleland Papers, Giamatti Research Center.
15. Vlasich, *Legend for Legendary*, 38; "Frick Will Do Fordham/New York University Game at Yankee Stadium for WOR," *New York Times*, November 14, 1931; and Frick, *Games*, 202.
16. "Baseball Hall of Fame to Be Museum Feature," *Freeman's Journal*, 1935, sundry newspaper clippings, Alexander Cleland Papers, Giamatti Research Center.
17. Jerome Holtzman, "35 Ball Helped Get Hallowed Hall Rolling," *Chicago Tribune*, August 3, 1986, sundry newspaper clippings, Alexander Cleland Papers, Giamatti Research Center.
18. Vlasich, *Legend for Legendary*, 41–44.
19. "Plan Hall of Fame for Diamond Stars," *New York Times*, August 16, 1935.
20. Alexander Cleland to Kenesaw Mountain Landis, May 3, 1935, Alexander Cleland Papers, Giamatti Research Center; Alexander Cleland to Leslie O'Connor, June 4, 1935, Alexander Cleland Papers, Giamatti Research Center; and Kenesaw Mountain Landis to Alexander Cleland, June 6, 1935, Alexander Cleland Papers, Giamatti Research Center.
21. National League Winter Meetings, December 11, 1935, box 7, folder 19, 99–100, Giamatti Research Center; and Special Meeting of the National League Baseball Clubs, November 26, 1935, box 7, folder 18, 9, Giamatti Research Center.
22. Joint Meeting of the National and American League Baseball Clubs, December 12, 1935, box 7, folder 19, 49–50, Giamatti Research Center.
23. Vlasich, *Legend for Legendary*, 45–47.

24. Joint Meeting of the National and American League Baseball Clubs, December 8, 1937, box 4, folder 2, 72–81, Giamatti Research Center.
25. Reisler, *Great Day in Cooperstown*, 137–43. Vlasich, *Legend for Legendary*, 108–11, discusses the role of public relations.
26. Ford Frick to Alexander Cleland, June 14, 1938, Alexander Cleland Papers, Giamatti Research Center. There are numerous letters from Cartwright, who expected his expenses to be paid to attend. The ultimate solution was inducting Cartwright, not Doubleday. Subsequent research questions Cartwright's role. Thorn, *Baseball in the Garden of Eden*, especially 25–32.
27. "Dedication of National Baseball Museum and Hall of Fame," June 12, 1939, Alexander Cleland Papers, Giamatti Research Center; and "The Cavalcade of Baseball," June 12, 1939, Alexander Cleland Papers, Giamatti Research Center. The other players inducted in 1939 were Grover Cleveland Alexander, George Sisler, and Eddie Collins. Farley's role is discussed in Reisler, *Great Day in Cooperstown*, 18–19.
28. Frick, *Games*, 202–3.
29. John Drebinger, "Baseball Pays Tribute to Landis by Picking Him for Hall of Fame," *New York Times*, December 11, 1944.
30. Dick Conners, "Shrine Game, Landis Tribute Crowd Cooperstown for Day," *The Sporting News*, June 26, 1946, 11; and Louis Effrat, "Landis Honored at Cooperstown," *New York Times*, June 14, 1946, 25.
31. "Boston Overcomes Bombers in Tenth," *New York Times*, July 22, 1947; and "Baseball Typical of 4 Freedoms, Says Ford Frick at Cooperstown," *New York Times*, July 25, 1950.
32. "Frick Defends Baseball," *New York Times*, July 24, 1951.
33. Barney Kremenko, "'An Amazing Thing!' Says Casey of Shrine Election," *The Sporting News*, March 19, 1966, 4.
34. "Baseball Writers Honor Frick at Dinner: Landis Is among the 140 Guests Present," *New York Times*, December 6, 1934.
35. John Kiernan, "Mr. Frick Tells All," Sports of the Times, *New York Times*, April 23, 1936.
36. "Ford Frick Strikes Out Casey at the Bunt; Kathy Now Batting," *New York Times*, April 25, 1962.
37. "Stengel's Path to Hall of Fame is Cleared by Change in Ruling," *New York Times*, January 31, 1966.
38. Joseph Durso, "Stengel Elected to Hall of Fame in Surprise Balloting," *New York Times*, March 9, 1966; and Arthur Daley, "A Most Proper Coronation Ceremony," Sports of Our Times, *New York Times*, March 9, 1966.
39. Dick Conners, "Ted and Casey Stars of Shrine Show," *The Sporting News*, August 6, 1966, 5.

40. "St. Louis Trophies Will Be Duplicated at Shrine," *The Sporting News*, February 24, 1968, 38. There was always a library, but now it was in its own wing.
41. Lee Allen, "Cooperstown Corner," *The Sporting News*, August 10, 1968, 6; and Jack Lang, "Shrine Doors Open for Coveleski and Hoyt," *The Sporting News*, February 15, 1969, 23.
42. "Frick, Combs and Haines Selected for Baseball Hall of Fame by Old-Timers," *New York Times*, February 2, 1970.
43. Russell Schneider, "Satch Walks in Shrine's Front Door," *The Sporting News*, August 28, 1971, 5; and "Broeg Succeeds Stockton on Cooperstown Group," *The Sporting News*, August 28, 1971, 33. It was sportswriters, through the BBWAA, who lobbied for equal treatment.
44. "Frick, Combs and Haines Selected . . . ," *New York Times*, February 2, 1970; and Jack Lang, "Frick, Combs and Haines New Hall of Famers," *The Sporting News*, February 14, 1970, 29. The article mentions Frick completed the "trifecta" for integrating baseball, joining Robinson and Rickey. Chandler reacted negatively, calling Frick "a dummy" and asserting all he did was sleep longer than Rip Van Winkle. Insiders Say, *The Sporting News*, February 21, 1970, 4.
45. Jerome Holtzman, "Frick Proud of His Role in Birth of Hall of Fame," *The Sporting News*, February 19, 1977, 35; and "Stack New Hall President; Kerr Retires after 16 Years," *The Sporting News*, February 19, 1977, 55.
46. Neil Amdur, "Old Baseball Feats Recalled at Hall of Fame Induction," *New York Times*, July 28, 1970.
47. Edgar Munzel, "Frick Aims Shrine Message at Youth of U.S.," *The Sporting News*, August 8, 1970, 5.

BIBLIOGRAPHY

The three major sources are the National League and joint meeting minutes from 1933 through 1957, congressional hearings on baseball during Frick's tenure, and three newspapers covering his thirty-one years in baseball. The league minutes, found at the Giamatti Research Center at the National Baseball Hall of Fame and Museum, are exceptionally detailed until shortly after World War II and are a valuable source of information about baseball's executive functions and issues. The congressional hearings from 1951 through the mid-1960s are rich in detail in antitrust and other concerns and offer numerous insights into Frick's policy positions. Three newspapers during Frick's baseball career were utilized: the *New York Times*, the *Chicago Tribune*, and *The Sporting News*. The two dailies were chosen because they were the only cities with two Major League teams during much of Frick's career. *The Sporting News* provided the most comprehensive weekly coverage of baseball.

ARCHIVES AND MANUSCRIPT MATERIALS

Colorado College Library.

Pikes Peak Nugget. Colorado Springs: 1918–19.

Giamatti Research Center, National Baseball Hall of Fame and Museum, Cooperstown NY.

Alexander Cleland Papers.

Celler's Subcommittee on Study of Monopoly Power, boxes 1–4.

Ford Frick newspaper clippings.

Joint Meetings of Major League Baseball Clubs, December 1933–March 1957. Joint meetings generally followed separate league meetings.

Meetings of the National League of Professional Baseball Clubs, November 1933–October 1957. For sixty-five years, Major League Baseball has restricted the availability of all minutes from league or joint meetings. There were usually three meetings a year—the scheduling meeting in early February, the Summer Meetings during the All-Star break, and the Winter Meetings in early December.

Special meetings are also included. Minutes after 1950 are summarized and very limited.
Miscellaneous records: audited financial statements. Commissioner's Office Report of Examination audited by Ernst & Ernst, 1951–65.
National League Board of Directors Meetings, November 1934–December 1945.
Porter, Paul A. "Organized Baseball and the Congress: A Review & Chronological Summary of the Past 10 Years." Prepared at the Request of Commissioner Ford Frick, February 25, 1961.
Sundry commissioner files on Minor Leagues, radio contracts, and rules.
Sundry newspaper clippings on Hall of Fame origins and opening.

Noble County Court House, Albion IN.
Transfer Books of Noble County, 1848–1854. Land transfers, 1848–54.
Transfer Books of Noble County, 1887–1894.
Transfer Books of Noble County, 1895–1903.

Noble County Library, Albion IN.
Directory of Noble County, 1908.
Marriage records, books 1–7, 1859–99.
Scrapbook of M. F. Owen, 1880–1931, vols. 20, 22, 23, 25, and 26.
Will abstracts, 1859–99.

Roy O. West Library Archives, DePauw University.
DePauw University Catalogue, 1913–14.
DePauw University Catalogue, 1914–15.
DePauw University trustees file, 1941–65.
Mirage yearbooks. Greencastle IN: 1911–15.
Phi Kappa Psi records, 1910–29.
Yellow Crab (humor publication), 1915.

University of Kentucky Library, Lexington.
Albert Benjamin "Happy" Chandler Papers.

U.S. Census.
Bronxville, New York, 1930, 1940.
Denver, Colorado, 1920.
Noble County, Indiana: Elkhart Township, 1850–1940.
Noble County, Indiana: Orange Township, 1900–1940.
Noble County, Indiana: Perry Township, 1920–40.
Tuscarawas County, Ohio: Dover Township, 1850.

PUBLISHED WORKS

Abrams, Roger I. *Legal Bases: Baseball and the Law*. Philadelphia: Temple University Press, 1998.

Alexander, Charles C. *Breaking the Slump: Baseball in the Depression Era*. New York: Columbia University Press, 2002.

Allen, Lee. *The National League Story: The Official History*. New York: Hill & Wang, 1965.

Alvord, Samuel E. *Alvord's History of Noble County*. Logansport IN: B. F. Bowen, 1902.

Appel, Marty. *Casey Stengel: Baseball's Greatest Character*. New York: Doubleday, 2017.

Armour, Mark. *Joe Cronin: A Life in Baseball*. Lincoln: University of Nebraska Press, 2010.

Armour, Mark L., and Daniel R. Levitt. *In Pursuit of Pennants: Baseball Operations from Deadball to Moneyball*. Lincoln: University of Nebraska Press, 2015.

Banner, Stuart. *The Baseball Trust: A History of Baseball's Antitrust Exemption*. New York: Oxford University Press, 2013.

Barber, Red. *1947: When All Hell Broke Loose in Baseball*. Garden City NY: Doubleday, 1982.

Barber, Red, and Robert Creamer. *Rhubarb in the Catbird Seat*. Garden City NY: Doubleday, 1968.

Barra, Allen. *Clearing the Bases: The Greatest Baseball Debates of the Last Century*. New York: St. Martin's Press, 2002.

Baughman. John J. *Our Past, Their Present: Historical Essays on Putnam County, Indiana*. Greencastle IN: Putnam County Museum, 2008.

Bavasi, Buzzie, and John Strege. *Off the Record*. Chicago: Contemporary Books, 1987.

Bellamy, Robert V., and James Robert Walker. "Did Televised Baseball Kill the 'Golden Age' of the Minor Leagues?" *Nine* 13, no. 1 (Fall 2004): 59–73.

Blau, Cliff. "The Real First-Year Player Draft." *Baseball Research Journal* 39, no. 1 (2010): 68–71.

Block, David. *Baseball before We Knew It: A Search for the Roots of the Game*. Lincoln: University of Nebraska Press, 2005.

Bohmer, David A. "Ford Frick and Jackie Robinson: The Enabler." In *Jackie: Perspectives on 42*, edited by Bill Nowlin and Glen Sparks, 114–21. Phoenix AZ: Society for American Baseball Research, 2021.

———. "Reshaping Baseball: The Positive Impact of Ford Frick." In *The Cooperstown Symposium on Baseball and American Culture, 2015–2016*, edited by William M. Simons, 198–215. Jefferson NC: McFarland, 2017.

———. "The Season That Almost Wasn't." *Nine* 27, no. 1 (2018): 25–40. https://dx.doi.org/10.1353/nin.2018.0003.

Bradlee, Ben, Jr. *The Kid: The Immortal Life of Ted Williams*. New York: Little, Brown & Company, 2013.

Briley, Ron. “Danny Gardella and Baseball’s Reserve Clause: A Working-Class Stiff Blacklisted in Cold War America.” *Nine* 19, no. 1 (Fall 2010): 52–66.

———, ed. *The Politics of Baseball: Essays on the Pastime and Power at Home and Abroad*. Jefferson, NC: McFarland, 2010.

———. “The Times They Were A-Changin’: Baseball as a Symbol of American Values in Transition, 1963–64.” *Baseball Research Journal* (1988): 54–60.

Buhite, Russell D. *The Continental League: A Personal History*. Lincoln: University of Nebraska Press, 2014.

Bullock, Steven R. *Playing for Their Nation: Baseball and the American Military During World War II*. Lincoln: University of Nebraska Press, 2004.

Burk, Robert F. *Much More Than a Game: Players, Owners, and American Baseball Since 1921*. Chapel Hill: University of North Carolina Press, 2001.

Caro, Robert A. *The Power Broker: Robert Moses and the Fall of New York*. New York: Albert A. Knopf, 1974.

Carvalho, John, and John Lofflin. “Ford Frick’s Big Leaguer: A Commissioner Takes a Swing at Baseball Fiction.” *Studies in Popular Culture* 39, no. 2 (Spring 2017): 38–57.

Carvalho, John, and Raymond Ankney. “Haunted by the Babe: Baseball Commissioner’s Column about Babe Ruth.” *American Journalism* 25, no. 4 (2008): 65–82.

Carvalho, John P. *Frick*: Baseball’s Third Commissioner*. Jefferson NC: McFarland, 2016.

Chandler, Happy, and Vance Trimble. *Heroes, Plain Folks, and Skunks: The Life and Times of Happy Chandler*. Chicago: Bonus Books, 1989.

Clavin, Tom, and Danny Peary. *Gil Hodges: The Brooklyn Bums, the New York Mets, and the Extraordinary Life of a Baseball Legend*. New York: New American Library, 2012.

———. *Roger Maris: Baseball’s Reluctant Hero*. New York: Simon & Schuster, 2010.

Cohen, Marilyn. *No Girls in the Clubhouse: The Exclusion of Women from Baseball*. Jefferson NC: McFarland, 2009.

Corbett, Warren. “Rickey’s Folly: How the Continental League Forced Baseball Expansion.” In *Time for Expansion Baseball*, edited by Maxwell Kates and Bill Nowlin, 21–26. Phoenix AZ: Society for American Baseball Research, 2018.

———. “The ‘Strike’ against Jackie Robinson: Truth or Myth?” *Baseball Research Journal* 46, no. 1 (2017): 88–93.

———. "Voices for the Voiceless: Ross Horning, Cy Block, and the Unwelcome Truth." *Baseball Research Journal* 47, no. 26 (2018): 78–82.

Cox, Joe. "Happy Helping? Inside Commissioner Chandler's Role in Jackie Robinson's Great Quest." In *Jackie: Perspectives on 42*, edited by Bill Nowlin and Glen Sparks, 68–72. Phoenix AZ: Society for American Baseball Research, 2021.

Crepeau, Richard. "Landis, Baseball and Racism—A Brief Comment." *Baseball Research Journal* 38, no. 1 (2009): 31–32.

D'Antonio, Michael. *Forever Blue: The True Story of Walter O'Malley, Baseball's Most Controversial Owner, and the Dodgers of Brooklyn and Los Angeles*. New York: Penguin Group, 2009.

Dickson, Paul. *Bill Veeck: Baseball's Greatest Maverick*. New York: Walker & Company, 2012.

———. *Leo Durocher: Baseball's Prodigal Son*. New York: Bloomsbury USA, 2017.

Dodson, Tim. "Coal Ball: Baseball and Its Role in the Colorado Fuel and Iron Coal Towns of Southeastern Colorado, 1900–1910." *Nine* 23, no. 2 (Spring 2015): 53–67.

Duquette, Jerold J. *Regulating the National Pastime: Baseball and Antitrust*. Westport CT: Praeger Publishers, 1999.

Edmonds, Ed. "Over a Century in the Making: Myths and Misconceptions about Major League Baseball's Antitrust Exemption, Part 1." *Outside the Lines* 28, no. 2 (Fall 2022): 23–32.

———. "Over a Century in the Making: Myths and Misconceptions about Major League Baseball's Antitrust Exemption, Part 2." *Outside the Lines* 29, no. 1 (Spring 2023): 20–31.

———. "Remembering Earl—Not George—Toolson: The Plaintiff Who Took the New York Yankees to the U.S. Supreme Court." *National Pastime* 37 (2017). https://sabr.org/journal/article/remembering-earl-not-george-toolson-the-plaintiff-who-took-the-new-york-yankees-to-the-us-supreme-court/.

Edmonds, Ed, and Frank Houdek. *Baseball and the Law: A Chronology of Decisions, Statues and Other Legal Events*. Jefferson NC: McFarland, 2017.

Ellsworth, Peter. "The Brooklyn Dodgers' Move to Los Angeles: Was Walter O'Malley Totally Responsible?" *Nine* 15, no. 1 (Fall 2005): 19–40.

Epplin, Luke. *Our Team: The Epic Story of Four Men and the World Series That Changed Baseball*. New York: Flatiron Books, 2021.

Eskenazi, Gerald. *Bill Veeck: A Baseball Legend*. New York: McGraw-Hill, 1988.

Fitts, Robert K. *Mashi: The Unfulfilled Baseball Dreams of Masanori Murakami, the First Japanese Major Leaguer*. Lincoln: University of Nebraska Press, 2020.

Fitts, Robert K., Bill Nowlin, and James Forr. *Nichibei Yakyu: US Tours of Japan*. Vol. 1, *1907–1958*. Phoenix AZ: Society of American Baseball Research, 2022.

Ford, Orville Stevens, William H. McEwen, and William H. McIntosh, eds. *History of Northeast Indiana*. 2 vols. Chicago: Lewis Publishing Company, 1920.

Frick, Ford C. *Games, Asterisks, and People: Memoirs of a Lucky Fan*. New York: Crown Publishers, 1973.

Garratt, Robert F. *Home Team: The Turbulent History of the San Francisco Giants*. Lincoln: University of Nebraska Press, 2017.

———. "Horace Stoneham and the Breaking of Baseball's Second Color Barrier." *Nine* 22, no. 2 (Spring 2014): 42–53.

Gietschier, Steven P. *Baseball: The Turbulent Midcentury Years*. Lincoln: University of Nebraska Press, 2023.

Goldberger, Paul. *Ballpark: Baseball in the American City*. New York: Alfred A. Knopf, 2019.

Goldstein, Richard. *Spartan Seasons: How Baseball Survived the Second World War*. New York: Macmillan Publishing, 1980.

Green, G. Michael, and Roger D. Launius. *Charlie Finley: The Outrageous Story of Baseball's Super Showman*. New York: Walker, 2010.

Guszhow, Stephen D. "The Exemption of Baseball from Federal Antitrust Laws: A Legal History." *Baseball Research Journal* (1994): 69–74.

Helyar, John. *Lords of the Realm: The Real History of Baseball*. New York: Villard Books, 1994.

Hensler, Paul. "A Farewell to Arms: The Major Leagues in 1968 and the Transition to a New Modern Era." *Baseball Research Journal* (2008): 101–4.

Hill, John Paul. "Commissioner A.B. 'Happy' Chandler and the Integration of Major League Baseball: A Reassessment." *Nine* 19, no. 1 (Fall 2010): 28–51.

Hirsh, Paul. "Walter O'Malley Was Right." *National Pastime* 31 (2011): 81–83.

Holtzman, Jerome. *The Commissioners: Baseball's Midlife Crisis*. New York: Total Sports, 1998.

———. *No Cheering in the Press Box: Recollections—Personal and Professional—by Eighteen Veteran American Sportswriters*. New York: Holt, Rinehart and Winston, 1973.

———. *On Baseball: A History of Baseball Scribes*. Champaign IL: Sports Publishing, 2005.

Jacobson, Steve. *Carrying Jackie's Torch: The Players Who Integrated Baseball—and America*. Chicago: Lawrence Hill Books, 2007.

James, Bill. *The New Bill James Historical Baseball Abstract*. New York: The Free Press, 2001.

Jordan, David, Larry Gerlach, and John Rossi. "A Baseball Myth Exploded: Bill Veeck and the 1943 Sale of the Phillies." *National Pastime* 18 (1998): 3–13.

Jozza, Frank P., Jr., and John J. Guthrie Jr. *Relocating Teams and Expanding Leagues in Professional Sports: How the Major Leagues Respond to Market Conditions*. Westport CT: Quorum Books, 1999.

Kahn, Roger. *The Era 1947–1957: When the Yankees, the Giants and the Dodgers Ruled the World*. New York: Ticknor & Fields, 1993.

———. *Rickey & Robinson: The True, Untold Story of the Integration of Baseball*. New York: Rodale, 2014.

Katz, Jeff. *The Kansas City A's and the Wrong Half of the Yankees: How the Yankees Controlled Two of the Eight American League Franchises During the 1950s*. Hingham MA: Maple Street Press, 2007.

Knee, Stuart. "Jim Crow Strikes Out: Branch Rickey and the Struggle for Integration in American Baseball." *Culture, Sport, Society* 6 (June 2003): 71–87.

Kolbert, Jered Benjamin. "Major League Baseball During World War II." *National Pastime* 14 (1994): 102–5.

Korr, Charles P. *The End of Baseball as We Knew It: The Players Union, 1960–81*. Urbana: University of Illinois Press, 2002.

Krell, David. *1962: Baseball and America in the Time of JFK*. Lincoln: University of Nebraska Press, 2021.

Kuhn, Bowie. *Hardball: The Education of a Baseball Commissioner*. Lincoln: University of Nebraska Press, 1997.

Lamb, Chris. "Baseball's Whitewash: Sportswriter Wendell Smith Exposes Major League Baseball's Big Lie." *Nine* 18, no. 1 (Fall 2009): 1–20.

———. *Conspiracy of Silence: Sportswriters and the Long Campaign to Desegregate Baseball*. Lincoln: University of Nebraska Press, 2012.

Lanctot, Neil. *Campy: The Two Lives of Roy Campanella*. New York: Simon & Schuster, 2011.

Landon, Bill, Robert C. Gagen Jr., and Sarah Knopp. *History of Early Schools in Noble County*. Albion IN: Noble County Historical Society, 2006.

Leahy, Michael. *The Last Innocents: The Collision of the Turbulent Sixties and the Los Angeles Dodgers*. New York: HarperCollins Publishers, 2016.

Leavy, Jane. *The Big Fella: Babe Ruth and the World He Created*. New York: HarperCollins Publishers, 2018.

Lerner, Marc. *A Laboratory of Liberty: The Transformation of Political Culture in Republican Switzerland, 1750–1848*. Boston: Brill Publishing, 2012.

Levitt, Daniel R. *The Battle That Forged Modern Baseball: The Federal League Challenge and Its Legacy*. Lanham MD: Ivan R. Dee, 2012.

Lewis, Robert F. "Bud Selig's Use of Smart Power." In *The Politics of Baseball: Essays on the Pastime and Power at Home and Abroad*, edited by Ron Briley, 190–205. Jefferson NC: McFarland, 2010.

Lowenfish, Lee. *Branch Rickey: Baseball's Ferocious Gentleman*. Lincoln: University of Nebraska Press, 2007.

———. "The Gentlemen's Agreement and the Ferocious Gentleman Who Broke It." *Baseball Research Journal* 38, no. 1 (2009): 33–34.

———. *The Imperfect Diamond: A History of Baseball's Labor Wars*. Lincoln: University of Nebraska Press, 2010.

Lowenfish, Lee, and Tony Lupien. *The Imperfect Diamond: The Story of Baseball's Reserve System and the Men Who Fought to Change It*. New York: Stein and Day Publishers, 1980.

MacDonald, Neil W. *The League That Lasted: 1876 and the Founding of the National League of Professional Baseball Clubs*. Jefferson NC: McFarland, 2004.

Macht, Norman L. "Does Baseball Deserve This Black Eye? A Dissent from the Universal Casting of Shame and Blame on Kenesaw Mountain Landis for Baseball's Failure to Sign Black Players before 1946." *Baseball Research Journal* 38, no. 1 (2009): 26–30.

Macht, Norman L., and Robert D. Warrington. "The Veracity of Veeck." *Baseball Research Journal* 42, no. 2 (2013): 17–20.

Madden, Bill. *1954: The Year Willie Mays and the First Generation of Black Superstars Changed Major League Baseball Forever*. Boston: Da Capo Press, 2014.

Mandell, David. "Danny Gardella and the Reserve Clause." *National Pastime* 26 (2006): 41–44.

———. "The Suspension of Leo Durocher." *National Pastime* 27 (2007): 101–4.

Manhart, George B. *DePauw through the Years*. Vol. 1, *1837–1919*. Chicago: Lakeside Press, 1962.

Mann, Arthur. *Baseball Confidential: Secret History of the War among Chandler, Durocher, MacPhail and Rickey*. Philadelphia: David McKay, 1951.

Marshall, William. *Baseball's Pivotal Era: 1945–1951*. Lexington: University of Kentucky Press, 1999.

McClure, Rusty, David Stern, and Michael A. Banks. *Crosley: Two Brothers and a Business Empire That Transformed the Nation*. Cincinnati OH: Clerisy Press, 2007.

McCue, Andy. "A History of Dodger Ownership." *National Pastime* 13 (1993): 34–42.

———. *Mover and Shaker: Walter O'Malley, the Dodgers, and Baseball's Westward Expansion*. Lincoln: University of Nebraska Press, 2014.
———. *Stumbling around the Bases: The American League's Mismanagement in the Expansion Eras*. Lincoln: University of Nebraska Press, 2022.
McCue, Andy, and Eric Thompson. "Mis-Management 101: The American League Expansion for 1961." *National Pastime* 31 (2011).
McKelvey, G. Richard. *The MacPhails: Baseball's First Family of the Front Office*. Jefferson NC: McFarland, 2000.
Melville, Tom. *Early Baseball and the Rise of the National League*. Jefferson NC: McFarland, 2001.
Miller, Marvin. *A Whole Different Ball Game: The Sport and Business of Baseball*. New York: Carol Publishing Group, 1991.
Moffi, Larry. *The Conscience of the Game: Baseball's Commissioners from Landis to Selig*. Lincoln: University of Nebraska Press, 2006.
Moffi, Larry, and Jonathan Kronstadt. *Crossing the Line: Black Major Leaguers, 1947–1959*. Jefferson NC: McFarland, 1994.
Montgomery, Wynn. "Georgia's 1948 Phenoms and the Bonus Rule." *Baseball Research Journal* 39, no. 1 (Summer 2010): 72–82.
Moore, Joseph Thomas. *Larry Doby: The Struggle of the American League's First Black Player*. Mineola NY: Dover Publications, 2011.
Murdock, Eugene C. *Ban Johnson: Czar of Baseball*. Westport CT: Greenwood Press, 1982.
Murphy, Robert E. *After Many a Summer: The Passing of the Giants and Dodgers and a Golden Age in New York Baseball*. New York: Union Square Press, 2009.
Noble County History Book Committee. *The History of Noble County, Indiana*. Dallas: Taylor Publishing, 1986.
Nusbaum, Eric. *Stealing Home: Los Angeles, the Dodgers, and the Lives Caught in Between*. New York: Public Affairs, 2020.
Obemeyer, Jeff. "War Games: The Business of Major League Baseball During World War II." *Nine* 19, no. 1 (Fall 2010): 1–27.
Parrott, Harold. *The Lords of Baseball: A Wry Look at the Side of the Game the Fan Seldom Sees—the Front Office*. New York: Praeger Publishers, 1976.
Pessah, Jon. *The Game: Inside the Secret World of Major League Baseball's Power Brokers*. New York: Little, Brown and Company, 2015.
Phillips, Christopher J. *Scouting and Scoring: How We Know What We Know about Baseball*. Princeton NJ: Princeton University Press, 2019.
Phillips, Clifton J., and John J. Baughman. *DePauw: A Pictorial History*. Greencastle IN: DePauw University, 1987.

Pietrusza, David. *Judge and Jury: The Life and Times of Judge Kenesaw Mountain Landis*. South Bend IN: Diamond Communications, 1998.

———. *Major Leagues: 18 Professional Baseball Organizations, 1871 to Present*. Jefferson NC: McFarland, 1991.

Quirk, James, and Rodney D. Fort. *Pay Dirt: The Business of Professional Team Sports*. Princeton NJ: Princeton University Press, 1992.

Rader, Benjamin G. *Baseball: A History of America's Game*. 2nd ed. Urbana: University of Illinois Press, 2002.

Ree, Dorothy Rose. *Walsenburg: Crossroads Town*. Walsenburg CO: Independent Nocturn Publishing, 2006.

Reisler, Jim. *A Great Day in Cooperstown: The Improbable Birth of Baseball's Hall of Fame*. New York: Carroll & Graf Publishers, 2006.

Riess, Steven A., ed. *Major Problems in American Sport History*. Boston: Houghton Mifflin Company, 1997.

Robinson, Jackie. *Baseball Has Done It*. Philadelphia: Lippincott, 1964.

———. *I Never Had It Made*. New York: Putnam, 1972.

Rosengren, John. *Hank Greenberg: The Hero of Heroes*. New York: New American Library, 2013.

Rossi, John. "The Nugent Era: Phillies Phlounder in Phutility." *National Pastime* 25 (2005): 15–18.

———. *A Whole New Game: Off the Field Changes in Baseball, 1946–1960*. Jefferson NC: McFarland, 1999.

Ruth, George Herman. *Babe Ruth's Own Book of Baseball*. Lincoln: University of Nebraska Press, 1992.

Selig, Bud, and Phil Rogers. *For the Good of The Game: The Inside Story of the Surprising and Dramatic Transformation of Major League Baseball*. New York: HarperCollins Publishers, 2019.

Seymour, Harold, and Dorothy Seymour Mills. *Baseball: The Early Years*. New York: Oxford University Press, 1960.

———. *Baseball: The Golden Age*. New York: Oxford University Press, 1971.

Shapiro, Michael. *Bottom of the Ninth: Branch Rickey, Casey Stengel, and the Daring Scheme to Save Baseball from Itself*. New York: Henry Holt and Company, 2009.

Simpson, Allan, ed. *The Baseball Draft: The First 25 Years*. Durham NC: American Sports Publishing, 1990.

Snyder, Brad. *A Well-Paid Slave: Curt Flood's Fight for Free Agency in Professional Sports*. New York: Viking Penguin, 2006.

Soderholm-Difatte, Bryan. *The Golden Era of Major League Baseball: A Time of Transition and Integration*. Lanham MD: Rowman & Littlefield, 2015.

———. *Tumultuous Times in America's Game: From Jackie Robinson's Breakthrough to the War Over Free Agency*. Lanham MD: Rowman & Littlefield, 2019.

Spink, J. G. Taylor. *Judge Landis and Twenty-Five Years of Baseball*. New York: Thomas Y. Crowell Company, 1947.

Stuart, Jeffrey Saint John. *Twilight Teams*. Gaithersburg MD: Stark Publishing, 2000.

Sullivan, Dean A. *Late Innings: A Documentary History of Baseball, 1945–1972*. Lincoln: University of Nebraska Press, 2002.

———. *Middle Innings: A Documentary History of Baseball, 1900–1948*. Lincoln: University of Nebraska Press, 1998.

Surdam, David George. *Wins, Losses, and Empty Seats: How Baseball Outlasted the Great Depression*. Lincoln: University of Nebraska Press, 2011.

Sweet, William Warren. *Indiana Asbury-DePauw University, 1837–1937*. New York: Abington Press, 1937.

Thomas, G. Scott. *A Brand New Ballgame: Branch Rickey, Bill Veeck, Walter O'Malley and the Transformation of Baseball, 1945–1962*. Jefferson NC: McFarland, 2022.

Thorn, John. *Baseball in the Garden of Eden: The Secret History of the Early Game*. New York: Simon & Schuster, 2011.

Treder, Steve. "Baseball's New Frontier: The Expansion of 1961." *Nine* 12, no. 2 (Spring 2004): 29–61.

———. *Forty Years a Giant: The Life of Horace Stoneham*. Lincoln: University of Nebraska Press, 2021.

———. "Open Classification: The Pacific Coast League's Drive to Turn Major." *Nine* 15, no. 1 (Fall 2006): 88–109.

Tygiel, Jules. *Baseball's Great Experiment: Jackie Robinson and His Legacy*. New York: Oxford University Press, 1984.

———. *Past Time: Baseball as History*. New York: Oxford University Press, 2000.

———. "Revisiting Bill Veeck and the 1943 Phillies." *Baseball Research Journal* 35 (2006): 109–14.

U.S. Congress. *Bills to Amend the Antitrust Laws to Protect Trade and Commerce Against Unlawful Restraints and Monopolies*. 85th Cong., 1st sess., June–August 1957. Washington DC: U.S. Government Printing Office, 1958.

———. *Bill to Authorize the Adoption of Certain Rules with Respect to the Broadcasting or Telecasting of Professional Exhibitions in Interstate Commerce and Other Purposes: Hearings Before Subcommittee of the Committee on Interstate and Foreign Commerce*. 83rd Cong., 1st sess.,

May 6–8 and 11, 1953. Washington DC: U.S. Government Printing Office, 1954.

———. *Hearings on Antitrust Dichotomy in Sports*. 86th Cong., 1st sess., September 2 and 4, 1959. Washington DC: U.S. Government Printing Office, 1960.

———. *House of Representatives Hearings Before the Subcommittee on Monopoly and Antitrust of the Committee of the Judiciary: Organized Baseball*. 82nd Cong., 1st sess., July 30, 31, August 1, 3, 6–8, 10, and October 15–19, 22–24, 1951. Washington DC: U.S. Government Printing Office, 1952.

———. *Organized Baseball Report of the Subcommittee of Monopoly Power and Antitrust of the Committee on the Judiciary*. 82nd Cong., 2nd sess., May 27, 1952. Washington DC: U.S. Government Printing Office, 1952.

———. *Telecasting of Professional Sports Contests*. 87th Cong., 1st sess., August 28, 1961. Washington DC: U.S. Government Printing Office, 1962.

———. *To Limit the Applicability of the Antitrust Laws so as to Exempt Certain Aspects of Designated Professional Team Sports and for Other Purposes*. 85th Cong., 2nd sess., July 9, 15–18, 22–24, 28–31, 1958. Washington DC: U.S. Government Printing Office, 1958.

———. *To Limit the Applicability of the Antitrust Laws so as to Exempt Certain Aspects of Designated Professional Team Sports and for Other Purposes*. 88th Cong., 2nd sess., January 30–31, February 17–18, 1964. Washington DC: U.S. Government Printing Office, 1964.

———. *To Make the Antitrust Laws Applicable to Professional Baseball Clubs Affiliated with the Alcoholic Beverage Industry*. 83rd Cong., 2nd sess., March 18, April 8, and May 25, 1954. Washington DC: U.S. Government Printing Office:, 1954.

———. *To Make the Antitrust Laws Applicable to the Organized Professional Team Sport of Baseball*. 86th Cong., 2nd sess., May 19–20, 1960. Washington DC: U.S. Government Printing Office, 1960.

———. *To Make the Antitrust Laws Applicable to the Organized Professional Team Sport of Baseball and to Limit the Applicability of the Antitrust Laws as to Exempt Certain Aspects of Designated Professional Team Sports and for Other Purposes*. 86th Cong., 1st sess., July 28–31, 1959. Washington DC: U.S. Government Printing Office, 1960.

Vanderberg, Bob. *Frantic Frank Lane: Baseball's Ultimate Wheeler-Dealer*. Jefferson NC: McFarland, 2013.

Veeck, Bill, and Ed Linn. *The Hustler's Handbook*. New York: Fireside, 1989.

———. *Veeck as in Wreck*. Chicago: University of Chicago Press, 2001.

Vincent, Fay. *The Last Commissioner: A Baseball Valentine*. New York: Simon & Schuster, 2002.

Vincent, Ted. *The Rise and Fall of American Sport: Mudville's Revenge*. Lincoln: University of Nebraska Press, 1994.
Vlasich, James A. *A Legend for the Legendary: The Origin of the Baseball Hall of Fame*. Bowling Green OH: Bowling Green State University Popular Press, 1990.
Voigt, David Quentin. *American Baseball*. Vol. 3, *From Postwar Expansion to the Electronic Age*. University Park: Pennsylvania State University Press, 1983.
Walker, James R. *Crack of the Bat: A History of Baseball on the Radio*. Lincoln: University of Nebraska Press, 2015.
Walker, James R., and Robert V. Bellamy. *Center Field Shot: A History of Baseball on Television*. Lincoln: University of Nebraska Press, 2008.
Walton, Chris. *Richard Wagner's Zurich: The Muse of Place*. Rochester NY: Camden House, 2007.
Warfield, Don. *The Roaring Redhead—Larry MacPhail—Baseball's Great Innovator*. South Bend IN: Diamond Communications, 1987.
Warrington, Robert D. "Departure without Dignity: The Athletics Leave Philadelphia." *Baseball Research Journal* 39, no. 1 (2010): 95–115.
Weintraub, Robert. *The Victory Season: The End of World War II and the Birth of Baseball's Golden Age*. New York: Little Brown and Company, 2013.
White, Bill, and Gordon Dillow. *Uppity: My Untold Story about the Games People Play*. New York: Grand Central Publishing, 2011.
White, G. Edward. *Creating the National Pastime: Baseball Transforms Itself, 1903–1953*. Princeton NJ: Princeton University Press, 1996.
Wisensale, Steven K. "The Cold War, a Red Scare, and the New York Giants' Historic Tour of Japan in 1953." In *Nichibei Yakyu: US Tours Of Japan*, vol. 1, *1907–1958*, edited by Robert K. Fitts, Bill Nowlin, and James Forr, 221–31. Phoenix AZ: Society for American Baseball Research, 2022.
Young, Bill. "From Mexico to Quebec: Baseball's Forgotten Giants." *National Pastime* 37 (2017): 80–84.
Zimbalist, Andrew. *Baseball and Billions: A Probing Look Inside the Big Business of Our National Pastime*. New York: Basic Books, 1992.
———. *In the Best Interests of Baseball? The Revolutionary Reign of Bud Selig*. Hoboken NJ: John Wiley & Sons, 2006.
Zimniuch, Fran. *Baseball's New Frontier: A History of Expansion, 1961–1998*. Lincoln: University of Nebraska Press, 2013.

INDEX